THE
FINANCIAL SERVICES
REVOLUTION

Innovations in Financial Markets and Institutions

Editors: Robert A. Eisenbeis and Richard W. McEnally
University of North Carolina at Chapel Hill
Chapel Hill, North Carolina USA

This series seeks to expand our understanding of the forces driving current changes in financial markets and the instruments traded in these markets. The objective is to increase our knowledge of their implications for the functioning, structure, and regulatory policies affecting financial markets.

Copublished by the
Cato Institute

THE
FINANCIAL SERVICES
REVOLUTION

POLICY DIRECTIONS
FOR · THE · FUTURE

edited by Catherine England
and Thomas Huertas

Kluwer Academic Publishers
Boston/Dordrecht/Lancaster

Distributors

---

for the United States and Canada: Kluwer Academic Publishers, 101
Philip Drive, Assinippi Park, Norwell, MA, 02061, USA

for the UK and Ireland: Kluwer Academic Publishers, MTP Press
Limited, Falcon House, Queen Square, Lancaster, LA1 1RN, UK

for all other countries: Kluwer Academic Publishers Group,
Distribution Centre, P.O. Box 322, 3300 AH Dordrecht, The
Netherlands

Library of Congress Cataloging-in-Publication Data

The Financial services revolution / edited by Catherine England,
    Thomas F. Huertas.
        p. cm.—(Innovations in financial markets and institutions
series)
    Proceedings of a conference held Feb. 26–27, 1987, sponsored by
the Cato Institute.
    Includes index.
    ISBN 0-89838-251-3 : $50.00 (est.)
    1. Banking law—United States—Congresses. 2. Banking law—
Canada—Congresses. 3. Banks and banking—United States—History—
Congresses. 4. Banks and banking—Canada—History—Congresses.
I. England, Catherine. II. Huertas, Thomas F. III. Cato Institute.
IV. Series.
KDZ260.A6   1987
346.73′082—dc19   87–24143
[347.30682]   CIP

Printed in the United States of America

CONTENTS

1

THE FINANCIAL SERVICES REVOLUTION: INTRODUCTION

Catherine England and Thomas F. Huertas

The Financial Services Revolution: Policy Directions for the Future, held February 26 and 27, 1987, was the fifth in a series of annual conferences sponsored by the Cato Institute examining public policy toward the monetary and banking systems. The 1987 conference focused specifically on the regulation of depository institutions, and from that conference grew this book.

The emphasis at the conference, and hence in the book, was placed on the regulation of depository institutions and especially banks, for several reasons. First is the intensity of the debates currently taking place in Washington over proposed changes in the regulatory structure. Second is the traditional importance of banks to the economy. And third is the fact that the government's attitude toward banks is often key in determining its attitude toward other questions of financial regulation.

The conference centered around three questions that are at the heart of the current debate on financial regulation: Who should be allowed to own a bank? In what activities should a bank's affiliates be allowed to engage? And how should banking organizations be regulated and supervised? How these issues are ultimately resolved depends to a great extent on the assumptions that participants bring to the debate. Consequently, the conference and book alike set out to examine the assumptions on which the existing regulatory structure is based, and to ask some important, but often overlooked questions about them. Were these assumptions ever valid? Are they valid now? If not, what does that imply for future regulation?

The book is divided into three broad areas. It begins with papers that examine the history of banking and bank regulation, both in the United States and in Canada. In taking a look at the past, Chapters 2 through 6 question many of the generally accepted facts about banking and should raise anew questions concerning the validity of the historical support for regulation.

The second section considers whether the current regulatory structure can be viewed as successful in meeting its stated goals. Chapters 7 through 11 also consider how regulations designed to promote safety and stability may be weakening the nation's depository institutions.

The third section looks to the future and to what sorts of changes might be appropriate.

Banking History

In Chapter 2, George Kaufman attempts to dispel many of the myths associated with bank runs. He describes the role bank runs traditionally have played as a means of disciplining badly managed banks, and he provides evidence concerning the historical unimportance of contagion. Kaufman also shows how depositors fared in an environment without deposit insurance. He ends by calling for the federal regulatory authorities to reinstitute closure rules that force recapitalization, reorganization, or closure as near as possible to the time an institution first reaches zero net worth.

In Chapter 3, Bert Ely sets out to determine the causes of the banking collapse of the early 1930s. The roots of the 1930s problem are found, Ely argues, in structural weaknesses of the banking industry as it emerged from the 1920s. These structural weaknesses were a result of regulatory rigidities imposed on a banking industry facing changing market conditions. Through a detailed analysis, Ely concludes that many of the lessons commonly drawn from the 1930s experience in this country are mistaken, that questions should be asked instead about the ability of U.S. banks to adapt to new economic and competitive conditions and about the impact of macroeconomic monetary policy on the environment facing banks.

In his chapter, Ely notes that the Canadians suffered no bank failures during the 1930s, raising questions about the differences in their system and that of the United States. Ely points out that Canadian banks were free to branch anywhere, and in Chapter 4, Michael Bordo and Angela Redish reveal that the Canadians also had no central bank until 1935. Bordo and Redish consider the possible justifications for the Canadians' establishing their central bank in 1935, and conclude that the decision was a result of political preferences rather than a response to any clear need on the part of the banking system or the Canadian economy for a central bank.

In Chapter 5, William Shughart also considers the part that politics played in banking legislation during the 1930s, but he looks at the banking legislation passed in the United States. Shughart draws particular attention to the provisions in the Banking Act of 1933 that required the separation of commercial and investment banking activities. Applying a public choice analysis, Shughart asks who gained from the provisions, and he concludes that the commercial banking industry, the investment banking industry, and the U.S. Treasury Department can all be said to have benefited in the years immediately following the passage of the act. Richard Timberlake, in his comment, extends Shughart's analysis to show how the federal government manipulated the monetary policy of the 1930s for its own benefit.

The history of the regulation of the savings and loan industry is the subject of Chapter 6. James Barth and Martin Regalia examine the way in which regulation of the industry has evolved since the first savings and loan was established in the 1830s. They conclude that the stated purpose of regulation appears to have changed, even while the regulations themselves often have not. Barth and Regalia provide some important insights into the contribution of thrift regulation to the current problems facing the industry as well as some suggestions about the direction reform should—and should not—take.

Current Regulation

The first two papers in Part II examine the contribution of the federal deposit insurance system to the problems now plaguing the federal banking industry and its regulators. In Chapter 7, Gerald O'Driscoll describes the moral hazard problem caused by deposit insurance—especially government-sponsored deposit insurance. He discusses how market incentives and a system of private deposit insurance might be substituted for the current federal guarantees and regulatory system.

In his paper, O'Driscoll discusses briefly the fact that an extensive regulatory system was deemed a necessary adjunct to federal deposit insurance when it was introduced. In Chapter 8, Roger Garrison, Eugenie Short, and Gerald O'Driscoll illustrate in more detail how specific regulations can be interpreted as attempting to offset many of the bad incentives implicit in federal deposit insurance. They conclude that the regulatory system designed to control the moral hazard and risk-taking introduced by deposit insurance has failed to meet its goals. Garrison, Short, and O'Driscoll suggest more market discipline as the key to controlling bankers' behavior.

Mark Toma examines the behavior of competitive and monopoly regulators of banking in Chapter 9. Specifically, he takes both a theoretical and a practical look at the ability of the Federal Reserve to enforce reserve requirements both when it competed against state banking supervisors in establishing the reserves banks were required to hold and now that the 1980 Monetary Control Act has given the Fed monopoly power. Many of Toma's insights can be applied to broader questions being raised about the desirability and efficiency of our dual system of bank regulation.

In Chapter 10, Gillian Garcia considers the financial state of the Federal Savings and Loan Insurance Corporation. She argues that the widespread insolvency in the industry and the inability of the FSLIC to close bankrupt institutions in a timely fashion has also made it extremely difficult for the Federal Home Loan Bank Board or the savings and loan insurance fund to fashion regulatory policies that make sense for both healthy and insolvent thrifts. As the contingent liabilities of the FSLIC seem to be growing larger each day, Garcia argues it is long past time for Congress to take the steps necessary to resolve the industry's problems.

In Chapter 11, Catherine England looks at the so-called nonbank bank loophole and provides an overview of the changing economic conditions facing the banking industry. She argues that the world for which much of banking regulation was designed no longer exists, and that to protect the stability of the nation's banking system, far-reaching regulatory changes are needed.

The Future

Robert Litan explores the arguments for reuniting commercial and investment banking in Chapter 12. He discusses the Swiss-cheese nature of the Glass-Steagall Act restrictions as well as examining both the risks and benefits associated with commercial bank entry into the securities underwriting business. Litan also describes various policy alternatives through which investment and commercial banking could be more fully united in the United States.

Thomas Huertas takes an even broader view of the range of activities in which banking organizations should be allowed to engage in Chapter 13. He reviews the history of business combinations including both banking and commerce and points out that restrictions on such combinations were introduced only 30 years ago. Huertas concludes there is no inherent danger introduced into the business of banking by its association through a holding company with commercial enterprises.

Finally, in Chapter 14, Catherine England uses both economic theory and historical evidence to speculate about how depositors might protect themselves in the absence of federal deposit insurance. She notes that in many markets some individuals give over to others control of funds for a specified period of time. Stockholders and bondholders are common examples. England examines the mechanisms used in these markets to protect the parties to the agreement and then asks what similar arrangements might evolve in a banking system without deposit insurance. Finally, she turns to the history of free banking in Scotland and the United States to determine whether depositors were, in fact, able to protect themselves.

Several themes unite the papers in this volume. First, and perhaps most important, all the papers implicitly argue that the current regulatory system is no longer in the best interest of the financial services industry or of the country at large. Second, there is general agreement that standard banking histories err when they emphasize the inherent instability of the banking industry. Third, although the authors offer many different policy recommendations, all envisage more market discipline and more freedom for all types of financial firms. Finally, all agree that rapid changes in the environment facing financial institutions make misperceptions about the past a luxury the country can no longer afford; reform of financial institution regulation is urgently needed.

PART I

THE HISTORY OF BANKS AND BANK REGULATION

2

THE TRUTH ABOUT BANK RUNS
George G. Kaufman

Bank runs have taken a bum rap. A shout of "run" strikes the same fear into most of us as a shout of "fire" in a crowded room might. After all, it is better to be safe than sorry. Not only will depositors run to the affected bank to withdraw their funds, but depositors elsewhere may also run on unaffected banks. Bank runs are frequently viewed as contagious, with people thinking, "If my neighbor's bank is in trouble, maybe mine is also." Thus, a run on one bank is believed capable of causing not only that bank to fail but also, domino fashion, the failure of a large number of banks nationwide, thus destabilizing the financial system if not the economy as a whole.[1] This belief is not uncommon even among students of bank-

---

The author is with Loyola University of Chicago and a consultant to the Federal Reserve Bank of Chicago. Partial funding for this paper was provided by the Cato Institute and the American Enterprise Institute. The author would like to thank Herbert Baer, George Benston, Robert Eisenbeis, Edward Kane, Allan Meltzer, Larry Mote, Edward Nash, Anna Schwartz, Steven Strongin, and Walker Todd for helpful comments on earlier drafts.

[1]Indeed, it is often believed that spreading "rumors" about a bank that can start a run is a crime subject to penalties. No such federal law exists, although some states may have such statutes. In early December 1986, the Magnet Savings Bank, the largest thrift institution in West Virginia, experienced a run when a proposed merger was canceled. Depositors withdrew about $1 million within 24 hours. In response, the bank offered a $5,000 reward for information leading to the conviction of those starting the rumor. The president of the bank explained that the bank had recently paid a $3,000 reward to catch a bank robber and that he considered the act of spreading rumors at least as serious as robbery. (See "Magnet Bank Cites Rumors in Run," *American Banker*, December 11, 1986, pp. 2, 9.) Attempts to penalize individuals who doubt the ability of banks to redeem their claims are not new in the United States. Dewey and Chaddock (1911, vol. 4, p. 74) noted that

> many in the earlier period of the [nineteenth] century considered it improper and injurious to call upon a bank for specie in payment of its bills. "Brokers who sent home the bills of country banks were denounced as speculators and bloodsuckers, whose extirpation would be a public benefit." Respectable men defended the conduct of banks in interposing obstacles to the payment of their notes to brokers who had brought them up to discount. A Boston broker was brought before a grand jury of Vermont for demanding payment in specie for the bills of one of its banks.

ing. For example, Norcross (1986, p. 318) warned in the *Banking Law Journal* that

> Bank failures are no longer isolated and self contained. . . . Today's bank failure is a crisis failure—a failure that will spread to other banks and financial institutions even during economic prosperity. The spark that ignites the flames of failure may still be grounded in mismanagement or fraud, but by the time the regulators douse today's fires, they will have ravaged the credit relationships of banks, businesses and individuals from coast to coast and, possibly, around the world.

During the Continental Illinois National Bank crisis, Comptroller of the Currency C. T. Conover (1984, pp. 287–88) defended the policy of guaranteeing the par value of all deposits and liabilities of the bank and the holding company by arguing that if

> Continental had failed and been treated in a way in which depositors and creditors were not made whole, we could very well have seen a national, if not an international, financial crisis the dimensions of which were difficult to imagine. None of us wanted to find out.

For many Americans, the term "bank run" conjures up images of the Great Depression. As a result, official public policy has been directed in recent years at preventing whenever possible any and all runs on depository institutions.

In examining whether the bad reputation of bank runs is deserved, we will in this chapter analyze the causes of bank runs; examine how runs have historically affected the bank(s) in which they occurred, other banks, the financial system, the community, and the national economy; review the history of bank runs; and explore alternative policy prescriptions for eliminating the potentially harmful effects of bank runs.

Anatomy of a Bank Run

Banks are depository intermediaries that borrow funds from lenders and lend them to borrowers. They do this more efficiently than individual lenders and borrowers can do on their own. Banks' profits are derived from the value added by transforming the denomination, maturity (or term to repricing), credit quality, and so forth of the securities sold to lenders or bought from borrowers and from assuming the associated risks. Contemporary banks typically raise most of their funds by selling short-term fixed-value debt securities (deposits), many of which contain put options exercisable by the depositor at par at any time. They invest their funds in, among other things, loans and securities that generally are not fixed-value and do not contain put options exercisable by the bank at par at any time. Thus, the banks assume the risk that the market value of their assets may decline to or below that of their deposit liabilities.

To protect themselves against possible loss, depositors, like any other creditors, will, in the absence of federal deposit insurance, monitor both the risk/return profile of their banks' asset and liability portfolios and the amount of capital (equity and subordinated debt) the banks hold. The poorer a bank's risk/return profile and the smaller its capital base, the greater is the probability that a shock will wipe out its capital and that depositors will experience a loss if the bank is not recapitalized or liquidated as soon as the market value of its net worth drops to zero. It seems reasonable to assume that the greater the probability that depositors place on this occurring, the more likely they are to withdraw their funds at the deposits' maturity date or the exercise date of the put option, whichever is earlier. The earlier the depositor is able to withdraw the deposit, the more likely he is to receive the full amount on time. As long as the cost of transferring deposits is smaller than the value of the ongoing banking relationship, the rational depositor will pursue a better-safe-than-sorry strategy. If a large number of a bank's depositors simultaneously assign a high probability of potential loss, the bank will experience many simultaneous requests for deposit withdrawals—that is, the bank will experience a run.

Depositors, of course, may be correct or incorrect in their assessment of a bank's financial strength. The implication of the run both for the bank and for the depositors depends in large part on the accuracy of the depositors' assessment.[2] If the depositors underestimated a bank's financial integrity and ignite a run on an economically solvent bank (one whose assets' current market value exceeds that of its liabilities) the main problem will be the bank's probable need for quick additional liquidity to meet deposit withdrawals. It can obtain the necessary liquidity by borrowing (which includes the sale of new deposits), by selling assets, or by a combination of the two. If other banks, including those that gain the deposits withdrawn, believe that the affected bank is economically solvent, it is in their mutual interest to recycle the funds quickly at market rates of interest either by lending to the bank or by purchasing the bank's assets. If a central bank exists, it is in society's interest for that bank to assist in the

---

[2]The process of a bank run is described in greater detail in Benston et al. (1986, particularly chapter 2) and in Benston and Kaufman (1986). For an analysis of the causes of bank runs, see Gorton (1986).

speedy recycling through appropriate use of the discount window or open market operations. In this scenario, the bank does not encounter a serious liquidity problem. The run will do little harm to the affected bank, other banks, or the economy, although it may produce a relatively small social cost by increasing uncertainty and causing depositors to expend shoe leather transferring funds.

If the bank does not get organized assistance from other banks or the central bank, it will be forced to tap the financial markets and may encounter more serious liquidity problems. The less developed these markets are, the higher will be the interest rates at which the bank can borrow funds quickly and the lower the prices at which it can sell assets quickly. The adverse consequences of the bank run will be more severe. The affected bank may incur "fire-sale" losses (selling assets at below-normal prices or borrowing at a higher-than-normal rate) because normal search time is not available to search out the best trading partner. At some point, the bank may be driven into fire-sale insolvency, where for the moment the market value of its assets is less than that of its deposits, although this would not be true if its assets were valued at equilibrium prices based on more normal search times. The liquidity problem has begotten a solvency problem, albeit a temporary one.

Unless such a bank is declared legally insolvent by the regulatory authorities as soon as it is economically insolvent, those depositors who ran fastest to withdraw their funds from the bank first would benefit the most, as they would receive payment in full. Those who were slower in seeking payment would be harmed the most, as they would be unlikely to receive full or timely payment. Indeed, one of the major reasons for the bank to be declared legally insolvent as soon as it is economically insolvent is to ensure that all depositors are treated fairly and are permitted to share alike in the distribution of the remaining assets. Such protection of creditors is the major rationale behind bankruptcy laws for nonbanking firms. In the scenario just presented, a bank run could drive an economically solvent bank into economic, albeit fire-sale, insolvency. Losses will accrue to shareholders and possibly to depositors. Because the economic/social cost of providing liquidity to a sound bank experiencing an unexpected demand for cash is smaller than the economic/social cost of allowing the institution to become "fire-sale" insolvent and forcing it to be recapitalized, sold, or liquidated, it is not in society's best interests to treat a fire-sale insolvency in the same fashion as a regular insolvency. Thus, under most circumstances, a run will not drive an economically sound bank into economic insolvency.

If the depositors are correct in their assessment of the bank and it is insolvent on the basis of equilibrium market values so that it cannot under current conditions expect to meet all of its deposit claims successfully, the fastest depositors will again benefit from beating slower depositors to the bank until the bank is declared legally insolvent and closed. An open insolvent bank can continue to pay deposit claims as long as the bank has enough assets to sell or can promise high enough interest rates to attract new deposits. However, in the absence of federal deposit insurance, an insolvent bank cannot be expected to borrow from other banks that are aware of its financial predicament and would thereby be endangering their own funds. Nor will the central bank enhance social welfare by providing the liquidity to maintain in operation an economically insolvent bank that uses the newly borrowed funds to repay previous depositors. Although the run may increase the bank's losses by forcing progressively greater fire-sale losses from the sale of progressively less liquid assets, in this case the run is the result of the insolvency, not the cause.

The effects of a bank run on other banks and beyond depend upon the response of depositors to the new information about the financial condition of the bank or banks that gave rise to the initial run. Individual depositors have three choices when they withdraw their funds from the insolvent bank. They can: 1) redeposit their funds at another bank that they perceive to be safer; 2) purchase a financial security (for example, a Treasury security) or real asset that they perceive to be safer; or 3) hold the funds in the form of currency outside the banking system.

Their choice depends on their analysis of the situation. If depositors' fears are restricted to a specific bank or to a few banks whose capital is perceived to be in jeopardy, they are likely to redeposit the funds immediately in other nearby banks that are perceived to be sounder financially. The net result is primarily a transfer of deposits and reserves from Bank A to, say, Bank B with no change in aggregate reserves, deposits, and credit. This is not to imply that in the "redeposit" scenario simultaneous runs may not occur on groups of banks, particularly if they are subject to the same actual or perceived market conditions. Regional contagion may occur—but it only involves a larger and more widespread churning of funds within the aggregate banking system. As long as depositors view some banks as safe for redeposits, total deposits will remain basically unchanged, contagion will be contained, and national or systemwide failure may be ruled out. Some small contraction in deposits may occur if banks increase their excess reserves to better protect themselves against runs, but

13

bank runs will not seriously destabilize the financial system. Some loan customers may be forced to transfer to another bank if Bank A is unable to regain the lost deposits quickly or to finance the deposit loss by the sale of investment securities, but that should be viewed as merely an inconvenience. Although the evidence is not strong, this cost may be expected to be relatively minor both in private and social terms.

Depositors who question the financial viability of all the banks in their market area may make the second choice mentioned above: to use their deposits to purchase securities they believe to be safe substitutes, such as U.S. Treasury securities. In this "flight to quality," ownership of the deposits is transferred to the seller of the securities, who now has the option of keeping the balances in the buyer's bank, transferring them to another bank, or withdrawing currency. Because security transactions are likely to be relatively large in dollar terms, the seller may be expected both to have a wider range of available banks and to be unlikely to want to hold the balance in the form of currency outside the banking system. Except for drug trafficking, currency is basically used only to finance smaller transactions.[3]

The wider the range of banks available to the seller of the security, the greater the probability of his finding a safe bank and the more likely it is that the funds will be transferred from the buyer's bank to the seller's. This indirect redeposit is equivalent to the direct redeposit scenario in terms of its effect on total deposits in the banking system. There will, however, also be other effects. The demand for riskless securities will push up the price and lower the yield on federal government securities relative to private securities. This may reasonably be expected to discourage private investment without automatically increasing public spending. At the same time, the churning of deposits among banks may be expected to be greater than with direct redeposits. This will further increase uncertainty in the economy and reinforce any downward pressures on economic activity. The increased churning of deposits will also require increased recycling of funds by the deposit-gaining banks and/or the central bank. But these costs are much smaller than those associated with nationwide systemic bank failures.

If both depositors and the sellers of safe securities fear the insolvency of all banks, neither group will redeposit funds in the banking

[3]Nor can any business organization but the very smallest use currency as an efficient medium of exchange. Nevertheless, in 1907 Henry Ford threatened to "build a vault to take our money out of the banks and put it in the vault, so we can pay our men in cash." Ford did not follow up on his threat. See Kennedy (1973, p. 92).

system and both will hold their balances as currency. Then the run is not on one bank but on the banking system. The flight to currency is equivalent to a drain of reserves from the banking system, and it will both ignite a multiple contraction in money and credit and increase the number and seriousness of bank fire-sale insolvencies. Unless a flight to currency is offset by an injection of reserves from the central bank equal to the currency drain, bank failures will be contagious nationwide, tumbling otherwise innocent solvent banks in domino fashion, breaking long-standing bank-customer loan relationships, destabilizing the financial sector, and adversely affecting all economic activity. This is the feared crisis or panic scenario that is vividly spelled out in money and banking textbooks. The private and social costs of a systemwide run are very high and of justifiably great concern to public policymakers. The process by which runs on individual banks turn into runs on the banking system has rarely been considered rigorously in the literature, however. Most writers do not seriously question that it occurs almost automatically and have accepted it as a matter of faith. For example, John Kareken (1986, pp. 36–37) has recently written:

> there is . . . [an] argument: that the failure of a bank, unlike the failure of any company not engaged in banking, has third party effects. I have always had difficulty with that argument; I have never been able to understand as well as I would have liked why there are third-party effects. . . . The third-party effects of a bank failure may be real or imagined. Whichever, there is reason enough for me to go on to how banks ought to be regulated.[4]

Unfortunately, the conditions under which runs on individual banks do turn into runs on the banking system are too important to be ignored, and the belief that the first automatically leads to the second is too important to be left to faith. The process needs to be analyzed carefully. Clearly, completely different public policies are appropriate if runs on individual banks endanger the entire system than if they do not.

The History of Bank Runs

Which of the options depositors are likely to choose during a bank run depends on the nature of the initial shock causing the loss of

---

[4]Indeed, a run on the banking system as a whole frequently is the only type of run analyzed in the academic literature. See, for example, Diamond and Dybvig (1983). Their article also considers only runs from bank deposits into consumption rather than currency. Such runs, however, effectively represent indirect redeposit runs and are not likely to lead to nationwide contagion or contraction in total bank deposits. Moreover, runs from deposits into consumption should increase income, which is inconsistent with both theory and observation.

depositor confidence and the institutional arrangements in place at the time. A review of U.S. history before the establishment of the FDIC in 1934 indicates that the national contagion scenario has not occurred very frequently.[5] If a net currency drain is a prerequisite for such a scenario, then analysis of annual data suggests that it is likely to have occurred in only four periods—1878, 1893, 1908, and 1929–33—when currency increased relative to bank deposits along with a decrease in total deposits (money). Further analysis suggests that nationwide bank contagion was probable in only two of these periods—1893 and 1929–33.[6] In 1893, nearly 500 banks failed, and between 1929 and 1933, the total number of commercial banks declined by 40 percent, from some 25,000 to 14,000.

In other years, the story was quite different. From the end of the Civil War through 1919, there were only 8 years besides 1893 in which more than 100 banks failed and none in which more than 200 banks failed. This is despite the existence of about 10,000 banks by 1895, 20,000 by 1905, and 30,000 (twice the current number of banks) by 1920. Indeed, the average bank failure rate in this period was below that for nonbanks, although the annual variance was higher. Aggregate losses to depositors were also small. The FDIC estimated that such losses averaged only 0.20 percent of total deposits at all banks annually, although individual depositors at failed institutions suffered considerably greater losses.

While the number of bank failures jumped to nearly 600 a year in the 1920s, failures for the most part involved small agricultural banks in small towns in the plains states and had little impact on banks elsewhere or on the aggregate economy.[7] Most of these failures, like those occurring today, reflected the severe problems in agriculture caused by a continuing sharp decline in commodity and land prices after an even sharper runup. Ninety percent of the banks that failed in this period had capital of less than $100,000, had loans and investments of less than $1 million, and were located in towns with populations below 5,000. Even after adjusting for the sixfold increase in prices since that period, these were Ma and Pa banks by any measure and were unlikely to have been diversified greatly or managed professionally. It appears that much of the current fear of bank fail-

---

[5]See Benston et al. (1986, chap. 2). A recent study by Schwartz (1987, forthcoming) suggests that major banking crises occurred even less frequently in foreign countries.

[6]Even in the 1929–33 period, regional rather than national contagion appears to have been the case until late 1932 when Nevada declared the first state banking holiday. See Willis and Chapman (1934, p. 9) and Wicker (1980).

[7]See Benston et al. (1986, chap. 2); Ely (1986); and Kindleberger (1985).

ures, at least in the United States, stems from the harrowing but unique experience of the Great Depression.

Although the number of bank failures was quite small until the 1920s, financial articles and history books are awash with stories of bank runs and document them convincingly. Thus, it appears that bank runs did not automatically lead to bank failures. Indeed, a study for the American Bankers Association in the late 1920s was summarized by a reviewer as relegating "the run as a real reason for [bank] suspensions . . . to a position of minor importance. It is found to be an effect of banking difficulties rather than a cause as a general proposition which is contrary to the fixed ideas of the public and even many bankers."[8] The evidence also suggests that problems in the nonfinancial sector of the economy caused problems in banking and not the other way around. That is, both bank runs and bank failures were an effect of and not the cause of aggregate economic contractions and hardships.[9] While accounts of financial panics and losses experienced by shareholders, some depositors, and loan customers of the failed banks indicate that the bank runs were not harmless, almost all bank runs resulted in either direct or indirect redeposits and did not develop into runs on the system.

How can we account for the failure of the runs on individual banks or groups of banks to lead, in most cases, to runs on all banks, despite the absence of an FDIC? The explanation seems to be that greater market discipline on bank management, combined with the timely closure of individual banks when they became economically insolvent, put banks in shape to weather most runs successfully. With all of their deposits at risk, depositors had more incentive to be concerned about the goings-on at their banks, to monitor bank operations carefully, and to exert discipline by either withdrawing their deposits or charging a higher interest rate for them if the banks' portfolios became too risky or their capital bases too small. The very threat of a run served as a powerful source of market discipline. At the turn of the century, capital ratios at banks were close to 25 percent and effectively even higher, as shareholders at national banks and some state banks were subject to double liability up to the initial par value of the shares. This led to an ex-post settling up in case of losses at failed banks, and although they were not fully effective, assessments were made on shareholders of failed banks and at least some funds were collected and paid to depositors. The inability to pursue share-

---

[8]See Thorndyke (1929, p. 1222). Schwartz (1987) also notes that few bank failures appear to be attributable to runs.

[9]See, for example, Cagan (1965) and Gorton (1986).

holders across state lines appears to have been a major barrier to fuller collections.

The threat of such assessments probably provided more incentive for shareholders to monitor their banks and exert pressure on management to operate prudently. They already had two good reasons to do so. To begin with, higher capital ratios meant shareholders had more of their own funds at stake. Moreover, the relatively swift closure of failed banks did not give them a free second or third chance to recoup their losses using the depositors' funds.

In the absence of deposit insurance, knowledgeable lenders, including other banks, were not likely to place their funds in banks they perceived to be economically insolvent. Indeed, they acted as quickly as possible to withdraw any funds they had on deposit at such a bank. Under these conditions, it did not take long for the bank to fail to meet a payment either by running out of currency or by not meeting its end-of-day debt to the clearinghouse. Such a bank was forced to suspend operations and subject itself to examination by the authorities to determine whether it was illiquid but solvent (satisfying minimum capital requirements) or illiquid and insolvent (having net worth below the minimum required capital). If the bank was solvent, it was permitted to reopen. If it was insolvent, it was required to recapitalize itself or be liquidated. Thus, liquidity served as an effective constraint to the continued operation of economically insolvent institutions.[10]

Lawrence White's (1984) book on banking in Scotland in the first half of the 1800s helps to explain the importance then of capital to banks and bank customers.[11] Bank shareholders were subject to unlimited personal liability. When the Fife Bank failed in 1829, for example, each holder of a £50 sterling share was assessed £5,500. In effect, the shareholders were general partners. This protected depositors and greatly diminished the incentive for bank runs. Bank failures and panics were infrequent and, when they did occur, losses to depositors were insignificant. White (1984, p. 143) quotes one contemporary observer as saying, "A run upon any bank, such as happens in England sometimes, or a panic, are terms the meaning of which is hardly understood in Scotland."

There is also evidence that depositors and noteholders in the United States cared about the financial condition of their banks and carefully

---

[10]See Kaufman (1986). A list of the reasons national banks could be declared insolvent and a receiver appointed in the period before 1930 appears in Upham and Lamke (1934, p. 19).

[11]For a somewhat different interpretation, see Rockoff (1986).

scrutinized bank balance sheets. Rolnick and Weber (1984, 1985) have shown that this clearly happened before the Civil War. Cleveland and Huertas (1985) demonstrated the importance of bank capital to depositors by noting that Citibank in its earlier days prospered in periods of general financial distress by maintaining higher than average capital ratios and providing depositors with a relatively safe haven.[12] Lastly, an analysis of balance sheets suggests that before the establishment of the FDIC banks at the very least assumed less interest rate risk than is the case today. Although some short-term loans were more or less automatically rolled over at maturity, they were repriced at the new market interest rate, making them equivalent to floating rate loans.[13]

The incentive structure for market discipline by private parties appears to have worked reasonably well. Many banks were able to survive runs through the sale of liquid assets and/or borrowing from others, including other banks that believed in their solvency. The recycling of funds from deposit-gaining to deposit-losing banks was generally undertaken under the leadership of the local clearinghouse, which had a strong direct stake in the survival of its member banks.[14] This facility acted to save solvent but illiquid banks and to prevent a run on one bank from setting off runs on other members. When there was a run on a member bank, the clearinghouse examined the bank and if it was determined to be solvent the clearinghouse arranged for loans from the other member banks. It also published the aggregate current balance sheet of its member banks to demonstrate their collective solvency and ability to satisfy all claims in full and on time. In emergencies, banks would suspend converting deposits into currency or specie (and earlier bank notes into specie), although they continued to provide all other services, including the making of loans.[15] At such times, the clearinghouse often would issue certifi-

---

[12]Recently, Citibank may be returning to this strategy. See Truell (1987).

[13]Most early students of banking from Adam Smith on argued that commercial banks should concentrate their lending on short-term self-liquidating loans in order to be able to meet potential currency and deposit losses. This represented a "real bills" micro bank management strategy as opposed to a "real bills" macro monetary policy strategy. This strategy also underlies the development of special banks for longer-term lending, such as for agriculture and residential housing, which would be financed by longer-term deposits. See Miller (1972), Fein (1986), and Merris and Wood (1985).

[14]For an account of clearinghouses, see Timberlake (1984) and Gorton (1985).

[15]The National Bank Act of 1863 effectively guaranteed the par value of national bank notes until their retirement in 1935, so that runs on banks to redeem notes were no longer of significance, particularly as notes of state banks were taxed out of existence after 1865. According to the 1952 annual report of the FDIC (p. 66):

The national banking system was essentially an extension on a national scale of

cates on itself to its member banks to assist in the clearing process and, on occasion, it also issued certificates in small denominations for its member banks to distribute to the public as a temporary replacement for currency. In this way, solvent banks were provided with time to work out their liquidity problems and avoid fire-sale insolvencies. The evidence strongly suggests that the clearinghouses were successful more often than they were not.

Indeed, their very success appears to have contributed to their decline, the establishment of the Federal Reserve System, and, ironically, to the most costly failure of the banking system. The clearinghouses performed well, but some of their actions, such as the distribution of certificates, were technically illegal although undertaken with the tacit approval of the authorities. This made some parties uneasy; they preferred a completely legal and aboveboard process. Furthermore, the financial system did not work perfectly and runs occurred that, although not nationally contagious, were highly visible and generated significant social and private costs. Ways were sought, therefore, to improve the structure. The result was the establishment of the Federal Reserve System, designed to serve as a national clearinghouse. The system was intended to expedite the recycling of funds to banks losing deposits as a result of runs, from banks gaining the deposits, by giving the Federal Reserve System direct access to the reserves of all banks in the country and by allowing the Fed to issue legal certificates in the form of currency. The liquidity role of the clearinghouses at the time of crises was thereby transferred to the Fed, and the clearinghouses restricted their operations to the

---

the free banking system established earlier in many States. That is, subject to certain restrictions, banking was open to all persons who qualified under the law and note issues were secured by the posting of collateral, in this case United States bonds. However, one important difference between the State systems and that adopted by the Federal Government was that the primary guaranty for the notes was the credit of the Government rather than the value of the posted collateral.

Holders of notes of a failed national bank were to be paid immediately and in full by the United States Treasury regardless of the then existing value of the bonds posted and whether or not any difficulty was encountered in disposing of the bonds. As the Comptroller of the Currency stated in his first report to Congress:

> If the banks fail, and the bonds of the government are depressed in the market, the notes of the national banks must still be redeemed in full at the treasury of the United States. The holder has not only the public securities but the faith of the nation pledged for their redemption.

It was apparently not foreseen early in the 1860s that deposits, rather than circulating notes, would come to constitute by far the largest portion of the nation's circulating medium. In 1860 the two items were about equal in amount. By 1870 deposits were about twice, and by the end of the century seven times, circulating notes.

See also Friedman and Schwartz (1963, pp. 21–23).

mechanics of clearing and paying interbank claims in the normal course of business. Contrary to expectations, the Fed, in part because it did not have the same direct incentives as the clearinghouses to maintain the solvency of the banks, failed to perform as well during the 1929–33 crisis as the clearinghouses had during earlier panics.[16]

The Role Runs Served

In the pre-FDIC scenario described above, bank runs had both good and bad effects. The good effect was the strong market discipline exerted on bank management to steer a prudent course and to avoid the substantial penalties for failure. The bad effect was their potential to spread damage to other innocent banks, the financial system, and the national economy. The costs of any severe crisis, however infrequent, are great enough that the perceived immediate benefits from preventing a recurrence take precedence, at least momentarily, over the costs of distorting incentives whose unfortunate effects will not be felt immediately. The introduction of the FDIC in 1934 effectively removed the bad effects of bank runs, but also, less visibly, significantly weakened the good effects. It is only in recent years, when changes in the economic, institutional, and technological environments have combined to reduce the costs and increase the payoffs for risk taking, that the implications of these distorted incentives have become generally visible.[17] On the whole, bank runs do not appear to deserve their bad reputation. They did a dirty job in maintaining market discipline—but someone had to do it. Eliminating dirty jobs per se does not eliminate the problems for which the jobs arose.

The problem of market discipline still exists. The authorities have been unable to develop clean ways of dealing with it effectively and are unwilling to assume "dirtier" ways. The consequences of the distortion introduced by deposit insurance have become very costly in dollar terms, but the authorities have preferred to delay recording the costs in the hope that conditions would reverse and the costs would decline or disappear. Economically insolvent institutions have not been closed and near-failed institutions have not been required to recapitalize. But the incentive structure was not changed. As a result, the strategy of buying time has been, on the whole, counterproductive. One can point to occasions when insolvent or near-insol-

[16]See Gorton (1986) and Friedman and Schwartz (1963). The Federal Reserve was also significantly less interested in the plight of nonmember banks than in that of member banks. This reduced its ability to serve as a national clearinghouse.

[17]See, for example, Benston et al. (1986) and Kane (1985, 1986a, 1986b).

vent institutions have improved their performance substantially given time, but the average bank in trouble is not so lucky. Assuming that markets are efficient and include in the assessments of any asset's value all available information, the ex ante probability of an independent event improving or worsening a bank's performance will be close to 50-50.[18]

Moreover, because the penalties for failure have been postponed and thereby weakened, a bank in trouble is likely to take greater risks than otherwise and the odds of success become even less favorable.[19] Thus, the policy of forbearance has served primarily to increase further the unbooked but very real losses accrued. In light of the large number of recent failures of depository institutions and the large associated accumulated losses, estimated to exceed $30 billion for savings and loan associations alone, changes in public policy are urgently required to protect the safety and efficiency of the banking system and to reduce the direct cost to the insurance agencies and the indirect cost to the U.S. Treasury and taxpayer. These changes need to correct the distortions in the incentive structure for risk taking introduced by the current structure of federal deposit insurance. Delay in reforming the system will only increase instability and the associated costs further.

[18]It might appear in retrospect that forbearance was successful for the thrift industry in the early 1980s when most of the institutions were economically insolvent because of the effects of high interest rates on their greatly mismatched asset-deposit duration structures. Many of these institutions were solvent again by 1986 after interest rates had declined sharply. Indeed, this conclusion was reached in a study of forbearance policy by the U.S. General Accounting Office. But this conclusion is not necessarily warranted. The sharp decline in interest rates cannot be attributed to management skills. It would have occurred regardless of who was in charge of the associations at the time. If the insolvent institutions had been "nationalized" when they first became economically insolvent, the subsequent gain in net worth would have accrued to the FSLIC and the taxpayers. If instead they had been sold to new owners who had expected interest rates to decline as sharply as they actually did, the FSLIC would have obtained premiums equal in present value dollar magnitude to the subsequent gain. Under forbearance, the gain accrued to the previously insolvent managers/owners. But what if interest rates had not declined? The FSLIC would have suffered all the additional loss. In retrospect, savings and loan association management was lucky, not skillful. Even in Las Vegas the customers win nearly half the time, but not on average over time. Moreover, the forbearance policy reduced the pressure on management/ shareholders to change their strategy and reduce their risk exposure. Thus, many associations have recently widened their asset-deposit duration mismatch again by returning to long-term fixed-rate mortgages. This is likely to lead to a repeat of the interest-rate risk game, but not necessarily with the same favorable outcome for the FSLIC. Other institutions found other ways to increase their bets on little or none of their own capital. See General Accounting Office (1986b).

[19]A rigorous statement of the incentive structure appears in Jensen and Meckling (1976) as well as in Kane (1985).

Perverse Incentives from Insurance

Earlier research has clearly established that the present structure of deposit insurance changes the incentives of insured depositors in ways that can cause individual depository institutions to take on more than the socially optimal degree of risk, increase the likelihood of losses by the insurance agency, and make it difficult to treat depository institutions equitably in assessing their insurance premiums.[20] It does so in three ways.

First, insurance of any type makes the insured party somewhat less careful because the costs or penalties from loss are expected to be less than if they were uninsured. Deposit insurance makes depositors less careful about evaluating and monitoring the financial integrity of their banks, at least up to the legal $100,000 maximum, and thereby reduces the degree of market discipline they exert. The increase in account coverage from the original $2,500 in 1934 to the present $100,000—in particular, the sharp jump from $40,000 to $100,000 in 1980—was a far greater adjustment for inflation than was justified to protect the "small" depositor. On the other hand, the increases in coverage made it easier and cheaper for larger depositors to divide up their funds among different institutions in fully insured chunks with or without the help of brokers. When banks are paying up to 150 basis points (1.50 percent) above the national average on insured deposits, what do depositors believe the banks are doing with their funds—and why should they care? As a result of depositor indifference, insured banks are less restrained about increasing their risk exposure.[21] With the help of technological advances, risk-prone banks can expand quickly by attracting funds from beyond local markets. It is unlikely that in the absence of deposit insurance commercial banks could operate with capital-asset ratios of only 6 percent and thrift institutions with ratios barely above zero.

Second, premiums for federal deposit insurance are proportional to the insured bank's total domestic deposits rather than related to the institution's risk exposure. Thus, risky institutions pay no more for the same insurance coverage than less risky institutions do. Because average losses on risky opportunities are larger than average losses on less risky opportunities, a flat-rate premium structure is inequi-

---

[20]This literature is described in Benston et al. (1986) and in Kane (1985). These problems are not limited to the United States. See, for example, Dowd (1987).

[21]An interesting empirical documentation appears in Clair (1984). In addition, a number of credit union officials have noted that the credit unions increased their risk exposure after the introduction of federal share insurance in 1971. See National Credit Union Administration (1983).

table. Although the promised revenue payoff on risky opportunities is greater, the cost of insured funds to finance these ventures does not increase proportionately. Thus, the bank's expected net return is greater for risky ventures. This is a strong incentive for insured banks to increase their risk exposure. Because few of the bigger bets are likely to pay off, the insurance agency can expect to absorb greater losses from the banks' greater risk exposures. Before federal deposit insurance, riskier banks had to pay higher interest rates for funding riskier ventures, so the opportunity for higher net returns on such ventures was reduced.

Third, because depositors need not be concerned about the safety of their funds up to the legally insured maximum amount, federal deposit insurance permits banks that are economically insolvent but that have not yet been declared insolvent and closed by bank regulators to attract funds not only to meet deposit losses, interest on deposits, and payrolls, but also to make additional loans and investments and to expand. Thus, the managers/owners of these institutions are able to continue operating for an indefinite time and are likely to increase their losses further.[22] This has been the experience of many insolvent savings and loan associations since the late 1970s. Before federal deposit insurance such operations were referred to as "Ponzi" schemes and viewed with disdain.

Barth et al. (1986) examined the cost to the FSLIC of all savings and loan associations that were merged with financial assistance or liquidated between 1982 and 1985. They reported that the most important determinant of the costs absorbed by the insurance fund was the delay between the date that an institution became insolvent on the basis of generally accepted accounting practices (GAAP) and the date that it was declared insolvent and closed by the FSLIC. The average delay was almost five months and cost the FSLIC about $300,000 per month per institution. Similarly, Easton (1986) reported that it cost the FSLIC, on average, 15 percent of a failed association's assets in 1984 to close or merge it. In 1985, this figure had risen to 25 percent.

Easton also described the deterioration in the net worth of a sample of the worst savings and loan associations that had been taken over by the FSLIC and were being operated by a management appointed by and responsible to the Federal Home Loan Bank Board. This management consignment program was begun in hopes of reversing the performance of unprofitable S&Ls. At least for these institutions it has not worked. The Sunrise Savings and Loan in Boynton Beach,

---

[22]See Kane (1985, chap. 2; 1987) and Kaufman (1987).

Florida, was liquidated in October 1986, about one year after it was placed in the program. During this period, its net worth declined from − $38 million on $1.5 billion of assets to − $368 million. Similarly, the Southern California Savings and Loan in Beverly Hills experienced a decline in net worth from − $57 million to − $218 million on $1.1 billion in assets in the one year ending June 1986 in which it was in the program. The net worth of the Bell Savings and Loan Association in San Mateo, California, declined from − $23 million to − $257 million on $1.4 billion in assets in about the same period. Two caveats are in order. On the one hand, the new management very likely recognized previously unbooked losses that should have been recognized sooner, so the initial net worth was probably overstated. On the other hand, the net worth data reported are computed on the basis of GAAP, which allows numerous procedures of dubious economic meaning that may have been used by the new managers to increase reported net worth above its market value.

If institutions could be closed precisely at the instant that the market value of their net worth declines to zero, there would be no losses to depositors and therefore no losses to the deposit insurance agency.[23] The term "closed" is misleading, however. To the public, it conjures up images of physically boarding up an institution so that it disappears as a provider of banking services to the community. The term "reorganized" is more accurate. Financially, closing a bank refers only to closing down the old shareholders and senior management unless they recapitalize the bank themselves or through sale or merger. Only if these alternatives fail is the bank liquidated and closed physically.

Reform, Not Abolition

Although federal deposit insurance creates many incentives for risk taking, abolition of federal insurance is not the solution to the problem. Some minimum federal deposit insurance, although not necessarily $100,000 per account, is necessary as long as Federal Reserve actions are sufficiently uncertain to preserve the stability of the system as a whole by eliminating the need for depositors to withdraw funds from all institutions simultaneously—that is, to prevent depositors from running on the system. Reform of the insurance structure is more promising. Most recommendations for reform are aimed at correcting the first two problems: the moral hazard from

---

[23]See, for example, Bierwag and Kaufman (1983) and Barbara Bennett (1984).

insurance per se and the increased risk incentive from flat-rate premiums.[24]

The proposed solutions go in two opposite directions. Some focus on increased regulatory and legislative discipline to limit an institution's potential risk exposure. Others would rely on market mechanisms to achieve the same result more efficiently. To intensify the degree of market discipline exerted by depositors, the de jure $100,000 maximum deposit insurance should be reduced, or at least neither de facto nor de jure insurance should be increased further. Depositor market discipline is already effectively nonexistent in thrift institutions, where all deposits are in effect fully insured, as almost all are in denominations of $100,000 or less. To reduce the rewards to depositories for risk taking, the market-oriented reformers also suggest scaling insurance premiums (or capital requirements) to a bank's risk exposure. Substantial opposition has developed to both the proposals for more market discipline and more regulator discipline. Regardless of their academic merits, both would, in the opinion of many, be difficult to implement.[25]

More Timely Failure Resolution

Less attention has been focused on solutions to the third problem—the increased risk incentive from capital forbearance.[26] Recapitalizing, selling, merging, or, as a last resort, liquidating institutions when

---

[24]See, for example, Federal Home Loan Bank Board (1983); Federal Deposit Insurance Corporation (1983); Working Group of the Cabinet Council on Economic Affairs (1985); and General Accounting Office (1986a).

[25]Much of the criticism focuses on the theoretical and practical difficulties of measuring risk accurately and developing appropriate premium scales. One of the earliest criticisms of these proposals was by Kareken (1983). Kareken is also one of the first proponents of replacing federal deposit insurance by establishing uninsured "money market" bank affiliates, which would offer transaction deposits and invest only in near riskless securities. Other types of deposits would be offered by other affiliates of the bank or bank holding company, which could invest in risky securities and would not be federally insured. See also Kareken (1986); Golembe and Mingo (1985); and Litan (1985). For a criticism of these proposals, see Benston and Kaufman (forthcoming).

Allan Meltzer and Thomas Huertas have proposed a variant on this proposal in which financial institutions that offer transactions balances may invest only in assets that can be marked to market. Thus, depositors could easily monitor their institutions' financial conditions. A side benefit of this proposal would be to encourage the development of procedures for marking to market assets that are currently not so valued as a by-product of banks' attempts to expand the range of permissible investments. However, as argued later in this paper, all these proposals still require a clear and enforced closure rule to be effective.

[26]Previous studies of the relationship of bank capital and deposit insurance include Pyle (1984 and 1986).

the market value of their net worth is equal to zero would help to counteract reduced market discipline from both shareholders and depositors that arises as a result of the existing regulatory structure. The incentives for institutional risk taking would be, therefore, greatly reduced.[27] Any rule governing such closure/reorganization would need to be both clearly enunciated and strictly enforced.

Except for major fraud, losses to the deposit insurance agencies would be effectively eliminated because no losses accrue to depositors, so timely failure resolution offers three further significant bonuses that may increase its attractiveness and thereby its prospects of adoption. First, assuming the current structure of federal deposit insurance, the effective elimination of losses from bank failures reduces the need for insurance premiums except those that pay the FDIC's and FSLIC's operational expenses, including upgraded and more frequent monitoring of insured institutions and the development of accurate market value accounting systems. The authority to close banks should be transferred from the chartering agencies, which bear none of the dollar costs of delayed bank closures and frequently fear official recognition of a failure as a blot on their records, to the insurance agency, which bears the full cost of such hits.[28] The FDIC and FSLIC may then be viewed as unusual insurance firms that can determine the magnitude and timing of their own losses by controlling the outcomes of insured events.[29] This makes it clear that federal deposit insurance is not really insurance but a guaranty. Thus, to the extent that insurance premiums are required and intended to be

---

[27]Because of problems of monitoring and the possibility of abrupt declines or jump processes in the market value of an institution's net worth, it may be desirable to reorganize the institution before the market value of its net worth declines to zero, say at some small positive percentage of assets such as 2 or 3 percent. If any ex post losses are incurred, they should be borne pro rata by the federal deposit insurance agencies on the de jure insured deposits and by the uninsured depositors. Alternatively, the reorganization/closure rule could be specified at some higher positive level of capital defined in nonmarket terms, for example, book value. Existing shareowners would be provided with an opportunity to recapitalize the bank at that point. If they failed to do so, the institution would be transferred to the regulators. It may reasonably be assumed that shareholders have better information about the "true" market value of their institutions than do the regulators, and that they would be willing to provide additional capital if this value were positive and would walk away if it were negative. These alternative closure schemes are analyzed more carefully in Benston and Kaufman (forthcoming).

[28]See Benston et al., chap. 5. Because it is unlikely that private insurance firms will be legally permitted to reorganize institutions when their capital approaches zero, private deposit insurance is likely to be more costly and less efficient than federal insurance.

[29]Reasons policymakers want to affect the timing of closures are discussed in Bierwag and Kaufman (1983).

actuarially fair to cover the insurance agencies' expected losses, they need to be scaled to the costs of monitoring the activities of the bank and the legal and political ability of the insurer to close institutions in a timely manner rather than to the riskiness of particular activities or the bank. Activity risk and difficulty of monitoring may or may not be correlated. This weakens the theoretical case for risk-sensitive insurance premiums. (See Bierwag and Kaufman 1983.)

Second, the risk characteristics of banks would be unimportant. There would be little justification for regulating or legislating the nature of the activities in which banks may or may not engage solely on considerations of risk. Activity restrictions based on other considerations, such as conflicts of interest, excess concentration, or the undesirability of bringing the activity under the surveillance of bank regulators would remain. To date, many restrictions on bank activities have been justified as restricting risk. These include the Glass-Steagall prohibitions on full-line securities activities and limitations on insurance underwriting, and some nonfinancial activities. If banks were closed or reorganized promptly, how much risk a bank wished to assume could be left up to its management, which might be expected to be sensitive to the penalties for failure. Decisions to take portfolio risk would be more likely to be based on the belief that the bank's capital is sufficient, rather than on the belief that the insurance agency will cover any losses. Greater risk would be undertaken only with greater capital.

Third, in some measure because of the different dollar losses that may be experienced by the insurance agency and uninsured depositors, present closure policy does not treat all failed banks equally. Uninsured depositors at large failed banks are reimbursed fully regardless of the bank's condition, while those at small failed banks are frequently assessed losses relative to the market value of the bank's assets. Obviously, this policy is inequitable to smaller banks and their customers. By effectively eliminating depositor losses, timely closure permits more equal treatment of banks regardless of their size, location, or the nature of their business. No bank would be "too large to fail."

As a result of the lower premium costs to banks, the greater freedom from regulation of bank risks and activities, and greater equity in treating banks in similar financial predicaments similarly, a policy of timely reorganization may be more efficient and attract less opposition than either reduced insurance coverage or risk-sensitive premiums. Opposition to it may be expected to center on 1) the application of a different, more stringent standard of insolvency for banks than for nonbanking firms, 2) the high cost to the community of bank failure, and 3) the difficulties of implementing market (current) value accounting and more frequent, almost online monitoring of bank activities.

Arguments against Timely Failure Resolution

A nonbank firm is generally declared involuntarily bankrupt, and remedies for creditors started, when it fails to pay a major scheduled payment on time and in full. Economic insolvency, per se, is not generally considered sufficient grounds for creditors to file for involuntary bankruptcy and request remedies, although it may be grounds for voluntary bankruptcy. (See Weintraub and Resnick 1986.) Thus, nonbank firms may be permitted to continue to operate after they become economically insolvent. Banks are different from nonbank firms in many ways, however, and different and more timely failure resolutions may be justified, in part as payment for federal deposit insurance.

As noted earlier, bank debt differs from the debt of nonbank firms in that much of it (deposits) contains a put option that is exercisable at par at the discretion of the depositor and much of the rest of it is very short term. Thus, in the absence of deposit insurance, attempts by some depositors to withdraw their funds out of concern about the bank's solvency could result in immediate large-scale demands from other depositors that the bank could not accommodate. Economic insolvency for banks is therefore only one inevitable step short of the necessary condition for involuntary bankruptcy for nonbank firms. Action to declare a bank in this condition legally insolvent represents, therefore, effectively equal treatment for the two types of firms. It is counterproductive to permit banks to default if it is not economically necessary. More timely failure resolution based on market valuations that would in a noninsurance environment ignite the inevitable run and bring on the solvency crisis appear to be a cheaper and more efficient remedy.

Evidence that more timely closure reduces losses to creditors is quite strong. Until recently, the FDIC closed banks reasonably quickly after it became evident that the market value of their assets had declined below that of their liabilities and, except in the cases of major fraud, experienced minor losses if any. (See Benston et al., chap. 4.) In the absence of major fraud, the market values of banks are unlikely to decline abruptly overnight. Rather, they will generally deteriorate slowly through time and can be monitored reasonably accurately. Through 1931, losses at failed and swiftly closed national banks were estimated to be about 10 cents on the dollar, compared to 90 cents on the dollar at nonfinancial firms.[30] In a recent study of defaulted corporate bonds, Altman and Nammacher (1985) estimated that the immediate loss in market bond values from 1974 through 1984 was about 60 percent. This is consistent with the loss ratios estimated by W. B. Hickman (1958) for the 1900 to 1943 period. These losses to creditors reflect the delay in initiating involuntary bankruptcy procedures for nonfinancial firms.

The fear of the high cost of bank failures is based on a belief that one or more of the following occurs: 1) failed banks are liquidated and disappear; 2) bank services are unique and even a brief interruption is exceptionally harmful to the community; and 3) the failure of one bank can set in motion a domino effect, with one bank after another tumbling throughout the country, disrupting the payments system.[31] The weight of available evidence suggests that none of these fears is justified. Liquidation of failed banks or any other type of firm is generally limited to smaller institutions. The others tend to be recapitalized, merged, or sold. Some time may be required to work out a least-cost solution for larger institutions, but recent proposals, some already implemented, for the FDIC to establish "bridge" or "trusteeship" banks would provide the necessary time to work out solutions for these larger banks. As already noted, the Federal Home Loan Bank Board operates failed savings and loan associations under a management consignment program until they can be sold or privately recapitalized.[32]

Even liquidations do not necessarily indicate that a community is left without banking facilities. Between 1927 and mid-1932, near the height in the decline in the number of banks, less than 4 percent of

[30]See Lawrence (1935). Losses tended to be greater from 1921 through 1930, at smaller banks, in smaller cities, where bank failures were greatest, and at liquidated banks. In this period, losses to depositors at fully liquidated banks were about 50 percent, but these were the smaller banks. Depositors at 50 percent of failed banks with loans and investments in excess of $1 million received 100 percent of their deposits and 70 percent of these depositors received 80 percent or more. See Upham and Lamke (1934, chap. 7).

[31]See Corrigan (1982) and Volcker (1986).

[32]Recently, strong political opposition has developed to regulators' declaring institutions insolvent in areas where large numbers of institutions are in financial difficulties. This appears to reflect a coalition of a number of interested parties, including managers, who prefer to keep their positions; shareholders, who are hoping to recover their losses in ways described in the text; debtors in default, who fear that new managers would be harsher in restructuring their loans and who view the status quo as not much different from a debt moratorium; and provincialists, who fear loss of control to nonlocal outsiders. See, for example, Garsson (1987) and Apcar and Yang (1987) describing actions by Speaker of the House Jim Wright (D-Tex.) to scale down the administration's FSLIC proposal.

the more than 10,000 cities in the United States with populations of 1,000 or more lost their only commercial bank, and only 17 of the nearly 1,000 cities with populations of 10,000 or more were left without a bank.[33] More recently, the number of savings and loan associations has declined by almost 50 percent (from 6,200 to 3,200) in the 20 years between 1965 and 1985 and by 30 percent in the 5 years since 1980 alone. This is not much less than the decline in the number of commercial banks in the 1920–33 period. Yet there has been no major outcry by consumers about a loss of services. In large part, this may be explained by a sharp increase in the number of branches so that the total number of savings and loan association offices more than doubled from 9,200 to 20,300 between 1965 and 1985 and declined by less than 1,000 between 1980 and 1985.

In a recent article in the *American Banker,* Bennett (1986) analyzed the effects on communities of the closing of their only banks. According to the author, the communities that lost their only local source of banking services in recent years were generally very small towns with populations under 300. These towns tend to be too small to support another independent bank or even a branch of a distant bank. The only bank's departure was not only inconvenient, it led to reduced revenues and even the closing of neighboring business firms, generally retail shops. Consumers had to travel to nearby cities for personal banking services, and those who used to bank and shop locally transferred some of their business to shops nearer to their new banks. But these effects are hardly different from the repercussions when a community loses its only movie theater, department store, or even supermarket. To provide local financial services in one of the affected communities, 11 imaginative residents contributed $100 apiece to form a local credit union. Within a year, the credit union had about $700,000 in deposits, equal to 15 percent of the deposits at the old bank. In addition, business has picked up again at community stores and a few new stores have opened. There is little validity, then, to the argument that closing a local bank devastates its community. Capital forbearance is primarily forbearance for guilty or unlucky bank owners and managers rather than for bank customers.

In addition, it is costly to society to carry insolvent institutions. In a market economy, failure is the market's way of indicating that customers are not satisfied with the products offered or prices charged by suppliers. Economically insolvent suppliers of banking services

---

[33]See "No Banking Adjustment in 68% of All Cities and Towns." *Bankers Monthly* (October 1932): 585–88.

are kept in business only through subsidies from bank authorities. The welfare of the economy would be improved if the institutions were permitted to close and the resources shifted elsewhere. Restrictions on exit are in effect also restrictions on the entry of new firms and result in the misallocation of scarce resources.

Although banks at some earlier time may have produced unique liquidity and payments mechanism services by virtue of their charters, the availability of which has been restricted at least since the Great Depression, recent dramatic advances in computer and telecommunications technology effectively permit anyone with a large computer system to offer similar services anywhere on short notice. In addition, different types of chartered financial institutions are now permitted to offer services previously restricted to only one type of institution. Surveys indicate that hardly any household now uses only one financial institution, that fully 60 percent use three or more, and that more than half of all small business firms use two or more (see Whitehead 1982 and Veronica Bennett 1984). Larger firms may reasonably be expected to use even more. Thus, failure and even liquidation of a bank is highly unlikely to leave many customers stranded.

The presence of federal deposit insurance has all but eliminated the threat of systemic bank failures. Except for errors in public policy, bank runs will not drive an economically solvent bank into insolvency nor spread to innocent banks. Although not discussed here, bank failures are also not serious threats to a payments system that sufficiently restricts or prohibits daylight overdrafts. Like federal deposit insurance, the Federal Reserve guaranty of each item entering its clearing process reduces the incentives for banks to carry sufficient clearing balances and capital. Computer breakdown, as occurred at the Bank of New York, is a much more serious threat. Even so, little research or evidence has been developed on the consequences of gridlock and unwinding transactions. Yet the regulatory authorities frequently predict the end of the economy as we know it if participants in the payments system default. These predictions are similar to those still made about the failure of large banks such as the Continental Illinois Bank, despite overwhelming evidence to the contrary.[34] It is unlikely that one or a few hours' delay in payments will cause all the lights in the world to go off!

Market Value Accounting

This is not to argue that more timely closure is without costs or difficulties. Market value accounting is not easy, particularly for infre-

[34]See, for example, Kaufman (1985); Ireland (1986); and Benston et al. (1986, chap. 2).

quently traded and nonfinancial assets.[35] Yet it underlies almost every proposal for reform. How is it possible for policymakers to evaluate the condition of a bank, or for management to manage the bank systematically, without an accurate statement of its accounts? To successfully map how to reach a target, one has to know where one is starting. Indeed, the use of book value accounting in banking was promoted by bank regulators in the 1930s to deliberately mask the banks' poor financial condition.[36] It continues to be used for this purpose today.[37]

It is interesting to note that the banks' increased reliance on book value accounting corresponds with their decreased allegiance to the "real-bills" strategy for asset management. One of the public's major misconceptions about banking is that one needs to have faith in one's bank and banker.[38] Nothing could be further from the truth! Faith belongs in churches; good assets belong in banks. If the value of the bank's assets is insufficient to meet its deposit liabilities in full and on time, those depositors who have the most faith will be the last to try withdrawing their funds and will suffer the largest losses. Market discipline requires depositor skepticism, not faith. Depositor faith only permits banks to assume greater risk exposure than otherwise. Brumbaugh (1986) looked at failed savings and loan associations and found that although losses to the FSLIC from these institutions were greater the smaller the net worth as computed on a market value basis, the losses were greater the greater the institutions' net worth as computed according to GAAP and the even less meaningful regulatory accounting practice (RAP). Indeed, if intangible faith and trust were required to operate a safe banking system, government intervention or formal industry self-regulation would be required to establish standards, including possible accreditation of bank managers, and to monitor compliance.

---

[35]See, for example, Benston et al. (1986, chap. 8); Kane (1985, chap. 4); Benston (1982); Johnson and Patterson (1984); and Leah et al. (1986).

[36]See "Revision in Bank Examination Procedure and in Investment Securities Regulation of the Comptroller of the Currency," *Federal Reserve Bulletin*, July 1938, pp. 563–66.

[37]When in the early 1980s even book value accounting proved insufficient to show positive net worth for savings and loan associations, the Federal Home Loan Bank Board invented regulatory accounting practice (RAP), which included a wider range of intangible and imaginary assets, to avoid having to reorganize insolvent institutions. Similar practices occur in other federal agencies. See Bailey and McCoy (1987).

[38]For example, Gerald Corrigan (1987, p. 21), president of the Federal Reserve Bank of New York, has recently argued that "the business of banking and finance is essentially the business of public and mutual confidence."

The market value of a bank's net worth may be obtained either directly from the transactions data for its stock or indirectly from assigning values to its assets and liability items, including off-balance sheet accounts, good will, franchise value, and other intangibles. The direct method is both cheaper and more accurate. Unfortunately, the shares of only a small number of the largest bank holding companies are traded publicly. Thus, the introduction of market value accounting will occasionally require imprecise and arbitrary estimations and appraisals. Although many bank assets and liabilities are not marketable and do not have a market price, a rapidly increasing number of them do as a result of both increased computerization of bank accounts and increased securitization of previously nonmarketable loans, for example, residential and mortgage loans, automobile loans, and business loans. Many larger business loan customers also issue bonds, and there is even a thin market for loans to less developed countries. A proxy price can now be obtained for most bank assets.

Moreover, in practice market value accounting need not be perfectly accurate to represent an improvement, only closer to the true value than book value accounting. That is not a difficult goal to achieve! Indeed, it is what bank loan officers themselves are trained to do when assessing their own loan customers. In recognition of possible errors that may understate the true market value of a bank's capital, however, the criterion for declaring a bank insolvent by the authorities may be set, at least during a transition period, at minus 1 or 2 percent of total assets rather than at zero percent. In addition, a procedure for speedy appeal should be established.

Similarly, frequent and accurate monitoring is difficult, but it is becoming easier, as bank managers themselves have discovered the need for quick, accurate on-line information. Indeed, it appears that opposition to market value accounting comes less from the banks themselves than from the regulators. Nevertheless, serious problems exist. By definition, fraud cannot be easily detected until after the event. Nor do changes in financial conditions occur either smoothly or continuously. Statistical jump processes can cause net worth to become suddenly negative and impose losses on the insurance agency even under perfect monitoring. Thus, substantial research efforts are needed to improve both market value accounting and monitoring procedures. This is likely to be expensive, but the cost is unlikely to come close to the estimated \$30 billion cost to the government of carrying today's insolvent savings and loan associations. Additional efforts are also needed to design workable and timely procedures for closing/reorganizing and unwinding the affairs of economically insolvent institutions. But these difficulties and costs should not delay consideration of a policy of more timely failure resolution. As noted earlier, alternative policies that have been proposed to increase the safety and efficiency of the financial structure appear to be economically more costly and politically less acceptable.

Conclusions

More timely resolution of bank failures, while neither easy nor costless, deserves greater immediate attention as a politically acceptable, economically efficient, and equitable solution for offsetting the undesirable incentive effects of deposit insurance; reducing the frequency, cost, and disruption of bank failures; and substantially reducing the degree of regulation over the amount of capital and types of activities in which a bank or bank holding company may engage. In such an environment, bank runs are unlikely to invoke fear or panic in depositors or the public. The good effects of timely bank closure/ reorganization will outweigh its bad effects and help to make the banking system both safer and more efficient at minimum cost.[39] The bad reputation bank runs have reflects both bad public policy and undue concern over losses to bank owners and managers. Public policy should shift the focus of concern from the stability of individual banks, which is little more important than the stability of individual grocery stores or gas stations, to the stability of the banking system as a whole, which is of critical importance and requires limited federal deposit insurance and/or more intelligent central bank policy. To the extent that these are in place, public policy toward

---

[39]To help increase the public acceptability of bank runs, I have written new lyrics to the readily singable tune of "Let It Snow! Let It Snow! Let It Snow!"

LET THEM RUN! LET THEM RUN! LET THEM RUN!
Oh, the depositors outside are threatening
But our vault is so protecting
And if you pardon the pun
Let them run, let them run, let them run.

Well, they don't show signs of stopping
So we're selling assets nonstopping
And until our work is done
Let them run, let them run, let them run.

Now the run is slowly dying
Our cash has stopped the crying
The work has become more fun
Let them run, let them run, let them run.

So, the moral is clearly revealing
If a bank is not concealing
And its capital is like a ton
Let them run, let them run, let them run.

banking can be greatly simplified. Because runs on individual banks have been confused in the public mind with runs on the banking system, bank runs have been given a bad rap. Public policy can change this by permitting at least the threat of their occurrence at poorly managed individual institutions. The challenge is not to eliminate bank runs, but to harness their power in such a way that the financial system is made safer and more efficient.

References

Altman, Edward I., and Nammacher, Scott A. "The Default Rate Experience on High Yield Corporate Debt." *Financial Analysts Journal* (July/August 1985): 25–41.

Annual Report of the Federal Deposit Insurance Corporation, 1952. Washington, D.C.: Federal Deposit Insurance Corporation, 1953.

Apcar, Leonard M., and Yang, John E. "Texans Are Holding Sway on Bank, S & L Regulation." *Wall Street Journal* (February 11, 1987): 6.

Bailey, Jeff, and McCoy, Charles F. "To Hide Huge Losses, Financial Officials Use Accounting Gimmicks." *Wall Street Journal* (January 12, 1987): 1, 14.

Barth, James R.; Brumbaugh, R. Dan; and Sauerhaft, Daniel. "Failure Costs of Government-Regulated Financial Firms: The Case of Thrift Institutions." Working Paper, Federal Home Loan Bank Board, June 1986.

Bennett, Andrea. "Small Town Businesses Don't Stick Around When the Only Bank Closes Its Doors." *American Banker* (December 2, 1986): 40, 32.

Bennett, Barbara A. "Bank Regulation and Deposit Insurance: Controlling the FDIC's Losses." Federal Reserve Bank of San Francisco *Economic Review* (Spring 1984): 16–30.

Bennett, Veronica. "Consumer Demand for Product Deregulation." Federal Reserve Bank of Atlanta *Economic Review* (May 1984): 28–37.

Benston, George J. "Accounting Numbers and Economic Values." *Antitrust Bulletin* (Spring 1982): 161–215.

Benston, George J.; Eisenbeis, Robert A.; Horvitz, Paul M.; Kane, Edward J.; and Kaufman, George G. *Perspectives on Safe and Sound Banking.* Cambridge, Mass.: MIT Press, 1986, pp. 49–77.

Benston, George J., and Kaufman, George G. "Risks and Failures in Banking: Overview, History, and Evaluation." In *Deregulating Financial Services.* Edited by George G. Kaufman and Roger C. Kormendi. Cambridge, Mass.: Ballinger Press, 1986.

Benston, George J., and Kaufman, George G. "Deposit Insurance and Risk Regulation." Washington, D.C.: American Enterprise Institute, forthcoming.

Bierwag, G. O., and Kaufman, George G. "A Proposal for Federal Deposit Insurance with Risk Sensitive Premiums." *Proceedings of a Conference on Bank Structure and Competition.* Federal Reserve Bank of Chicago, 1983, pp. 223–42.

Brumbaugh, R. Dan. "Empirical Evaluation of the Determinants of Losses for the Federal Savings and Loan Insurance Corporation (FSLIC)." Working Paper, Federal Home Loan Bank Board, February 1986.

Cagan, Philip. *Determinants and Effects of Changes in the Stock of Money, 1875–1960*. New York: Columbia University Press, 1965.

Clair, Robert T. "Deposit Insurance, Moral Hazard, and Credit Unions." Federal Reserve Bank of Dallas *Economic Review* (July 1984): 1–12.

Cleveland, Harold van B., and Huertas, Thomas F. *Citibank, 1812–1970*. Cambridge, Mass.: Harvard University Press, 1985.

Conover, C. T. Testimony before the Subcommittee on Financial Institutions Supervision, Regulation and Insurance of the Committee on Banking, Finance and Urban Affairs, U.S. House of Representatives. Inquiry into Continental Illinois Corp. and Continental Illinois National Bank: Hearings. 98th Congress, 2nd Session, 1984.

Corrigan, F. Gerald. "Are Banks Special?" *Annual Report, 1982*. Minneapolis: Federal Reserve Bank of Minneapolis, 1982.

Corrigan, F. Gerald. *Financial Market Structure: A Longer View*. New York: Federal Reserve Bank of New York, January 1987.

Dewey, Davis R., and Chaddock, Robert E. *State Banking Before the Civil War*. Washington, D.C.: National Monetary Commission, 1911.

Diamond, Douglas W., and Dybvig, Philip H. "Bank Runs, Deposit Insurance and Liquidity." *Journal of Political Economy* (June 1983): 401–19.

Dowd, Kevin. "Some Lessons from the Recent Canadian Bank Failures." Working Paper, University of Sheffield, England, January 1987.

Easton, Nina. "Costs to FSLIC Skyrocket as Delays on Sales of Failed Thrifts Drag On." *American Banker* (December 15, 1986): 1, 20–21.

Ely, Bert. "The Big Bust: The 1930–33 Banking Collapse—Its Causes, Its Lessons." *Proceedings of a Conference on Bank Structure and Competition*. Federal Reserve Bank of Chicago, 1986, pp. 19–63.

Federal Deposit Insurance Corporation. *Deposit Insurance in a Changing Environment*. Washington, D.C.: Federal Deposit Insurance Corporation, April 1983.

Federal Home Loan Bank Board. *Agenda for Reform*. Washington, D.C.: Federal Home Loan Bank Board, March 1983.

Fein, Melanie L. "The Separation of Banking and Commerce in American Banking History." In Appendices to the Statement of Paul A. Volcker before the Subcommittee on Commerce, Consumer and Monetary Affairs of the Committee on Government Operations, U.S. House of Representatives. Washington, D.C.: Board of Governors of the Federal Reserve System, June 1986.

Friedman, Milton, and Schwartz, Anna J. *A Monetary History of the United States, 1867–1960*. Princeton, N.J.: Princeton University Press, 1963.

Garsson, Robert. "Speaker Backs Scaled-Down Aid for FSLIC." *American Banker* (February 10, 1987): 1, 23.

General Accounting Office. *Deposit Insurance*. Washington, D.C.: General Accounting Office, 1986a.

General Accounting Office. *Thrift Industry: Cost to FSLIC of Delaying Action on Insolvent Savings Institutions*. Washington, D.C.: General Accounting Office, September 1986b.

Golembe, Carter H., and Mingo, John J. "Can Supervision and Regulation Ensure Financial Stability?" In *The Search for Financial Stability: The Past Fifty Years,* pp. 125–46. San Francisco: The Federal Reserve Bank of San Francisco, 1985.

Gorton, Gary. "Clearinghouses and the Origin of Central Banking in the United States." *Journal of Economic History* (June 1985): 277–83.

Gorton, Gary. "Banking Panics and Business Cycles." Working Paper 86–9, Federal Reserve Bank of Philadelphia, March 1986.

Hickman, W. B. *Corporate Bond Quality and Investor Experience.* Princeton, N.J.: National Bureau of Economic Research, 1958.

Ireland, Oliver I. "Payments System Risk." In Appendices to the Statement by Paul A. Volcker before the Subcommittee on Commerce, Consumer and Monetary Affairs of the Committee on Government Operations, U.S. House of Representatives. Washington, D.C.: Board of Governors of the Federal Reserve System, June 1986.

Jensen, Michael C., and Meckling, William H.' "Theory of the Firm: Managerial Behavior, Agency Costs and Ownership Structure." *Journal of Financial Economics* (October 1976): 305–60.

Johnson, Ramon E., and Petterson, Paul T. "Current Value Accounting for Savings and Loans: A Needed Reform." *Journal of Accountancy* (January 1984): 80–85.

Kane, Edward J. *The Gathering Crisis in Federal Deposit Insurance.* Cambridge, Mass.: MIT Press, 1985.

Kane, Edward J. "Appearance and Reality in Deposit Insurance." *Journal of Banking and Finance* (June 1986a): 175–88.

Kane, Edward J. "Confronting Incentive Problems in U.S. Deposit Insurance: The Range of Alternative Solutions." In *Deregulating Financial Services.* Edited by George G. Kaufman and Roger C. Kormendi. Cambridge, Mass.: Ballinger Press, 1986b.

Kane, Edward J. "Dangers of Capital Forbearance: The Case of the FSLIC and 'Zombie' S&Ls." *Contemporary Policy Issues* (January 1987): 77–83.

Kareken, John H. "Deposit Insurance Reform or Deregulation Is the Cart, Not the Horse." Federal Reserve Bank of Minneapolis *Quarterly Review* (Spring 1983).

Kareken, John H. "Federal Bank Regulatory Policy." *Journal of Business* (January 1986): 3–48.

Kaufman, George G. "Implications of Large Bank Problems and Insolvencies for the Banking System and Economic Policy." Federal Reserve Bank of Chicago *Staff Memoranda,* 85-3, 1985.

Kaufman, George G. "Banking Risk in Historical Perspective." *Proceedings of a Conference on Bank Structure and Competition.* Federal Reserve Bank of Chicago, 1986, pp. 231–49.

Kaufman, George G. "Bank Capital Forbearance and Public Policy." *Contemporary Policy Issues* (January 1987): 84–91.

Kennedy, Susan F. *The Banking Crisis of 1933.* Lexington: University of Kentucky Press, 1973.

Kindleberger, Charles P. "Bank Failures: The 1930s and the 1980s." In *The Search for Financial Stability in the Past Fifty Years,* pp. 7–34. San Francisco: Federal Reserve Bank of San Francisco, 1985.

Lawrence, Joseph S. "What Is the Average Recovery of Depositors?" *American Bankers Association Journal* (February 1931): 655–56, 722–23.

Leah, David, et al. "Section VIII—The Measurement of Bank Risk-Market Value Accounting." *Proceedings of a Conference on Bank Structure and Competition.* Federal Reserve Bank of Chicago, 1986, pp. 311–68.

Litan, Robert E. "Evaluating and Controlling the Risks of Financial Product Deregulation." *Yale Journal on Regulation* (Fall 1985): 1–52.

Merris, Randall C., and Wood, John. "A Deregulated Rerun: Banking in the Eighties." Federal Reserve Bank of Chicago *Economic Perspectives* (September/October 1985).

Miller, Harry F. *Banking Theories in the United States Before 1860.* Cambridge, Mass.: Harvard University Press and New York: Augustus Kelley, 1972.

National Credit Union Administration. *Credit Union Share Insurance: A Report to the Congress.* Washington, D.C.: National Credit Union Administration, 1983.

Norcross, Robert W., Jr. "The Bank Insolvency Game: FDIC Superpowers, the D'Oench Doctrine, and Federal Common Law." *Banking Law Journal* (July/August 1986).

Pyle, David H. "Deregulation and Deposit Insurance Reform." Federal Reserve Bank of San Francisco *Economic Review* (Spring 1984): 5–15.

Pyle, David H. "Capital Regulation and Deposit Insurance." *Journal of Banking and Finance* (June 1986): 189–201.

Rockoff, Hugh. "Institutional Requirements for Stable Free Banking." *Cato Journal* (Fall 1986): 617–34.

Rolnick, Arthur J., and Weber, Warren E. "The Causes of Free Bank Failures." *Journal of Monetary Economics* (October 1984).

Rolnick, Arthur J., and Weber, Warren E. "Banking Instability and Regulation in the U.S. Free Banking Era." Federal Reserve Bank of Minneapolis *Quarterly Review* (Summer 1985).

Schwartz, Anna J. "Financial Stability and the Federal Reserve Safety Net." Working Paper for the American Enterprise Institute, February 1987.

Schwartz, Anna J. "Comments on 'The Big Bust' and 'The Truth about Bank Runs.' " *Cato Journal* (forthcoming).

Thorndyke, Gilbert. "Fiction and Fact on Bank Runs." *American Bankers Association Journal* (June 1929).

Timberlake, Richard H. Jr. "The Central Banking Role of Clearinghouse Associations." *Journal of Money, Credit and Banking* (February 1984): 1–15.

Truell, Peter. "Citicorp's Reed Takes Firm Stance on Third-World Debt." *Wall Street Journal* (February 4, 1987): 6.

Upham, Cyril B. and Lamke, Edwin. *Closed and Distressed Banks.* Washington, D.C.: Brookings Institution, 1934.

Volcker, Paul A. Statement before Subcommittee on Commerce, Consumer and Monetary Affairs of the Committee on Government Operations, U.S. House of Representatives, June 11, 1986 and Appendices.

Weintraub, Benjamin, and Resnick, Alan N. *Bankruptcy Law Manual.* Boston: Warren, Gorham and Lamont, 1986.

White, Lawrence H. *Free Banking in Britain*. Cambridge: Cambridge University Press, 1984.

Whitehead, David D. "The Sixth District Survey of Small Business Credit." Federal Reserve Bank of Atlanta *Economic Review* (April 1982): 42–47.

Wicker, Elmus. "A Reconsideration of the Causes of the Banking Panic of 1930." *Journal of Economic History* (September 1980): 571–83.

Willis, H. Parker, and Chapman, John. *The Banking System*. New York: Columbia University Press, 1934.

Working Group of the Cabinet Council on Economic Affairs. *Recommendations for Change in the Federal Deposit Insurance System*. Washington, D.C., 1985.

3

THE BIG BUST:
THE 1930–33 BANKING COLLAPSE—ITS
CAUSES, ITS LESSONS
Bert Ely

Public policy failings, not bank mismanagement, caused the 1930–33 banking collapse. These public policy failings unnecessarily exposed the American banking system to excessive monetary and structural risks in the absence of which the banking system would not have collapsed. To make this case, this paper is divided into three major sections. The first establishes a framework to explain why the banking collapse occurred. The second applies this framework to American banking history from 1920 to the 1933 bank holiday. The paper closes with seven lessons for today that can be drawn from this research.

Framework

The framework used herein is built on the premise that banking is more vulnerable than other types of business enterprises to systemic risk. Systemic risk is triggered by major events, often government-induced, that simultaneously afflict many banks. Banks are particularly susceptible to two types of systemic risk: monetary risk and structural risk. Business risk, the third risk facing banks, encompasses events that afflict individual banks, and hence will not be explored in this paper except as it is aggravated by monetary and structural risk.

Monetary Risks

There are two types of monetary risk: unanticipated price level changes and mismanagement of monetary policy. Although each of these risks will be discussed separately, they are not totally unrelated.

Unanticipated price level changes. Unanticipated price level changes can be either inflationary or deflationary. Deflationary trends

---

The author is president of Ely and Company, a financial institutions consulting firm in Alexandria, Virginia.

have two components. The first, disinflation, occurs when the rate of price increases is slowing; the second, deflation, occurs when prices are actually falling from previous levels. Unanticipated *disinflation* is more likely to harm a commercial bank than unanticipated *inflation,* and unanticipated *deflation* can cause even greater harm. It can kill a bank by making it market value insolvent; that is, unanticipated deflation can cause the market value of a bank's assets to fall below the face value of its liabilities.[1]

Unanticipated deflation is especially damaging to banks because their balance sheets are extreme in two ways when compared to other types of businesses. First, a very high proportion (usually 90 to 95 percent) of banks' assets are the debts of others. Second, banks are much more highly leveraged than other types of business firms.

Bank assets fall into two categories: debt of others and equity interests. Although the market value of equity interests can range from less than zero to near infinity, the potential market value of debts, particularly those of an adjustable rate nature, is asymmetric. That is, debts are more likely to decline in market value than to increase above their face value.

This asymmetric nature of debt can work against a bank. If a bank borrower gets into financial difficulty, his debt (the bank loan) loses value because the ability of the borrower to repay his loan decreases. In the extreme, of course, the debt may become uncollectible and the bank's asset worthless. On the other hand, if the borrower's income increases, for example, then his loan can gain some value as a result of reduced default risk, but the gain will be limited. Thus, the bank's potential for gain is much less than its potential for loss. This explanation also is true for debt securities owned by a bank.

The probability of default is the credit risk faced by banks, and credit risk increases in the face of disinflation or deflation. Though debt carrying a fixed rate of interest can increase in market value as interest rates decline, two offsetting factors will limit these market value increases and may even depress debt values.

First, although nominal interest rates may appear low, real interest rates may be high and rising during a deflationary period. Those who purchase debt securities will not accept a negative rate of return, even on riskless Treasury securities, when they can hold riskless

---

[1]Thrift institution insolvencies during the early 1980s are an obvious exception to this general statement about the impact of price level changes on commercial banks. Thrifts became market value insolvent when skyrocketing interest rates shrank the market value of their fixed-rate mortgage loans. Since market, or nominal, interest rates declined during the banking collapse, insolvencies caused by long-term, fixed-rate lending will not be addressed in this paper.

government-issued currency as a substitute. Thus, the nominal rate of interest on riskless government debt securities will not fall below zero. While deflation continues, a zero nominal interest rate still implies a positive rate of return. If deflation becomes more severe, the real rate of return rises on securities offering a zero or positive interest rate. Thus, in a deflationary environment, the real rate of interest paid by debtors holding fixed-rate loans will be increasing.

Second, during deflations, a rising default risk can quickly offset any market value appreciation of a debt arising from declining nominal interest rates. The market value of the debt will then decline even though the fixed-rate debt will have a very high apparent yield to maturity. This high yield effectively includes a substantial premium to compensate for default risk.[2]

The default risk rises dramatically as deflation becomes more severe for two reasons. First, the debtor's cash flow may decline as deflation depresses his revenues more than his expenses. Second, deflation will reduce the market value of the borrower's assets or collateral, thus reducing the ability of the bank to recover its principal should the borrower's assets have to be sold to repay the loan. Debt securities, or bonds, are subject to the same pressures, and not surprisingly, increases in the default risk premium will be concentrated in the lower-quality debt issues.

High leverage is the other reason banks are so susceptible to price declines. Leverage is the ratio of the bank's deposits and other liabilities to its equity capital or net worth. Even in the absence of deposit insurance,[3] banks have always been highly leveraged when compared to the business firms to whom they lend money or whose securities they purchase. This is because banks are, themselves, major debtors. Furthermore, bank liabilities do not lose nominal value during a deflation. Thus, a slight decline in a bank's asset values has a greatly magnified and adverse impact on the bank's net worth.

By contrast, banks can preserve the market value of their equity capital during an unanticipated inflation if they have written loan

---

[2]Irving Fisher (1933, p. 343) observed that "money interest on safe loans falls but money interest on unsafe loans rises" during a depression. He did not explain in this article why the interest rate on unsafe loans rises. However, it is apparent from the context of the article that the nominal interest rate on unsafe loans rises during deflationary times as default risks rise.

[3]So-called deposit insurance, at least federal deposit insurance, really is not insurance, since it lacks one central element of any true insurance plan—risk-related pricing. Federal deposit insurance is more properly called depositor protection. So-called deposit insurance premiums really are a special tax on depositors that serves to spread the cost of regulatory and monetary policy failures across all deposits.

contracts with adjustable interest rates. Inflation also increases the nominal value of any equity interests they hold, particularly in physical assets. Just as inflation often bails out debtors, so too does it bail out their banks.

Mismanagement of monetary policy. Deflationary pressures can be caused by forces outside or inside the monetary system. This paper will discuss only internal deflationary pressures, that is, those caused by government mismanagement of monetary policy. Before proceeding, though, it is important to understand the downward deflationary spiral.

In many regards, the downward deflationary spiral mirrors an inflationary spiral.[4] The downward spiral is driven by six deflationary forces that feed upon each other:

(1) High real interest rates trigger increased debt defaults and lead to the disinvestment processes discussed below.

(2) The money supply contracts.

(3) Asset sales are made at distressed or "fire sale" prices. As a result, they reduce the market value net worth of all holders of comparable assets, possibly forcing these individuals or businesses to sell assets, liquidate debts, and/or trim investment spending.[5] In addition, depressed prices on existing physical assets reduce or eliminate the profit incentive to manufacture or construct comparable new assets.

(4) Fixed asset disinvestment occurs. Businesses will not replace their depreciable assets as fast as they are wearing out or becoming obsolete because the real rate of return on holding cash, even in a non-interest-bearing form, exceeds the rate of return on tangible assets. Cash flows are retained in the business or paid to stockholders instead. This disinvestment process reduces demand for capital goods, leading to a decline in the real level of economic activity.

(5) Inventory liquidation occurs for the same reason as fixed asset disinvestment. Higher returns are earned by shrinking inventories and holding money balances. New inventory will be purchased only when it is absolutely needed, allowing inventories to be replaced at lower nominal unit costs. The high real interest cost of holding inventories also encourages inventory liquidation.

(6) Trade credit contracts. Trade credit, which usually carries no nominal interest charge, becomes very expensive in real terms during a deflation. The disincentive to incur trade credit further accelerates the inventory liquidation process.

---

[4]Fisher (1932, p. 25) first described the "the vicious spiral downward."
[5]See Minsky (1963, p. 107).

Monetary policy mismanagement can accelerate the downward deflationary spiral in three ways. First, fixed exchange rates and commodity clauses (usually gold clauses) in private and public contracts can drive the downward spiral when the price of the monetized commodity (that is, gold or silver) is increasing relative to the price of nonmonetized commodities. Second, the government monetary authority or central bank (the Federal Reserve System in the United States) can stand idly by during a deflationary contraction of the aggregate quantity of money and credit. Third, a lender of last resort (LLR) can permit a contagion during which a run on one or a few banks sparks simultaneous, panic-driven deposit withdrawals from numerous banks. However effected, monetary policy mismanagement can greatly compound and accelerate the adverse effects of external deflationary pressures.

Under fixed rates of exchange, a government monetary authority agrees to exchange a predetermined quantity of a precious commodity, usually gold or silver, for a unit of currency issued by the central bank or the national government. If the currency can be exchanged freely for bank deposits denominated in that currency, these deposits are indirectly convertible into the precious commodity at the fixed exchange rate.

Under a gold clause, debts and contractual obligations are payable either in a unit of account, such as a dollar, or in a fixed quantity of gold. Thus, when a gold clause is in widespread use there effectively are two mediums of exchange operating in the economy. Depending on the terms of the contract, this duality may permit a creditor to demand payment in either medium, in which case he will opt for payment in the medium that offers the greatest purchasing power at the time of the exchange. Although gold clauses are meant to protect creditors against inflation, there is a pernicious aspect to gold clauses during a deflation—the gold clause unilaterally transfers wealth from debtor to creditor as the precious metal increases in value against other goods. This increase in value occurs because deflation expands demand for the precious metal, as those who hold it earn high real rates of return as long as the deflation, the metal's link to a currency, and limited supplies of the metal continue.

Fixed exchange rates and gold clauses are closely linked in economies where both exist. The link can become destructive during a deflation because changing or abandoning a fixed exchange rate does not alter the exchange rate incorporated in the gold clause in contracts. The link will not be completely broken unless gold clauses are abrogated. Monetary policy mismanagement occurs during a deflation when the central bank and the government do not act in a coordinated fashion to devalue both the national currency and the exchange rate incorporated in contractual gold clauses. As Green (1986, p. 8) points out, government interference with gold clauses has occurred for centuries.

Unchecked, the supply of money and credit contracts automatically during a deflation. Declining business activity leads to reduced levels of accounts receivable and inventories. The cash proceeds from the shrinkage of these assets are used by businesses to pay down working capital loans. At the same time, purchases of new fixed assets financed with bank loans decline. Repayments on existing loans soon exceed extensions of new loans. Very high real interest rates accelerate this debt liquidation process by giving debtors a tremendous incentive to reduce their very expensive debt burdens.

A bank failure also can lead to a contraction of money and credit in the market area served by a failed bank if the credit supplied by the bank is not quickly replaced by another bank or by recapitalizing and reopening the failed bank.

The central bank has two principal tools it can use to attempt to reinflate the economy by arresting and reversing the downward trend of prices and real interest rates. First, it can conduct open market and rediscounting operations in an effort to increase the aggregate money supply sufficiently to at least neutralize if not reverse the deflationary spiral. Open market activities also expand bank reserves and thus increase the banking system's potential for increasing the money supply through new credit extensions.

Second, the central bank can reduce its discount rate in an effort to reduce other interest rates in the economy. The central bank cannot reduce the discount rate below zero, however, if the public has the ability to convert bank deposits into currency. Thus, discount rate cuts are not very effective during a severe deflation.

Contagion occurs when a run on one or a few banks triggers panic-driven runs on other banks. From society's point of view, panic-driven runs on solvent banks are irrational because they cause real economic losses. Those participating in a run often see their actions as rational, however, because their individual loss may increase if they do not run.

Contagions pose a severe systemic risk for a banking system, in part by accelerating a downward deflationary spiral as bank reserves shrink when people withdraw currency from the banking system. The money supply is thus contracted until the central bank reinjects reserves back into the banking system through open market operations.

The lender of last resort (LLR) can provide, or advance, liquidity to the distressed bank, usually in the form of loans or deposits. These advances replace departing deposits; in effect, the LLR becomes a substitute depositor in the distressed bank. The LLR's advances enable the bank to avoid suddenly shrinking its balance sheet by selling assets and calling loans. By avoiding such drastic actions and the associated losses, the bank can minimize the impact of the run on its net worth.

Two risks generally have existed when a banking system relies on clearinghouses or a central bank to act as LLR. First, not every depository institution has an LLR. If a depository without an LLR experiences a run, it closes and nearby banks brace themselves for a run. Second, LLRs usually lend only against acceptable collateral and oftentimes only to solvent banks. If a bank exhausts its acceptable collateral or becomes insolvent while it is still experiencing a run, it will be forced to close.

If through highly restrictive discounting policies an LLR fails to provide the banking system with sufficient currency during a contagion, then banks will feel compelled to maintain higher reserves in the future, and thus provide less credit to the economy, than prior to the contagion.

Contagious bank runs cause four types of economic damage: "fire sale" losses in banks experiencing runs, declines in the market value net worth of asset holders, credit contractions, and payments system disruptions.

Fire sale losses occur when a bank experiencing a run has to hurriedly sell assets to raise the cash needed to meet deposit withdrawals and pay off other liabilities that are called or cannot be rolled over. The fire sale loss is the difference between what an asset could be sold for in an orderly manner and what it will bring in a quick sale. Fire sale losses reduce a bank's net worth; severe fire sale losses can drive a bank into insolvency.

Market value losses are experienced by persons who happen to be holding, but do not immediately sell, assets identical or similar to the assets being sold by banks in the fire sale. Their market value losses are paper losses until their assets return to their pre–fire sale value or until the assets are sold for a loss. Paper losses also increase an individual's leverage, or personal debt to assets ratio. At a minimum, this greater leverage may restrain the affected individual from taking on new debt. It may even provide the incentive to liquidate some of his assets in order to bring his leverage back down to an acceptable level.

Credit contraction and disruption, which are in effect a money supply contraction, occur when liquidity pressures force a bank to raise cash by calling in loans, refusing to make new loans, declining to roll over existing loans, and using loan principal payments for liability reduction instead of new credit extensions. At a minimum, this process disrupts the flow of bank credit into the economy. If depositors withdraw their deposits in the form of currency, which they do not redeposit elsewhere, then aggregate credit contraction occurs if the central bank does not offset the currency withdrawals with open market purchases of government securities. Depressions, of course, spring from credit contractions.

Payments system disruptions can quickly create payments system gridlock, which develops when banks close, freezing transaction accounts. If the closed banks are numerous or large enough, an entire payments system can grind to a halt.

The LLR function is supposed to minimize contagion losses by lessening liquidity pressure on banks. When the LLR does not perform as expected or to the extent it could, then banks and the overall economy suffer unwarranted contagion losses. The 1930–33 banking collapse clearly demonstrated that inadequate LLR performance is a very real systemic banking risk.

Structural Risks

Structural risk is the risk that the structure of the marketplace will change in such a manner and degree that most if not all participants will have to materially alter the way they do business. Thus, structural risk is more than just the continual entry and departure of individual participants in a marketplace.

There are two types of structural risks in every marketplace: market risks and government-induced risks. Banks face greater government-induced risks than participants in most markets because banking historically has experienced heavy government regulation. Regulation materially increases market risk if, as has been true for banking, the regulation is ill-conceived, obsolete, and/or driven by political forces that ignore marketplace realities. Market risks in banking will not be discussed here except as they relate to government-induced risks.

Government increases banking risk by imposing certain rules, constraints, and obligations on banks that lessen their ability to respond to changes in the marketplace. In effect, these regulations force banks to operate in a manner that is not marketplace- or management-driven. Instead, regulation attempts to define the banking marketplace and then tells the participants how to operate.

The principal risks the federal and state governments imposed on banking before 1933 involved the widespread restrictions on branching. Other restrictions, justified as a means of increasing the safety and soundness of the banking system, were feeble attempts to offset weaknesses imposed on the banking system through branching restrictions. In a sense, government attempted to protect with one hand what it weakened with the other.

The single greatest risk branching restrictions impose on a banking system is the inability of individual banks to efficiently diversify their portfolios. While risk diversification can take several forms, geographical risk diversification is the most effective. A small unit bank in a single-crop or single-industry region can achieve some degree of risk diversification by buying securities issued elsewhere, placing deposits in other banks, and participating in loans made by other banks. But despite these efforts, unit banks inevitably have a higher percentage of their risks concentrated in the region they serve directly than would larger banks with a broader base of operations. This would be true even if the larger bank lent and invested the same amount in the region as did the small bank. Thus, loan losses in the region will hit the unit bank proportionally harder than they will hit the large bank.

Branching restrictions also increase bank run risk, which varies inversely with bank size. Bank run risk is greatest in the small unit bank because unit banks couple a high degree of geographical risk concentration with a heavy funding dependence on deposits drawn from the small regions they serve. Consequently, depositors quickly become aware of losses that will drive the unit bank into insolvency, and they will act to protect themselves by running to the bank, hoping to withdraw their deposits before their neighbors do.

Banks lack managerial specialization and the opportunity to capture economies of scale when they are very small, particularly in number of employees. Low employee head counts limit banks to manual techniques for recording and processing basic banking transactions and also limit the range of services that a bank can offer. The median-sized bank in the 1920s had approximately three full-time employees, while the bank at the 75th percentile in size in 1930 had approximately eight employees. These banks could not capture whatever economies of scale there were in banking during the 1920s.

Branching restrictions foster correspondent banking, by which small banks obtain services they cannot produce internally or services that require an agent in a distant city. In effect, branching restrictions push what otherwise would be interbranch transactions into the correspondent banking marketplace. While correspondent banking integrates the banking system into a whole, it is a less than optimal substitute for unrestricted branching in terms of banking efficiencies.

Many banks failed during the 1920s because of fraudulent acts by bank employees and officers. Branching restrictions increase the probability of fraud, and the probability that fraud will lead to bank failure, by forcing the creation of banks that are too small to protect themselves against fraud. Thus, branching restrictions, by increasing the probability of fraud and embezzlement in banks, materially add to the structural risk of banking.

Branching restrictions can lead to various ownership subterfuges, designed to achieve at least some of the benefits of branching without running afoul of the law. Bank chains, for example, consist of several banks with a common owner or owners. But branching is superior to group or chain banking because depositors and creditors are better protected from insolvency and banks can achieve greater operating efficiencies. Thus, the subterfuges created by branching restrictions add yet another element of structural risk to banking.

To avoid failing during a local depression, unit banks need to achieve at least some geographical risk diversification. At the same time, a unit bank is constrained in its local lending by a lack of deposits and low capital levels. Thus, it must diversify its risk by exporting deposits while simultaneously importing credit through loan participations and overline lending. However, the deposit-exporting/credit-importing process conducted in a unit banking system imposes inefficiencies and creates structural risk not found in a branch banking system. This structural risk exists regardless of the number of unit banks serving a given region. Although the region's risks may be spread over several unit banks, each bank is still just as subject to the risk of a regional downturn.

Branching restrictions prevent an optimal deployment of equity capital in a banking system. Because individual risk exposures in a small bank often are geographically concentrated and relatively large when compared to its total assets, the small bank needs a higher equity capital ratio to protect itself against insolvency than a big bank with many branches would need. These higher capital ratios draw excessive equity capital into the banking system, and because equity capital costs more than the deposits used to fund a bank's assets, small banks experience lower returns on equity capital than do banks with branch networks.

Two types of structural changes can occur in a banking system. First, an individual banking office can be closed through failure or relocation, consolidated with another banking office, or reduced in size or range of services. Second, structural changes can affect many banking offices within a short period of time. Extensive branching restrictions increase the traumatic effect of each type of structural change by building an unsustainable rigidity into the banking system that delays change and makes it more wrenching and costly when it does occur.

Finally, branching restrictions increase the cost of and/or restrict the availability of banking services in small or isolated communities or in areas with low population densities. This creates structural risk by creating an unhealthy fringe of small, marginally profitable unit banks. Because unit banks withdraw from the banking system in a more painful fashion than branches, failures within this fringe during a time of economic stress will create higher insolvency losses for the banking system than will the contraction of a branch banking network. In effect, the branching process provides a more efficient mechanism for contracting the banking system when contraction is called for than exists in a unit banking system.

History and Analysis

The 1920s—Prelude to Disaster

American banking structure and bank failures. Unit banks dominated American banking in the 1920s. In 1921, 98.2 percent of the country's 30,456 banks were unit banks, and in 1929, unit banks still accounted for 96.9 percent of the industry.[6] Most of these banks were tiny. The median-sized bank in 1920 had total loans and investments of $335,000. By 1930, that figure had risen to just $385,000.

Small banks were becoming increasingly uneconomic in the 1920s. According to the Federal Reserve System's (1932) study on branch, group, and chain banking, national banks with less than $150,000 in loans and investments (roughly equal to deposits) barely broke even. Banks in the $150,000 to $250,000 size range were profitable, but they made only half as much per $100 of loans and investments as banks in the $750,000 to $1 million size range (Federal Reserve System 1932, vol. 9, Table 10, p. 38). This was despite the fact that the small banks, as a group, had 27 percent more capital per $100 of loans and investments than the larger banks (Federal Reserve System 1932, vol. 9, Table 16, p. 48). Consequently, smaller banks earned only marginal returns on equity capital while larger banks enjoyed more reasonable returns. During the 1926–30 period, for example, banks in the $250,000 to $500,000 size range earned an average return on equity capital (presumably book value) of 3.87 percent while

---

[6]The total number of banks is taken from Bureau of the Census (1975, series X588). The number of banks with branches is taken from Federal Reserve Board of Governors (1943, Table 73).

banks in the $1 million to $2 million size range averaged a 6.56 percent return. By contrast, banks over $50 million in size averaged an 8.64 percent return (Federal Reserve System 1932, vol. 9, Table 16, p. 48).

Higher loan losses were the principal reason smaller national banks were less profitable than their larger brethren. Without exception, the larger the bank size class, the lower were the bank's net loan losses per $100 of loans and investments (Federal Reserve System 1932, vol. 9, Table 12, p. 40). These losses most likely resulted from a lack of diversified lending opportunities. It also appears that small banks with loans and investments under $250,000 were significantly less efficient intermediators of funds than even moderately sized national banks with $750,000 to $1 million in loans and investments (Federal Reserve System 1932, vol. 9, Table 14, p. 44).

The distribution of banks by the population of the area in which they were located provides further insight into the unit banking problem. Almost one-half of all banks in 1920 were located in towns and villages with fewer than 1,000 people. In that year, such communities each had an average of 1.37 banks. From 1920 to 1930, though, 86 percent of the banking contraction occurred in places with fewer than 2,500 people. The 1920s banking contraction was almost totally a rural and small town phenomenon!

Between 1921 and 1929, 5,712 banks failed. On average, 2.26 percent of all banks failed each year during the 1920s, 4.4 times the average suspension rate during the previous 30 years and 6.6 times the average suspension rate during the previous decade.[7] Failures during the 1921–29 period accounted for 90 percent of the contraction in the total number of banks between 1920 and 1930. The banks that failed generally were the smaller-than-average banks. The average failed bank during the 1920s had total deposits of just $284,000,[8] which in 1987 dollars would be approximately $2.1 million in deposits. The average failed bank probably had the equivalent of just two or three employees, its loans and deposit accounts probably numbered in the hundreds, and it may not even have been a full-time operation.

By contrast, large bank failures during the 1920s were relatively rare events, particularly for banks over $10 million in size. (In 1987

[7]These comparisons are calculated from data in Bureau of the Census (1975, series X742–44 and X588). Comparative average suspension rates over the three previous decades are as follows: 1891–1900—1.08 percent of all banks closed; 1901–1910—0.42 percent; 1911–1920—0.34 percent. For years prior to 1896, the data are drawn from Bureau of the Census (1975, series X634 and X683).

[8]This figure is calculated from the 1983 FDIC Annual Report, p. 41.

dollars, these would be banks with deposits in excess of $75 to $80 million.) The annualized failure rate during the 1921–29 period was 0.09 percent for banks over $10 million in loans and investments, or even lower than the 0.12 percent annualized failure rate experienced by banks with more than $80 million in deposits between 1977 and 1985.

The gap between the average-sized failed bank and the average-sized nonfailed bank increased steadily during the 1920s, illustrating that the bank failures of that era were largely among small unit banks. The failures were concentrated in two geographic areas—the grain states west of the Mississippi, including, to some extent, Oklahoma and Texas, and the southeastern states of South Carolina, Georgia, and Florida.

The ratio of bank failures to commercial business failures was 3.4 times higher during the 1921–29 period than during the previous 31 years. Between 1921 and 1929, this ratio averaged 2.19 to 1, while between 1890 and 1920, the ratio had averaged just 0.64 to 1. Apparently a unit banking system suitable for the late 19th century was becoming increasingly obsolete and economically unsound by the third decade of the 20th century.

American banking contracted in large part during the 1920s because farmers and other rural residents gained greater mobility. Fewer than one farm in three had a car or truck in 1919; by 1930, four out of five had some form of off-the-farm motor transportation. Surfaced rural highway mileage also grew steadily during these years, permitting farmers to go farther in a given period of time than they could on earlier mud roads. As farmers sped off to larger, more distant towns and cities, they bypassed smaller, local businesses, including the local bank.

Agriculture is often cited as one of the economy's weak spots during the 1920s, which, if true, would have adversely affected banking, as approximately 10 percent of the country's gross domestic product originated in the farm sector.[9] Nationally, farming was relatively strong financially, however. Both net farming income and cash flow per acre, indexed for changing price levels, reached a post–World War I peak in 1925 and continued there until 1929. These conditions prevailed even though farm prices were declining because farm productivity increased during these years.

Agriculture's debt burden, as a percentage of farm assets, was the exception to this relative overall prosperity. This burden increased for two reasons: (1) By 1924, farm property values had fallen an

[9]Bureau of the Census (1975, series F127).

average of 23 percent per acre from peak values in 1920; and (2) total farm debt increased 14 percent during the same period. Consequently, farm debt rose to 23 percent of farm property values in 1923 from 15 percent in 1920, and it did not drop below 21 percent for the rest of the decade. This debt burden was high by prewar standards (13 percent in 1914) and thus probably oppressive. It helps explain why farmers paid down their total indebtedness by $1.8 billion, or 13 percent, between 1921 and 1927. They achieved this even though farm cash flow dropped 60 percent between 1919 and 1922 and did not fully recover until 1925. Despite these high debt loads, and probably because of farming's relative prosperity, the total number of farms and farm acreage began to increase after 1925.

Even though American agriculture was relatively healthy during the 1920s, there were a number of regional problems in the farming sector. For example, gross revenues per acre of wheat declined from $18.37 in 1925 to $13.52 in 1929[10] while gross revenues per acre of cotton declined from $7.91 in 1924 to $5.03 in 1926.[11] Droughts, boll weevils, and other afflictions caused localized stresses, and small unit banks, largely dependent on the fortunes of local farmers and farm-related businesses, survived or failed as their customers won or lost their war against nature and world agricultural prices. By contrast, the banks with large, more geographically diverse portfolios of farm loans, such as the large California banks, could more easily absorb localized losses while profiting from the overall profitability of farming.

The Canadian system: strength through branching. The Canadian banking system experienced a period of contraction and consolidation during the 1920s comparable to that in the United States, but the Canadian consolidation occurred primarily through mergers and branch closings.

The number of Canadian banking offices reached a peak in 1920 after a sharp postwar buildup to accommodate employees returning from the war. (The number of American banking offices reached its peak in 1922.) Beginning in 1922, the Canadian banks began reducing the number of offices they operated at an even faster pace than U.S. banking offices were disappearing. And even though Canadian banks increased their office count again in the late 1920s, by 1929, the number of Canadian banking offices had contracted from its 1920 peak by a slightly greater proportion than the number of American banking offices had contracted from its 1922 peak. Still, in 1929, the

[10]Calculated from Bureau of the Census (1975, series K506–8).
[11]Calculated from Bureau of the Census (1975, series K553–55).

54

11 Canadian banks operated 4,069 branches. There was a major difference between the two contractions, however. With the exception of the Home Bank failure in 1923, in which depositors lost at least $15 million, the Canadian banking contraction occurred without losses to depositors.[12] In the United States, by contrast, depositors in banks failing between 1921 and 1929 lost an estimated $565 million.[13] Stockholder losses in U.S. banking failures totaled an additional $400 million.[14]

Another interesting contrast between the U.S. and Canadian experiences is that the Canadian banks were able to successfully operate branches that were smaller in terms of deposits and population per branch than were U.S. unit banks. This undoubtedly reflects the inherent operating efficiencies of branch banking over unit banking, particularly where branch banking is conducted over geographically large and economically diverse areas. It also appears that despite its contraction, the Canadian banking system continued to maintain offices in more relatively small towns and villages, particularly after 1930.

Although the Canadian banking system proved the greater resilience of branch banking, unit banking persisted in the United States and became even more entrenched with the passage in 1927 of the McFadden Act. This law, which gave national banks virtually the same branching rights as state banks, was intended to slow the switching of national banks to state bank charters in states such as California that had liberal branching laws, and many who supported the bill saw it as liberalizing banking law. The detrimental effect of the act, however, was to permit state law to govern national bank branching. Thus, the McFadden Act can properly be called the "Unit Bank Perpetuation Act."[15]

The 1930–33 Banking Collapse

The year prior to the start of the banking collapse. The October 1929 to October 1930 period was characterized by declining industrial production, falling wholesale prices, and reduced corporate profits. The Federal Reserve's index of industrial production (seasonally unadjusted) declined 25 percent, from 60.4 in October 1929 (1947–

[12]See Jamison and Mackintosh (1979, pp. 59–63).

[13]Calculated from the 1983 FDIC Annual Report, p. 41.

[14]Estimated from Federal Reserve System (1932, vol. 5, Table 57, p. 112).

[15]Although discussions of the McFadden Act abound, the Federal Reserve System's analysis of the act is particularly effective in capturing the emotional tenor of the opposition to branch banking in any form whatsoever. See Federal Reserve System (1932, vol. 2, pp. 117–54).

49 = 100) to 45.5 in October 1930, after hitting a peak of 61.3 in September 1929. Wholesale prices (for all commodities) declined 13 percent from October 1929 to October 1930, falling from 49.0 (1967 = 100) to 42.8. After-tax corporate profits, as measured in the national income accounts, dropped by two-thirds, from \$8.6 billion in 1929 to \$2.9 billion in 1930.[16] Despite these conditions, until October 1930, the recession that started in August 1929 actually was less severe than the 1920–21 recession.

Monetary and financial conditions did not deteriorate as rapidly as overall economic activity. The money supply declined 4.6 percent from October 1929 to October 1930,[17] only one-fifth the estimated 24 percent decline in GNP during the same 13 months.[18] Although the general business failure rate rose from 1.04 percent in 1929 to 1.22 percent in 1930, it was only slightly higher than the 1.20 percent rate in 1922.[19] There were only slightly more bank failures, on a seasonally adjusted basis, from October 1929 to October 1930 than there were during the 1921–28 period. Deposits in failed banks, although 50 percent higher than the 1921–28 experience, still were not significantly out of line with the year-to-year variability of the 1920s.[20] The deposit/currency ratio, supposedly a barometer of public confidence in banks, dipped slightly during this period, but by October 1930, the ratio was 11.54, or almost equal to October 1929's ratio of 11.57.[21]

The first segment of the collapse. The banking collapse began in November 1930. The bank failure rate for November and December 1930 was more than four times the previous experience for that time of year. During the first 15 months of the banking collapse, from November 1930 to January 1932, the bank failure rate was four times the 1920s rate; the amount on deposit in failed banks increased 10-fold. These sharp increases in measures of bank failure reflect the vicious downward deflationary spiral then under way in the economy

---

[16]Bureau of the Census (1975, series F181).

[17]See Friedman and Schwartz (1963, Table A-1, column 9). The money supply data include currency plus deposits in commercial and mutual savings banks and in the postal savings system.

[18]Because only annual GNP data are available prior to 1946, I have estimated annualized GNP on a monthly basis for the period from January 1929 to February 1933. I multiplied each month's industrial production index (seasonally unadjusted) by the consumer price index for that month and then adjusted that product by a factor to make the estimated monthly GNP figures for a year equal to reported GNP, measured in current dollars, for that year.

[19]Bureau of the Census (1975, series V23).

[20]Data on failed banks and deposits in failed banks have been taken from the *Federal Reserve Bulletin* (September 1937), pp. 907, 909.

[21]Calculated from Friedman and Schwartz (1963, Table A-1, columns 1 and 4).

as declining economic activity and other economic shocks finally caught up with the banking system. From November 1930 to January 1932, the money supply shrank an additional 12.9 percent (measured from October 1929) while the deposit/currency ratio dropped 44 percent, from 11.54 to 6.47. Wholesale prices plunged an additional 16 percent (measured from October 1929) while the rate of decline in industrial production dropped an additional 20 percent (measured from October 1929), or about 1.33 percent per month, and annualized GNP dropped an additional 17 percent (measured from October 1929) during the first 15 months of the banking collapse.

The second segment of the collapse. Between February 1932 and the bank holiday in early March 1933, the rate of bank failures actually declined by almost one-half compared to the first 15 months of the collapse, from an average of 216 failures per month to 118 per month.[22] The monthly average of deposits in failed banks dropped by two-thirds. In no month after January 1932 did the number of bank suspensions or the deposits in suspended banks exceed the January figures.

This moderation in bank failures may have reflected the fact that the economic decline was starting to decelerate. The money supply, prices, and industrial production all experienced slower rates of decline during this 13-month period than they had during the previous 15 months. In effect, the downward spiral started to slow as the economy bottomed out. The money supply, including time deposits, hit a low point in September 1932, bounced up slightly by November, and then started back down to an even lower turning point in April 1933, and although wholesale and consumer prices did not hit their lows until February and April 1933, respectively, their rates of decline slowed somewhat during the second half of 1932. Wholesale prices were essentially flat from April to October 1932. Industrial production actually dropped to its pre–bank holiday trough in July 1932 before bouncing up to a turning point in October 1932 and then dropping to a second bottom in March 1933. Nominal interest rates also dropped during the second half of 1932, implying that real interest rates had started to decline, although they still remained at quite high levels. For the last four months of 1932, the real interest rate on Aaa-rated corporate bonds was almost 13 percent, and on Baa-rated corporate bonds, it was over 16 percent.

---

[22]These figures exclude banks closed during state bank holidays because these bank holidays were triggered by liquidity crises, not insolvency. For the same reason, this analysis also excludes the 3,553 banks closed during the national bank holiday that did not reopen afterward.

The final banking crisis. The final crisis was as much a political crisis as it was a banking crisis. For banks, the final crisis was caused by a lack of liquidity, not by widespread insolvencies. The state bank holidays and eventually the national bank holiday were triggered by runs to gold and currency, not by a new wave of bank suspensions.

In a political sense, the final banking crisis spanned the four-month period between Franklin Roosevelt's election on November 8, 1932, and the start of the bank holiday on March 6, 1933, two days after Roosevelt was inaugurated. This four-month interregnum was laced with political tension between Roosevelt and Hoover, tension that led to a number of political and monetary blunders. These blunders turned a fading banking collapse into an unnecessary and destructive crescendo driven by illiquidity within the banking system. One can reasonably surmise that the New Deal banking legislation was shaped as much, if not more, by what transpired during this interregnum, particularly its last 45 days, than by what had transpired during the first two years of the banking collapse.

The first blunder was the public deliberation by Roosevelt and his aides, starting in December 1932, about devaluing the dollar against gold.[23] Although this devaluation was long overdue, Hoover and many others opposed it, and as Roosevelt's inauguration drew closer, and, more important, as he refused to deny the rumors of an impending devaluation, a run to gold occurred.[24] Wigmore (1986, p. 11) estimates that the New York Fed alone lost $756 million in gold between January 31, 1933, and March 4, the day Roosevelt was inaugurated. This run to gold pulled reserves out of the banking system and undoubtedly raised fundamental concerns about the soundness of the dollar and the banks.

The second blunder occurred when, in January 1933, Congress directed the Reconstruction Finance Corporation (RFC) to publish the names of the banks it had made loans to prior to August 1932 (Friedman and Schwartz 1963, p. 331). There is every indication that depositors interpreted RFC assistance as a sign of weakness and instituted runs on the assisted banks (Friedman and Schwartz 1963, p. 325).

The third blunder was the Fed's mismanagement of the liquidity crisis in early 1933. This crisis, triggered by the run to gold and growing currency runs on banks, quickly led to widespread state banking holidays. The first major state bank holiday was declared in Michigan on February 14, 1933, almost three weeks before the start

[23]See Wigmore (1986, p. 8).
[24]See Friedman and Schwartz (1963, p. 332).

of the national bank holiday (Wigmore 1986, p. 8). According to Friedman and Schwartz (1963, Table A-1, column 9), currency holdings increased $609 million, or 12 percent, between January 27 and February 24, 1933. Wigmore (1985, p. 444) reports that currency in circulation rose by $1.5 billion in the final days before the national bank holiday, probably as spreading state bank holidays encouraged people to withdraw currency from banks that were still open. Friedman and Schwartz (1963, p. 332) report that the Fed panicked and not only failed to meet all currency demands but also failed to urge a suspension of the conversion of deposits into currency. Similar partial suspensions that allowed banks to remain open and continue conducting most business had successfully broken past panics, most recently in 1907 (Friedman and Schwartz 1963, pp. 156–68). There was no reason a partial suspension would not have worked again in 1933. By March 4, the last banking day before the start of the national bank holiday, almost half the states had declared holidays.

The severity of the final banking crisis may have been caused as much by the U.S. Constitution as by anything else. At that time, four months elapsed between the popular election of a president and his inauguration. In fact, the final banking crisis might not have occurred had the 20th Amendment to the Constitution become effective in 1932 instead of one year later. The worst of the final crisis transpired during the 43 days between January 20, the post-1933 inaugural date, and March 4.

The Federal Reserve's failures during the banking crisis. As the U.S. central bank, the Fed failed the American banking system in at least three ways during the 1930–33 period.

First, it failed as America's lender of last resort, particularly during the final banking crisis.

Second, the Fed permitted a contracting money supply, which was contributing to an already severe deflation, to sharply boost real interest rates as the depression worsened. Interest rates on government and Aaa-rated corporate bonds in 1930 exceeded the rates in all years since 1922. In 1930 and 1931, real interest rates on top-quality bonds were in the 14 percent to 16 percent range. Even in 1933, real rates averaged 7 percent. The same pattern held true for Baa-rated corporate bonds, on which real interest rates averaged 8.5 percent in 1930 and over 18 percent during the 1931–32 period. These high real interest rates magnified the debt-servicing burdens of debtors and triggered a massive disinvestment in tangible assets.

Apparently the Fed failed to respond adequately to these punitively high real interest rates because it was unable to distinguish between real and nominal rates.[25] In addition, the Fed was concerned about renewed inflation even though price levels had been declining since 1925. The Fed could have broken the downward spiral and lowered real interest rates by sharply boosting the money supply through open market operations and by dropping the nominal discount rate to zero until such time as real rates returned to a more normal level.

Third, the Fed ignored, and probably did not even understand, the twin problems of the gold standard and the gold clauses in public and private bonds and contracts. Consequently, the Fed provided no leadership in dealing with these related problems, which were a principal cause, if not the principal cause, of the deflation that was racking the American banking system. The Fed could have provided leadership by advocating an early departure from the gold standard and the abrogation of gold clauses. As radical as this suggestion may seem, that is precisely what the Roosevelt administration did after the gold standard had done almost incalculable damage to the American economy.

A gold standard can transmit international price deflation into a domestic economy as the price of internationally traded commodities declines in terms of the price of gold. This is what happened to the United States in 1925, as Great Britain returned to the gold standard in April with its pound overvalued by 10 percent (Friedman and Schwartz 1963, p. 284).[26] U.S. wholesale prices hit a peak in November 1925 and then declined by 8 percent between then and August 1929,[27] the month in which the Great Depression started. Consumer prices also hit a peak in November 1925 before declining by 4 percent by the start of the Great Depression. These falling prices occurred despite a 3 percent increase in the nominal money supply per adult between November 1925 and August 1929.[28]

It would have been insufficient, though, if the federal government had only devalued the dollar against gold, because gold clauses were so prevalent in public and private contracts. Green (1986, p. 5) estimates that in 1933 the par value of all debt obligations with gold clauses was about $100 billion (plus or minus $25 billion), or approx-

[25]See Meltzer (1976, p. 468).

[26]This overvaluation of the pound, and effectively of other currencies linked to the pound, set off price declines in internationally traded commodities.

[27]Wholesale prices for all commodities dropped from 53.9 in November 1925 to 51.9 in August 1929 (1967 = 100).

[28]Calculated from Friedman and Schwartz (Table A-1, column 9). The money supply definition includes mutual savings and postal savings system deposits. The calculation is based on the average of the June and July money supply figures for 1925 and 1929.

imately 60 percent of all private and public debt outstanding in the United States that year. Since gold clauses had been widely used in contracts and bond issues since the late 19th century, the percentage of contracts with gold clauses in the late 1920s was probably comparable to 1933. Permitting gold clauses to operate would have continued the transmission of deflation into the American economy if gold as a medium of exchange was not devalued while the dollar was.

Issues Cutting Across the 1920s and 1930s

Bank failure patterns before and during the banking collapse. Banking structure contributed much more to the high rate of bank failures between November 1930 and the 1933 bank holiday, a period during which 4,801 banks failed,[29] than it had during the prior 10 years. Most bank failures were concentrated in small communities. Between 1930 and 1941, locales with fewer than 2,500 people lost 6,077 banks, or 44 percent of the banks operating there in 1930, continuing a pattern of closures that had begun in the 1920s. The bank offices closed in such towns represented 71 percent of all bank offices closed during that period. Thus, many small communities (over half of those with fewer than 1,000 residents) did not have local banking services by 1941 because branching restrictions prevented viable branches from operating where unit banks could not.

Towns and cities with more than 10,000 people did not experience a significant loss of banking offices until the 1930s, however. In 1920, 42 percent of America's population lived in such towns and cities, and 48 percent lived there in 1930 and 1940.[30] During the 1920s, these communities had a net loss of 127 banks, or just 2.7 percent of the bank offices they had in 1920. Between 1930 and 1941, however, cities and towns with more than 10,000 people suffered a net loss of 1,442 banks, or 31.2 percent of the banks they had in 1930.[31]

The failure experience of the 1930–32 period is instructive in two regards. First, the failure rate for the smallest banks (less than $500,000 in loans and investments) increased 3.3 times over the 1921–29 rate, indicating that banks in this size range generally were operating under even greater stress during the 1930s than they were in the

---

[29]Derived from Friedman and Schwartz (1963, Table 13); the 1983 FDIC annual report, p. 41; and the *Federal Reserve Bulletin* (September 1937).

[30]Bureau of the Census (1975, series A57–A72).

[31]This reduction in banks was not offset by an increase in the number of bank branches. Between 1930 and 1941, the total number of bank branches in the United States increased just 1 percent, from 3,522 in 1930 to 3,558 in 1941, based on data in Federal Reserve Board of Governors (1943, Table 73).

1920s. Second, the annual failure rate among America's larger banks skyrocketed in 1930–32 from the low levels of the 1921–29 period, increasing by 7.8 times for banks in the $2 million to $5 million size range, by 14.5 times for banks in the $5 million to $10 million size range, and by 29.4 times for banks over $10 million in size. Even though the failure rate for the larger banks increased dramatically, only 8 percent of the banks over $10 million in size failed during the 1930–32 period while 31 percent of the banks under $250,000 in size failed during that three-year period.

Currency preferences in the interwar period. The extent to which people lost confidence in the American banking system as a result of the banking collapse is doubtful. Currency holdings on both an actual and a price-adjusted basis declined steadily during the 1920s until the fall of 1930, just before the start of the banking collapse. This decline, which paralleled the rise in the deposit/currency ratio, may indicate, in fact, that many Americans entered the banking system for the first time during the 1920s, enabling them to conduct more of their financial transactions with checks and fewer with currency. But why were there new entrants? It may be that the rapid increase in cars, trucks, and paved highways in rural America gave more people physical access to the banking system, something they had previously lacked.

From November 1930 on, actual currency per adult started to climb; on a price-adjusted basis, currency climbed even more rapidly. Did this steady climb indicate declining faith in the banking system and a shift from bank deposits to currency in the mattress? Not necessarily. These data may indicate that growing numbers of Americans, particularly rural Americans, once again lost their access to the banking system because of the closure of thousands of small rural banks that could be reached by horse and buggy. In 1930, almost every small town and village had a bank. By 1940, though, at least 5,400 towns with populations of fewer than 2,500 people had no bank. In addition, farmers were losing their cars and trucks. From 1930 to 1933, the number of farms without a car or truck doubled, rising from 1.26 million in 1930 to 2.48 million in 1933.[32] Thus, by 1933, many rural Americans had neither access to a nearby bank nor a car or truck they could use to get to a more distant bank.

Three relatively sharp monthly increases in currency per adult occurred in 1931 and 1932. Each jump corresponds with a spike in the number of bank failures. Although spurts of bank failures may

---

[32]This datum assumes no more than one car *or* truck per farm; thus, it understates the number of farms without motorized, off-the-farm transportation during these years.

have undermined the confidence of some in banks, these clumps of failures also may have forced yet more people into an all-currency existence if they suddenly lost access to the banking system. The sharp upswing in currency holdings just before the bank holiday largely reversed itself within a few months, before the introduction of federal deposit insurance on January 1, 1934. On both a price-adjusted and an actual basis, currency holdings were back to their October 1932 levels by August 1933. This reversal probably reflects the steady reopening of banks after the bank holiday.

Federal deposit insurance apparently did pull some currency back into the banks, as evidenced by a drop in currency holdings between December 1933 and January 1934. On a price-adjusted basis, however, currency holdings per adult stayed above their November 1931 level until at least the end of 1941. Actual currency holdings per adult exhibited a similar pattern and never dropped below the level they reached in September 1931.

The failure of currency holdings per adult to decline to pre–bank holiday levels could mean that deposit insurance did not restore full faith in U.S. banks. The continued high level of currency holdings may instead reflect that millions of Americans did not regain access to the banking system for many years after the bank holiday due to a lack of motorized transportation and fewer banking offices in rural America. This raises a more basic question: Did Americans ever lose faith in the banking system, except possibly for a few days just before the 1933 bank holiday? Or did they instead lose faith in individual banks, as evidenced by bank runs, and/or did they lose physical access to the banking system because of restrictive branching laws?

Why didn't the banking system collapse in 1921? The 1929–30 recession and deflation were in some ways less severe than the 1920–21 recession and deflation. Yet the American banking system did not collapse after the first recession, while it did at the end of the second. There are three reasons why.

First, small banks were more viable in 1920 and 1921 than they were a decade later. Rural America still had few cars, trucks, and paved roads in 1921. The increased size differential between failed and nonfailed banks during the 1920s indicates that bank failures in 1921 more closely represented a cross-section of American banking; by 1929, failures provided evidence of a large, uneconomic fringe of small banks within the banking system.

Second, there was a substantial difference between the 1920–22 and the 1929–33 deflations. The earlier deflation canceled out the inflation of World War I and the immediate postwar period, representing an easily anticipated correction of the price level. During the later deflation, however, prices dropped to levels last reached decades earlier, and the decline was not easily anticipated. Price index data will illustrate this point. The wholesale price index essentially hit its immediate postwar low of 48.2 in June 1921, 56 months after passing that point during the prewar inflation.[33] The consumer price index hit its immediate postwar low of 49.7 in August 1922, only 40 months after passing that point during the 1919–20 inflation. During the 1930s, however, the wholesale price index hit a low of 30.8 in February 1933, a level it had not reached since 1904. The consumer price index hit its low of 37.6 in April 1933, a level it had not reached since April 1917.

Third, the economy rebounded from its postwar deflation in 1921 and 1922, something that did not happen in 1930–31. Thus, banks were saved during the earlier period from the extremely debilitating effects of a prolonged downward deflationary spiral. There appear to be two reasons why the earlier deflation ended more quickly. First, price levels worldwide did not exert strong deflationary price pressures after 1921, perhaps in part because Great Britain and other countries had not yet returned to the gold standard. Second, the money supply started to expand in September 1921 after having dropped 7 percent in 12 months from its postwar peak. By September 1922, the money supply had fully recovered from its 1920–21 decline.[34]

Three factors that did not cause the banking collapse. Numerous false causes have been offered to explain the banking collapse. Unfortunately, they have been used to justify much of the post–bank holiday regulation that still encumbers the banking industry. Three of these myths are discussed below.

Myth No. 1: Banks paid excessive interest rates that forced them to make risky loans. The data do not support this contention. Bank interest rates in the late 1920s were amazingly flat, and even declining in the case of interbank deposits; bank time deposit rates were lower than other rates, and increasingly so in the late 1920s. The Federal Reserve System's (1932) study on branch, group, and chain banking reported that the average interest rate paid by banks in different size ranges varied primarily with their mix of time and demand deposits. Thus, the largest banks, with loans and invest-

[33]The wholesale price index did dip slightly below 48.2 between December 1921 and April 1922, to a low of 47.1. However, that dip occurred after what was in effect the end of the postwar deflation.

[34]According to Friedman and Schwartz (1963, Table A-1, column 9), the money supply, including time deposits, hit a peak of $40.205 billion in September 1921, declined to a low of $37.418 billion one year later, and then rose back up to $40.428 billion by September 1922.

ments over $50 million, paid the lowest average rate of interest in the 1926–30 period because they relied least on time deposits for their funding. Banks in the $5 million to $10 million size range paid the highest average rate during the 1926–30 period but also held a high percentage of time deposits.

Myth No. 2: Bad lending in the 1920s led to large loan losses in the 1930s. The price deflation beginning in 1929 eventually caused bank loan losses. These losses caused some banks to fail after 1930 and certainly contributed to the overall operating losses experienced by Fed member banks (and by extension, nonmember banks) in 1932, 1933, and 1934.[35]

Extraordinary loan losses experienced by Fed members between 1930 and 1936—that is, loan losses exceeding normal loss rates— equaled 5.15 percent of the total member bank loans outstanding in October 1929, their pre-Depression peak. This represents slightly more than one-third of the 15 percent average price deflation the American economy experienced during the 1930–36 period (as measured by the GNP deflator against a 1929 base year). Thus, the extraordinary loan losses experienced by commercial banks after 1929 appear to be due largely to the 1929–33 price deflation and the economy's very slow post-1933 recovery from it.[36] Deflation caused extraordinary loan losses by driving collateral values below loan balances, triggering loan defaults, and by increasing business failures and, hence, losses on business loans.

Myth No. 3: Investment banking activities undermined commercial banks. The Glass-Steagall Act of 1933 separated commercial from investment banking. Yet bank failures in the 1920s and during the banking collapse offer no evidence that mixing the two types of banking had increased bank failures.

According to Peach (1941, pp. 82–87), 566 commercial banks in 1930 were engaged in investment banking activities, that is, underwriting and selling corporate securities. Peach's count excludes banks that owned only finance and real estate holding companies, managed investment trusts, or made markets in their own stocks. There were 555 banks in 1930 with loans and investments in excess of $10 million. Assuming most of these banks engaged in investment banking, then most of the 566 banks with investment banking activities exceeded $10 million in size. The remaining banks engaged in investment

---

[35]Federal Reserve Board of Governors (1943, Table 57).

[36]The GNP deflator (1982 = 100) was 14.6 in 1929. It bottomed out in 1933 at 11.2. By 1936, it had recovered only to 12.6. The deflator did not return to its 1929 level until 1942, when it reached 14.7.

banking were most likely among the 595 banks in the $5 million to $10 million size range. Because larger banks failed during the banking collapse at a much lower rate than smaller banks, securities affiliates do not appear to have increased the failure rate of their parent banks.

Lessons from the 1930–33 Banking Collapse

The 1930–33 banking collapse offers these seven lessons for 1987 and the future.

One, restrictions on branch banking enormously magnify banking system problems. Economic distress is hard on banks; fragmenting the banking system in an unnatural manner, as branching restrictions do, worsens the distress. The Canadian experience, in which some banks operated hundreds of branches nationwide, demonstrates that widespread branching is especially safe and desirable during an era of severe price deflation.

Two, unanticipated price disinflation and particularly deflation are a bank killer, particularly of small and/or undiversified banks. Stable prices are key to keeping bad bank failures to a minimum.

Three, a hesitant lender of last resort adds instability to the banking system and increases the likelihood that the money supply will decline inadvertently, thereby causing deflation, bank failures, and a continuing downward spiral in the economy.

Four, the banking collapse offers absolutely no justification for interest rate controls, including the continuing ban on interest paid on corporate demand deposits. Banks did not pay excessive interest rates to attract deposits during the 1920s and 1930s; nor has any credible evidence been offered to support the contention that interest rate competition led to bank failures.[37]

Five, the banking collapse does not justify separating commercial from investment banking. Some underwriters of the era, including some commercial bankers, engaged in abusive and fraudulent practices, but that issue was addressed by the 1933 and 1934 securities acts.

Six, excessive competition caused few, if any, bank failures prior to the bank holiday. Bank chartering and branching restrictions imposed after the bank holiday were not justified.

Seven, the banking collapse does not justify the federal deposit insurance schemes enacted after the bank holiday. First, the history

---

[37]Benston (1964, pp. 431–49) found that high interest rates on demand deposits in the 1920s did not lead to unsafe lending and investment practices by bankers or to bank failures.

of the deposit/currency ratio suggests that depositors did not lose faith in the banking system. Second, the protection offered by federal deposit insurance is not insurance because it lacks risk-related pricing. Third, the lender of last resort, not the deposit insurer, protects a banking system against liquidity risk. Fourth, a severe deflation will bankrupt a deposit insurer just as it will destroy banks saddled with numerous uneconomic and/or undiversified risks.

References

Benston, George J. "Interest Payments on Demand Deposits and Bank Investment Behavior." *Journal of Political Economy* (October 1964): 431–39.

Board of Governors of the Federal Reserve System. *Banking and Monetary Statistics, 1914–1941.* Washington, D.C., 1943.

Bureau of the Census. *Historical Statistics of the United States, Colonial Times to 1970, Bicentennial Edition.* Washington, D.C., 1975.

Federal Reserve System. *Report of the Federal Reserve Committee on Branch, Group, and Chain Banking.* Washington, D.C., 1932.

Fisher, Irving. *Booms and Depressions.* New York: Adelphi Co., 1932.

Fisher, Irving. "The Debt-Inflation Theory of Great Depressions." *Econometrica* 1 (October 1933).

Friedman, Milton, and Schwartz, Anna J. *A Monetary History of the United States, 1867–1960.* Princeton, N.J.: Princeton University Press, 1963.

Green, Steven L. "The Abrogation of Gold Clauses in 1933 and Its Relation to Current Controversies in Monetary Economics." Federal Reserve Bank of Dallas *Economic Review* (July 1986): 1–17.

Jamison, A. B., and Mackintosh, W. A. *Chartered Banking in Canada.* Toronto: Ryerson Press, 1979.

Maisel, Sherman J., ed. *Risk and Capital Adequacy in Commercial Banks.* Chicago: University of Chicago Press, 1981.

Meltzer, Alan H. "Monetary and Other Explanations of the Start of the Great Depression." *Journal of Monetary Economics* 2 (November 1976): 455–71.

Minsky, Hyman P. "Can 'It' Happen Again?" In *Banking and Monetary Studies.* Edited by Deane Carson. Homewood, Ill.: R. D. Irwin, 1963.

Peach, W. Nelson. *The Security Affiliates of National Banks.* Baltimore: Johns Hopkins Press, 1941.

White, Lawrence H. *Free Banking in Britain: Theory, Experience and Debate, 1800–1845.* Cambridge: Cambridge University Press, 1984.

Wigmore, Barrie A. *The Crash and Its Aftermath.* Westport, Conn.: Greenwood Press, 1985.

Wigmore, Barrie A. "Was the Bank Holiday of 1933 a Run on the Dollar Rather than on the Banks?" Unpublished manuscript, 1986.

4

WAS THE ESTABLISHMENT OF A CANADIAN CENTRAL BANK IN 1935 NECESSARY?*

Michael D. Bordo and Angela Redish

The Bank of Canada began operations in March 1935, considerably later than the central banks of most other Western industrial economies. We examine two questions suggested by this event: Why did Canada not develop a central bank earlier, and, that given, why did the central bank evolve at all?

The current debate over regulatory reform of the banking system has led to a reexamination of the need for government intervention in the monetary sector. One of the central issues in the debate is the role of central banks, and historical evidence on the circumstances leading to their establishment is crucial. Some economists argue that in every case central banks were imposed by revenue-seeking or power-hungry governments, while others argue that central banks, specifically in their role as lender of last resort, evolved naturally from a fractional reserve banking system.[1]

The relatively late appearance of central banking in Canada suggests that its experience may shed some light on the debate. We examine three competing hypotheses concerning the introduction of central banking in Canada: (1) the bank evolved naturally as a lender of last resort to the fractional reserve banking system; (2) the bank was introduced to provide an anchor for a largely unregulated mon-

---

*This article is a slightly revised version of "Why Did the Bank of Canada Emerge in 1935?" *Journal of Economic History* (June 1987). It is used with permission of the *Journal of Economic History* and the Economic History Association.

Michael D. Bordo is a professor of economics at the University of South Carolina. Angela Redish is an assistant professor of economics at the University of British Columbia. They wish to thank Greg Bloss and Shirley Haun for research assistance and the Bank of Nova Scotia Archives for access to its material. Helpful comments on an earlier draft were supplied by Lance Davis, Steven Easton, Steven Ferris, Debra Glassman, Charles Goodhart, Mark Rush, Anna Schwartz, Ronald Shearer, Charles Stuart, Dean Taylor, and Kenneth White.

[1]See Smith (1936) and Hayek (1976) for the view that central banks were primarily a response to political and historical forces and Goodhart (1985) for the natural evolution hypothesis.

etary system that had just left the certainties of the gold standard; and (3) the bank's emergence was prompted primarily by political factors independent of the preceding two hypotheses.[2] We find most support for the third hypothesis.

We argue that by 1935, the Canadian banking system had developed alternative institutions to perform the functions traditionally associated with a central bank. At the same time, the Bank of Canada was considered by its framers to be a complement to, not a substitute for, the gold standard, and we find support for this position in econometric analysis.

The Natural Evolution Hypothesis

The traditional approach to the origins of central banking views it as part of the natural evolution of a modern banking system. A competitive banking system, with bank money convertible into gold or some other dominant (outside) money, will periodically face the problem of runs on individual banks, reflecting the public's fears about the solvency of a particular institution. Because the public is unable to distinguish between the illiquidity and insolvency of other banks also suffering an increased demand for outside moneys, a liquidity crisis and banking panic often will follow. Goodhart (1985) effectively argues that because of an information asymmetry, a central bank is necessary to act as lender of last resort and cannot be operated on profit-maximizing lines because of potential conflicts of interest between the competitive central bank and other banks in the system.

Goodhart's explanation for the evolution of central banking in England and other European countries is that the first central banks evolved from commercial banks that had the special privilege of being the government's bank. Because of their sound reputation, position as holder of the nation's central gold reserve, ability to obtain economies by pooling reserves through a correspondent banking system, and ability to provide extra cash by rediscounting, such banks evolved into bankers' banks and lenders of last resort in a liquidity crisis. Once such banks assumed the role of lender of last resort, "moral hazard" on the part of other banks (now free to follow a more risky strategy) provided a rationale for the central bank to develop some form of supervision or regulation. Goodhart further argues that the conflict between the public functions of such an institution and

[2]The traditional explanation given for the establishment of the Bank of Canada in the 1930s is the failure of the prevailing set of monetary arrangements to increase the money supply during the Great Depression. See, for example, Noble (1937).

its need to satisfy its shareholders made the transition from a competitive bank to a central bank lengthy and painful.

The counterargument has been put most clearly by Vera Smith (1936), who argued that central banks did not, in fact, evolve naturally but were established through monopoly privileges granted by the government of the day upon receipt of some special consideration—for example, the regular purchase of government debt at a favorable price. Milton Friedman and Anna Schwartz (1986), while agreeing with Smith, have suggested that the case against some form of government role as a lender of last resort is inconclusive. Although private insurance schemes could handle individual bank insolvencies, federal deposit insurance has been necessary in the United States to allay incipient liquidity crises in the unit banking system.

The structure of the Canadian banking system changed considerably between the emergence of the first chartered bank in 1822 and the 1930s, but the process of evolution did' not result in the introduction of central banking. The government's involvement in the monetary sector was through regulation of financial institutions and the issue of convertible and, in part, fiduciary Dominion notes. Dominion notes were legal tender and were generally issued in small denominations for hand-to-hand currency (the government had a monopoly over the issue of notes of $5 or less) and large denominations (over $10,000) used as reserves by the banks.[3] The government held a fractional reserve against its notes, up to a limit above which 100 percent reserves were required to be held. (The limit rose from $9 million to $50 million between 1860 and 1930.)

The degree of bank regulation was mixed. There were no required reserves, but banks usually kept substantial levels of reserves because the refusal to convert their notes and demand deposits into specie or Dominion notes would result in suspension or forfeit of their charter. In addition, there were no restrictions on the formation of branch banks. In the early years of this century, the Canadian banking system was comprised of 36 competitive fractional reserve banks, each permitted to operate branches nationwide, with a total of about 1,000 branches. The banks, however, required a government charter to commence operations and some minimum level of paid-up capital. In 1900 the minimum paid-up capital was $250,000, which was said to explain the lack of entrants into the industry (Bond 1969). In addition, lending was restricted to real bills, which excluded loans

---

[3]These notes were a more secure form of reserve than gold, since they were numbered and therefore identifiable. Thus the banks were used to introduce both the large and small Dominion notes.

secured by real estate, accommodation paper, and most plant and equipment. Finally, banks legally were not permitted to charge an interest rate of more than 7 percent on loans.

Although Canada had a competitive fractional reserve banking system throughout the 19th century, no central bank evolved. Virtually all the elements of traditional central banking had emerged by the beginning of the 20th century, undertaken either by private institutions or directly by the government.

First, the Canadian banking system had developed an efficient and elastic note issue (bank notes generally traded at par throughout the country). The clearinghouse in Montreal was maintained by the Canadian Bankers' Association (CBA), which in 1901 was recognized by the Bank Act as "an agency for the supervision and control of certain activities of the banks" (Watts 1972, p. 18). Second, the nationwide branch system avoided the problem of seasonal liquidity crises so evident in the United States after the Civil War, lessening the need for a lender of last resort.

Third, the Bank of Montreal (founded in 1817) emerged very early as the government's bank, performing many central bank functions. The Bank of Montreal, however, never evolved into a full-fledged central bank as did the Bank of England (or the government's bank in other countries) perhaps because of the rivalry of other large Canadian banks (for example, the Royal Bank). Fourth, Canadian banks kept most of their reserves on "call" in the New York money market. Such outside reserves were used occasionally to satisfy the public's demand for liquidity, again precluding the need for a central bank. On two occasions, in 1907 and 1914, these reserves proved inadequate to prevent a liquidity crisis and the Canadian government had to step in to provide adequate reserves.[4]

Fifth, the 1914 Finance Act, passed to facilitate wartime finance, provided chartered banks with a liberal rediscounting facility. This act included a clause permitting issuance of unbacked Dominion notes. By pledging appropriate collateral (and this was broadly defined), banks could borrow Dominion notes from the Treasury Board. The clause, which was extended after the wartime emergency, provided a discount window/lender of last resort for the Canadian banking system.

Providing a Substitute for the Gold Standard

The key macroeconomic function of a central bank under the gold standard was to maintain the convertibility of its liabilities into gold.

---

[4]In 1907 the government lent Dominion notes to the banks, and in 1914 the government introduced the Finance Act described below. See Rich (1984).

In Canada, overissue by individual banks was prevented through the operation of the clearing mechanism, while convertibility for the system as a whole was maintained through the holding of outside reserves. Discretionary monetary policy (for debt management purposes and to finance the government's bonds) rarely conflicted with the gold standard constraint and was carried out by the government using the Bank of Montreal as its fiscal agent. Thus, under the gold standard that prevailed before 1914, there seemed to be little need for a central bank in Canada.[5]

In 1926, Canada returned to the gold standard it had abandoned in November 1914. In December 1928, Canada de facto suspended the gold standard again. The banks "cooperated" with the government by suspending gold exports from their own accounts and by raising the price of gold for U.S. banks.[6] Because Dominion notes were de facto inconvertible, the Canadian exchange rate was no longer constrained at par. On the other hand, and in contrast to the 19th-century suspension of convertibility, internal convertibility was maintained; that is, Canadian banks were still required to convert their notes into Dominion notes on demand. The informal suspension continued (more or less) until October 1931, when, following the British suspension of the gold standard, a formal embargo was placed on gold exports. Consequently, one possible rationale for the establishment of a central bank was to provide an anchor to the money supply, the price level, and hence the exchange rate, in the absence of gold convertibility. A central bank could prevent unregulated profit-maximizing private banks from expanding their money issues without limit.[7]

There is considerable evidence that this hypothesis is at best incomplete. We have argued elsewhere that suspension of the gold standard did not create an explosion of the price level as a consequence of profit-maximizing banks expanding their money issues, as suggested by traditional models of inflationary finance. Banks' expectations that the gold standard would be resumed at some traditional

---

[5]Chisholm (1983) argues that the Bank of Canada was equally unnecessary in the 1930s, since the government of Canada had shown that it could manage the Canadian currency both before and after the suspension of free gold convertibility.

[6]The cost for a Canadian bank to export gold to New York was very small, and therefore the gold points for this transaction were very narrow. (The costs were higher for private individuals, and for shipments to the U.K.) In practice, the exchange rate did not fall below the narrow gold export points. See Shearer and Clark (1979).

[7]See Friedman (1959). For the counterargument that competing banks would provide a determinant price level, see Klein (1974).

par constrained the issuance of bank money.[8] This view is supported by the almost identical deflationary behavior of the Canadian and U.S. price levels during the period from 1929 to 1933, and the tendency of the exchange rate to stay close to par for three years after Canada had left the gold standard.

In addition, the evidence gathered by the Macmillan Commission, established in 1933 to investigate the desirability and potential structure of a central bank in Canada, suggests that the central bank was not viewed as an alternative to the international gold standard, but rather as a necessary institution in a gold standard world. The commission conducted hearings across Canada before reporting on September 27, 1933, in favor of the establishment of a central bank, with two dissenting opinions. Moreover, the evidence presented to the commission shows that it was widely believed that the suspension of the gold standard was temporary. Jackson Dodds, speaking for the CBA, stated (RCBC 1933, p. 3225): "It is logical to assume that the gold standard (perhaps with modifications) will be resumed in due time by the great trading nations and that the Dominion would naturally desire to follow suit." Frank Knox, a leading academic economist, stated (RCBC 1933, p. 3063):

> It may be assumed that sooner or later the major trading countries of the world will have to come to some agreement as to a common monetary standard and that they will stabilize their several currencies with respect to each other probably by making them convertible once more into gold. Supposing this to have taken place Canada's monetary policy is clearly to join such a group.

The debate about the need for a central bank therefore focused on the need for central banking in a gold standard world and the argument that the automatic gold standard of the pre-1914 era had been replaced by a managed gold standard. Macmillan's report stated his position (Royal Commission on Banking and Currency: Report 1933, p. 59): "The gold standard was restored in a world which called for continuous direction and cooperation on the part of the various national authorities."[9] Indeed the dissenting commissioners stated that while they realized a central bank might be appropriate at some later date, they felt it should wait for the reestablishment of the international gold standard. Macmillan, on the other hand, argued that the present

---

[8]Bordo and Redish (1987). In this paper we argue that the government did not expand the Dominion note issue because it wished to avoid a currency depreciation, and that the government's behavior conditioned the expectations of the banks and the public.

[9]This view found support from both bankers and academics. See, for example, the evidence of T. E. Gregory (RCBC 1933, p. 2995) and J. A. MacLeod (RCBC 1933, p. 50).

time was particularly advantageous for establishing the bank because it would not be subject to the day-to-day discipline of the gold standard until the central bankers had developed some experience.

An empirical analysis of the impact of the establishment of the Bank of Canada on such key macroeconomic variables as the price level, exchange rates, and interest rates can provide indirect evidence of the reasons for the bank's emergence. The hypothesis that the bank was necessary as a substitute for the gold standard implies that the introduction of a central bank with the power to control the money supply would lead to very different price level behavior than under a regime in which monetary variables were determined by a private banking system.

In the absence of sufficient data to estimate a structural model of the macroeconomy that would permit identification of the channels and magnitude of the bank's impact, time-series models were used to examine the bank's effect on the macroeconomy. The impact of the bank's formation on the level of the money stock itself is difficult to gauge because the definition of such variables as currency in the hands of the public and reserves changed the day the bank began operations. The nature of the demand for reserves was altered by the introduction of a required reserve ratio, and the high-powered money component of currency in the hands of the public changed from Dominion notes in circulation to Bank of Canada notes in active circulation.[10] Thus, although the impact of the bank's emergence on monetary variables is of interest, our serious doubts about the consistency of the measurement of high-powered money led us to restrict our analysis to the behavior of such nominal variables as the price level and exchange rate.

We estimated univariate models of the price level and the exchange rate (data on Canadian interest rates were not available). We also estimated two multivariate models of the price level in which the independent variables were the U.S. price level and the money stock—variables that economic theory suggests would affect the price level. In each case, the impact of the formation of the bank was tested by an analysis of the stability of the regression and by an examination of the regression residuals.

The methodology and results are described in detail in the Appendix, and we present here a summary of the results. We performed a Chow test for each model to see if there was a structural break in

[10]The active circulation of Bank of Canada notes in March 1935 was double the Dominion notes in the hands of the public in February 1935, which we attribute primarily to a change in measurement rather than a doubling of currency holdings.

March 1935. In all cases but one, the hypothesis of a structural break was rejected. When the M1 definition of money was employed, there was a structural break in March 1935, which we suspect reflects the change in reporting techniques for the "currency in the hands of the public" component of high-powered money discussed above. We therefore reestimated the model using M1 less the high-powered currency component as the monetary variable. In this model the hypothesis of structural stability could not be rejected.

We next examined the regression residuals to test whether any particular period represents an outlier. Figure 1 (in the Appendix) shows the standardized residuals, so that a value greater than 1.97 in absolute value can be considered an outlier. Figure 1 shows that late 1929, the period from October 1931 through 1933, and late 1939 were the main outliers. Thus, the battery of tests largely supports the conclusion that the introduction of the Bank of Canada in 1935 did not alter the money supply process in Canada and did not affect the evolution of the key nominal variables in the economy.

The annual reports of the governor of the Bank of Canada (1935–39) suggest that the result was not unintentional. In the first annual report the governor described the bank's functions and how they were being implemented (Bank of Canada 1935). The five functions listed were: to manage domestic credit, manage the exchange rate, advise the government, cooperate with other central banks, and manage the bank rate. The bank, however, took a rather agnostic approach to these activities. After admitting that because the Canadian dollar was inconvertible, the bank could control the level of domestic credit, the governor argued that the objective of such control was the level of income, which "can grow and does grow without any definite connection between such growth and a growth in bank deposits or notes in circulation" (Bank of Canada 1935, p. 12).

With respect to the exchange rate, the governor noted that "the Canadian dollar has exhibited a remarkable tendency, when not at parity with the pound or U.S. dollar to take up an intermediate position." But he took no credit for the level or stability of the exchange rate and rather attributed it to institutional arrangements: "The existence of so many Canadian bonds payable in 2 or 3 currencies . . . has had a tendency to restrict fluctuations." Finally, with respect to the bank discount rate: "It is quite out of touch with Treasury Bill rates, but this fact is not at present of any significance" (Bank of Canada 1935, pp. 13, 16).

The governor's report reflects more concern with the housekeeping details of the transfer to the bank of various activities previously managed by the government (the issue of currency and the management of the government debt) than with macroeconomic objectives. This is consistent with our econometric analysis, which finds that the formation of the bank had virtually no macroeconomic impact.

The Political Forces

Canada's central bank was not intended to replace the gold standard, and it was not considered a necessary part of a fractional reserve banking system. The emergence of the Bank of Canada, we believe, reflected a conjuncture of political imperatives. Domestically, in an environment wherein traditional trust in the beneficial nature of the market system was eroding and a spirit of nationalism was rising, political pressure was mounting to halt the deflation that was frequently blamed on the concentrated banking industry. Internationally, monetary cooperation was said to depend on a system of central banks.

The demand for inflation, while clearly important, was rather ambiguous. The popular demand was succinctly expressed in an article in *Maclean's* (1 July 1933):

> The point which our bankers seem to miss is that what the Canadian people want in a central bank is not to supply the other banks with rediscount facilities which they already have or to save us from future panics [as, it is previously noted, U.S. experience shows they do not], but they do want an institution that will effectually control the whole of the money and credit of the nation, now under the control of the other banks and which will somehow be able to make that money and credit available in sufficient volume wherever legitimately needed, and on terms much more fair and equitable than at present.

The ambiguity arises because there was no stated desire to abandon the gold standard. In addition, the Canadian government clearly did not oppose the deflation and the stability of the Canadian dollar, and it should have been clear that a central bank would not diverge from such a policy. Government representatives had frequently stated that the dollar would not be depreciated, although a monetary expansion was attempted in late 1932 by forcing the banks to borrow under the Finance Act. The new borrowing was used primarily to pay off older borrowings and had little inflationary impact. The government continued to refuse to undertake the direct inflationary policies of either increasing the fiat limit on Dominion notes or reducing the gold backing of notes beneath the limit.

The demand for inflation was often linked to attacks on the monopoly power of the banking system. In 1930, there were only 10 banks, and, of these, 3 owned 75 percent of industry assets. The CBA provided a forum for explicit collusion, and the collusion was admitted on occasion in such areas as Western branch closures.[11] Opposition members in Parliament complained that "farmers were innocent victims of the policy of deflation instituted by the banks" (Stokes 1939, p. 62).

These attacks came at the same time as more general attacks on the efficacy of the market system. Historian Donald Creighton (1970, p. 215) noted that "a fairly large and increasing number of Canadians were rapidly reaching the conclusion that positive action by the state must remedy the admitted weakness of economic liberalism." The political manifestation of this sentiment was the formation of the socialist Cooperative Commonwealth Federation (CCF) in 1932, which by 1934 had become the official opposition in the provincial governments of Ontario and Saskatchewan. A central platform of the CCF was the nationalization of all financial institutions. Schemes for increased government intervention also appeared from the right— the Social Credit party, founded on the doctrines of Major C. H. Douglas, and the Bloc Populaire, a proto-fascist party, in Quebec.[12]

There were, in addition, more subtle political pressures. The Canadian government had been a party to the 1920 International Financial Conference in Brussels, which urged all countries without a central bank to establish one. Moreover, the World Monetary and Economic Conference in 1933 had stated that all developed countries without a central bank should create one to facilitate monetary cooperation and recovery. In an article analyzing the need for a central bank, Queen's University economists stressed the need for a central bank to send representatives to world monetary conferences: "There are few countries . . . more vitally interested in international cooperation in the monetary and economic fields than Canada and yet we lack any institution which would permit effective participation in such cooperation" (Department of Political and Economic Science 1933, p. 439).

The establishment of the central bank was also part of a more general program to create sovereign institutions.[13] In laying the foun-

[11]See, for example, Vancouver *Province* (December 30, 1935).

[12]Major Douglas believed that a shortage of purchasing power inevitably caused underconsumption in a capitalist economy, and that the state of unemployment could be remedied by injecting fiat money into the economy. See Douglas (1931). In Alberta the government of William Aberhart, following Douglas's precepts, promised a national dividend of $25 per month to all adult Albertans. In 1938 this practice was declared *ultra vires* by the Supreme Court of Canada. See McIvor (1961).

[13]We would like to thank historian Fred Armstrong at the University of Western Ontario for pointing out this argument.

dation for a national airline, for example, Prime Minister R. B. Bennett remarked (Creighton 1970, p. 215): "The Americans can fly on their side of the line but we are quite capable of doing all the flying in or over Canada." The Canadian Radio Broadcasting Commission was also established in 1932. Indeed, it was not until 1931 that Canada's independence from Britain was solidified by the Statute of Westminster, which gave her Dominion status and authority over her own external affairs. Speaking in December 1933, Bennett declared that he had decided in December 1931, after Britain left gold, to establish a central bank (Stokes 1939, p. 65):

> I learned to my surprise that there was no direct means of settling international balances between Canada and London, that the only medium was New York, and the value of the Canadian dollar would have to be determined in Wall Street. I made up my mind then and there that this country was going to have a central bank because there must be some financial institution that can with authority do business for the whole of the Dominion with the other nations of the World. If Canada was to be financially independent there had to be a means of determining balances, of settling international accounts; and a central bank would furnish this.

Whether or not Bennett was speaking with hindsight, there is considerable evidence that the decision to introduce a central bank was made before the Macmillan Commission handed down its report. Bryce (1986, p. 82) states that W. C. Clark "agreed to become deputy minister of finance [in late 1932] only when he had found out that the Prime Minister was prepared to accept in principle the establishment of a central bank for Canada." Indeed, the appointment of Lord Macmillan (a staunch advocate of central banking) as head of the commission left little doubt about the outcome of the investigation. The president of the CBA, writing in August 1933 to a colleague, stated: "Confidentially, I think it was decided before Lord Macmillan left London that some kind of a central organization should be established in Canada."[14] One week after the Macmillan Commission handed down its report, Prime Minister Bennett announced that he would introduce a bill to establish a central bank "to regulate credit and currency in the best interests of the economic life of the nation, to control and protect the external value of the national monetary

---

[14]J. A. MacLeod to Hector MacInnes, August 25, 1933, in Archives of the Bank of Nova Scotia, B.N.S. docs sec. #8, file 3. Earlier in August, a newspaper report stated that Eastern financial circles were taking it for granted that a central bank would be created and that the banks would lose their rights to note issue (Vancouver *Sun*, August 11, 1933).

unit and to mitigate by its influence fluctuations in the general level of production, trade, prices and employment."

Conclusion

Examination of the available evidence has led us to reject the hypotheses that the Bank of Canada's emergence merely reflected evolutionary necessity or the need to anchor a monetary system cast adrift by the suspension of the gold standard. The qualitative evidence suggests that the emergence of the bank reflected political, rather than economic, imperatives. Domestically, the government needed to be seen as taking active measures in response to the Depression. The reduced faith in the omnipotence of the market system, coupled with public hostility toward the banking system, meant that the introduction of a central bank was politically popular. Internationally, foreign governments and international organizations were urging nations to create central banks to facilitate international monetary cooperation. These factors, rather than strict economic efficiency, prompted establishment of Canada's central bank.

References

Bank of Canada. *Annual Report of the Governor of the Bank of Canada*. Ottawa, 1935.

Belsley, David A., Kuh, Edwin, and Welsch, Roy E. *Regression Diagnostics*. New York: John Wiley and Sons, 1980.

Bond, David. "The Merger Movement in Canadian Banking, 1890–1920." Discussion paper no. 21, University of British Columbia, May 1969.

Bordo, Michael, and Redish, Angela. "The Supply of Inconvertible Money in the Absence of a Central Bank: Canada's Interwar Experience." Manuscript. University of British Columbia, 1987.

Box, George E. P., and Jenkins, Gwilym M. *Time Series Analysis*. San Francisco: Holden-Day, 1976.

Bryce, Robert B. *Maturing in Hard Times*. Kingston: McGill–Queen's University Press, 1986.

Chisholm, Derek. "La Banque de Canada était-elle nécessaire?" *L'actualité économique* 59 (September 1983): 551–74.

Creighton, Donald. *Canada's First Century*. Toronto: Macmillan Company of Canada, 1970.

Department of Political and Economic Science, Queen's University. "The Proposal for a Central Bank." *Queen's Quarterly* 40 (August 1933): 424–40.

Douglas, C. H. *The Monopoly of Credit*. London: Chapman and Hall, Ltd., 1931.

Friedman, Milton. *A Program for Monetary Stability*. New York: Fordham University Press, 1959.

Friedman, Milton, and Schwartz, Anna. "Has Government Any Role in Money?" *Journal of Monetary Economics* 19 (January 1986): 37–62.

Goodhart, Charles. *The Evolution of Central Banks: A Natural Development?* London: London School of Economics Suntory-Toyota International Center for Economics and Related Disciplines, 1985.

Hayek, Friedrich. *Denationalization of Money.* London: Institute of Economic Affairs, 1976.

Klein, Benjamin. "The Competitive Supply of Money." *Journal of Money, Credit and Banking* 6 (November 1974): 423–53.

McIvor, R. Craig. *Canadian Monetary, Banking and Fiscal Development.* Toronto: Macmillan Company of Canada, 1961.

Mishkin, Frederic S. *A Rational Expectations Approach to Macroeconometrics.* Chicago: University of Chicago Press, 1983.

Noble, S. R. "The Monetary Experience of Canada during the Depression." In *The Lessons of Monetary Experience*, pp. 117–28. Edited by Arthur Gayer. New York: Rinehart and Co., 1937.

Royal Commission on Banking and Currency in Canada: Report. Ottawa, 1933.

RCBC. *Royal Commission on Banking and Currency: Evidence.* Ottawa, 1933.

Rich, Georg. "Canadian Banks, Gold, and the Crisis of 1907." Paper presented at the 13th Conference on Quantitative Methods in Canadian Economic History, March 1984.

Shearer, R. A., and Clark, Carolyn. "The Suspension of the Gold Standard, 1928–1931." Discussion paper no. 79-36, University of British Columbia, November 1979.

Smith, Vera. *The Rationale for Central Banking.* London: P. S. King, 1936.

Stokes, Milton L. *The Bank of Canada.* Toronto: Macmillan Company of Canada, 1939.

U.S. Department of Commerce. *Statistical Abstract of the U.S.* Washington, D.C.

Watts, George S. "The Origins and Background of Central Banking in Canada." *Bank of Canada Review* (May 1972): 15–27.

Appendix
The Empirical Methodology

A univariate model of the Canadian price level was estimated using monthly seasonally adjusted price data.[1] Box-Jenkins (1976) methods identified the following estimating equation as the appropriate univariate model:

$$P_t - P_{t-1} = \alpha (P_{t-1} - P_{t-2}) + \epsilon_t$$

where ϵ_t is a white noise error term. The estimated value of α was 0.48 with a t statistic of 6.98.

The objective of the estimation was to determine whether the evolution of the price series changed after the introduction of the Bank of Canada. The first test examined the structural stability of the equation. Three potential structural breaks were examined: January 1929, when Canada suspended gold convertibility; March 1933, when the United States suspended gold convertibility; and March 1935. If the Bank of Canada had created a new monetary regime, the equation should have a structural break in 1935. Chow tests for the three periods showed that the null hypothesis of no break should be accepted for each of the three periods.

An alternative method of determining the stability of the regression is to examine the regression residuals and to find those residuals that have a disproportionate influence on the estimated model. Figure 1a presents the "studentized" residuals for the model.[2] If the formation of the Bank of Canada altered the monetary regime, then the month when the bank began business or when the bill establishing the bank was passed (June 1934) would have a studentized residual greater than 1.97 in absolute value. In the equation for the entire period, four residuals are significant: July 1929, July 1933, August 1933, and September 1939. The first date marks the peak of the business cycle in the late 1920s; the months of 1933 are part of the brief hiatus from March 1933 to January 1934 when the gold price of the U.S. dollar

[1]The data sources are as follows: Canadian wholesale price index—*Prices and Price Indexes*, Dominion Bureau of Statistics, Canada; the exchange rate—monthly average noon buying rate for the Canadian dollar in New York, Board of Governors of the Federal Reserve System, from *Federal Reserve Bulletin*; U.S. wholesale price index—U.S. Department of Commerce, *Statistical Abstract of the U.S.*, M1 and M2—calculated from the returns published in the Canada *Gazette* (available from the authors on request). All data were seasonally adjusted using the SAS X-11 program.

[2]One interpretation of the "studentized" residuals is as follows: If the regression were rerun with a dummy variable for the ith observation, the t-statistic on the coefficient of the dummy variable would be the same as the "studentized" residual for that observation. See Belsley, Kuh, and Welsch (1980, p. 20).

fluctuated; the last date marks the beginning of World War II. The absence of a significant residual in March 1935 (or in June 1934) provides evidence that the Bank of Canada had little effect on macroeconomic variables.

Similar analysis was conducted for the behavior of the exchange rate between the Canadian dollar and the U.S. dollar. The data again did not reject the hypothesis that the equation was stable throughout the period. The results of the influence tests are shown in Figure 1b. All the significant residuals (other than that for September 1939) lie within the period from September 1931 to November 1933, when the normal relationship between the pound and the U.S. dollar was disrupted, while there is no evidence of a change in the relationship in March 1935.

The third model is a multivariate model including lagged and contemporaneous U.S. price level terms as well as lagged Canadian price level terms as determinants of the Canadian price level. Since the Canadian dollar was very close to par with the U.S. dollar for the period July 1926 to September 1939 (with the exception of the period from October 1931 to March 1933), we would expect Canadian prices to be strongly correlated with U.S. prices. Furthermore, because Canada had many of the features of a small open economy, we would expect the world price level to be exogenous for the Canadian economy. The independent variables of the estimating equation were the contemporaneous U.S. price level and six lags of the Canadian price level and of the U.S. price level.[3] The Chow tests suggested a structural break only in March 1933, and the analysis of the residuals (Figure 1c) again showed no significant residual in March 1935.

Finally, a multivariate model in which the current price level depends on lagged prices and lagged and contemporaneous money stock was estimated separately with M1 and M2.[4] We used the same methodology to determine lag length as in the previous model, and 12 lagged values of the dependent variable and 6 of the money stock variable were included. When the M2 definition of money was used, the results are quite similar to those of the other models. The only structural break occurred in March 1933, and again there was no significant residual in March 1935 (Figure 1e).

When the M1 definition of money was employed, no structural break was found in January 1929 or March 1933, although, as reported

---

[3]The lag lengths were determined by the method of Mishkin (1983, p. 22).

[4]M1 comprises Dominion notes in the hands of the public, chartered bank notes in circulation, plus public (including provincial government) demand deposits. M2 includes M1 and notice deposits.

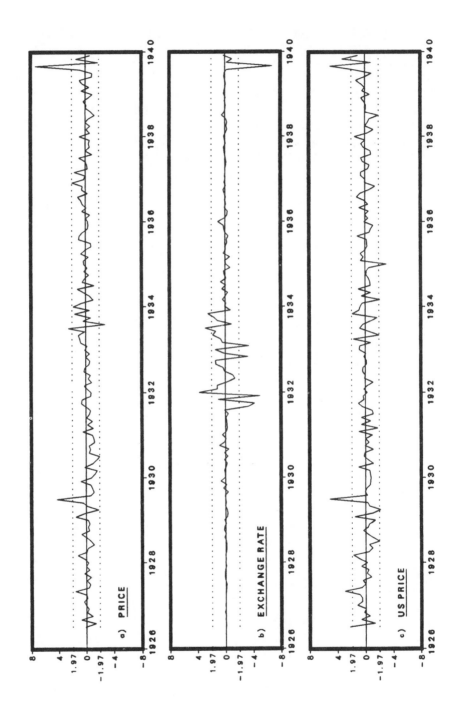

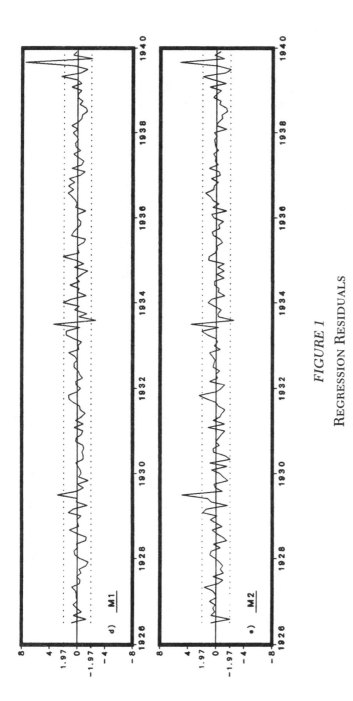

FIGURE 1
Regression Residuals

in the text, there was a structural break in March 1935. As we suspected that this break reflects changes in methods of reporting the data, we reestimated the model using M1 less the high-powered currency component as the monetary variable. In this model the hypothesis of structural stability could not be rejected. The studentized residuals were similar to those for M2 (see Figure 1d).

Thus the evidence suggests that the formation of the Bank of Canada in 1935 did not affect the stochastic processes generating the price level and the exchange rate.

5

A PUBLIC CHOICE PERSPECTIVE OF THE BANKING ACT OF 1933

William F. Shughart II

Against a background of an unprecedented number of commercial bank failures, the Banking Act of 1933 laid out the basic framework of modern banking regulation in the United States. Among its other provisions, the legislation established federal deposit insurance, reaffirmed the restrictions on branch banking imposed in 1927 by the McFadden Act, authorized the Federal Reserve to set ceilings on the interest rates payable on savings and time deposits at member banks, and prohibited the payment of interest on demand deposits. The Banking Act of 1933 also contained four provisions, commonly referred to as the Glass-Steagall Act, that effectively separated commercial and investment banking in the United States.[1] This was accomplished by prohibiting banks from engaging in the activities of underwriting, promoting, or selling securities either directly or through an affiliated brokerage firm. For their part, securities dealers were precluded from engaging in the business of deposit banking.

The Glass-Steagall Act is typically viewed as a public-spirited attempt by Congress to protect depositors against several problems alleged to arise when the activities of commercial and investment banking are combined. It is suggested that commercial bank security holdings raise concerns about the liquidity and, hence, soundness of banks' asset portfolios. This is because the relatively long terms to maturity of marketable securities may not match up well with the short-term nature of banks' deposit liabilities. Moreover, security

The author is affiliated with the Center for Study of Public Choice, George Mason University. He would like to thank Henry Butler, Roger Congleton, Thomas Huertas, Jonathan Macey, Fred McChesney, Clark Nardinelli, Richard Timberlake, Walker Todd, and Robert Tollison for comments on earlier drafts. Participants in a Clemson University Economics Department seminar also provided valuable suggestions.

[1] I am well aware that the names of Glass and Steagall are more properly associated with legislation enacted in 1932 that allowed the Federal Reserve to use U.S. government securities as collateral for note issues. However, because "Glass-Steagall Act" is widely used in the literature to refer to the 1933 act, I have chosen to perpetuate the error in this paper.

holdings make banks' asset portfolios vulnerable to unanticipated capital losses caused by fluctuating market securities prices.

In addition, combining commercial and investment banking activities is thought to create a conflict of interest that may increase the riskiness of banks' loan portfolios. Of particular concern is that banks will make loans on preferential terms to customers who purchase securities underwritten by the bank or that such securities will be accepted as collateral for loans. In short, if banks both purchase securities for their own accounts and make loans to customers who use securities underwritten by banks as collateral, a downturn in the securities market will simultaneously lower the value of banks' asset portfolios and increase the likelihood of default on their loan portfolios. If a deposit outflow occurs at the same time, the banking system's ability to meet the cash demands of its customers will be impaired. This vulnerability to failure is thought to be greater for a combined commercial-investment banking system than for a system in which the two activities are kept separate.

Indeed, a large measure of the blame for the banking crisis of late 1932 and early 1933 was placed on the then fairly common practice of commercial banks underwriting the sale of securities through their bond departments or through separate but affiliated securities firms. Hearings on the bill that would eventually be enacted in 1933 produced testimony on a wide variety of abuses in the securities activities of commercial banks, including insider trading and outright fraud.[2] Senator Glass himself went so far as to claim that the activities of the securities affiliates of commercial banks were a major cause of the Great Depression: "These affiliates, I repeat, were the most unscrupulous contributors, next to the debauch of the New York Stock Exchange, to the financial catastrophe which visited this country and was mainly responsible for the depression under which we have been suffering since" (Kelly 1985, p. 53).

The public-interest explanation for the Glass-Steagall Act suggests that the members of the 73d Congress, which convened in March 1933, successfully set aside political considerations to impose a series of regulations that would restore safety and soundness to a banking system badly battered by the great crash and ensuing depression. In particular, the formal separation of commercial and investment banking required by the Glass-Steagall Act protected depositors by

[2]Many of these horror stories surfaced during hearings before the Senate Banking and Commerce Committee (often referred to as the Pecora hearings, after the committee's counsel, Ferdinand Pecora). See Kennedy (1973, pp. 108–28) for a description of the practices of one of the committee's main targets, National City Bank and its securities affiliate, National City Company.

removing a risky asset from banks' portfolios and by eliminating the conflict of interest between the business of accepting deposits and making loans on the one hand and that of underwriting securities on the other.

The remainder of this paper examines these arguments in more detail. First, some historical background is provided through discussions of the growth of commercial banks' securities activities prior to 1933, the role of securities activities, if any, in precipitating the banking panic of 1929–33, and the main events in the legislative debate on the Glass-Steagall Act. Then comes a summary of the available evidence supporting an alternative, private-interest explanation for the legislation that separated commercial and investment banking. After that, some concluding remarks are presented.

Historical Background

Alleged securities market abuses by commercial banks and their affiliated brokerage firms played a large role in creating an environment conducive to the regulation of investment banking in the United States. The following is a brief review of the events leading up to the enactment in June 1933 of the bill cosponsored by Senator Glass and Representative Steagall.

Commercial Bank Securities Activities before 1933

The involvement of commercial banks in the securities business predates the 1920s. Indeed, one of the principal motives behind the establishment of a federal chartering option for banks by the National Banking Act (1863) was to create a convenient outlet for U.S. government securities by allowing member banks to issue notes (currency) against collateral in the form of Treasury bonds. These activities expanded rapidly during World War I and the years immediately thereafter when a large number of banks participated heavily in the distribution of Liberty Bonds issued to finance the war effort (Flannery 1985, pp. 67–68).

Although national banks were encouraged to deal in U.S. government securities, they were prohibited from underwriting corporate securities prior to the McFadden Act (1927). Many of the larger commercial banks were able to avoid this restriction, however, by establishing separate but affiliated securities firms to apply to private securities issues the experience they had gained in purchasing and selling Treasury bonds.[3] The creation of these securities affiliates

[3]The owners of the bank and the securities affiliate were often the same. Kennedy (1973, p. 111) notes that the stock of National City Company was printed on the opposite side of the shares of its parent, National City Bank.

boosted the involvement of commercial banks in the underwriting business during the 1920s, but the fact that federal regulations continued to restrict national banks from participating directly in such activities raised concerns about the banks' ability to compete effectively with state-chartered institutions that were not so constrained. These concerns were given weight by the development of a trend in which member banks either established state-chartered affiliated banks to deal in corporate securities or simply dropped out of the Federal Reserve System. The McFadden Act attempted to arrest this trend by "reaffirming" the authority of member banks to underwrite certain corporate securities. National banks' underwriting activities were limited initially by the Comptroller of the Currency to debt securities, but were later expanded to include certain equities as well (Flannery 1985, p. 68; Kelly 1985, pp. 42–43).

The establishment of securities affiliates and the lifting of some of the federal restrictions on underwriting activities by the McFadden Act enabled commercial banks to become prominent actors in the securities business by the end of the 1920s. In 1929, for example, 459 U.S. banks were underwriting securities directly through their bond departments and an additional 132 were sponsoring securities issues through an affiliate (Flannery 1985, p. 68). (See Table 1 for data on the growth of commercial banks' securities activities beginning in 1922.) By 1930, commercial banks were underwriting 54.4 percent of all new securities issues (Kennedy 1973, p. 212).

The increased involvement of commercial banks in underwriting activities was reflected to an extent in their own securities holdings. Table 2 reports on the composition of banks' securities portfolios from 1920 to 1933, showing a slight trend during the period toward larger holdings of "other" securities—obligations of domestic corporations, those issued by government agencies but not guaranteed by the United States, and foreign securities. Securities holdings were somewhat more important to member institutions of the Federal Reserve System. By the end of 1933, for instance, U.S. government bonds and other securities accounted for 21.41 percent and 15.5 percent, respectively, of member banks' total assets (Flannery 1985, p. 73).

Securities Affiliates and the Panic of 1929–33

The panic that swept the U.S. banking system following the stock market crash of October 1929 is well documented.[4] From 1929 through 1933, nearly 10,000 banks failed as depositors and bank owner-man-

---

[4]See, especially, Friedman and Schwartz (1963, pp. 299–419).

TABLE 1

SECURITIES ACTIVITIES OF NATIONAL AND STATE BANKS,
1922–33

	National Banks		State Banks		
Year	Directly Engaged in Securities Business	Operating Securities Affiliates	Directly Engaged in Securities Business	Operating Securities Affiliates	Total
1922	62	10	197	8	277
1923	78	17	210	9	314
1924	97	26	236	13	372
1925	112	33	254	14	413
1926	128	45	274	17	464
1927	121	60	290	22	493
1928	150	69	310	32	561
1929	151	84	308	48	591
1930	126	105	260	75	566
1931	123	114	230	58	525
1932	109	104	209	53	475
1933	102	76	169	32	379

SOURCE: Peach (1975, p. 83).

agers scrambled for liquidity; 4,000 banks closed their doors in 1933 alone. Considered in context, however, depositor losses were not of sufficient magnitude to threaten the survival of the entire commercial banking industry. Mergers and other forms of reorganization transferred the deposit liabilities of many failed banks to institutions on sounder footing. When this was not possible, depositors received some compensation from the liquidation of bank assets. Even at the height of the panic, therefore, only a little more than 2 percent of total commercial bank deposits were irretrievably lost. (Details concerning the effects of the crisis on banks and depositors are shown in Table 3.)

Hardest hit were small, state-chartered banks located away from major financial centers. Eighty-eight percent of the banks that suspended operations between 1921 and 1929, for example, had capital of less than $100,000 (Kelly 1985, p. 44).[5] This is the pattern that continued into the 1930s. The institutions that failed over the next

[5]Burns (1974, p. 5) reports that over half the banks that failed between 1921 and 1929 were located in communities with populations of 2,500 or less and that more than 50 percent of the failures occurred in banks each having a capital stock of not more than $25,000.

TABLE 2

SECURITIES HOLDINGS OF COMMERCIAL BANKS AS
PERCENTAGE OF TOTAL ASSETS, 1920–33

Year	U.S. Government Obligations	Obligations of State and Local Governments	Other Securities[a]
1920	7.66	1.99	8.03
1921	7.47	2.39	9.29
1922	8.72	2.60	9.90
1923	9.73	2.50	9.59
1924	8.50	2.76	10.05
1925	8.19	2.81	10.61
1926	7.77	3.03	10.72
1927	7.62	3.24	11.46
1928	8.01	3.25	12.24
1929	7.80	3.13	10.98
1930	7.60	3.29	11.55
1931	10.19	4.12	12.27
1932	13.50	4.97	12.37
1933	18.50	5.60	10.65

[a]Includes obligations of domestic corporations, those of government agencies not guaranteed by the United States, and foreign securities.
SOURCE: U.S. Department of Commerce (1975, p. 1021).

four years were similarly smaller, on average, than those banks able to weather the storm (see Table 4).

What role did the securities activities of commercial banks play in the crisis of 1929–33? Although a definitive answer to this question is not possible, most of the available evidence points to the conclusion that factors other than securities dealings were more important in explaining the wave of bank failures that followed the crash. Despite the fact that congressional hearings on the subject generated much rhetoric on the harm to the safety and soundness of commercial banks allegedly caused by their investment banking activities, securities affiliates were identified as a proximate cause of failure only in the case of the Bank of the United States (Flannery 1985, p. 75). Moreover, although the collapse of the Bank of the United States in December 1930 was spectacular and contributed greatly to a weakening of public confidence in the banking system, it was due less to the operations of the bank's securities affiliate per se than to inept management and outright fraud (Kennedy 1973, pp. 1–5).

Systematic evidence in this regard has recently been reported by White (1986, p. 40). He notes that while 26.3 percent of all national

TABLE 3
BANK SUSPENSIONS, 1921–33

Year	Banks		Deposits		Depositors	
	No. of Suspensions	Failed Banks as Percent of All Banks	Deposits of Failed Banks ($'000)	Deposits of Failed Banks as Percent of All Banks	Losses of Depositors ($'000)	Losses of Depositors per $100 of All Banks' Deposits
1921	506	1.16	172,806	0.62	59,967	0.21
1922	366	1.15	91,182	0.30	38,223	0.13
1923	646	2.10	149,601	0.46	62,142	0.19
1924	775	2.58	210,150	0.61	79,381	0.23
1925	617	2.08	166,937	0.44	60,799	0.16
1926	975	3.28	260,153	0.66	83,066	0.21
1927	669	2.39	199,332	0.49	60,681	0.15
1928	498	1.84	142,386	0.34	43,813	0.10
1929	659	2.47	230,643	0.54	76,659	0.18
1930	1,350	5.29	837,096	2.01	237,359	0.57
1931	2,293	9.87	1,690,232	4.42	390,476	1.01
1932	1,453	6.94	706,187	2.43	168,302	0.57
1933	4,000	20.53	3,596,708	14.23	540,396	2.15

SOURCES: Flannery (1985, p. 77) and Friedman and Schwartz (1963, p. 438).

TABLE 4

AVERAGE SIZE OF FAILED BANKS VERSUS SURVIVING BANKS, 1929–33

	Deposits per Bank ($ '000)	
Year	Failed Banks	All Banks
1929	349.99	1,977.77
1930	620.07	2,165.08
1931	737.13	2,183.29
1932	486.60	1,903.38
1933	899.18	2,257.90

SOURCES: Friedman and Schwartz (1963, p. 438) and U.S. Department of Commerce (1975, pp. 1021–22).

banks failed between 1930 and 1933, "only 6.5% of the 62 banks which had affiliates in 1929 and 7.6% of the 145 banks which conducted large operations through their bond departments closed their doors." More importantly, using data for 1931, the year when the largest number of banks with securities affiliates failed, White (p. 41) finds that holding other things equal, the presence of an affiliate appears to have reduced the probability of bank failure.

Friedman and Schwartz (1963, p. 354) observe that "if there was any deterioration at all in the ex ante quality of loans and investments of banks, it must have been minor, to judge from the slowness with which it manifested itself." Simply put, banks would have failed at a much higher rate as the economy moved into depression if the composition of the asset and loan portfolios they had built up during the 1920s had been a major contributor to impaired safety and soundness. Further evidence against the culpability of securities affiliates in precipitating the pre-1933 banking crisis is that it was the smaller, rural institutions that accounted for the majority of bank failures throughout the 1920s and early 1930s, and virtually none of these were likely to have been much involved in underwriting activities.

There remains the question of whether the securities affiliates of the larger banks contributed in any way to the collapse of smaller institutions. In fact, Senator Carter Glass charged that "great banks in the money centers choked the portfolios of their correspondent banks from Maine to California with utterly worthless investment securities" (Flannery 1985, p. 72). "Country" (non money center) banks did indeed hold larger proportions of their assets in the form of private bonds, stocks, and securities than did the average member bank—19.50 percent of total assets at the end of 1929 versus 6.90

percent for banks located in New York City (Flannery 1985, p. 73). There is little to go on in assessing how important the quality (or lack thereof) of these securities was in explaining the failure of the smaller banks, however. A competing explanation deserving of at least as much consideration is that these small, rural banks were hurt severely by the effects of depression on agricultural activity. Falling farm prices caused the default rate on agricultural loans to be sufficiently high that many of these institutions would have failed in any case.

Legislative History of the Glass-Steagall Act

The separation of commercial and investment banking in the United States became a public policy issue soon after the October 1929 stock market crash—President Hoover called upon Congress to consider such a measure in his first State of the Union message in December 1929—but it would take almost three years of legislative maneuvering before the Glass-Steagall bill became law. In response to the president's request, the Senate passed a resolution in May 1930 directing the Committee on Banking and Currency to conduct a "complete survey" of the Federal Reserve System; one month later, Senator Glass introduced the first bill, which provided only for the regulation of commercial banks' securities affiliates and to which the origins of the Glass-Steagall Act can be traced (Kelly 1985, p. 43).

The hearings conducted under the auspices of the Senate's resolution (chaired by Glass himself) convened in early 1931 and produced testimony on a number of ways in which the operations of a securities affiliate could adversely affect the safety and soundness of its parent bank. Most of the problems identified by the subcommittee centered on the conflict of interest between the two businesses. It was basically alleged that the existence of a securities affiliate would induce the bank to make a variety of ill-advised managerial and investment decisions that it would not otherwise undertake, including lending money to the affiliate or its customers on preferential terms and purchasing securities from the affiliate to relieve it of excess holdings. For their part, securities affiliates were charged with such practices as being less cautious in their investment decisions because of their access to the parent bank's resources and with manipulating the market for the bank's own stock (Kelly 1985, pp. 46–47).

No specific legislative action followed the Senate hearings. In January 1932, though, Senator Glass introduced a new bill that would have separated commercial and investment banking by the device of prohibiting corporations from depositing funds in any institution except a chartered commercial bank. This proposal quickly foundered on nearly unanimous opposition, including that of the president of the Federal Reserve Bank of New York, who argued that the bill would essentially divorce "the banking system and the capital market" (Kelly 1985, p. 48). Glass then revised his bill introducing in April 1932 a measure that with some amendment, would eventually become the Glass-Steagall Act (Kelly 1985, pp. 48–49).

More hearings were held, but again no action was taken for the remainder of 1932. Increasing pressure for investment banking regulation was brought to bear, however, by revelations of stock-exchange abuses in testimony before another Senate subcommittee and by the deepening of the banking crisis.[6] The logjam was broken in March 1933 by the announcement of Winthrop Aldrich, the newly appointed chairman of Chase National Bank, that his bank would divest its securities affiliate so that Chase would no longer be tainted with "the spirit of speculation" (Kennedy 1973, p. 212). Aldrich went on to propose that the separation of commercial and investment banking be brought about by prohibiting securities dealers from accepting deposits (Kelly 1985, p. 53). The Aldrich plan was quickly incorporated into the new legislative initiative introduced by Senator Glass when the 73d Congress convened later that month. After a short debate in which a few changes in language were adopted, the bill was passed by the Senate in May. Its provisions were written into the House version of the bill sponsored by Representative Henry Steagall, and the Congress approved the conference report on June 13. President Roosevelt signed the measure into law three days later (Kelly 1985, p. 54).

Private Interests at Work

The conventional wisdom is that the Glass-Steagall Act resulted from action of a public-spirited Congress moving to restore safety and soundness to an industry badly weakened by commercial banks' involvement in the business of investment banking. As in the case of most public interest justifications for government intervention in the private economy, the conventional wisdom about the Glass-Steagall Act cannot be taken seriously. The notion that depositors were the main beneficiaries of the purging of securities from commercial banks' asset portfolios overlooks the critical fact that most banks that had securities affiliates survived the wave of panic that swept the banking system during the early 1930s. Even if this were not true, however, the creation of federal deposit insurance by other provisions of the Banking Act of 1933 made the separation of commercial

---

[6]The abuses of National City Bank and its securities affiliate, National City Company, were especially important in creating a climate favorable to regulation. See footnote 2.

96

and investment banking redundant from the point of view of depositors. Simply put, if a customer's deposit is insured, the composition of his bank's asset portfolio becomes irrelevant to him; his account is protected even if a collapse in asset values causes the bank to fail.

The public interest argument that a separation of commercial and investment banking was needed to prevent an owner-manager from compromising his bank's liquidity by purchasing unnecessarily risky assets or making unnecessarily risky loans similarly fails on the historical evidence of the ability of institutions having securities affiliates to survive the 1933 panic. The argument also fails in terms of the incentives faced by commercial bank owner-managers to minimize downside risk. A profit maximizing commercial bank undertakes investments in such a way that the ex ante risk-adjusted rate of return on its asset portfolio is at a maximum. Such forces would induce the bank not to overinvest in any asset, including any securities it may have underwritten. The market value of equities can fall unexpectedly, but this is true of all other assets that the bank may hold. It is therefore disingenuous to accuse bankers of bad management after the fact when unanticipated events have caused the realized rate of return on a particular asset to be less than expected.

Clearly, the public interest argument does not hold up well under close scrutiny. What follows here is a brief description of an alternative explanation based on identifying whose interests were served by the separation of commercial and investment banking.

First, the legislation benefited brokerage firms by eliminating an important competitor from the business of underwriting, promoting, and selling securities. Some support for this proposition is provided by the fact that by 1930, the securities affiliates of commercial banks were sponsoring over 54 percent of all new securities issues (Kennedy 1973, p. 212). Second, commercial bankers were the beneficiaries of the Glass-Steagall regulations precluding securities dealers from entering the business of deposit banking. Given that successful brokerage houses develop experience in making loans by managing their customers' margin accounts, commercial bankers may have been concerned with the possibility that securities firms not affiliated with commercial banks could use their expertise to provide other cash-management services, including checkable deposits, blurring the distinction between stock brokering and banking. Under this interpretation, the Glass-Steagall Act represented an early attempt by commercial bankers to block the kinds of innovations in the financial services industry that ultimately did appear in the 1970s and that provided the impetus for recent deregulation legislation.

In addition to the private interests identified above, the Glass-Steagall Act may also have provided an important benefit to the U.S.

Treasury. By purging private securities from banks' asset portfolios, the legislation helped expand the market for U.S. government securities by eliminating a competitor to the Treasury for banks' loanable funds.

The Interests of Commercial and Investment Bankers

One way of interpreting the Glass-Steagall Act is in terms of a government-sponsored market-sharing agreement for the financial services industry. Under the regulations enacted in 1933, commercial bankers would specialize in the business of accepting deposits and making loans, and investment bankers would specialize in the business of underwriting, promoting, and selling securities. Simply put, the Glass-Steagall Act erected barriers that prevented any direct competition between commercial and investment banking. Such an agreement on how a market is to be divided is a classic example of a dimension of collusion through which the members of a cartel can maximize their joint profits.

Some support for explaining the Glass-Steagall Act as a cartel market-sharing agreement is given by the fact that the new regulations allowed bankers one year to choose between the two businesses (Kennedy 1973, p. 213). Those institutions having a comparative advantage in accepting deposits and making loans thereby had an opportunity to divest their securities affiliates and become members in good standing of the commercial banking industry. Similarly, the grace period allowed those institutions having a comparative advantage in underwriting securities to choose to become investment banking firms by dropping out of the business of accepting deposits. Thus, the Glass-Steagall Act did not require any institution to give up what it thought to be its most profitable line of business.

The legislation enacted in 1933 gave the force of law to a division of the financial services market that benefited both commercial and investment-banking interests. Investment bankers benefited by having an important competitor eliminated from the securities underwriting business.[7] As mentioned earlier, this was of consequence because securities affiliates of commercial banks were sponsoring over half of all new securities issues by 1933 (Kennedy 1973, p. 212). The emerging success of commercial banks as securities dealers has been traced by White (1986) to significant complementarities in the production of financial services. Economies of scope allowed banks to become "the contemporary equivalents of 'discount brokers' with

---

[7]The protection against new competition would soon be made more secure by the Securities Act of 1933 and the Securities Exchange Act of 1934.

fees of about one-quarter the New York brokerage commission" (White 1986, p. 36).

The hypothesis that the Glass-Steagall separation decree solely benefited investment bankers at the expense of commercial bankers has been put forth by Macey (1984). His argument is based in part on a 1971 Supreme Court decision striking down a ruling by the Comptroller of the Currency that authorized commercial banks to operate mutual funds.[8] Specifically, Macey (1984, p. 17) reports that Justice John Marshall Harlan's dissenting opinion recognized that in granting standing to the Investment Company Institute's challenge to the Comptroller's decision, the Court was in effect concluding that Congress intended to protect investment bankers against competition from commercial bankers.

Controversy over what constitutes a "security" has plagued efforts to enforce the Glass-Steagall Act since its passage.[9] This is because borrowing funds from a commercial bank and selling stock are interchangeable methods for firms to raise capital. That the Glass-Steagall Act created a dichotomy between two businesses that is more apparent than real provides further support for the legislation's private interest basis (Macey 1984, p. 7). There was also a substantial cost imposed on investment bankers (and a corresponding benefit to commercial bankers) associated with the Glass-Steagall Act's provision excluding them from the business of accepting deposits, however.[10]

The suggestion that commercial banks may also have benefited from the Glass-Steagall Act is borne out by recent events leading to the banking deregulation initiatives of the early 1980s. Deregulation was precipitated by an innovative cash management service offered to the market by a brokerage firm, Merrill Lynch, which allowed customers to withdraw funds deposited in securities accounts on demand using a financial instrument identical to a bank check in all respects except name. This innovation was soon copied by other brokers, putting securities firms in direct competition with commercial banks for short-term deposit liabilities. Moreover, because the

[8]*Investment Co. Institute* v. *Camp*, 401 U.S. 617 (1971).

[9]In contrast to *Camp*, the decision rendered in *Board of Governors* v. *Investment Co.*, 450 U.S. 46 (1981) held that the Glass-Steagall Act does not prohibit a commercial bank or its affiliate from offering a closed-end mutual fund. The "subtle hazards" that arise when commercial and investment banking are combined have been held to prohibit banks from underwriting commercial paper, but not to prevent a commercial bank affiliate from engaging in securities brokerage (*Securities Industry Ass'n* v. *Board of Governors*, 104 S.Ct. 2979, 3003 (1984)). See Fischel, Rosenfield, and Stillman (1986).

[10]Evidence of the profitability of deposit banking is provided by the ability of state-chartered banks to survive despite being taxed out of the business of issuing notes by the National Banking Act. See Perkins (1971, p. 488).

securities industry was not constrained by regulations limiting either their entry into other lines of business (insurance, real estate, and so on) or the interest rates they could pay on customers' accounts, commercial banks were increasingly at a competitive disadvantage. The resulting shift of deposits from banks to brokerage firms created calls for reform that were resolved ultimately in the form of deregulation of commercial banking.

Thus, the Glass-Steagall Act may have represented an early attempt by commercial bankers to forestall the kinds of innovations in the financial services industry that in recent years have caused a breakdown of their market-sharing agreement with investment banking firms. Commercial bankers may have been concerned in 1933 with the possibility that unaffiliated securities firms could use their cash management expertise to offer financial services that would compete directly with commercial bank deposits. The elimination of this potential competition would have been particularly important in view of the provisions of the Banking Act of 1933 authorizing the Federal Reserve to limit the interest rates payable on deposits at member banks.

In this regard it is noteworthy that in 1933,

> [m]any . . . affiliates were . . . in process of liquidation, or had been previously dissolved, either because final passage of the Glass bill was anticipated or because banks welcomed the opportunity to rid themselves of affiliates which they had thought necessary or highly desirable during the twenties (Peach 1975, p. 158).

The data in Table 1 indeed suggest that commercial banks were leaving the securities business prior to the passage of the Glass-Steagall Act—more than 200 institutions did so between 1929 and 1933. The implication is that the cost to commercial banks of giving up their underwriting activities was less than the benefit gained by eliminating a potential competitor from the business of accepting deposits.[11] This observation helps explain Winthrop Aldrich's announcement of his willingness to divest Chase National Bank's securities affiliate, a decision that lent crucial support to the bill introduced by Senator Glass.[12]

Evidence that can be gathered from congressional hearings concerning the relative benefits and costs of the Glass-Steagall Act to commercial and investment bankers is mixed. Eight witnesses tes-

---

[11]Perkins (1971, p. 522) claims that by 1933 the investment banking business was "dormant."

[12]Fear of a new congressional investigation into the practices of other bank affiliates may also have played a role (Perkins 1971, p. 523).

tified in favor of a complete separation of the two businesses during the 1931 Senate hearings conducted under the auspices of the resolution passed in May 1930. Of these, four were members or former members of government regulatory agencies, two were bankers from the Midwest, one represented a New York commercial bank that had not engaged in investment banking activities, and one was a Harvard economist. Most of the sixteen witnesses who opposed the separation were representatives of large commercial banks (Perkins 1971, pp. 506–10). Both the Investment Bankers Association of America and the American Bankers Association issued statements in late 1932 and early 1933 criticizing the Glass proposal (Perkins 1971, pp. 521–22). It is difficult to tell, however, how much of this opposition was to the idea of separation per se rather than to specific elements of the plan as it then stood, such as the length of the grace period the various institutions would be given to comply with the separation decree.

By April 1933, the American Bankers Association had apparently been won over. The Association's Economic Policy Commission issued a report recommending immediate enactment of the Glass bill (Burns 1974, p. 82). It is important to note, however, that on the eve of the bill's final passage, the controversy over the provision requiring separation of commercial and investment banking had subsided, with most of the debate now focusing on the issue of deposit insurance and on the nature and extent of the increased regulatory powers to be given to the Federal Reserve System, especially as they related to state-chartered institutions.[13] Thus, the many and diverse motives that were ultimately responsible for the passage of the separation decree itself cannot be completely disentangled.

What is clear, though, is that the Glass-Steagall Act did provide significant private benefits to both the commercial and investment banking industries. As Perkins (1971, pp. 524–25) has put it,

> Perhaps in the end the bankers themselves . . . were relieved to have the assurance that no competitive pressures would be allowed to emerge in the future, as they had in the past. . . . Certainly, the older investment banking firms welcomed relief from aggressive commercial bank competitors. Hereafter, competition would be

[13]Indeed, deposit insurance, the legislative brainchild of Rep. Henry B. Steagall, may have been the most controversial provision of the Banking Act of 1933. President Roosevelt's opposition to the idea nearly killed the entire bill. See Golembe (1960) for details. Benston (1982) highlights the role of several provisions of the Banking Act of 1933 in providing a "horse-trading" explanation for the bill's passage. Specifically, he cites deposit insurance as a victory for small unit banks, the prohibition of interest payments on demand deposits as a compensating payoff to large banks, and the Glass-Steagall separation decree as the act's main benefit for securities dealers.

contained within the narrow functional banking fields of commercial and investment banking.

The Treasury's Interests

Whether intentional or not, the U.S. Treasury also obtained a substantial benefit from the Glass-Steagall Act. By 1940, as Friedman and Schwartz (1963, p. 452) observe, 70 percent of commercial bank investments were in the form of U.S. government securities. Part of the explanation for the sharp increase in commercial banks' holdings of Treasury obligations during the period immediately following the passage of the Glass-Steagall Act lies in the continuation of a trend, dating back to as early as 1929, toward greater liquidity in banks' asset portfolios. Less than 40 percent of banks' investments in 1929 were in the form of U.S. government securities, and nearly three-quarters of these were relatively long-term Treasury bonds. By 1933, U.S. government securities accounted for over 50 percent of investments and the average term to maturity of Treasury obligations held by banks had fallen by nearly one-half. This shift in the composition of banks' asset portfolios was a rational response to the increased cash demands of depositors. Indeed, "the banks that survived understandably placed far greater weight on liquidity than the banks in existence in 1929" (Friedman and Schwartz 1963, p. 449).

The increased demand for liquidity on the part of commercial banks is also reflected in Table 5 (basically a continuation of the data in Table 2), which shows the securities holdings of banks as a percentage of total assets from 1934 to 1940. In 1933, banks held 18.5 percent of their assets in the form of U.S. government securities. This

TABLE 5

SECURITIES HOLDINGS OF COMMERCIAL BANKS AS PERCENTAGE OF TOTAL ASSETS, 1934–40

Year	U.S. Government Obligations	Obligations of State and Local Governments	Other Securities
1934	22.95	5.25	9.49
1935	26.13	5.50	8.73
1936	27.61	5.17	8.75
1937	25.63	4.92	8.36
1938	25.06	4.95	7.56
1939	25.63	5.35	6.48
1940	24.48	5.32	5.29

SOURCE: U.S. Department of Commerce (1975, p. 1021).

figure jumped to nearly 23 percent in 1934, rose again in both 1935 and 1936, and then stabilized at around 25 percent for the remainder of the decade.[14] A portion, but certainly not all, of the increase in commercial banks' U.S. government securities holdings came at the expense of "other" securities, which declined steadily as a proportion of total assets throughout the period.

A shift in the liquidity preferences of banks no doubt accounts for most of the shift in the composition of asset portfolios that began in 1929.[15] However, it seems reasonable to assign to the Glass-Steagall Act at least some of the responsibility for the increase in the banking system's U.S. government securities holdings between 1933 and 1934. Simply put, the 5 percentage point rise in commercial banks' purchases of Treasury obligations, which equaled the largest single-year jump between 1929 and 1940, may have been driven in part by a need to replace the private securities purged from their portfolios by the new banking regulations. As such, the Glass-Steagall Act caused an increase in the demand for Treasury securities. Although the bill would probably not have been enacted had its sole purpose been to eliminate a competitor to the Treasury for banks' investment funds, such considerations may have played a role in pushing through the separation of commercial and investment banking.

In sum, the conventional wisdom that the separation of commercial and investment banking served the public interest does not hold up well under close scrutiny. There were private interests at work, and these were successful in giving the force of law to a market-sharing agreement in the financial services industry that virtually eliminated competition between commercial and investment banks for roughly 40 years. That the distinction between commercial and investment banking is now in the process of breaking down may be taken by some as evidence that the Glass-Steagall Act has outlived its usefulness and should therefore be repealed. The evidence presented herein suggests, however, that the Glass-Steagall bill should never have been enacted in the first place.

Conclusion

This paper has argued that the private interests of commercial and investment bankers were the driving force behind the regulations

---

[14]The decline in U.S. government securities holdings between 1936 and 1937 can be partly explained as a reaction by member banks to the fact that the Federal Reserve's Board of Governors doubled reserve requirements during this period.

[15]This is the major factor identified by Friedman and Schwartz (1963, p. 453). They discount the importance of changes in the demand for or supply of assets.

imposed on the financial services industry by the Glass-Steagall Act. The principal alternative justification for the law, which suggests that the separation of commercial and investment banking was necessary to protect the public against the speculative activities of commercial banks' securities affiliates, is particularly ironic in view of the creation of federal deposit insurance by separate provisions of the Banking Act of 1933. Such insurance made the equity-ownership and underwriting ban redundant from the point of view of depositors. Thus, the Glass-Steagall Act generates no apparent benefits for depositors but it clearly entails costs. Allowing commercial banks to purchase equities would simply give them an extra degree of freedom, an additional asset over which to spread downside risk. Prohibiting them from doing so precludes commercial banks from holding an efficient asset portfolio and this may have raised, not lowered, the probability of bank failure.[16]

The development of futures markets has further eroded the public interest basis for regulating the activities of commercial and investment banks. Futures and options contracts are now available on a number of equity market indexes, as well as on a wide range of financial assets, including Treasury securities, commercial paper, and foreign currencies. Such contracts allow asset holders to shift downside risk to other market participants, creating a hedge against unanticipated reductions in the values of these assets. Empirical evidence suggests that even the losses from equity underwriting can be reduced to a relatively low level by participation in the options market (Giddy 1985). Thus, the argument that securities are inherently more risky than other assets that commercial banks may hold is simply not valid.[17] There is no reason to believe that allowing commercial banks to deal in securities—or allowing investment banks to accept deposits—would materially increase the riskiness of either type of institution. More importantly, however, breaking down the barrier between commercial and investment banking would further increase the by now widely apparent benefits that would accrue to depositors through deregulation of the financial services industry.

References

Benston, George J. "Why Did Congress Pass New Financial Services Laws in the 1930's? An Alternative Opinion." Federal Reserve Bank of Atlanta *Economic Review* (April 1982): 7–10.

[16]This point is also made by Macey (1984, p. 12). Prohibiting banks from purchasing securities would lower the probability of failure only if all stocks are inherently more risky than all other assets banks may hold. This is clearly not the case.

[17]The opportunity for self-insurance provided by futures markets also raises questions about the continued need for federal deposit protection.

Burns, Helen M. *The American Banking Community and New Deal Banking Reforms, 1933–1935*. Westport, Conn.: Greenwood Press, 1974.

Fischel, Daniel R., Rosenfield, Andrew M., and Stillman, Robert S. "The Regulation of Banks and Bank Holding Companies." Unpublished manuscript, November 1986.

Flannery, Mark J. "An Economic Evaluation of Bank Securities Activities before 1933." In *Deregulating Wall Street: Commercial Bank Penetration of the Corporate Securities Market*, pp. 67–87. Edited by Ingo Walter. New York: John Wiley & Sons, 1985.

Friedman, Milton, and Schwartz, Anna J. *A Monetary History of the United States, 1867–1960*. Princeton, N.J.: Princeton University Press, 1963.

Giddy, Ian H. "Is Equity Underwriting Risky for Commercial Bank Affiliates?" In *Deregulating Wall Street: Commercial Bank Penetration of the Corporate Securities Market*, pp. 145–69. Edited by Ingo Walter. New York: John Wiley & Sons, 1985.

Golembe, Carter H. "The Deposit Insurance Legislation of 1933: An Examination of its Antecedents and its Purposes." *Political Science Quarterly* 76 (1960): 181–200.

Kelly, Edward J., III. "Legislative History of the Glass-Steagall Act." In *Deregulating Wall Street: Commercial Bank Penetration of the Corporate Securities Market*, pp. 41–65. Edited by Ingo Walter. New York: John Wiley & Sons, 1985.

Kennedy, Susan E. *The Banking Crisis of 1933*. Lexington, Ky.: University of Kentucky Press, 1973.

Macey, Jonathan R. "Special Interest Groups Legislation and the Judicial Function: The Dilemma of Glass-Steagall." *Emory Law Journal* 33 (Winter 1984): 1–40.

Peach, W. Nelson. *The Security Affiliates of National Banks*. New York: Arno Press, 1975. Reprint of 1941 edition published by Johns Hopkins Press.

Perkins, Edwin J. "The Divorce of Commercial and Investment Banking: A History." *Banking Law Journal* 88 (June 1971): 483–528.

U.S. Department of Commerce, Bureau of the Census. *Historical Statistics of the United States, Colonial Times to 1970*. Washington: Government Printing Office, 1975.

White, Eugene N. "Before the Glass-Steagall Act: An Analysis of the Investment Banking Activities of National Banks." *Explorations in Economic History* 23 (1986): 33–55.

NEW DEAL MONETARY LEGISLATION FOR THE WELFARE OF THE GOVERNMENT

Richard H. Timberlake

William F. Shughart II's paper (1987) discusses the public choice aspects of the Banking Act of 1933, which was passed by Congress on June 16 of that year.

This act had its origins in the second of two bills proposed by Sen. Carter Glass of Virginia and Rep. Henry B. Steagall of Alabama to regulate commercial banking and the Federal Reserve System. The first bill, passed on February 27, 1932, and called the Glass-Steagall Act, allowed the Federal Reserve Banks to use government securities as collateral for the issue of Federal Reserve notes. Because this legislation was named the Glass-Steagall Act, the second act could not be identically labeled, so it was simply titled the Banking Act of 1933 (a more formal, if not better, choice than, say, the Carter-Henry Act, based on their first names).

Besides separating commercial banking from investment banking (the provision Shughart analyzes), the Banking Act of 1933 also granted additional powers to the Federal Reserve Board and Federal Reserve Banks to oversee loans and investments of member banks. The idea was to discourage speculative trading activity in securities, real estate, and commodities. The act also contained several other provisions, including prohibition of interest on demand deposits and Federal Reserve authority to set ceiling rates of interest on time deposits.

Shughart notes immediately the security overdose in the 1933 act: If deposit insurance was a general requirement for banks—including as it subsequently did 98.4 percent of all deposit accounts—the separation of investment banking from commercial banking was an unnecessary flourish as far as the safety of depositors was concerned. They were already well protected. Shughart then looks at the two special interest groups that might have benefited from the cartel-like separation of the two banking functions. He finds that commercial

---

The author is a Professor of Economics at the University of Georgia.

banks probably benefited more than investment banks. The evidence for this conclusion is the current direction taken by deregulation; that is, investment houses and others have again gone into the manufacture of demand deposits.

Shughart also notes that the U.S. Treasury received substantial benefits from the 1933 Act. The act encouraged banks to invest in U.S. government securities, both because of the conditioned need for liquidity the banks felt after the recent liquidity debacle, and because of the purging of private securities from the banks' portfolios in accordance with the provisions of the new act. For the nonbank public, ceiling rates of interest on time deposits and zero interest rates on demand deposits also tended to make commercial bank deposits appear less attractive than, say, holding U.S. government securities. Interest rate ceilings on bank deposits, therefore, had the effect of holding down market interest rates on government securities.

Shughart's paper has persuasive arguments. By picking up this one bit of legislation and showing that it was written and passed to further the special interests of at least one of two private groups—or both—in alliance with the government, his investigation opens the door for the same question about other "critical" legislation passed at that time. What follows is the legislative pattern that developed between 1932 and 1934—the years during which congressional acts regulating the monetary, banking, and financial services industry abounded.

The legislation that began the federal government's monetary and banking activities during the early 1930s was the act to form the Reconstruction Finance Corporation (RFC), passed on January 22, 1932. This government corporation was capitalized by the U.S. Treasury with $500 million from general taxpayer revenues. The RFC could then issue its own bonds, debentures, and notes to raise an additional $1,500 million. Its mission was to lend to banks, other corporations, and government agencies that could not get help from conventional sources (Harris 1933, pp. 685–87; White 1935, pp. 697–702).

In the pre-RFC era the most "conventional" source, of course, had been the 12 Federal Reserve Banks. They were the touted lenders of last resort, the legalized descendants from the "extralegal" and illegal clearinghouse associations. However, the Federal Reserve Banks had turned out to be lenders of next-to-last resort. Their managers' concept of "eligibility" for the collateral paper on which they made loans to banks had proven to be procyclical; it had effectively sterilized the vast amount of lending power that the Federal Reserve Banks had at their disposal throughout the early 1930s.

Congress and the administration, unable to persuade the Fed to promote an extensive and consistent lending policy either for the banks or for the government, decided to create an even more fundamental lender of last resort. The RFC was that institution. After two and three-quarter years of operation (up to November 1, 1934), the RFC had loaned $6.3 billion. Banks received 41 percent of total loans made, and government agencies and state governments came next, with a combined 27 percent (White, p. 699).

The absurdity of this burgeoning of institutions is immediately apparent. Why was an RFC necessary to make loans to needy banks when the elaborate Federal Reserve System has been put in place 20 years earlier to do just that? The RFC, at best, had no net leverage on the monetary system. It could not create monetary base materials. It was similar to a commercial finance corporation in that it borrowed from the securities market after its first endowment of taxpayers' money, and then made loans with the proceeds. True, it made loans to commercial banks when the Federal Reserve Banks would not. It could do so because it was allowed to broaden the eligibility concept to include assets that, although not eligible where the Fed was concerned, were sound and acceptable backing for RFC loans (Harris, p. 686; White, p. 699).

The Glass-Steagall Act of 1932 made an attempt to go in the same direction as the RFC. It relaxed collateral security requirements for member bank discounts at Federal Reserve Banks. It also allowed Fed Banks to use government securities as collateral for the issue of Federal Reserve notes, thereby establishing a formal basis for the government seigniorage operations that were to occur within the next two years. By the end of 1933, as a matter of fact, eligible paper plus government security holdings of member banks were over $7 billion, or 10 times the amount of Federal Reserve lending to member banks at that time (White, p. 703).

The Emergency Banking Act was signed into law on March 9, 1933. It allowed President Roosevelt to declare a banking holiday. More important, it gave the executive branch through the Treasury Department the power to call in all gold coin and gold certificates owned domestically, thereby setting the stage for further seigniorage operations (White, p. 705).

In May 1933, Congress passed the Thomas amendment to the Agricultural Adjustment Act. This "inflation bill," as it was dubbed, allowed the Federal Reserve Banks to buy $3 billion more in government securities on the basis of which they could issue an equivalent amount of new Federal Reserve notes. In addition, it gave the president the power to reduce the gold content of the gold dollar by as much as 60 percent (White, pp. 709–10).

Next, on June 5, 1933, Congress passed the act that abrogated all gold clauses in contracts, including those made by the government in the bonds financing the Liberty and Victory loans (White, pp. 712–13). The Banking Act of 1933 was then passed on June 16. This act was advertised as antispeculative, but it pointedly exempted all security issues of the federal government, state governments, municipalities, and government agencies from the class of investment securities denied to commercial banks (White, p. 718).

The federal government now had the path cleared for expropriating a large fraction of the monetary system's real gold stock. By his authority under the Gold Reserve Act passed January 30, 1934, President Roosevelt raised the price of gold to $35.00 per ounce. He then called in all the gold to the U.S. Treasury, but paid for it at the old price of $20.67 per ounce (White, pp. 720–21). Because all gold clauses had been nullified, the government did not have to share its seigniorage profits of $2.8 billion with private speculators and other "malefactors of great wealth." Two billion dollars of this total was put into the Exchange Stabilization Fund to fix exchange rates, but was used to buy government securities until the money was needed for exchange-control purposes.

Finally, the Silver Purchase Act of 1934 concluded the government's extensive housekeeping revenue-accruing operations. By this act, the Treasury could buy silver at $0.50 per ounce or less, and it could then issue silver certificates as though its silver was worth $1.29 per ounce—the historic fixed price for monetization of silver. During the next two years, the Treasury realized silver seigniorage worth over $300 million (Friedman and Schwartz, pp. 465–70).

All of these congressional acts taken together suggest a pattern of incentives and strategies that is consistent. First, the evil that provoked the Great Contraction and ensuing depression was unchecked speculation. The evidence for this opinion was the dramatic stock market boom. The need, therefore, was to rein in speculation through the Federal Reserve System's imposition of its version of the "moral" use of credit. Unfortunately, in depriving the Speculative Devil of his sustenance, the Federal Reserve also starved the innocent banking institutions it was supposed to nourish. In doing so, it likewise deprived the government of its ability to generate tax revenues.

In the presence of a Federal Reserve System that had so bungled, government policy was to intervene in the financial markets to ensure that its own inflow of resources was secure. By this time, tax revenues were not manipulable. Seigniorage from gold and silver expropriation, however, provided at least a one-time bonanza. The government's "profit" of $2.8 billion from the revaluation of the gold was, by one pen-stroke, almost the equivalent of one year's ordinary tax revenues. That same federal government almost 100 years earlier, in 1835–37, had returned its fiscal surplus to the states. The government of 1934 legislated the revenue into existence and kept all of the proceeds for itself.

The second source of government revenue, especially on account of the cyclical dearth of taxes, was the sale of U.S. Treasury (and other government agency) securities. Almost all of the new laws encouraged or stimulated a demand for securities from all levels of government, and from government agencies. Commercial banks, Federal Reserve Banks, the RFC, the 12 regional banks of the Federal Home Loan Bank System, the Exchange Stabilization Fund—all were induced to purchase government securities by a number of legislative devices. That some of these purchases might have helped revive the private sector was largely irrelevant to government spokesmen, although they professed otherwise as part of their political rhetoric. As it was, most of the legislation that established government corporations, such as the RFC, simply bled off resources from the private sector that private institutions could have used more efficiently.

References

Friedman, Milton, and Schwartz, Anna J. *A Monetary History of the United States, 1867–1960*. Princeton, N.J.: Princeton University Press, 1963.

Harris, Seymour E. *Twenty Years of Federal Reserve Policy, Vol. 2: The Monetary Crisis*. Cambridge: Harvard University Press, 1933.

Shughart, William F, II. "A Public Choice Perspective of the Banking Act of 1933." Chapter 5 in this book.

White, Horace. *Money and Banking*. New edition, revised and enlarged by Charles Tippetts and Lewis Froman. New York: Ginn and Co., 1935.

6

THE EVOLVING ROLE OF REGULATION IN THE SAVINGS AND LOAN INDUSTRY

James R. Barth and Martin A. Regalia

The financial system in a modern economy facilitates the transfer of resources from savers to borrowers. Such a transfer allows the productive sectors to invest in capital necessary for growth. The financial system also allows consumers to adjust to variations in income so as to smooth consumption.

An integral part of any modern financial system consists of firms called financial intermediaries, which differ from their nonfinancial firm counterparts in that they transfer direct claims to resources into indirect claims. They do not contribute directly to economic growth in the sense that manufacturing firms do; rather, they facilitate the interactions of borrowers and lenders and thereby grease the wheels of a production economy.

Financial intermediaries exist because they minimize information and transactions costs while providing individuals with the benefits of diversification of risk, flexibility in maturity of and divisibility in assets and liabilities, and expertise regarding the monitoring of contractual obligations. All these activities increase the allocational efficiency of an economy.

Financial intermediaries can be divided into depository and nondepository institutions, depending on whether deposits are included among their liabilities. In addition, depository institutions have long been subdivided further into commercial banks, savings and loan associations, mutual savings banks, and credit unions on the basis of the maturity and liquidity or "moneyness" of their deposits and whether their assets consist primarily of commercial loans, consumer loans, or mortgages. (See Table 1, which presents historical data on the relative size of these different types of financial intermediaries.)

The authors are, respectively, a professor of economics at George Washington University and vice president and chief economist at the National Council of Savings Institutions. This paper was completed while Dr. Regalia was with the Congressional Budget Office. They acknowledge helpful comments and suggestions from Dan Brumbaugh, Don Bisenius, and Ned Gramlich.

TABLE 1

PERCENTAGE OF TOTAL U.S. FINANCIAL ASSETS HELD BY
MAJOR FINANCIAL INTERMEDIARIES, 1900 TO 1985

	1900	1929	1933	1945	1955	1965	1975	1985
Commercial Banks	66	60	51	65	44	36	37	30
Savings & Loan Associations	3	7	7	3	9	14	16	16
Mutual Savings Banks	16	9	12	7	8	6	6	3
Credit Unions	—[b]	—	—	1	1	1	2	2
Life Insurance Companies	12	16	23	18	21	17	13	12
Other Institutions[a]	3	8	7	6	17	26	26	33
Total Assets ($ billion)	15	110	90	247	424	921	2136	6603

[a]Includes such financial intermediaries as private pension funds, state and local government retirement funds, finance companies, other insurance companies, and money market funds.
[b]A dash indicates less than 1.
SOURCES: Goldsmith (1958) and Board of Governors of the Federal Reserve System.

Thus, depository financial institutions play a particularly important role in the financial system both because their liabilities are considered money or near-money and thus are the foundation of the payments mechanism, and because they have been associated with sectors of the economy, such as housing, that have great social significance.

The important role played by financial institutions in general and depository institutions in particular has not escaped the attention of the regulatory authorities. As a result, the financial industry, particularly the depository institutions segment, is one of the most heavily regulated industries in America.[1] The extent of the regulation is so pervasive that it has heavily influenced not only the course of evolution of the entire financial industry but also the future of all those real sectors of the economy served by financial institutions. Thus, questions arise as to the appropriate magnitude and scope of regulation of the financial industry and who should determine the evolution of the financial and real sectors of the economy—the regulators or the market.

Rather than deal with this issue immediately, it is useful to explore the development of the savings and loan industry and the role played by the regulators and thereby see if history holds any clues to the future.

[1]See appendix 1 for a listing of the major federal legislation affecting the financial sector.

Origin and Development of Savings and Loan Associations

The First Hundred Years: 1830–1930

The first American savings and loan institution, the Oxford Provident Building Association, was founded in Frankford, Pennsylvania, on January 3, 1831.[2] The association was organized to enable its member shareholders, most of whom were textile workers, to pool their savings so that a subset of them could obtain the necessary financing to build or purchase homes. Every member was to be afforded the opportunity, over time, of borrowing funds for this purpose, with the association terminating after the last member was accommodated. Association membership was geographically restricted and no loans were made for homes located more than five miles from Frankford.

This first savings and loan association was organized as a mutual institution and therefore was owned by its shareholder members. New members were elected by ballot at shareholder meetings. Shareholders were expected to remain with the institution throughout its life, but those wishing to withdraw their shares were allowed to do so if they gave a month's notice and paid a penalty of 5 percent of their withdrawal. The association's balance sheet consisted of mortgage loans as assets and ownership shares as liabilities, with relatively little net worth. These shares were the precursor of the savings deposits held today.[3]

The founders of this first savings and loan envisioned an institution with a limited life in which the shareholders and the borrowers eventually became one and the same. The institution served the important role of consolidating the savings of a group of local individuals and rechanneling the funds to these same individuals in the form of mortgage loans. Only much later were borrowers and savers

---

[2]Originally, institutions of this type were called building societies because they actually purchased land and built homes. When they began lending to members to build their own homes, they were referred to as building and loan associations. After the 1930s, they tended to be called savings and loan associations, following the name given to federally chartered associations. Until recently, all new federal associations had to begin as mutuals. With the passage of the Garn–St Germain Depository Institutions Act of 1982, however, the Federal Home Loan Bank Board (FHLBB) can now federally charter new stock associations.

[3]The Housing and Urban Development Act of 1968 authorized federal savings and loan associations to offer savers deposit accounts rather than share accounts. The FHLBB adopted a regulation implementing this legislation, and all federal associations began offering deposit accounts the following year.

separated not just intertemporally but completely.[4] Thus, the first savings and loan association was founded specifically to gather savings and finance home building and home ownership, a niche that was woefully underserviced by the financial institutions already in existence at the time.

Perhaps it is not surprising that this particular financial need went largely unfulfilled by the commercial banks and mutual savings banks.[5] Although both types of financial entities preceded the development of savings and loan associations, neither catered to the home market. Commercial banks issued liabilities consisting primarily of currency and demand deposits that were acceptable to their customers because they were backed by self-liquidating commercial loans. These banks therefore developed an informational comparative advantage by becoming directly involved in the payments system and catering to the short-term business loan market. Mutual savings banks did not issue currency or accept demand deposits, but were involved with the savings of the general public. Unlike savings and loans, however, they were originally philanthropic. Their intent was to provide financial services for the small saver, which required that their deposits be more flexible in terms of amounts and maturities and correspondingly required a much more flexible asset portfolio than just mortgages. Each type of institution, therefore, specialized in a particular market, and the specialization was reflected in the balance sheets of these financial firms.

Following the organization of the first savings and loan association, similar institutions spread throughout the United States—for example, entering New York in 1836, South Carolina in 1843, and what is now Oklahoma in 1890. Accurate data on the number and assets of savings and loan associations prior to 1893 are not available. However, data for that year show that the total number of such institutions then in existence was 5,598. (See Table 2, which presents historical data on the number and assets of savings and loan associations as well as similar data for commercial banks and mutual savings banks.) By 1930, before growth was interrupted by the Great Depression, the number of savings and loans had grown to nearly 12,000. Total assets in the savings and loan institutions increased substantially before 1930 as the number and income of shareholders grew.

---

[4]The first savings and loan associations were essentially finite-lived mutual funds, investing shareholders' savings solely in residential mortgage loans. There were no maturity mismatch problems, and informational problems were minimized by direct saver involvement in every aspect of the business.

[5]Credit unions did not come into existence until the early 1900s.

As these associations spread throughout the country, innovations began to occur. For example, the self-terminating type of institution was replaced by a more permanent type, and the borrowers were separated from the savers. Thus, these firms began to operate with a long-term horizon in mind, and they began to accept shareholders who were not obliged to take out mortgage loans. This not only enlarged the pool of potential shareholders but also emphasized the savings aspect of membership in an association. So the link between borrower and saver began to dissipate despite the mutual form of organization under which these firms usually operated. These institutions still generally did not take deposits per se; in many states, in fact, they were precluded by law from doing so. It was not until the advent of federal deposit insurance for savings and loan associations in the 1930s that the taking of deposits as such became widespread.[6]

Accompanying the growth of the savings and loan industry during its first century were state and eventually federal regulations. As the roles of saver and borrower became more distinct and as the shareholders or owners became less directly involved in the management of the associations, the public desire for monitoring and supervision grew. The state governments, which were the only chartering agents for the associations until the Great Depression, therefore became more involved with monitoring these early institutions.[7]

State supervision evolved from reports to state officials, to permissive examinations by state officials, and then to required periodic examinations by state officials.[8] In this way, states were able to show "their disapproval of loans for purposes not strictly within the building and loan field, which [was determined to be] the financing of single-family residences" (Bodfish 1931, p. 130). In addition, "a rather common power given to the state official in charge of the supervision of building and loan associations [was] that of refusing to grant charters where there [did] not seem to be a necessity for another building and loan" (Bodfish 1931, p. 129). Thus, the monitoring and supervision that developed were aimed not only at preventing and detecting fraud but also at limiting the lending activities of savings and loans to loans for residential homes as well as limiting the amount of competition within the industry. This less intrusive form of regulation was fostered by the fact that there were few reported failures of

[6]See Bodfish (1931, pp. 95–96).

[7]Apparently, the state governments initially became involved as a cost-effective means for the majority of the associations to impose some discipline on all associations so as to maintain the reputation of every association.

[8]In 1875, New York was the first state to pass legislation requiring the filing of annual reports.

TABLE 2
NUMBER AND ASSETS OF MAJOR DEPOSITORY FINANCIAL INSTITUTIONS, 1800 to 1985[a]

Year	Savings & Loan Associations		Commercial Banks		Savings Banks	
	Number	Assets ($ million)	Number	Assets ($ million)	Number	Assets ($ million)
1800	0	0	n.a.	n.a.	0	0
1810	0	0	88	n.a.	0	0
1820	0	0	297	30	10	1[b]
1830	0	0	293	34	36	7[b]
1850	n.a.	n.a.	716	489	108	43[b]
1860	n.a.	n.a.	1,284	851	278	149[b]
1870	n.a.	n.a.	1,420	1,231	517	550[b]
1880	n.a.	n.a.	2,726	2,517	629	882
1890	n.a.	n.a.	7,280	4,612	921	1,743
1900	5,356	571	12,427	9,059	626	2,328
1905	5,264	629	18,152	14,542	615	2,969
1910	5,869	932	24,514	19,324	637	3,598
1915	6,806	1,484	27,390	24,106	627	4,257
1920	8,633	2,520	30,291	47,509	618	5,586
1925	12,403	5,509	28,442	54,401	610	7,831
1930	11,777	8,829	23,679	64,125	594	10,164
1935	10,266	5,875	15,488	48,905	559	11,046
1940	7,521	5,733	14,534	67,804	542	11,925
1945	6,149	8,747	14,126	146,245	534	15,924

TABLE 2 (cont.)

NUMBER AND ASSETS OF MAJOR DEPOSITORY FINANCIAL INSTITUTIONS, 1800 to 1985[a]

Year	Savings & Loan Associations		Commercial Banks		Savings Banks	
	Number	Assets ($ million)	Number	Assets ($ million)	Number	Assets ($ million)
1950	5,992	16,893	14,146	156,914	530	22,252
1955	6,071	37,656	13,780	199,244	528	30,382
1960	5,320	71,476	13,503	243,274	516	39,598
1965	6,185	129,580	13,805	356,110	505	56,383
1970	5,669	176,183	13,690	534,932	497	76,373
1975	4,931	338,200	14,657	974,700	476	121,100
1980	4,613	629,800	14,870	1,543,500	460	166,600
1985	3,246	1,069,547	15,282	2,731,000	403	157,400

[a]Data before 1975 are for year ending June 30. Data after 1975 are for year ending December 31.
[b]Deposits rather than assets.
n.a. = not available.
SOURCE: U.S. Department of Commerce, Bureau of the Census.

savings and loan associations in their formative years. However, the number of failures increased during the economic downturn of the 1890s.

A major result of this downturn was the virtual elimination of the so-called national institutions. This type of institution developed in the 1880s by gathering deposits and making mortgage loans on a national scale through the use of branch offices and the mail. Although the downturn of the 1890s hit both nationally based and locally based institutions, local associations attributed their problems to the improper loan strategy and subsequent failures of the national institutions. They claimed that customers were unable to distinguish between the two types of firms during the panic of 1893.

The increased competition engendered by the nationals also led to the establishment of the U.S. League of Local Building and Loan Associations (the precursor to the present-day U.S. League of Savings Institutions). This group, which became very influential over the years, successfully lobbied the state legislatures to curb the activities of the national associations—a move that eventually drove the nationals out of business.[9]

Although the local savings and loan associations had effectively removed competition from the national associations, competition from commercial banks was beginning to develop. In the early 1900s, national banks were informed that they were not prohibited from accepting savings deposits. Moreover, Federal Reserve member banks were given an incentive to use this source of funds when a lower reserve requirement was placed on savings accounts than on demand deposits. On the asset side, competition for residential mortgages was also beginning to develop between savings and loans and banks, albeit to a much lower degree. Without active secondary markets and with still somewhat restrictive regulations, the two types of depository institutions found that comparative advantages in information collection and processing, as well as the favorable tax treatment afforded savings and loan associations, still led to fairly identifiable balance sheet differences.

Thus, as the economic boom of the 1920s began, the banks and savings and loan associations maintained different balance sheets, competed only indirectly, and were regulated to a different degree and by different levels of government. (See Table 3 and Table 4 for information on the balance sheets of the different types of depository institutions.) The federal regulators were most interested in commercial banks and the payments mechanism, and the state govern-

---

[9]See Bodfish and Theobald (1940, p. 54).

TABLE 3
NONFARM RESIDENTIAL MORTGAGE HOLDINGS BY TYPE OF INSTITUTION,[a] 1900 TO 1985

Year	Total Holdings (Millions of dollars)	Percent of Total Holdings				
		CBs	MSBs	S&Ls	LICs	Other
1900	1,917	5.4	21.7	12.7	6.3	53.9
1905	3,520	8.3	23.4	12.7	7.2	48.4
1910	4,426	10.1	25.1	15.6	9.1	40.1
1915	6,012	9.4	23.6	18.3	8.7	40.1
1920	9,120	8.8	19.5	20.4	6.1	45.2
1925	1,323	10.8	17.6	23.2	8.2	40.2
1930	27,649	10.3	15.9	22.2	10.4	41.2
1935	22,211	10.0	17.9	14.9	9.9	47.3
1940	23,810	12.6	16.4	17.1	12.1	41.7
1945	24,643	13.8	13.7	20.9	14.7	36.8
1950	54,362	19.2	13.0	24.1	20.3	23.4
1955	100,827	15.8	15.4	29.5	21.0	18.3
1960	161,540	12.6	15.0	34.9	17.8	19.7
1965	256,494	12.6	15.6	39.0	15.0	17.7
1970	354,464	12.9	14.1	38.3	12.0	22.7
1975	577,545	14.4	11.0	42.3	6.4	25.8
1980	1,097,512	15.8	7.6	40.9	3.4	32.5
1985	1,683,162	14.1	5.4	33.4	1.9	45.2

[a]Commercial banks (CBs), mutual savings banks (MSBs), savings and loans (S&Ls), life insurance companies (LICs), and "other."
SOURCES: U.S. Department of Commerce and Board of Governors of the Federal Reserve System.

TABLE 4
SELECTED BALANCE SHEET ITEMS FOR MAJOR DEPOSITORY FINANCIAL INSTITUTIONS, 1900 TO 1985

Institutions	Percent of Total Assets									
	1900	1920	1940	1960	1980	1981	1982	1983	1984	1985
Commercial Banks										
Mortgages	5.3	6.8	6.5	12.8[a]	20.4	20.4	20.0	20.2	20.7	21.2
Mortgage-Backed Securities	0	0	0	0	—[c]	—[c]	—[c]	—[c]	—[c]	—[c]
Transactions Accounts	48.0	45.4	49.4	55.0	25.9	25.1	24.7	23.7	22.7	23.1
Savings and Time Accounts	12.0	23.4	23.0	27.5	37.4	37.6	41.6	46.3	45.4	45.0
Mutual Savings Banks										
Mortgages	36.9	41.0	40.5	65.8	58.2	56.9	53.8	50.3	50.5	51.0
Mortgage-Backed Securities	0	0	0	0	8.1	7.9	8.0	9.4	9.4	9.0
Transactions Accounts	0	0	0	0	—[c]	—[c]	1.6	1.8	1.9	2.3
Savings and Time Accounts	91.5	92.3	89.0	89.6	88.5	87.1	87.0	86.1	85.1	81.7

TABLE 4 (cont.)

SELECTED BALANCE SHEET ITEMS FOR MAJOR DEPOSITORY FINANCIAL INSTITUTIONS, 1900 TO 1985

Institutions	1900	1920	1940	1960	Percent of Total Assets 1980	1981	1982	1983	1984	1985
Savings and Loan Associations										
Mortgages	82.9	91.8[b]	72.0	84.0	79.7	77.8	68.9	64.5	62.3	61.7
Mortgage-Backed Securities	0	0	0	0	4.3	5.0	8.5	10.8	11.0	10.2
Transactions Accounts	0	0	0	0	—[c]	0.1	0.1	0.2	2.8	3.3
Savings and Time Accounts	86.1	87.7[b]	75.4	86.9	80.6	78.2	76.5	77.4	73.6	72.1

[a]Data from 1960 onward for commercial banks are from the flow of funds and are reported as percentage of financial assets. In 1985, the ratio of financial assets to total assets was .92. Also, savings and time account numbers are net of large certificates of deposit.
[b]Data for 1922.
[c]Dashes indicate that these data were not available separately.
SOURCE: U.S. Department of Commerce and Board of Governors of the Federal Reserve System.

ments were most directly involved with savings and loan associations and their role in facilitating homeownership.

Savings and Loan Associations and the Depression

There appear to have been only two periods in the first 150 years of savings and loan institutions in which they have suffered large-scale failures. The first was the severe economic downturn of the 1890s, and the second was the Great Depression of the 1930s.

During the Depression, savings and loan associations did not accept demand deposits and therefore did not suffer the runs that reportedly plagued commercial banks. Nevertheless, they suffered deposit withdrawals as their members drew upon their savings to maintain consumption. Savings and loan associations were hard pressed to cope with these withdrawals because their assets were almost entirely mortgages, and they prided themselves on maintaining low liquidity levels. Moreover, reserves for losses were relatively low because "many state laws . . . discouraged the accumulation of reserves and some supervisory authorities practically forced the distribution of all earnings" (Bodfish 1931, p. 7). As withdrawals mounted and assets declined in value due to delinquencies and defaults, savings and loan associations failed. (See Table 5, which presents data on the number of failures and resultant losses for the period from 1920 to 1939 and also, for comparative purposes, the period from 1980 to 1985.) These failures during the Depression severely limited the flow of funds to housing.[10]

The disruption in the housing market to which such failures contributed finally changed the role of the federal government in the regulation of the savings and loan industry. First, the Home Owners' Loan Act was signed on June 13, 1933. Although the main purpose of the act was to facilitate the refinancing of existing mortgages in distress cases, many people merely seeking the more favorable interest rate and other terms offered by the government were also able to obtain loans. This desire to qualify for government loans on an especially favorable basis caused many borrowers deliberately to default on their existing loans, thus exacerbating the problems of the savings and loan associations.[11]

Another purpose of the act was to allow the Federal Home Loan Bank Board (FHLBB) to charter federal savings and loan associations.

---

[10]According to Bodfish (1935, p. 22), "One-half of the counties in the United States as a result of the Great Depression now had no mortgage loan institutions or facilities."
[11]See Bodfish (1935, p. 21).

The chartering of federal institutions was not an attempt to drive the state-chartered institutions out of business but rather to provide for associations in localities where the state institutions were providing insufficient service. Furthermore, the federal associations were to be mutual-type associations and to operate only in the local areas in which they were chartered.[12]

Meanwhile, on July 22, 1932, almost a year before the Home Owner's Loan Act became law, the Federal Home Loan Bank Act was signed by President Hoover. This act set up the Federal Home Loan Bank System, consisting of 12 regional Federal Home Loan (FHL) Banks under the supervision of the FHLBB in Washington. The main purpose of the system was to financially strengthen member savings and loan associations by providing them with an alternative and steady source of funds so as to promote home ownership.[13] Member savings and loan associations included all federal associations and those state-chartered institutions that voluntarily chose to and qualified to be members. The system was designed so that the FHL Banks could issue bonds in the capital markets and thus be able to provide advances to healthy and reasonably safe institutions. It was not intended to bail out failing thrifts.[14]

Finally, Title IV of the National Housing Act, which was enacted on June 27, 1934, created the Federal Savings and Loan Insurance Corporation (FSLIC) to provide deposit insurance for savings deposits at savings and loan associations. Membership in the FSLIC was made compulsory for federal associations and optional for state-chartered associations. With the establishment of the FSLIC, the savings and loans were placed on an equal footing with commercial banks, which were insured by the Federal Deposit Insurance Corporation (FDIC). For the federally insured institutions, the insurance amount was $5,000 per account (this was later raised to $10,000 in 1950, $15,000 in 1966, $20,000 in 1969, $40,000 in 1974, and $100,000 in 1980).

The rationale for deposit insurance, as well as the potential abuses caused by it, was understood from its inception. As Bodfish and Theobald (1940, p. 482) observed, "Deposit insurance plans have developed as a means of combating a universal lack of confidence in financial institutions which has adversely affected the sound banks otherwise able to survive the acute financial crisis." But, they also

[12]The act specified that most loans had to be mortgage loans and had to be secured by houses within 50 miles of the association's home office.

[13]The institutions initially eligible for membership were savings and loan associations, insurance companies, and mutual savings banks. The latter two types of institutions generally did not join the system.

[14]See Bodfish and Theobald (1940, p. 30).

125

TABLE 5

SAVINGS AND LOAN ASSOCIATION FAILURES AND LOSSES, 1920 TO 1939, 1980 TO 1985

Year	Total Number	Total Assets ($ million)	Number of Failures	Ratio of Failed to Total Institutions	Losses ($ thousand)	Ratio of Losses to Total Assets
1920	8,663	2,520	2	0.000	1	0.000
1921	9,255	2,891	6	0.000	92	0.003
1922	10,009	3,343	4	0.000	159	0.005
1923	10,744	3,943	9	0.000	133	0.003
1924	11,844	4,766	18	0.002	398	0.000
1925	12,403	5,509	26	0.002	500	0.000
1926	12,626	6,334	12	0.001	381	0.000
1927	12,804	7,179	21	0.002	1,013	0.000
1928	12,666	8,016	23	0.002	568	0.000
1929	12,343	8,695	159	0.013	2,313	0.000
1930	11,777	8,829	190	0.016	24,677	0.003
1931	11,442	8,417	126	0.011	22,328	0.003
1932	10,997	7,750	122	0.011	20,337	0.003
1933	10,727	6,978	88	0.008	43,955	0.006
1934	10,919	6,450	68	0.006	10,174	0.002
1935	10,266	5,875	239	0.023	15,782	0.003
1936	10,042	5,772	144	0.014	9,052	0.002
1937	9,225	5,682	269	0.029	15,775	0.003
1938	8,762	5,632	277	0.032	11,281	0.002
1939	8,006	5,597	183	0.023	27,040	0.005

TABLE 5 (cont.)

SAVINGS AND LOAN ASSOCIATION FAILURES AND LOSSES, 1920 to 1939, 1980 to 1985

Year	Total Number	Total Assets ($ million)	Number of Failures	Ratio of Failed to Total Institutions	Losses ($ thousand)	Ratio of Losses to Total Assets
1980	4,002	618,466	35	0.009	166,644	0.000
1981	4,002	651,068	81	0.020	1,018,243	0.002
1982	3,343	692,663	252	0.075	1,212,907	0.002
1983	3,040	819,168	101	0.033	1,020,595	0.001
1984	3,167	978,514	42	0.013	833,054	0.001
1985	3,246	1,069,547	45[a]	0.014	948,698	0.001

[a]There were also an additional 25 institutions placed into the newly created management consignment program but for which no loss data are available.
SOURCES: Harr and Harris (1936); Kendall (1962); and Barth, Brumbaugh, and Sauerhaft (1986).

noted (pp. 480–81), "insurance of commercial bank deposits and of savings and loan accounts does not meet all assumptions of insurance theory, for it admittedly deals with expectancies that have no actuarial history or measurement because of the unpredictable and incalculable changes that accompany the business cycle." One disadvantage pointed out very early was that

> "insurance may tend to eliminate differences among associations. It may reduce the incentive for good management because, on the one hand, some institutions may become dependent upon insurance, and because, on the other hand, sound and efficiently staffed institutions may be penalized for the careless policy and poorly trained personnel of others. Further, the public may become indiscriminate in selecting the association with which it wishes to deal" (Bodfish and Theobald 1940, p. 502).[15]

Postwar Growth and Diversification

Following the Great Depression and World War II, savings and loan associations experienced tremendous growth for close to four decades. They surpassed mutual savings banks in terms of total assets for the first time in 1954 and grew to half the size of the commercial banking industry by the end of 1980. (See Table 2.) This dramatic expansion was spread throughout the entire industry, with both large and small institutions participating.

The magnitude of the redistribution is remarkable. Private financial assets in 1945 totaled $247 billion. Of this amount, savings and loan associations held a meager 3 percent, compared to 65 percent for commercial banks. By 1975, however, savings and loan associations had increased their share of the total to 16 percent, while the share for commercial banks had dropped to 37 percent. Both mutual savings banks and life insurance companies also lost considerable ground during this period. Moreover, although the share of total financial assets accounted for by all of the depository financial services firms declined to 51 percent from 76 percent, the share of savings and loan institutions managed to quintuple.

The relative growth in savings and loan associations is even more impressive in light of the increased competition among financial institutions. In the 1950s and 1960s, more than half of the deposits in commercial banks were non-interest-bearing checking accounts

---

[15]It may be noted that on March 30, 1932, in testifying on the bill to provide federal insurance for depositors in commercial banks, Irving Fisher stated that the bill should be changed so that "the comptroller—or some other authority—may add to said premium 25 percent, 50 percent, or 100 percent in individual cases which are regarded by him as extra hazardous or may refuse to insure altogether" (Hearings 1932, p. 153).

or demand deposits (which savings and loans did not offer). However, by the late 1970s, demand deposits made up only about one-fourth of commercial bank deposits. At savings and loans over this same period, time and passbook savings accounts remained about the same, 75 to 80 percent of total deposits, and S&Ls offered virtually no transactions accounts. The commercial banks were therefore beginning to compete more directly for the saver's dollar, but savings and loan associations had not yet received unrestricted permission to compete for the commercial banks' bread-and-butter accounts.

In addition to facing competition from other depository institutions, some nondepository financial institutions were being developed to help the small savers combat the ravages inflicted on their portfolios by inflation and high interest rates. Laws and regulations generally prohibited savings and loan associations and other depository institutions from paying interest on checking deposits and limited the rates of interest and maturities on savings and time deposits. As a result, customers of these institutions began increasingly to go to the relatively unregulated nondepository financial firms in search of higher interest rates.

This interaction between market interest rates and regulatory constraints led to the development of money market mutual funds. These funds attracted customers by offering a new type of account. Not being subject to depository institution regulations, this account offered higher rates of interest than other financial depository service firms could pay, and it included limited check-writing privileges. By the late 1970s, these money market funds, which had been introduced in 1972, had grown large enough to be a serious competitive threat to depository financial institutions. This threat spurred the development and regulatory approval of new market-based accounts offered by depository institutions, such as the money market certificate in 1978, whose rate was tied to the six-month Treasury bill rate.

Moreover, in response to the unattractiveness of demand deposits paying no interest, financial depository institutions created interest-bearing checking accounts—credit union share drafts and negotiable orders of withdrawal (NOW) accounts—that were direct substitutes for demand deposits. These new accounts were first introduced in Massachusetts in 1972, spreading to six other Northeastern states by the mid-1970s before being authorized by Congress on December 31, 1980, for nationwide use by commercial banks, savings and loans, mutual savings banks, and credit unions.

Although the 1970s marked the beginning of what would become extensive changes on the liability side of the depository institutions' balance sheet, it was not until the 1980s that the asset side would catch up with the changes. Variable-rate mortgages, which existed in the early 1970s in some states such as Wisconsin and California, were rejected by Congress on a national basis in 1974. Although federally chartered savings and loans were allowed to issue variable-rate mortgages in states where state-chartered institutions were permitted to do so, it was not until January 1, 1979, that all federally chartered savings and loan associations were allowed to offer variable-rate, graduated-payment, and reverse-annuity mortgages on a national basis.

The postwar years were also a time of change for the FHLBB and the FSLIC. Several additional pieces of legislation were passed by Congress to strengthen the FSLIC against any unexpected and heavy demands for insurance payments. These included authority in 1950 to borrow up to $750 million from the U.S. Treasury; the establishment in 1961 of a secondary reserve, which was eliminated as of the end of 1986 when the FSLIC was declared insolvent; and the authority in 1965 to call for loans from all insured savings and loan associations. The FSLIC may also borrow from the FHL Banks, which it did for the first time in 1984.

Tax law in the savings and loan industry came into play in 1951. Before the Revenue Act of 1951, savings and loans were exempt from federal income taxes. Although this act terminated their tax-exempt status, savings and loans nonetheless were able to avoid paying taxes because they were permitted essentially to deduct up to 100 percent of taxable income through a bad-debt reserve. In 1962, however, another Revenue Act was passed that reduced the bad-debt deduction to 60 percent of taxable income, subject to a qualifying asset restriction. This restriction stated that for a savings and loan to be eligible for the maximum deduction, 82 percent or more of its assets had to consist of cash, U.S. government securities, and passbook loans, plus one-to-four family residential property loans. The bad-debt deduction was reduced by three-quarters of 1 percent for every 1 percent the qualified assets fell below 82 percent of total assets. The deduction was zero if these assets fell below 60 percent.

The Tax Reform Act of 1969 modified this restriction by permitting a savings and loan association to base its bad-debt deduction on taxable income, loss experience, or percentage of eligible loans. Because the vast majority of associations used the taxable-income method, the result was that the deduction was reduced in scheduled steps from 60 percent of taxable income in 1969 to 40 percent in 1979.[16] The Tax Equity and Fiscal Responsibility Act of 1982 further

---

[16]In 1975, 83 percent of all savings and loan associations used the taxable-income method. In 1982, the corresponding figure was 65 percent.

reduced the bad-debt deduction to 34 percent in 1982 and then to 32 percent in 1984. More recently, the Tax Reform Act of 1986 reduced the bad-debt deduction as a percent of taxable income to 8 percent in 1987. At the same time, this act reduced the maximum corporate tax rate from 46 percent to 34 percent, provided for an alternative minimum tax, and extended the time of the loss–carry-forward provision, all of which (unlike the reduced bad-debt deduction) benefit savings and loan associations. To be eligible for the maximum deduction under the 1986 act, a savings and loan only had to have 60 percent or more of its assets in qualifying assets (basically those mentioned above). Thus, over time, the tax laws have provided a large but diminishing incentive to invest in eligible mortgage-related assets.

In addition to the tax laws, there are regulations pertaining to FHLBB-member associations, FSLIC-insured associations, federal associations, and state associations. As regards the member associations, only two direct regulations exist. One pertains to the rate paid on savings deposits and the other to member associations' liquidity. The power to set liquidity requirements was granted to the FHLBB in 1950, with "liquidity" referring to the minimum amount of such assets as cash and U.S. Treasury securities that must be held as a percent of savings deposits. The Interest Rate Control Act of 1966, on the other hand, gave the FHLBB the authority to set rate ceilings, which until then had been nonexistent, on the savings deposits of member associations. This ceiling was set initially at one-half of 1 percent—but later was reduced to one-fourth of 1 percent—above the ceiling rate that commercial banks were permitted to pay on savings deposits. The ceiling represented an attempt to provide a competitive edge to savings and loan associations to garner funds for the residential housing sector. This differential was abolished in January 1984, and all rate ceilings for depository institutions were eliminated in March 1986.

For FSLIC-insured institutions, the regulations are quite comprehensive and subject to change. They involve asset and liability restrictions, closure procedures, and net worth or capital requirements. Rather than discuss these regulations here, it will suffice to make two brief points. First, the Financial Institutions Supervisory Act of 1966 allows the FHLBB to issue cease-and-desist orders wherever an insured thrift is engaged in "unsafe and unsound practices."[17] Second, the net worth regulation was designed to provide a

---

[17]The FHLBB was actually granted this power in 1954, but legal appeals could delay compliance with the orders for considerable periods of time. The 1966 act required immediate compliance, with legal challenges to be resolved later.

buffer for asset value declines in bad times, and thereby to protect the insurance fund from losses due to failures. It was also used in 1964 to discourage fast-growing thrifts engaging in "risky" loan policies.[18]

The federal associations are subjected to the most control by the FHLBB. The reason, of course, is that they are subject to three sets of regulations because they are federal, member, and insured associations all in one. Accordingly, federal associations must examine three sets of regulations to determine whether they are complying with the law. Interestingly enough, "there are cases where the FHLBB has given federal associations certain powers . . . and then set tighter restrictions [for insured associations] taking away these powers" (Marvell 1969, p. 137).

The regulations for federal associations were initially quite direct in their intention to limit lending to local home-mortgage loans, which meant loans secured by houses within 50 miles of the association's home office. In 1964, federal associations were permitted to make unsecured, personal loans for college or educational expenses— the first time they had been allowed to make loans for any purpose other than acquiring real estate. In the same year, the geographical limit for mortgage loans was extended to 100 miles. This limit was extended in later years by the Congress to encompass the association's home state—and beyond that for the largest savings and loan associations. Then, in 1983, the FHLBB permitted federal associations to make loans nationwide. Unless prohibited by state law, state associations with FSLIC insurance were permitted to do the same. In 100 years, the savings and loan industry had come full circle— nationals were once again alive and well.[19] In 1986, however, the FHLBB proposed restricting somewhat the ability of savings and loan associations to make nationwide loans, but it dropped the proposal after considerable negative reaction.

Federal associations were also permitted in 1964 to issue mortgages and buy property in urban renewal areas and to buy securities issued by federal, state, and municipal governments. And then in

---

[18]An economist at the FHLBB in 1979 commented that the net worth requirements were "excessively complex." As evidence, he noted that "of 3,864 completed SF893 [net worth requirement forms] received by the Federal Savings and Loan Insurance Corporation for 1977, 2,700 contained errors" (see Horton 1979, p. 1, fn. 1). Appendix 2 contains the most recent net worth requirements.

[19]Before March 1981, however, FHLBB policy prohibited interstate branching by federally chartered savings and loan associations. Since then, the policy has been modified to permit federal associations to branch on equal terms with state associations and to branch more freely as a result of the acquisition of supervisory or failing institutions.

1968, these associations were allowed to make loans for mobile homes, second or vacation homes, and housing fixtures. Thus began the entry by savings and loans into business areas long viewed as the exclusive domain of commercial banks.

Those state-chartered institutions that are not members or federally insured are subject to regulations that vary from state to state.

The Turbulent 1980s

As interest rates rose unexpectedly and fluctuated widely early in the decade of the 1980s, it became very clear that many savings and loan associations were ill-equipped to handle the new financial environment in which they found themselves. Their newly authorized market-rate deposits were rapidly escalating the institutions' cost of funds, while the largely fixed-rate mortgage portfolios were painfully slow to turn over. The result was rapidly deteriorating profits and a significant increase in failures. The problems persisted—even as interest rates declined and the maturity-mismatch problem lessened—due to a growing deterioration in the quality of assets held by many associations. The savings and loan industry's ratio of net worth to total assets fell from over 5 percent at the end of 1979 to 3.4 percent at the end of 1985 (based upon generally accepted accounting principles). Over this same period, more than 500 savings and loan associations failed and an additional 400 or so were left with negative net worth. (See Table 6 and Table 7 for more detailed data regarding the plight of savings and loans during the 1980s.)

The turbulence of the early 1980s, however, has done much more than merely reduce the number of institutions. It has perhaps permanently affected the way in which savings and loans do business. Instead of just savings and time deposits, these institutions now offer transaction accounts, large certificates of deposit, and consumer-repurchase agreements—virtually as wide a selection as that of any commercial bank. On the asset side, these institutions now go beyond mortgages to also hold consumer loans, commercial loans, mortgage-backed securities, and a wide variety of direct investments. As such, savings and loans now differ from commercial banks more as a matter of degree than of kind.[20] The result is that the distinctions among the depository financial services firms may be forever blurred.

Whereas Congress and the regulatory agencies in the past had reacted to most financial change with the proverbial "long and vari-

---

[20]Indeed, savings and loan associations are now permitted to accept demand deposits and make commercial loans, which is a function that, according to the Bank Holding Company Act, legally defines a bank.

TABLE 6

THE SAVINGS AND LOAN INDUSTRY: THE TURBULENT 1980s

Year	Number of S&Ls	Assets ($ million)	Number of Failures	RAP Net Worth to Assets (Percent)	Number of S&Ls with RAPNW<0	GAAP Net Worth to Assets (Percent)	Number of S&Ls with GAAP<0 Net Worth	FSLIC Reserves ($ million)	FSLIC Reserves as Percent of Assets (Percent)
1980	4,002	618,466	35	5.26	17	5.26	17	6,462	1.04
1981	3,779	651,068	81	4.27	41	4.15	65	6,302	0.97
1982	3,343	692,663	251	3.69	80	2.95	201	6,331	0.91
1983	3,040	819,168	101	4.02	54	3.14	287	6,425	0.78
1984	3,167	978,514	42	3.86	71	2.87	434	5,606	0.61
1985	3,246	1,069,547	70[a]	4.38	123	3.39	450	4,557	0.43
1986 Sept.	3,234	1,143,298	86[b]	4.56	219	3.43	446	3,600	0.31

[a]Includes 25 MCP cases.
[b]Includes 46 MCP cases. Total is for entire year.

SOURCE: Barth, Brumbaugh, Sauerhaft, and Wang (1985b and 1986) and data compiled by the authors from information provided by the Federal Home Loan Bank Board.

Note: On September 31, 1986, tangible net worth as a percent of total assets for the industry as a whole was 1.25, with 655 institutions holding $359 billion in assets having negative tangible net worth.

TABLE 7

SELECTED DATA FOR FSLIC-INSURED SAVINGS AND LOAN INSTITUTIONS WITH GAAP NET WORTH LESS THAN ZERO AND NET INCOME LESS THAN ZERO

	1984		1985				1986	
	I	III	I	II	III	IV	II	III
Number of Institutions	223	255	268	210	235	229	269	297
Assets ($ billion)	50	56	62	51	55	55	67	72
RAP Net Worth ($ million)	564	441	147	−46	−496	−524	−2879	−4304
GAAP Net Worth ($ million)	−1853	−1967	−2336	−1736	−2390	−2371	−6074	−7015
Net Income ($ million)	−147	−212	−231	−413	−494	−671	−1451	−1483

SOURCES: Barth, Brumbaugh, Sauerhaft, and Wang (1985b); and data compiled by the authors from information provided by the Federal Home Loan Bank Board.

able lag," the reaction time in the 1980s has been much shorter, owing in no small part to the speed of financial change. The first major legislation of the decade, the Depository Institutions Deregulation and Monetary Control Act of 1980, provided for the gradual elimination of interest rate controls and the removal of the savings and loan differential by 1986. It also granted new powers to federal savings and loans, including the authority to operate remote service units, offer credit cards, engage in consumer and commercial lending, and offer NOW accounts. In exchange, the federal associations were made subject to Federal Reserve Board reserve requirements on their deposits. Savings and loans were also given equal access to the Federal Reserve System services, however, including the discount window for emergency borrowing purposes.

Following the passage of this particular federal legislation, the FHLBB began to loosen its regulatory grip on the savings and loan industry. This was done in a number of ways in 1980, 1981, and 1982. The FHLBB allowed federal associations to negotiate with borrowers any type of fixed- or variable-rate mortgage instrument. FSLIC-insured associations were permitted to borrow outside the FHLBB system without limit and to accept more liabilities maturing within a three-month period. Federal associations were given authority to invest in mutual funds and to invest up to 3 percent of their assets in service corporations. FSLIC-insured associations were permitted to make real estate loans without regard to the geographic location of the property securing the loan, and they were authorized to issue variable-rate savings accounts and certificates of deposit. Federal association service corporations were given permission to engage in a wider range of activities without prior approval and were permitted to deal with a broader range of customers.

The second major legislation of the 1980s was the Garn–St Germain Depository Institutions Act of 1982 (known for short as the Garn–St Germain Act). In broad terms, this act gave the FHLBB the authority to arrange mergers of failing savings and loan associations with other associations, commercial banks, savings and loan holding companies, bank holding companies, and nondepository companies. In addition, the act gave the FHLBB the authority to implement a capital-assistance plan for savings and loans with low net worth. It also expanded the balance sheet powers of savings and loans and granted greater freedom for them to operate in stock rather than mutual form.

Several of the provisions of this law were originally set to expire on October 15, 1985, but subsequently were extended until October 13, 1986. Congress is currently considering reinstating the provisions that pertain to dealing with financially troubled savings and loan institutions.

Under the 1982 act's program of capital assistance for associations with seriously low net worth, the FSLIC issues promissory notes to purchase net worth certificates from qualified associations. If the qualified associations recover from their troubles, the promissory notes and net worth certificates are retired. Otherwise, the FSLIC incurs losses by being forced to pay off the promissory notes.

In addition, the 1982 act granted the FHLBB authority to approve interstate merger transactions by permitting the FSLIC to override any state or federal law that would prevent a financially troubled FSLIC-insured association from merging with any other FSLIC-insured association or an FDIC-insured bank or being acquired by any person or company, including a bank holding company. The approval of a large number of transactions of this kind breaks down the walls separating different types of financial firms and increases the pressures to remove all banking restrictions.

The so-called permanent changes made by the 1982 act were indeed historic. They involved additional asset and liability powers, as well as greater freedom pertaining to organizational form and capital generation. More specifically, existing law had been biased against the stock form of organization, and that bias restricted the industry's access to capital markets, but this act permitted the creation of new federal savings and loan associations—whether on a de novo or a conversion basis or whether in the mutual or stock form—nationwide. Further, it permitted any federal association to convert from the mutual to the stock form, or the reverse, also without geographic restriction.

The Garn–St Germain Act also specifically provided for federal associations to make secured and unsecured loans for commercial, corporate, business, or agricultural purposes. The limit was set at 10 percent of assets invested in such loans as of January 1, 1984. Complementing this new commercial lending power, federal associations were authorized to offer demand deposits to persons and corporations with which the institution has a corporate, commercial, business, or agricultural loan relationship. Corporations could also establish demand deposits at federal associations into which individual customers could pay their bills. In other words, these particular changes permitting federal associations to accept demand deposits and to make commercial loans transformed them into banks, although they were exempt from being so classified under the Bank Holding Company Act. Instead, these associations were to be exclusively regulated by the Savings and Loan Holding Company Act as regards acquisitions or control by companies other than bank holding companies.

Under the 1982 legislation, federal savings and loan associations were permitted to invest up to 40 percent (up from 20 percent) of their assets in loans in nonresidential real estate. They were also permitted to invest as much as 30 percent of assets (up from 20 percent) in commercial loans, which, for the first time, could include inventory and floor-planning loans. The federal associations could also invest up to 10 percent of their assets in tangible personal property for lease or sale, thus enabling these institutions to compete with commercial banks in the commercial leasing business. The act enabled a federal thrift to invest up to 90 percent of its assets in commercial-type investments. It also permitted this type of institution to invest up to 100 percent of its assets in state or local government securities and, for the first time, to invest in other associations' time and savings deposits, and use such investments to help meet liquidity requirements.

Although the Garn–St Germain Act gave federal associations many banklike powers, it also imposed banklike branching restrictions under certain circumstances. More specifically, a federal association could have interstate branches only if it qualified as a saving and loan association according to the Internal Revenue Code. To qualify as an association under this code, an institution would have to meet the "thriftness test" of having a minimum of 60 percent of its assets in financing homeownership or other qualifying assets (such as mortgage-backed securities, cash, certain government securities, student loans, and passbook loans). Also, if an FSLIC-insured institution subsidiary of a unitary savings and loan holding company no longer qualified as a saving and loan association according to the Internal Revenue Code, the parent would have to either divest the association or come into compliance with the activities applicable to multiple savings and loan association holding companies.

Following passage of the Garn–St Germain Act, the FHLBB continued to issue a number of regulations affecting savings and loan associations. In 1983, FHL Banks were permitted to make advances for terms of up to 20 years (rather than 10 years). In 1984, federal associations were permitted to establish financial subsidiaries to issue securities for the parent institution. In that same year, FSLIC-insured institutions were required to establish policies for the management of interest-rate risk in the institutions' operations. In 1985, new net worth and direct-investment requirements were imposed. FSLIC-insured institutions had to increase their net worth depending on their respective rates of growth. Those institutions with more than

$100 million in assets had to seek permission from the FHLBB to grow faster than 25 percent a year. Greater net worth also was required for associations with direct investments. And, finally, the five-year averaging used to calculate net worth was gradually eliminated.[21]

As regards direct investments, or investments in equity securities, real estate, and service corporations, the FHLBB established a process of supervisory review and approval for such investments if they exceed 10 percent of assets or twice regulatory net worth, whichever is greater. Also associations that exceed the above guidelines were required to post a 10 percent reserve against all direct investments made after December 10, 1984. This particular asset restriction was quite controversial and therefore had a sunset provision so that it would expire on March 15, 1987, unless extended by the FHLBB. It was subsequently extended and was incorporated in final form on June 10, 1987, as part of the FHLBB regulation restricting equity risk investments.

In summary, much of the recent legislation and regulatory changes has been a response to the turbulence in the financial markets that has occurred in the 1970s and 1980s. The change in the legal environment has resulted in savings and loan associations becoming much more like commercial banks than anytime since their development in 1831.

Until relatively recently, these institutions encouraged savings and provided for home financing by having balance sheets consisting almost entirely of passbook saving accounts and home mortgage loans. At the end of 1985, however, passbook loans accounted for only 7.5 percent of deposits and home mortgage loans accounted for only 42 percent of assets (52.3 percent when mortgage-backed securities are included). As a result of these changes, the rationale for government regulation of savings and loans seems to be shifting from one based upon their role in savings and home financing toward one based upon their role in the payments mechanism, just like that of commercial banks. But, of course, this raises the question as to whether the payments role of depository institutions should simply be severed from their other activities, with the financial intermediary or saving-investment role being opened up to all types of activities by removing existing regulations.

Organizational Form and Government Regulation

Historically, most savings and loan associations have been mutual rather than stock-type organizations. (See Table 8.) At the time the

[21]See appendix 2 for details.

TABLE 8
ORGANIZATIONAL FORM OF SAVINGS AND LOAN INSTITUTIONS, 1980–85

	Number of Stock Institutions	Percent of All Insured	Assets of Stock Institutions ($ billion)	Percent of All Insured Assets	Number of Savings and Loan Holding Companies		
					Total	Multiple	Unitary
1980	789	19.7	168.0	27.2	n.a.	n.a.	n.a.
1981	791	20.9	188.4	28.9	155	9	146
1982	755	22.6	206.9	30.0	176	8	166
1983	738	24.3	298.2	39.5	229	18	211
1984	934	29.5	511.1	52.2	288	24	264
1985	1,087	33.5	601.6	56.2	342	29	313

SOURCE: Data compiled by the authors from information provided by the Federal Home Loan Bank Board.

Spence Act—the original holding company legislation for savings and loan institutions—was enacted in 1959, there were only 480 stock associations out of 6,223 S&Ls, accounting for 13 percent of all assets. One reason for this situation was that Congress and the FHLBB had imposed moratoriums on the conversion of federal associations from the mutual to the stock type of organization from 1955 to 1974. Although some state mutual associations did convert, there is relatively little information available about the number and amount of funds raised from these conversions.[22]

The rapidly deteriorating net worth position of the savings and loan industry during the early 1980s clearly demonstrated the need for associations to be able to have as much access as possible to the capital markets. Mutual associations, however, could increase their net worth only through retained earnings or through the sale of subordinated debt. They could not raise external equity capital. Although the FHLBB had been authorizing conversions on an experimental basis from 1974 to 1976, and thereafter on a more regular basis, between 1976 and 1982 only 142 conversions had been consummated, raising $600 million. With the passage of the Garn–St Germain Act in 1982, however, the conversion process was greatly facilitated. As a result, 255 conversions, raising $4,837 million, occurred between 1983 and 1985.

The first savings and loan holding company, Great Western Financial Corporation, was organized in 1955 by Lehman Brothers in New York. Beginning with one savings and loan association, it obtained six more within four years and eventually controlled at least twenty non–savings and loan subsidiaries, including an insurance agency, two land-development companies, and fifteen escrow companies.[23] Owing to this type of activity, Congress enacted the Spence Act, which was limited to FSLIC-insured institutions and to holding companies controlling more than one insured association. This act was viewed as an attempt to slow the growth in multi-association holding companies to gain time to study the issue. Eventually more comprehensive legislation was passed in 1968. Under the 1968 law and in subsequent legislation, a savings and loan holding company was defined as any company controlling an insured savings and loan institution or other savings and loan holding company.

Current law provides that it is unlawful to become a savings and loan holding company or to be an existing holding company that

[22]Before 1980, fewer than 20 states allowed stock savings and loan associations to operate.
[23]See Marvell (1969, p. 200).

acquires another insured or uninsured association without the prior approval of the FSLIC. Subject to the exceptions provided by the emergency provisions of the Garn–St Germain Act, no applications are to be approved that result in a multiple savings and loan holding company controlling FSLIC-insured associations in more than one state. Interestingly enough, under the Savings and Loan Holding Company Act, unitary savings and loan holding companies that meet the "thriftness test" of the Internal Revenue Code may engage without restriction in any activity, through non-FSLIC subsidiaries. This explains how Sears, Roebuck and Company can operate a retailing business, insurance company, securities firm, and a single savings and loan institution, all through a holding company and yet not violate the Savings and Loan Holding Company Act.[24]

Multiple savings and loan holding companies (and unitary companies failing to meet the thriftness test) may only engage in those activities determined to be permissible by the FSLIC. The FSLIC has thus far permitted savings and loan companies, and subsidiaries thereof that are neither insured institutions nor service corporations of insured institutions, to engage in such activities as conducting an insurance agency, operating an escrow business, processing data, developing unimproved real estate, and preparing federal and state tax returns.

Besides holding companies, it is also important to briefly mention service corporations, which are corporations organized under the laws of the state in which the savings and loan association has its home office and whose stock is available for purchase only by state or federal associations also having a home office in that state. Federal associations are currently authorized by law to invest up to 3 percent of their assets in the stock of service corporations. Utilizing these corporations, federal associations may engage in stock brokerage, insurance brokerage, and agency activities, among other activities, as well as join together in different states to carry out mutually advantageous ventures on a nationwide scale. By the end of September 1986, 4,286 service corporations had been authorized.

Trade Associations and Regulation

In addition to the state and federal authorities, there has been considerable private influence on the course of regulation in the savings and loan industry. The oldest national trade association for savings and loans is the U.S. League of Savings Institutions, which

[24]Citicorp was the first bank holding company permitted by both the Federal Reserve and the FHLBB to acquire a savings and loan association, which it did in August 1982.

was organized in April 1892.[25] Starting in 1897, the league collected data on savings and loan associations and filed annual reports on the industry. Each year, as state after state passed laws requiring their associations to file reports with a state official, these data were compiled for the annual report on savings and loan associations.[26]

In addition to collecting statistics, the league has taken an active interest in laws and regulations affecting savings and loan associations. This interest was and probably still is based upon the belief that "the savings and loan business desires uniformity along sound lines" (quoted in Bodfish and Theobald 1940, p. 616). This view was reflected in the opposition to national savings and loan associations in the 1890s, and it was also reflected in the federal government's early chartering restrictions limiting an association to making only residential mortgage loans and only within a 50-mile radius.

The league also played a large role in establishing the Federal Home Loan Bank System and the FSLIC. Indeed, according to one of the first members of the Federal Home Loan Bank Board, during the Great Depression "practically every plan or general proposal of the league was adopted by the government in full or in modified form and thrown into the breach to stabilize the situation and prevent a sweeping collapse" (quoted in Bodfish 1935, p. 17). Specifically, leaders of the league participated in the actual drafting of the Federal Home Loan Bank Act; the league's proposal regarding deposit insurance was included as Title IV of the National Housing Act; and the league was instrumental in maintaining the tax exemption for savings and loan associations until 1951.[27] Thus, the relationship between the FHLBB and the U.S. League has been very close over the years.[28]

These relationships are even more important when one considers that the FHLBB not only oversees federal savings and loan associations and state-chartered member savings and loans but also the FSLIC and the Federal Home Loan Mortgage Corporation (FHLMC). In evaluating the future course of regulation, it is important to deter-

[25]The earliest form of trade association in the savings and loan industry was the state league. The first was formed in Pennsylvania in 1877. See Bodfish and Theobald (1940, p. 591).

[26]See Bodfish (1931, pp. 152–53). It should also be noted that until the Great Depression, "the United States League and the several state leagues were primarily responsible for the supervision and public inspection or visitation of savings and loan associations" (Bodfish 1935, p. 9).

[27]See Bodfish (1935, p. 24).

[28]See Marvell (1969, p. 255).

mine the extent to which regulators are safeguarding the public trust and to what degree they represent industry interests.

Three Unresolved Issues

Having traced the economic and regulatory evolution of the savings and loan industry from its inception in 1831 to the present, it is essential to consider three unresolved issues, summarized below.

First, is the traditional rationale for using laws and regulations to maintain balance sheet distinctions between savings and loan associations and commercial banks still valid?

Traditionally, savings and loans were given special treatment because of their role in encouraging savings and supporting home financing. Today, however, consumers have ready access to a wide variety of relatively safe savings instruments offered by financial services firms other than savings and loan associations, and savings and loan associations offer transactions accounts just like commercial banks. In addition, it is no longer clear that savings and loans find themselves confined strictly to originating and holding mortgage loans. Indeed, by the end of September 1986, one-to-four family residential mortgages accounted for only 37 percent of the total financial assets of savings and loans.[29]

Instead, savings and loans now make commercial and consumer loans as well as directly invest in real estate, corporate stock, and service corporations engaging in a variety of nonresidential mortgage loan activities. (See Table 9 for data on the types and amounts of assets held by savings and loan associations in recent years.) Moreover, even to the extent that savings and loan associations do acquire residential mortgage loans, an increasing share of these take the form of mortgage-backed securities. By the end of September 1986, these securities accounted for more than 25 percent of all residential mortgage loans held by savings and loans. Many savings and loans are now increasingly behaving just like mortgage bankers—originating and servicing residential mortgage loans and then selling them in the secondary market rather than holding onto them. This process of transforming illiquid mortgage loans into capital market securities has resulted in other financial services firms, both here and abroad, channeling more funds into the mortgage market, thereby diminishing the role played by savings and loan associations. Thus, it appears that modern savings and loan regulation might better address the issues of safety and soundness, as does commercial bank regulation, rather than furthering traditional credit allocation motives.

[29]Even adding in mortgage-backed securities, the figure still was under 50 percent.

TABLE 9

DISTRIBUTION OF ASSETS HELD BY FSLIC-INSURED INSTITUTIONS (Percent)

Type of Asset	1977	1978	1979	1980	1981	1982	1983	1984	1985	1986 Sept.
Mortgage-Backed Securities	2.8	3.1	3.5	4.3	5.0	8.5	10.8	11.0	10.3	12.5
Home Mortgages	67.4	67.8	67.7	66.2	64.7	55.7	49.3	44.5	42.0	37.3
Subtotal	70.2	70.9	71.2	70.5	69.7	64.2	60.1	55.5	52.3	49.8
Multifamily Mortgages	6.7	6.6	6.2	5.8	5.4	5.3	5.8	6.3	6.8	6.8
Mortgages on Commercial Real Estate	7.3	6.8	6.5	6.2	6.2	6.3	7.2	8.4	9.1	8.8
Mortgages for Land and Land Development	0.9	0.8	0.9	0.9	0.9	0.9	1.5	2.3	2.8	2.7
Nonmortgage Commercial Loans	0.1	0.1	0.2	0.3	0.1[a]	0.1	0.4	1.1	1.5	1.7
Nonmortgage Consumer Loans	2.2	2.1	2.6	2.7	2.7	2.8	3.0	3.4	4.0	4.2
Repossessed Assets	0.3	0.2	0.1	0.2	0.2	0.4	0.5	0.5	0.9	1.3
Investment Real Estate	0.1	0.1	0.2	0.2	0.3	0.4	0.5	0.5	0.6	0.7
Cash, Deposits, and Securities	9.2	9.2	8.9	9.8	10.1	12.0	13.4	13.3	12.8	13.1
Fixed Assets	1.7	1.7	1.7	1.8	1.8	1.9	1.8	1.2[a]	1.2	1.2
Equity in Service Corps./Subsidiaries	0.3	0.3	0.4	0.5	0.6	0.8	1.0	1.6	1.9	2.1
Goodwill	[b]	[b]	[b]	[b]	1.8	0.2	2.3	3.6	3.9	2.1
Other	1.0	1.2	1.1	1.1	1.8	2.6	2.3	3.6	3.9	5.5
Total Assets ($ billion)	450	513	568	618	651	693	819	979	1,070	1,193

[a]Change in definition.
[b]Less than 0.05 percent.
SOURCE: Compiled by the authors from data provided by the Federal Home Loan Bank Board.

Second, how has the role of deposit insurance evolved, and is it appropriate to apply the same insurance framework to savings and loans and commercial banks?

The basic argument in support of regulation is that without it, banks would be subject to runs that could lead to widespread bank failures and a collapse of the payments system. Although the Federal Reserve System was established in 1913 to provide liquidity to solvent but illiquid banks facing massive deposit withdrawals, the Great Depression revealed weaknesses in this preventive device. Thus, federal deposit insurance was established as an additional layer of protection. But along with it came a different type of problem: although runs were largely eliminated, the problem of moral hazard arose. This occurs because insured financial institutions can gather deposits from individuals who have no incentive to monitor the activities of the institutions. To compound the problem, institutions pay a flat-rate premium for the insurance, regardless of risk, thus providing an incentive for insured institutions to increase the overall riskiness of their portfolios.

The government has a choice to make in this situation. It can introduce risk-sensitive insurance premiums, raise capital requirements, adopt restrictive asset and liability regulations, or move toward market-value accounting and become more aggressive in liquidating or merging institutions fast enough to impose zero costs upon the insurance agency.

A more dramatic change would simply be to isolate the payments system by separating the transactions account function of depository institutions from their intermediation function. This would mean that transactions accounts would be backed by a "completely" risk-free security or asset. Because it is presumably concern about the backing of demand and transactions deposits that would set off a run, secure backing for the transactions accounts should make runs less likely. Thus, the need for deposit insurance and the accompanying problems it creates would be diminished. In any event, one point seems clear: since savings and loan institutions and banks are now integrally involved in the payments mechanism, a consistent set of regulations must be applied to both types of institutions.

Third, while many savings and loan institutions are healthy, a significant number of them have failed but have yet to be closed. What should be done about all the insolvent savings and loan associations still open?

For several years now there has been a growing number of savings and loans that are insolvent yet still operating, whether one measures insolvency according to regulatory accounting principles (RAP) or generally accepted accounting principles (GAAP). The number of associations that are both insolvent and earning negative net income is also growing at an alarming rate. This situation is particularly troublesome because the cost of resolving the problem appears to be growing. Although the resolution costs resulting from liquidations and mergers are typically substantially understated by reported book value measures of capital or net worth, both RAP and GAAP measures of net worth were a negative $4.3 billion and $7.0 billion in September 1986, respectively, for the 297 institutions with GAAP net worth less than zero and net income less than zero.[30] With reserves available to the FSLIC of around $2 billion, even the book value measures of net worth underscore the inability of the FSLIC to handle properly the financially troubled institutions.

As a result of this delay in closing down insolvent savings and loans, the institutions are permitted to engage in "go-for-broke" strategies. To deal with this situation, Congress is considering legislation to recapitalize the FSLIC, with the aim of raising sufficient funds to close down all insolvent institutions. Controversy exists, however, on three major points: (1) whether sufficient funds will be raised to handle the entire problem; (2) whether too much is being raised and will thus be spent too fast, resulting in institutions being closed that would have overcome their problems if only they had been given more time; and (3) whether the financially healthy institutions can really afford to cover the tab for closing down the hundreds of institutions contemplated by the recapitalization legislation.

Even though funds must be obtained to close down (through liquidation or merger) these insolvent institutions as soon as possible to put a stop to their gamble for resurrection using insured deposits, now is not the time to be driven—as so often happened in the past—by a crisis environment. That is, the issue of failed but still operating institutions must be separated from the long-run role of savings and loan associations in the financial system.

Summary and Conclusions

This paper has surveyed 150 years of savings and loan history to describe the evolving role of regulation and to provide a backdrop for evaluating the regulatory framework of the future. At this point, the authors would like to reiterate a few of the most important conclusions.

---

[30]See Table 6 and Table 7 for detailed data regarding the financial plight of the bottom portion of the firms making up the savings and loan industry.

Although savings and loan associations are part of the same financial institutions community as commercial banks, the rationale for regulating them was far different from that for commercial banks. Savings and loan regulation was designed to ensure a stable flow of funds into the housing sector, whereas commercial banks were regulated with an eye toward preserving the safety and soundness of the payments mechanism. Clearly, there were times when these goals contributed to a different approach to regulation, but given that these institutions operated in distinct markets, a similarity in regulatory philosophy was not a necessity. As the financial markets evolved, though, the distinctions between the types of institutions blurred and the need for some consistency in regulation increased. This is not to say that all institutions should be the same, but rather that institutions that choose to operate in a similar manner should be regulated consistently.

Second, the regulatory authorities have to avoid the pitfall of crisis regulation. So often in the past, regulation was a myopic response to an immediate problem and, at best, provided short-lived symptomatic relief. The controversy over dealing with the current crisis of failing savings and loan institutions is a case in point. Any solution to this problem must allocate the costs in an equitable manner between the surviving institutions and the government regulators (that is, the taxpayers). In the long run, however, the regulators must address the root causes of the problem and design regulations with the long-term health of the industry in mind, rather than spending an inordinate amount of time assessing blame for past mistakes or engaging in a futile attempt to return the industry to the good old days.

Finally, if government regulation is to avoid the crisis-prevention rut of the past, it must take its cue from market forces. Although it is probably in the nature of regulation to be a restraining force to uninhibited market growth, regulation must be formulated more with the intent of promoting safe and sound financial practices than with artificially prolonging institutional differences or allocating credit flows.

References

Balderston, Frederick E. *Thrifts in Crisis: Structural Transformation of the Federal Savings and Loan Industry*. Cambridge, Mass.: Ballinger Publishing Co., 1985.

Barth, James R.; Bisenius, Donald J.; Brumbaugh, Dan R., Jr.; and Sauerhaft, Daniel. "The Thrift Industry's Rough Road Ahead." *Challenge* (September/October 1986): 38–43.

Barth, James R.; Brumbaugh, Dan R., Jr.; and Sauerhaft, Daniel. "Failure Costs of Government-Regulated Financial Firms: The Case of Thrift Institutions." Research working paper no. 123. Washington: Federal Home Loan Bank Board, Office of Policy and Economic Research, October 1986.

Barth, James R.; Brumbaugh, Dan R., Jr.; Sauerhaft, Daniel; and Wang, George H. K. "Insolvency and Risk-Taking in the Thrift Industry: Implications for the Future." *Contemporary Policy Issues* (Fall 1985a): 1–32.

Barth, James R.; Brumbaugh, Dan R., Jr.; Sauerhaft, Daniel; and Wang, George H.K. "Thrift Institution Failures: Causes and Policy Issues." *Proceedings of a Conference on Bank Structure and Competition.* Federal Reserve Bank of Chicago, 1985b, pp. 184–216.

Barth, James R.; Brumbaugh, Dan R., Jr.; Sauerhaft, Daniel; and Wang, George H. K. "Thrift Institution Failures: Estimating the Regulation's Closure Rule." Research working paper no. 125. Washington: Federal Home Loan Bank Board, Office of Policy and Economic Research, August 1986.

Barth, James R., and Keleher, Robert E. "Financial Crises and the Role of the Lender of Last Resort." Federal Reserve Bank of Atlanta *Economic Review* (January 1984): 58–67.

Benston, George J. *An Analysis of the Causes of Savings and Loan Association Failures.* Monograph Series in Finance and Economics, Monograph 1985-45. New York: Salomon Brothers Center for the Study of Financial Institutions, New York University.

Benston, George J., et al. *Perspectives on Safe and Sound Banking: Past, Present and Future.* Cambridge, Mass.: MIT Press, 1986.

Biederman, Kenneth R., and Tuccillo, John A. *Taxation and Regulation of the Savings and Loan Industry.* Lexington: D.C. Heath and Company, 1976.

Bisenius, Donald J. "An Analysis of the Proposed Capital Requirements for Thrift Institutions: A Staff Economic Study." Washington: Federal Home Loan Bank Board, Office of Policy and Economic Research, August 15, 1986.

Bodfish, Morton. *History of Building and Loans in the United States.* Chicago: U.S. Building and Loan League, 1931.

Bodfish, Morton. "The Depression Experience of Savings and Loan Associations in the United States." Address delivered in Salzburg, Austria, September 1935.

Bodfish, Morton, and Theobald, A. D. *Savings and Loan Principles.* New York: Prentice-Hall, 1940.

Committee on Government Operations. *Federal Regulation of Direct Investments by Savings and Loan Associations.* House report 99–358. Washington: Government Printing Office, November 5, 1985.

Ely, Bert. "This Savings and Loan Mess Won't Go Away." *Wall Street Journal,* July 17, 1986.

Ely, Bert. "Our S&Ls Are Obsolete." *Washington Post,* September 21, 1986.

England, Catherine. "Private Deposit Insurance: Stabilizing the Banking System." Cato Policy Analysis no. 54. Washington: Cato Institute, June 21, 1985.

England, Catherine. "Agency Costs and Unregulated Banks: Could Depositors Protect Themselves?" Chapter 14 in this book.

Fand, David I. "The Viability of Thrift Intermediaries as Financial Institutions." *Banca Nazionale Del Lavoro Quarterly Review* (September 1973): 235–68.

Giles, Thomas G.; Mayer, Thomas; and Ettin, Edward C. "Portfolio Regulations and Policies of Financial Intermediaries." In *Private Financial Institutions*, pp. 157–262. Commission on Money and Credit. Englewood Cliffs, N.J.: Prentice-Hall, 1963.

Goldsmith, Raymond A. *Financial Intermediaries in the American Economy Since 1900*. Princeton, N.J.: Princeton University Press, 1958.

Golembe, Carter H., and Holland, David S. *Federal Regulation of Banking 1986–87*. Washington: Golembe Associates, Inc., 1986.

Harr, Luther, and Harris, W. Carlton. *Banking Theory and Practice*. 2d ed. New York: McGraw-Hill Book Co., 1936.

Hearings on a Guaranty Fund for Depositors in Banks. Committee on Banking and Currency, U.S. House of Representatives, 1932.

Horton, Joseph. "A Critical Analysis of Asset-Based Risk-Related Capital Requirements for Savings and Loan Associations." Research working paper no. 83. Washington: Federal Home Loan Bank Board, Office of Policy and Economic Research, January 1979.

Horvitz, Paul M., and Pettit, R. Richardson. "Short-Run Financial Solutions for Troubled Thrift Institutions." In *The Future of the Thrift Industry*, pp. 44–67. Conference series no. 24. Federal Reserve Bank of Boston, October 1981.

Humphrey, Thomas M., and Keleher, Robert E. "The Lender of Last Resort: A Historical Perspective." *Cato Journal* 4 (Spring/Summer 1984): 275–318.

Kane, Edward J. "Accelerating Inflation, Technological Innovation, and the Decreasing Effectiveness of Banking Regulation." *Journal of Finance* (May 1981): 355–67.

Kane, Edward J. "S&Ls and Interest Rate Deregulation: The FSLIC as an In-Place Bailout Program." *Housing Finance Review* (July 1982): 219–43.

Kane Edward J. *The Gathering Crisis in Federal Deposit Insurance*. Cambridge, Mass.: MIT Press, 1985.

Kane, Edward J. "The Dangers of Capital Forbearance: The Case of FSLIC and the 'Zombie' S&Ls." *Contemporary Policy Issues* 5 (January 1987): 77–83.

Kaufman, George G., and Kormendi, Roger C., editors. *Deregulating Financial Services*. Cambridge, Mass.: Ballinger Publishing Co., 1986.

Kendall, Leon T. *The Savings and Loan Business*. Englewood Cliffs, N.J.: Prentice-Hall Inc., 1962.

Litan, Robert E. "Ending the Stalemate over Expanded Bank Powers." Unpublished paper, June 17, 1986.

Loeys, Jan G. "Deregulation: A New Future for Thrifts." Federal Reserve Bank of Philadelphia *Business Review* (January/February 1983): 15–26.

Marvell, Thomas B. *The Federal Home Loan Bank Board*. New York: Frederick A. Praeger, Publishers, 1969.

McCanan, David. "Failure of Bank Guaranty Plans." In *Federal Regulation of Banking*, pp. 161–71. Compiled by James Goodwin Hodgson. The Reference Shelf, vol. 8, no. 6. New York: H.W. Wilson Co., 1932.

Mingo, John J. "Short-Run Structural Solutions to the Problems of Thrift Institutions." In *The Future of the Thrift Industry*, pp. 81–106. Conference series no. 24. Federal Reserve Bank of Boston, October 1981.

Rolnick, Arthur, J. "Bank Regulation: Strengthening Friedman's Case for Reform." Federal Reserve Bank of Minneapolis *Quarterly Review* (Summer 1977): 11–14.

Scott, Kenneth E., and Mayer, Thomas. "Risk and Regulation in Banking: Some Proposals for Federal Deposit Insurance Reform." *Stanford Law Review* (May 1971): 537–82.

U.S. Department of Commerce, Bureau of the Census. *Historical Statistics of the United States: Colonial Times to 1970*, Part 2. Washington.

Vartanian, Thomas P. (general counsel, Federal Home Loan Bank Board). "Regulatory Restructuring of Financial Institutions and the Rebirth of the Thrift Industry." *Legal Bulletin* (January 1983): 1–22.

Walter, James E. "The Financial Soundness of Savings and Loan Associations," pp. 183–281. In *Study of the Savings and Loan Industry*, directed by Irwin Friend. Washington: Federal Home Loan Bank Board, July 1969.

White, Lawrence H. "Free Banking as an Alternative Monetary Unit." In *Money in Crisis*, pp. 269–302. Edited by Barry N. Siegel. Cambridge, Mass.: Ballinger Publishing Co., 1984.

Appendix 1:
Major Depository Financial Institution Legislation

Date of Enactment	Legislation	Key Provisions
September 17, 1787	U.S. Constitution	Granted the federal government the exclusive right to coin money and to regulate the value thereof.
February 25, 1791	First Bank of the United States	The first federally chartered bank—chartered for 20 years.
March 10, 1816	Second Bank of the United States	The second federally chartered bank—chartered for 20 years.
February 25, 1863	National Currency Act	Provided for the federal chartering of national banks under the supervision of the Comptroller of the Currency.
June 3, 1864	National Currency Bank	Superseded the act of February 25, 1863. (Under neither act could national banks make real estate loans.)
March 3, 1865	Act of 1865	Legislated state banks notes out of existence by imposing a tax of 10 percent (effective August 1, 1866) per annum on the circulating notes of state banks.
June 20, 1874	Act of 1874	Changed the name of the National Currency Act to the National Bank Act.
December 23, 1913	Federal Reserve Act	Provided for the establishment of the Federal Reserve System to furnish an "elastic currency," by advancing funds to illiquid but solvent member banks. Also increased supervision and regulation of banks. Gave national banks the power to make real estate loans, but only with respect to farm land.

Date of Enactment	Legislation	Key Provisions
February 25, 1927	McFadden Act	Enlarged the power of national banks to make real estate loans and permitted national banks to branch within the state in which they were located to the same extent permitted state banks. Prior to this act, national banks had no power to branch.
July 22, 1932	Federal Home Loan Bank Act	Established 12 Federal Home Loan Banks under the supervision of the Federal Home Loan Bank Board to advance funds to savings and loan associations to promote home ownership.
May 27, 1933 and June 6, 1934	Securities Act and Securities and Exchange Act	These two acts provided for the regulation of securities exchanges and brokers and dealers in securities to prevent manipulative and unfair practices in the securities markets. Established the Securities and Exchange Commission.
June 13, 1933	Home Owners' Loan Act	Created federal savings and loan associations. Also created the Home Owners' Loan Corporation to purchase delinquent home mortgages from financial institutions and refinance the mortgages over longer terms and at lower interest rates.
June 16, 1933	Banking Act of 1933 (and Glass-Steagall Act)	Created the Federal Deposit Insurance Corporation (FDIC), prohibited the payment of interest on demand deposits, established Regulation Q, and forced a separation between banking and the securities business.
June 26, 1934	Federal Credit Union Act	Authorized federal credit unions in all states. Maximum maturity of loans was initially two years.
June 27, 1934	National Housing Act	Created the Federal Savings and Loan Insurance Corporation. It also authorized the FSLIC to regulate savings and loan holding companies.

August 23, 1935	Banking Act of 1935	Amended the Banking Act of 1933 and the Federal Reserve Act to restructure the Federal Open Market Committee and the Federal Reserve Board. Also permitted national banks to make 5-year real estate loans.
May 9, 1956	Bank Holding Company Act (and Douglas amendment)	Prohibited interstate ownership of banks by companies owning more than one bank unless the law of the state of the bank to be acquired authorized it, and restricted the range of permissible nonbanking activities to those approved by the Federal Reserve Board. The act permitted the Federal Reserve Board to allow a bank holding company to engage directly in, or acquire shares of any company, the activities of which are found to be so "closely related to banking as to be a proper incident thereto," and which, if engaged in by a bank holding company, will result in a net public benefit.
September 23, 1959	Spence Act	The original holding company legislation for savings and loan associations. It provided for regulation of savings and loan holding companies by the FSLIC. Prohibited savings and loan holding companies from acquiring additional S&Ls, but did not prohibit the acquisition of a single S&L by a company that owned no other S&Ls.
October 23, 1962	Bank Service Corporation Act	Authorized banks to invest in service corporations to provide clerical and related financial services to investing banks.
September 2, 1964	Savings and Loan Service Corporation Act	Authorized federal savings and loan associations to acquire and operate service corporations to engage (up to 1 percent of their assets) in businesses not otherwise considered per-

155

Date of Enactment	Legislation	Key Provisions
		missable for a savings and loan institution to engage in directly, including stock brokerage, insurance brokerage, and agency activities.
July 23, 1965	Coinage Act	Declared that all coins and currencies of the U.S., including Federal Reserve notes are legal tender.
October 16, 1966	Financial Institutions Supervisory Act	Granted authority to the Comptroller of the Currency, Federal Reserve Board, FDIC, and the FSLIC to issue cease-and-desist and suspension and removal orders that are effective immediately.
September 21, 1966	Interest Rate Control Act	Extended deposit rate ceilings to the thrift institutions.
February 14, 1968	Savings and Loan Holding Company Act	Defined savings and loan holding company as being any company that directly or indirectly controls an insured institution (FSLIC–insured savings and loan or FDIC–insured federal savings bank) or other savings and loan holding company. Prohibited a multiple savings and loan holding company controlling insured institutions in more than one state (but later, under the Garn–St Germain Act of 1982, temporary authority was granted to the FSLIC to approve emergency acquisitions of insured institutions, including interstate and interindustry acquisition). Permitted unitary savings and loan holding companies (that meet the IRS thriftness test—60 percent of the assets must be obligations of the United States or states, residential real estate loans, or urban-renewal loans—included as part of the Garn–St Germain Act of 1982) to engage, through non–FSLIC-insured subsidiaries, in any

156

activity, even those unrelated to the savings and loan business (for example, Sears, Roebuck and Company). Multiple savings and loan holding companies were allowed to engage only in those activities approved by the FSLIC.

Date	Act	Description
July 24, 1970	Emergency Home Finance Act	Established the Federal Home Loan Mortgage Corporation to strengthen the secondary market for conventional mortgages, as well as for federally insured or guaranteed mortgages, through the purchase of residential mortgages from federally insured institutions.
October 19, 1970	Federal Credit Union Act	Established the National Credit Union Administration to charter federal credit unions and to provide federal insurance of credit union member accounts.
December 31, 1970	One-Bank Holding Company Act	Subjected one-bank holding companies to the same regulations as multiple-bank holding companies and restricted the definition of "bank" to institutions that accept demand deposits and make commercial loans.
November 10, 1978	Financial Institutions Regulatory and Interest Rate Control Act	Provided for FHLBB chartering of federal savings banks by permitting existing state-chartered mutual savings banks to convert to federal charters.
September 17, 1978	International Banking Act	Subjected foreign banks and foreign holding companies with branches or agencies in the United States to portions of the Bank Holding Company Acts of 1956 and 1970 to place them on an equal footing with U.S. institutions.
March 31, 1980	Depository Institutions	Authorized NOW accounts for individuals and not-for-profit

Date of Enactment	Legislation	Key Provisions
	Deregulation and Monetary Control Act	organizations at all federally insured depository institutions as of December 31, 1980; phased out Regulation Q over a 6-year period ending on March 31, 1986. Imposed mandatory reserve requirements set by the Federal Reserve Board on all depository institutions and permitted these institutions to utilize Federal Reserve services, including discount and borrowing privileges. Increased federal insurance of accounts from $40,000 to $100,000. Permanently authorized automatic transfer services and remote-service units. Preempted state usury ceilings. Authorized federal savings and loan associations to issue credit cards, to act as trustees, to operate trust departments, to make loans on the basis of commercial real estate, to invest up to 20 percent of their assets in a combination of consumer loans, commercial paper, and corporate debt securities, and to invest up to 3 percent of their assets in service corporations.
October 15, 1982	Garn–St Germain Depository Institutions Act	Expanded the authority of the FDIC and the FSLIC to provide direct aid to, and facilitate mergers of, insured depository institutions. Also, for the first time, permitted interstate and interindustry acquisitions of troubled financial institutions. More specifically, authorized the FDIC and FSLIC to increase or maintain capital of insured banks and savings and loan associations eligible for assistance through the purchase of capital instruments known as net worth certificates. Authorized commercial banks and thrifts to offer money market deposit accounts, and preempted state restrictions on the

enforcement by lenders of due-on-sale clauses. Authorized the FHLBB to charter and regulate federal savings and loan associations and federal savings banks, and granted them essentially similar powers (the savings banks could be organized in either stock or mutual form). Permitted federal associations to make commercial, corporate, business, or agricultural loans, which, after January 1984, could comprise up to 10 percent of an association's assets; to invest as much as 30 percent of assets (up from 20 percent) in consumer loans; to offer individual or corporate demand deposit accounts (although corporate checking accounts would be opened only by companies having other business with the association); to increase from 20 to 40 percent the investment of assets in loans secured by nonresidential real estate; to invest up to 10 percent of assets in personal property for rent or sale (thereby gaining access to the leasing business); to make educational loans for any educational purpose (rather than just for college or vocational training); to invest up to 100 percent of assets in state or local government obligations; and, for the first time, to invest in other savings and loan associations' time and savings deposits, and use such investments to help meet liquidity requirements. Abolished on all accounts on January 1, 1984, the slightly higher interest rate that savings and loan associations could pay relative to commercial banks.

Appendix 2: Net Worth or Capital Requirement for Savings and Loan Associations: February 1987

CAPITAL REQUIREMENT = LIABILITY COMPONENT + CONTINGENCY COMPONENT – MATURITY MATCHING CREDIT

I. Liability Component = base liabilities amount + increased liabilities amount

- Base liabilities amount = base liabilities × liability factor
  - Base liabilities: The lesser of total liabilities on January 1, 1987 (adjusted for branch purchases and sales) or total liabilities at the end of the quarter for which regulatory capital is being computed.
  - Liability factor: Initially equal to the sum of an institution's base factor, growth factor, and amortization factor (as defined by the capital regulation in effect prior to January 1, 1987), divided by total liabilities. This percentage rate increases (until 6% is reached) each July and January by a fraction of the industry's average ROA for the preceding year.[1]
- Increased liabilities amount = (total liabilities − base liabilities) × 6%.

II. Contingency Component =   2% of recourse liabilities
                                +2% of standby letters of credit
                                +20% of scheduled items
                                +Capital required for variable reserve elements

- Variable reserve elements are direct investments, land loans, and nonresidential construction loans.[2]
- Incremental capital required on variable reserve elements depends on an institution's level of capital and its portfolio concentration in the variable reserve element.
- Define three groups of institutions
  - Group A: institutions not meeting their capital requirement net of variable reserve elements
  - Group B: institutions meeting their capital requirement net of variable reserve elements but whose capital is less than 6% of liabilities[3]

- Group C: institutions whose capital is greater than 6% of liabilities[3]

% of Portfolio in Contingent Category	Incremental Capital on Direct Investments			Incremental Capital on Land Loans			Incremental Capital on Nonresidential Construction Loans		
	Group A	Group B	Group C	Group A	Group B	Group C	Group A	Group B	Group C
Less than 10%	10%	5%	0%	4%	2%	0%	4%	2%	0%
Between 10% and 20%	10%	10%	5%	4%	4%	2%	4%	4%	2%
Greater than 20%	10%	10%	10%	4%	4%	4%	4%	4%	4%

III. Maturity Matching Credit

- Based on an institution's 1-year and 3-year cumulative hedged gap from 6 months prior.
- Credit equals 1% of liabilities for each gap less than 15% in absolute value.
- Credit equals $[.02005 - (.067 \times [\text{the absolute value of the gap}])] \times$ total liabilities for each gap between 15% and 25%.
- Credit equals 0 for each gap above 25% in absolute value.

[1] The regulation ties the rate of increase in the liability factor to an institution's initial liability factor. The liability factor for institutions with an initial liability factor of less than 3 percent—the lower group—increases annually by 90% of the greater of the industry's ROA or the institutions own ROA. The liability factor for institutions with an initial liability factor of 3%—the standard group—increases annually by 75% of the preceding year's ROA. The liability factor for institutions with an initial liability factor above 3%—the higher group—remains constant until the standard group catches up. It then increases along with the standard group.

[2] Specific direct investments, land loans, or nonresidential construction loans made prior to 1986 and not subject to incremental capital requirements under the former regulation are not subject to incremental capital requirements under the new regulation. These assets do count towards portfolio concentration levels.

[3] The actual criterion is 6% of liabilities or the fully phased-in capital requirement net of variable reserve elements, whichever is greater.

SOURCE: Compiled by Donald J. Bisenius of the Federal Home Loan Bank Board.

PART II

A REGULATORY SYSTEM IN NEED OF REPAIR

7

DEPOSIT INSURANCE IN THEORY AND PRACTICE

Gerald P. O'Driscoll, Jr.

My purpose in this paper is to analyze how market incentives could substitute for government regulation of banks in controlling risk. The present system for insuring bank deposits is unique in conjoining insurance with a highly detailed system of government regulation. In what follows, I briefly describe and explain the current system.[1] Then I present the rationale for reforming the system by making a transition to private insurance of deposits. Finally, I suggest that privatizing deposit insurance might be only one part of a more general reform of the existing banking system.

The Risks Defined

Two risks need to be distinguished. First, an individual bank may fail and be incapable of paying off its depositors in full. This is a case of failure to fulfill a contract and by itself does not involve any serious third-party effects. Second, the failure of one bank may lead to failures of other banks. The mechanism for this domino effect may be either direct or indirect. It is direct if, for example, the failed bank served as a correspondent bank for other banks, and their losses lead to their insolvency. The mechanism is indirect if the first bank's failure causes fearful depositors to withdraw their funds from other

The author is an assistant vice president and a senior economist and policy adviser at the Federal Reserve Bank of Dallas. This version was revised in May 1987. The views expressed herein are the author's alone and should not be construed as representing the official position of any part of the Federal Reserve System. The comments of Eugenie D. Short, Robert T. Clair, Catherine England, and Eugene Nelson White are gratefully acknowledged, as are helpful comments from participants in a workshop of the School of Business at the University of Alabama.

[1]There are separate federal insurance agencies for, respectively, commercial banks and mutual savings banks, savings and loan associations, and credit unions. In this paper, I concentrate on the case of commercial banks and the FDIC. The principles and issues involved are the same for all depository institutions. An excellent analysis of thrift problems is contained in Kane (1985). Clair (1984) examines just the case of credit unions.

solvent but illiquid institutions. This "contagion" effect involves a classic banking panic, in which widespread depositor runs on banks occur. In this case, the payments mechanism itself is threatened. If a contagion effect exists, it would be a prime example of the possible third-party effects of a bank failure. In the economist's parlance, the third-party effects are externalities.

In examining whether there are externalities in bank failures, one must distinguish between the two types of risk associated with a failing bank. As I suggest below, policies designed to deal with one type of risk are not necessarily efficacious in controlling the other type. And, more important, the feasibility of a system of private deposit insurance very much depends upon which type of risk insurers would be facing.

Why Deposit Insurance?

The post–World War I period was characterized by a large number of bank suspensions. Between 1921 and 1928 (inclusive), suspensions averaged 552 per year (Friedman and Schwartz 1963, pp. 438–39). Approximately one-sixth of all banks failed during this period of general prosperity and price stability. Three features of suspended banks stand out. First, they tended to be small unit banks. Second, failures were concentrated in agricultural states, a fact reflecting the distress experienced by the agricultural sector throughout this period. Finally, agricultural states with unit banking were also likely to have enacted state deposit insurance systems.[2] I will reconsider this pattern of bank failures at the end of this paper.

Even in comparison to the extraordinary number of bank failures during the previous decade, the early years of the Great Depression saw a marked increase in failures. Between 1929 and 1933, 9,755 suspensions occurred; this was over one-third of the banks then in existence. Suspensions were more widespread and involved larger institutions than in the previous period. It was against this background that the existing system of federal regulation and deposit insurance was implemented.

The primary legislative purpose in creating the Federal Deposit Insurance Corporation (FDIC) was the avoidance of bank runs and the protection of the payments mechanism (Golembe 1960). The tide of bank closings and the concomitant contraction of the money supply together threatened the payments mechanism itself. If analyzed in

[2]In this century, state deposit insurance systems were enacted in Oklahoma, Kansas, Nebraska, South Dakota, Texas, Mississippi, North Dakota, and Washington. See White (1983, pp. 191–204).

terms of its subsequent history and policies, the FDIC makes much more sense as an agency established to control third-party risks of bank failures than as a protector of small depositors unable to bear losses incurred in the event of an individual bank failure (Kareken 1983, pp. 199–200). In fact, the FDIC has been so successful in pursuit of its goal that until recently it had virtually eliminated bank failures.[3]

The FDIC was created by the Banking Act of 1933 ("Glass-Steagall Act"), whose stated purpose was "to provide for the safer and more effective use of assets of banks, to regulate interbank control, to prevent the undue diversion of funds into speculative operations, and for other purposes." Among other things, the act prevented banks from being affiliated with any firm engaged in the securities business; established limits on loans made by banks to affiliates, including holding company affiliates; prohibited the payment of interest on demand accounts; and empowered the Federal Reserve Board to regulate interest rates paid on savings and time deposits. These regulations were intended to provide for the safety and soundness of the banking system.

It is no accident that federal deposit insurance and the modern federal regulatory system were created by the same act. The incentives established by the insurance system necessitated the regulatory framework. Specifically, from its inception, the FDIC has charged a flat-rate premium for insurance. The statutory rate is one-twelfth of 1 percent—approximately .0833 percent—of domestic deposits (not just insured deposits). Thus, larger banks pay larger premiums, but riskier institutions of a given size pay no more than conservatively managed ones. This premium system confounds sound insurance practices. Since institutions can increase their expected return by selecting a riskier portfolio, they have an incentive to do so. The FDIC's pricing of deposit insurance creates a subsidy to risk taking, a subsidy that can only be captured insofar as banks actually make their asset portfolio riskier.[4]

The incentive for risk taking constitutes a classic moral-hazard problem for the FDIC. Moral hazard occurs when the provision of insurance itself diminishes the incentives facing the insured to avoid

---

[3]"From 1921 through 1933, every year requires at least three digits to record the number of banks that suspended; from 1934 on, two digits suffice, and from 1943 through 1960, one digit, for both insured and uninsured banks" (Friedman and Schwartz 1963, p. 437).

[4]This point is well recognized in the literature. Benston (1983) contains an excellent bibliography. More recent papers include Kareken (1983); Short and O'Driscoll (1983a and 1983b); Flannery and Protopapadakis (1984); and Baer (1985).

risk, thereby increasing the occurrence of the risk insured against. Therefore, at the same time it implemented the present deposit insurance system, Congress enacted a system of binding regulations on banks. If banks wanted federal insurance, then they had to adhere to the new rules. National banks and state members of the Federal Reserve System were required to join the FDIC, and virtually all commercial banks now belong to the FDIC.

On its own terms, the system worked reasonably well for 30 or 40 years. It began unraveling, however, as competitive forces asserted themselves in financial markets. Inflation, which accelerated and became more volatile in the mid-1960s, appears to have been a catalyst in the process. Consequently, banks and other depository institutions experienced more funding pressure as regulatory ceilings on interest rates payable on deposits became binding. Depository institutions experienced outflows in a process known as disintermediation (O'Driscoll 1985, p. 3).

The emergence of money-market mutual funds and cash management accounts at brokerage firms fueled the competitive fire. From the perspective of depository institutions, the major impact of these new financial products was to alter the structure of their balance sheets. A large percentage of money-market funds' assets is held in certificates of deposit at commercial banks and other depository institutions. Funds withdrawn from depository institutions and placed in money-market funds wound up back in the banking system. In the process, however, deposits paying high money-market rates were substituted for low-yielding, regulated deposits, such as passbook savings accounts. Economic rents previously earned on regulated deposits were thereby competed away.[5]

As banks' funding costs came to reflect more fully the fluctuations in money-market interest rates, it became imperative that their assets also yield competitive returns. Banks responded to these pressures by, among other things, shortening the maturities of their assets and setting floating rates on a higher proportion of their loans (Merris and Wood 1985, pp. 74–75). The alarming increase in the failure rate among banks suggests that in their search for higher yields, banks may have also taken on more risk (Short 1987).

I have been describing the process by which the de facto deregulation of interest rates paid on deposits occurred. In 1980, Congress ushered in the beginning of de jure deregulation with the Depository

---

[5]The process probably also changed the distribution of assets among depository institutions, since money-market funds tend to purchase certificates of deposit only from larger depository institutions. Thrifts, in particular, probably suffered on net.

Institutions Deregulation and Monetary Control Act. This act created the Depository Institutions Deregulation Committee, whose purpose was to phase out controls on the interest rates that banks could pay on most accounts. In 1982, Congress passed the Garn–St Germain Depository Institutions Act, which accelerated the pace of deposit interest rate deregulation. That act also addressed the problem of insuring bank deposits in a deregulated environment. It mandated that each of the three federal agencies insuring depository institutions examine its insurance system and report to Congress on the feasibility of risk-based insurance. This requirement was the source of renewed interest in and research on deposit insurance.

Pricing Deposit Insurance

Risk-Based Premiums

The FDIC is well aware of the defects of its pricing system. As put in its report to Congress on the deposit insurance system: "Comprehensive government insurance of liabilities is inconsistent with deregulation of the institutions responsible for those liabilities; it is unlikely that government can allow deregulation to proceed much further without addressing the insurance connection."[6]

By referring to the "comprehensive" nature of federal deposit insurance, the FDIC focused attention on one of the most significant aspects of its settlement policy for depositors of most failed banks. For the past 30 years, the majority of bank failures and nearly all large bank failures have been settled by a purchase and assumption (P&A) transaction.[7] In a P&A transaction, the FDIC replaces the bad assets of a failed bank with cash. Another bank then purchases the remaining assets and assumes all the nonsubordinated liabilities of the failed bank. All depositors are thus made whole. The transaction typically occurs overnight, resulting in no disruption to depositors. The only change that they observe is in the name of the bank with which they are dealing.

Several justifications are offered for using P&A transactions, but the FDIC itself has identified the most important reason: "The P&A enables the FDIC to implement its monetary stability objective in a way that might be impossible if the FDIC had only the option of paying insured depositors directly."[8] Indeed, if protection of small

---

[6]In *Deposit Insurance in a Changing Environment* (Washington, D.C.: Federal Deposit Insurance Corporation, 1983), p. xiii.

[7]*Deposit Insurance in a Changing Environment*, p. x.

[8]*Deposit Insurance in a Changing Environment*, p. xi.

depositors were the main goal of the deposit insurance system, a payoff to them (and permanent closure of the failed bank) would be an equally sound policy.[9] Paying off insured depositors, however, raises the possibility of flight by large depositors from troubled banks in the future. In a payoff, uninsured depositors receive a pro rata payment and a contingent claim on any residual asset value of the failed bank. Large depositors, fearful of incurring at least a partial loss, would be inclined to flee troubled institutions in such an environment. It is believed that such behavior could result in additional bank failures through a contagion effect.

With the virtual collapse of Continental Illinois National Bank, the FDIC added a new wrinkle to the deposit insurance story. In that case, it made an explicit ex ante guarantee not only to all depositors but to all creditors (including those of the holding company). By making explicit (and extending) the blanket guarantee implied by federal deposit insurance, the FDIC starkly revealed the perverse incentives established by the current system. The rational depositor should now be indifferent to the quality of the assets held by any large bank likely to be settled by a P&A transaction.[10]

Recognizing the problems with the current system, the FDIC proposed instituting a three-tier system of risked-based deposit insurance premiums for normal, risky, and very risky banks. Short and O'Driscoll (1983b) examined that proposal. More recently, Flannery and Protopapadakis also offered a useful critique of the FDIC's proposal, in which they presented a public choice analysis of an agency's attempt to assess and price risk (Flannery and Protopapadakis 1985, p. 8):

> Public institutions' decisions are subject to public scrutiny. Such scrutiny can involve lengthy debates, appeal procedures, and compromises between economic efficiency and political needs. Even the most well-meaning and efficient public institutions move with glacial speed compared to the rapid assessment of information and the continuous reassessment of risk that takes place in the financial markets.

[9]Of course, the current $100,000 limit on deposit insurance negates any argument that deposit insurance exists to protect the small depositor.

[10]In the 1982 failure of Penn Square Bank, which had $470 million of deposits, the FDIC did not use a P&A transaction but paid off insured depositors. For a time it was believed that this case signaled a change in policy for handling large bank failures. Continental surely negated any such change and further constrained the FDIC. Further, the agency recognized the inequality of settling the failures of large and small banks differently. (See *Deposit Insurance in a Changing Environment,* chap. 1, p. 1.) Nonetheless, the FDIC has continued to settle some small bank failures through modified payouts to depositors.

As telling as their public choice argument is, Flannery and Proto-papadakis introduce another, even more compelling issue: different insurers will typically assess risks differently (Flannery and Proto-papadakis 1985, pp. 7–8). This argument goes to the most basic function of a competitive price system.

Complete information, including information on risk, is not something that individuals bring with them to markets. The market process itself is a source of needed information, information generated through a trial-and-error process. For example, some insurers will demand a relatively high premium for insuring a given risk, while others will charge a relatively low premium. Some insurers will avoid insuring a particular type of risk, while others will specialize in underwriting policies to cover that very risk.[11] This trial-and-error process, comprising innovation and imitation, yields information on the expected losses from insuring a particular risk. Given a good deal of other information (including that on its other risks), the individual insurer has a basis for setting premiums.

The information-gathering function of competitive markets is a continual and unending process. There is no once-and-for-all answer to the question, "What premium should be assessed?" New data constantly render previous calculations obsolete. Further, the process of adapting to these changes by each firm alters the underwriting environment for all others.[12]

Under its proposal, the FDIC would remain a monopoly provider of insurance. As such, it would lack the information generated by competitive markets. Accordingly, it would face an insoluble calculation problem in setting risk-based insurance premiums (O'Driscoll and Rizzo 1985, pp. 138–42). It may be that a system of competitively provided insurance is impolitic at this time, but a rational system of risk-based insurance premiums offered monopolistically by a public agency is simply impossible.

Competitive Deposit Insurance

Short and O'Driscoll (1983b, p. 17) presented a four-point transition proposal for moving to a system of competitively supplied deposit insurance. The plan envisioned a period in which the FDIC would be the chief if not exclusive provider of the basic or underlying policy covering deposits, and private firms would enter as suppliers of excess policies. The recommendations were as follows:

[11]See Short and O'Driscoll (1983a); compare Short and O'Driscoll (1983b, p. 17) and Flannery and Protopapadakis (1985, p. 7).
[12]See O'Driscoll and Rizzo (1985, pp. 73–74 and 99–109, especially pp. 101–02).

First, eliminate *de facto* coverage of deposits above statutory limits; reduce coverage limits; introduce some form of coinsurance. Second, eliminate the statutory requirement that national and state-chartered member banks, as well as banks in bank holding companies, purchase deposit insurance from the FDIC. Third, require the FDIC to utilize the best available information to determine risk categories; require that these risk classifications be used to set premiums that minimize cross-subsidization among risk categories. Fourth, require the FDIC to cover costs plus earn a reasonable return on capital.

The purpose of the proposal was to provide a framework within which private insurers could successfully operate. The first recommendation would provide private insurers an opportunity to enter the market initially by offering excess insurance to banks (or directly to depositors). In this case, risk would be priced at the margin. Some market discipline would thus be introduced into the market for deposits.

The purpose of the third and fourth points was to compel the FDIC to set up risk-based premiums on the basic or underlying insurance policy issued to banks. Further consideration of the economic calculation issue makes me less sanguine than I was two years ago about the feasibility of the FDIC's properly pricing the risk associated with even a limited insurance policy. The first and second points go to the heart of the pricing problem, however. If there is to be any market discipline in the market for banks' depository liabilities, the 100percent coverage of all deposits provided by P&A transactions must be eliminated. Even were this done, however, the present $100,000 statutory limit would be too high, especially if there is to be a market for excess insurance. Large depositors need only purchase $100,000 CDs from multiple institutions in order to have insured deposits of $1 million or more. The latter strategy is prevalent already among depositors in multi-bank holding companies.

This insight highlights the necessity of a deductible of some magnitude. Brokerage firms have developed a market for CDs in lots of $1,000. Simply lowering the limits would not address the problem, therefore.[13] Requiring depositors to coinsure, as is done for most medical policies, would add to market discipline.

The second point, urging elimination of the statutory requirement to purchase FDIC insurance, specifically addresses the issue of com-

---

[13]The FDIC promulgated a rule that would effectively end the practice of brokering retail deposits. Each brokerage house would only be insured for the first $100,000 of deposits, thus treating the broker and not the customer as the beneficial owner of the deposits. At this point, the FDIC has been unable to implement the rule because of successful court challenges.

petition, which, as I argue above, is absolutely necessary for rational pricing of deposit insurance. Eventually, it must at least be possible for competitors of the FDIC to underwrite basic policies for banks or individuals.

In terms of the feasibility of this proposal, I would emphasize three points. First, the plan envisages firms entering, as it were, on the fringe of the market and at low capital costs. Specifically, it provides the opportunity for private insurance companies to write excess policies for depositors. For example, even the present reserves of existing property and casualty companies would permit their writing *some* financial insurance. Over time, if the business were profitable, additional capital and new firms would be attracted to the industry. Second, the proposal does not envision that private insurers would ever be providing the present level of coverage. Reduction in the size of total coverage would presumably be an effect of reducing the limits. Third, and most important, private insurers would not be effectively insuring the payments mechanism or the money supply itself. In other words, the function of deposit insurance itself would change with its provision. *The risk against which protection would be offered would be different: limited protection of depositors, not of the payments mechanism.* This final point is key to the feasibility of introducing some competition into deposit insurance. It also raises more general issues for our banking system. If the payments mechanism is no longer being protected by deposit insurance, then something else must be substituted in its stead.

Further Considerations

Until now, I have focused only on reforming deposit insurance. The stringent regulatory system established by the Banking Act of 1933 makes sense, however, only as an offset to the incentives for incurring risk set up by deposit insurance. The effects of the regulatory system are to lessen competition between different types of financial institutions and to inhibit financial innovation. In addition, the act's limitations on banks' permissible activities have inhibited banks' diversification. This, in turn, has arguably lessened the stability of the banking system. The Banking Act of 1933 artificially froze lines of commerce, delimiting the activities in which it is legally permissible for commercial banks, investment banks, brokerage houses, and other financial firms to engage.

At the time the act was enacted, the distinction between, say, commercial banks and investment banks may have reflected commercial practice, but the distinction was already in the process of

173

breaking down.[14] Indeed, in examining banking and financial history, one is struck by how quickly the traditional business of financial institutions changes with changing market conditions. The business of a typical commercial or investment bank can, perhaps, be defined at a given time, but historically such a definition would not be valid for even a generation.[15]

At the time of Glass-Steagall's passage, branching by banks was either prohibited or severely constrained in most states. The McFadden Act firmly established that national banks had to conform to the policy of the states in which they operated. As a consequence, the United States had a system of thousands of small banks, undiversified with respect to either their deposit base or their loan portfolio. Branching restrictions exposed banks to the effects of downturns in the local economy. This problem particularly afflicted unit banks in rural areas and small towns. Agriculture is notoriously subject to economic cycles. At the very time that farmers would be under stress and payments on agricultural loans in arrears, agricultural banks would also tend to be suffering deposit outflows. Without branches, these banks had no other good local loan opportunities or sources of deposits.

Over the years, the system of interbank deposits had evolved in a way that, to some extent, substituted for a system of geographically diversified banks. By maintaining correspondent balances in money center banks, smaller banks indirectly gained access to other loan markets. Money center banks competed vigorously for funds by offering competitive rates on interbank deposits. In turn, a correspondent relationship provided small banks with access to funds to tide them over bad times or merely to meet seasonal variation in loan demand (White 1983, pp. 65–74).

By its prohibition of interest payments on interbank deposits, the Banking Act of 1933 crippled the interbank system.[16] The act's framers feared that a competitive market for interbank funds would "siphon off" funds in rural areas and small towns to urban financial centers. Of course, this might occur in times of poor loan opportunities resulting from a local downturn. This process is an aspect of the diversification provided by a competitive market for interbank funds. In times of financial crisis, however, money center banks actually increased

[14]White (1986) argues that commercial banks were attracted to the securities business because of economies of scope in the production of financial services.

[15]For a fascinating account of the evolution of British merchant banks that illustrates this point, see Chapman (1984).

[16]Only the development of the federal funds market restored some financial integration to our fragmented banking system.

their loans to their rural and small-town counterparts.[17] The federal guaranty of deposits was designed to provide financial stability without either competition or diversification. Fifty years of experience have clarified the flaws in this design.

There is thus a double symmetry in the banking act. On the one hand, the regulations offset the undesirable incentive effects of deposit insurance. On the other hand, deposit insurance offsets the destabilizing effects of the regulations. A combination of market forces and liability deregulation has undone the delicate balance. Like Humpty Dumpty, it is doubtful that we can put the pieces of the regulatory mosaic back together.

The value of financial diversification should not be underestimated. One need only compare the performance of the Canadian and U.S. banking systems in this century. Between 1920 and 1929, there were 6,008 suspensions and 3,963 absorptions and mergers in the United States. In the same period, only one bank failed in Canada. Contraction also occurred in Canada, but it did so by a 13.2 percent reduction in the number of bank *offices*. Similarly, there were no Canadian bank failures in the Great Depression. The number of Canadian bank offices declined by 10.4 percent, while 34.5 percent of all U.S. bank offices closed.[18]

The Canadian banking experience in the 1929–33 period is even more remarkable given that Canada and the United States experienced similar monetary shocks. Until Great Britain went off the gold standard in September 1931, Canada maintained a fixed exchange rate between its currency and the U.S. dollar. Since the Canadian dollar depreciated less than sterling after September 1931, Canada's national income and money supply were forced to contract in order to maintain external equilibrium at the new fixed exchange rate between the U.S. and Canadian dollars. Friedman and Schwartz (1963, p. 35) found that[19]

---

[17]"Critics charged that New York banks protected themselves in times of crisis and shortchanged their correspondents. The opposite was, in fact, true, and central reserve-city banks' loans rose in these periods, providing assistance to the interior banks. Interest rates on these loans did rise, but that was what any sound institution, commercial bank or central bank, would do" (White 1983, pp. 73–74).

[18]Compare Friedman and Schwartz (1963, pp. 352 and 457–58) and White (1984, pp. 131–32).

[19]Friedman and Schwartz present the following comparison. In the 1929–33 period, the U.S. money stock fell 33 percent while the Canadian money supply declined 13 percent. The decline in net national products for the two countries was nearly the same (53 percent versus 49 percent). The different behavior of velocity in the two countries explains the results. Velocity declined 29 percent in the U.S. but 41 percent in Canada.

though the required fall in both prices and income was sharp, the depreciation of the Canadian exchange rate permitted the percentage fall to be somewhat smaller than that in the United States. The stock of money fell sharply also, but by a much smaller percentage than in the United States. Even the smaller fall was, however, nearly one and a half times as large as the fall in any contraction in U.S. history since the Civil War except only the 1929–33 contraction. So it can hardly be regarded as minor.

The recent failures in 1985 of two small Canadian banks (Canadian Commercial Bank and Northland Bank) reinforce rather than rebut my thesis. Both failed banks were more like the typical U.S. rather than the typical Canadian bank. Neither of the two failed banks was widely branched, and they were specialized energy banks. The failures caused financial troubles for six of the remaining seven smaller Canadian banks, which had been experiencing deposit outflows in the absence of any obvious loan problems. There appears to have been a contagion effect from the failures. In other words, there were potential externalities to these two bank failures.

It is noteworthy, however, to see how the Canadian banking system dealt with the problem. The five major Canadian banks plus the next largest institution—not the Bank of Canada—provided loans to the troubled banks. Two of the affected institutions merged: Continental Bank with Lloyd's Bank and Mercantile Bank with the National Bank of Canada. The third-party effects of the bank failures were internalized by the remaining banks. Recognizing that all would suffer from the spread of the contagion effect, the stronger institutions were prepared to lend on the value of the sound assets of the weaker institutions. This is what economic theory would predict, of course. And this is the way our own clearinghouse system operated in the past to internalize the externalities of bank failures (Gorton 1984).

It would require a separate paper to deal with contagion effects more generally. A new literature is emerging, however, that disputes the conventional wisdom.[20] The new literature questions the existence of a contagion effect in the sense that one bank failure leads to the failure of other, sound institutions. The latter may experience brief runs, which is the justification for holding liquid reserves, but absent catastrophic macroeconomic policies, such as occurred in the 1930s, runs should not translate into failures of sound institutions.

---

[20]For example, see Benston (1986) and Rolnick and Weber (1982, 1985). For a succinct statement of the traditional view, see Gilbert and Wood (1986). Their paper clearly distinguishes between the problems of runs and of failures. Finally, see Kaufman (1987).

Even with bad macroeconomic policy, the Canadian experience demonstrates the vitality of a sound, diversified banking system.

I am certainly not suggesting that in the absence of branching restrictions, the U.S. banking system would be composed of as few as a dozen or so banking institutions. There are good reasons to believe that in a competitive system, banking institutions would number in the thousands. First, the U.S. population is 10 times that of Canada, suggesting room for more competitors. Second, the Canadian system is the product of a public policy that, until the 1970s, actively discouraged the entry of new independent commercial banks. California's banking system is probably a better source for an order-of-magnitude estimate of how many banks would exist nationwide if branching were unrestricted. California, the most populous state, has a long history of statewide branching and liberal chartering practices. In mid-1985, there were 470 insured banks in the state. If we extrapolate from this number (assuming the same ratio of banks to population nationwide as exists in California), there would be over 4,000 independent banking institutions nationwide. It is fair to conclude that if competition had reigned in North American banking, Canada would have had many more independent banks and the United States far fewer.

In any case, geographical deregulation is now proceeding rapidly in the United States. We will probably detour through a system of regional banks on the way to one of nationally branched commercial banks. In the end, however, we will have arrived at the very system that Glass-Steagall sought to prevent: a system of financially integrated, diversified national banks whose pricing of deposits and loans reflects market interest rates.

As the Canadian experience in the 1930s illustrates, a nationally branched banking system with diversified assets can withstand even severe shocks, both real and monetary. In other words, diversification by itself can help solve the stability problem that deposit insurance was intended to address. In the last few years, banks' liabilities have been substantially deregulated. Geographical deregulation is proceeding rapidly and could be completed by decade's end.

There has basically been no deregulation of banks' assets, however, and the Banking Act of 1933 remains an effective obstacle to asset deregulation.[21] This obstacle remains, yet the delicately balanced system of regulations joined with financial safety nets has been radically, if not permanently, changed. If the banking system itself

---

[21]I am using "assets" broadly, referring not only to the marketable financial assets in a bank's portfolio but also to the lines of commerce in which a bank may engage.

were to attain a self-reinforcing stability, this would take the pressure off the federal deposit insurance system as guarantor of the payments mechanism. In the presence of a more stable banking system, if deposit insurance were offered competitively, it would likely be no more widespread than portfolio insurance or insurance of municipal bond issues. As with other financial insurance, deposit insurance would be an option usually rejected. Most investors do not wish to sacrifice the necessary yield to immunize themselves from loss, and instead rely on diversification and sophisticated financial instruments (such as options and futures contracts) to protect themselves.

Competitive deposit insurance might take the form of performance bonds issued to depositors who place an extraordinary premium on safety. In such a system, however, insurance would truly protect individual depositors, not the payments mechanism itself. Similarly, the deposit insurance system would no longer be a destabilizing force whose incentive structure would need to be offset by a system of rigid regulations. Only time will tell how far along to a stable, competitive banking system market-driven changes alone can take us.

References

Baer, Herbert. "Private Prices, Public Insurance: The Pricing of Federal Deposit Insurance." Federal Reserve Bank of Chicago *Economic Perspectives* (September/October 1985): 45–57.

Benston, George J. "Deposit Insurance and Bank Failures." Federal Reserve Bank of Atlanta *Economic Review* (March 1983): 4–17.

Benston, George J., et al. *Perspectives on Safe and Sound Banking: Past, Present and Future.* Cambridge, Mass.: MIT Press, 1986.

Chapman, Stanley. *The Rise of Merchant Banking.* London: George Allen & Unwin, 1984.

Clair, Robert T. "Deposit Insurance, Moral Hazard, and Credit Unions." Federal Reserve Bank of Dallas *Economic Review* (July 1984): 1–12.

Deposit Insurance in a Changing Environment. Washington, D.C.: Federal Deposit Insurance Corporation, 1983.

Flannery, Mark J., and Protopapadakis, Aris A. "Risk-Sensitive Deposit Insurance: The Pricing of Federal Deposit Insurance." Federal Reserve Bank of Philadelphia *Business Review* (September/October 1985): 45–57.

Friedman, Milton, and Schwartz, Anna J. *A Monetary History of the United States, 1867–1960.* Princeton, N.J.: Princeton University Press for the National Bureau of Economic Research, 1963.

Gilbert, R. Alton, and Wood, Geoffrey E. "Coping with Bank Failures: Some Lessons from the United States and United Kingdom." Federal Reserve Bank of St. Louis *Review* (December 1986): 5–14.

Golembe, Carter H. "The Deposit Insurance Legislation of 1933." *Political Science Quarterly* 76 (June 1960): 181–200.

Gorton, Gary. "Private Clearinghouses and the Origins of Central Banking." Federal Reserve Bank of Philadelphia *Business Review* (January/February 1984): 3–12.

Kane, Edward J. *The Gathering Crisis in Federal Deposit Insurance.* Cambridge, Mass.: MIT Press, 1985.

Kareken, John H. "The First Step in Bank Deregulation: What About the FDIC?" *American Economic Review* 73 (May 1983).

Kaufman, George G. "The Truth about Bank Runs." Chap. 2 of this book.

Merris, Randall C., and Wood, John. "A Deregulated Rerun: Banking in the Eighties." Federal Reserve Bank of Chicago *Economic Perspectives* (September/October 1985).

O'Driscoll, Gerald P., Jr. "Money in a Deregulated Financial System." Federal Reserve Bank of Dallas *Economic Review* (May 1985).

O'Driscoll, Gerald P., Jr., and Rizzo, Mario J. *The Economics of Time and Ignorance.* Oxford and New York: Basil Blackwell, 1985.

Rolnick, Arthur J., and Weber, Warren. "Free Banking, Wildcat Banking, and Shinplasters." Federal Reserve Bank of Minneapolis *Quarterly Review* (Fall 1982): 10–19.

Rolnick, Arthur J., and Weber, Warren. "Banking Instability and Regulation in the U.S. Free Banking Era." Federal Reserve Bank of Minneapolis *Quarterly Review* (Summer 1985): 2–9.

Short, Eugenie D. "Bank Problems and Financial Safety-Nets." Federal Reserve Bank of Dallas *Economic Review* (March 1987): 17–28.

Short, Eugenie D., and O'Driscoll, Gerald P., Jr. "Deposit Insurance and Financial Stability." *Business Forum* (Summer 1983a).

Short, Eugenie D., and O'Driscoll, Gerald P., Jr. "Deregulation and Deposit Insurance." Federal Reserve Bank of Dallas *Economic Review* (September 1983b).

White, Eugene Nelson. *The Regulation and Reform of the American Banking System, 1900–1929.* Princeton, N.J.: Princeton University Press, 1983.

White, Eugene Nelson. "A Reinterpretation of the Banking Crisis of 1930." *Journal of Economic History* 44 (March 1984).

White, Eugene Nelson. "Before the Glass-Steagall Act: An Analysis of the Investment Banking Activities of National Banks." *Explorations in Economic History* 23 (1986): 33–55.

Toward a Sound Financial System

William S. Haraf

Gerald O'Driscoll's purpose in his paper (1987) is to analyze how market incentives could substitute for regulation in controlling risk taking by depository firms. This is a useful purpose in that regulation is costly to both consumers and regulated firms. Moreover, it may not be possible to regulate risk exposures in any meaningful sense. Regulation, rather than restraining potentially risky activities, is more likely to shift such exposures into new and unpredictable channels. Particularly, in today's aggressive, trading-oriented banking environment, it seems unlikely that regulation can substitute for market discipline in controlling risk taking by banking firms.

Although there is a lot I agree with in this paper, I am also left with the feeling that it glosses over some thorny issues. In particular, I do not think that this paper, by itself, will convince skeptics that we can rely on market solutions for banking in lieu of banking regulation and the existing federal safety-net apparatus.

O'Driscoll begins by making three very important points that are worth emphasizing. First, banking law and regulation have inhibited diversification across activities and geographic markets and as a result have contributed to the riskiness of banking. Removing such obstacles to bank diversification would be very important in reducing the problem of bank failures. Second, it is unlikely that the deposit insurance agencies will ever be capable of implementing a truly effective risk-based premium structure. Third, failure resolution techniques that have extended the level of safety-net protection to large depositors, other creditors, and managers of banks, thrifts, and their holding companies have greatly exacerbated the moral-hazard problem from deposit insurance. There would be important benefits associated with eliminating this type of de facto coverage.

The author is the J. E. Lundy Scholar and the director of the Financial Market Project at the American Enterprise Institute.

Ultimately, O'Driscoll would like to see the federal government out of the deposit insurance business. He proposes a four-point program that would allow private insurers to enter the market gradually, primarily as suppliers of insurance coverage in excess of statutory maximums. Over time, governmentally provided deposit insurance would be phased out.

The central argument in O'Driscoll's paper is that a nationally branched banking system with diversified assets would "attain a self-reinforcing stability" that would take the pressure off the deposit insurance system "as a guarantor of the payments mechanism or the money supply itself." O'Driscoll claims that with such a system it would be feasible for deposit insurance to be supplied privately. The evidence he cites is the Canadian banking experience during the 1930s, when there were no bank failures. He concludes that such a system "can withstand the severest shocks, both real and monetary."

This is an important and surely controversial argument. Unfortunately, the evidence in the paper on this critical point is weak. O'Driscoll does not provide information about other factors that could have influenced comparative failure rates, such as capital levels of Canadian and U.S. banks or monetary policy. Between 1929 and 1933, the U.S. money stock was permitted to decline by one-third, while the Canadian money stock fell by 12 percent. Although part of this difference might plausibly be attributed to differences in banking structures in the two countries, it is also likely to have been related to differences in monetary regimes. A full analysis of the effects of bank structure on failure experience would systematically examine the experience of a number of countries operating under distinct monetary and regulatory regimes.

Early in his paper, O'Driscoll recognizes that the feasibility of a system of private deposit insurance depends on whether the banking system is subject to contagious runs. Although he does not make the argument explicitly, O'Driscoll must believe that the risk of contagious runs is manageable in an environment with a nationally branched and well-diversified banking system.

Some scholars have recently argued that the risk of contagious bank runs has been exaggerated, irrespective of further product and geographic market diversification. Studies of bank runs prior to the establishment of federal deposit insurance by George Benston and George Kaufman (1986), Phillip Cagan (1965), Anna Schwartz (1985), Michael Bordo (1985), and Arthur Rolnick and Warren Weber (1983) lead to several important conclusions. First, true contagious panics have been rare. There are many periods in U.S. and British history in which bank failure rates were high, but widespread panics did not occur. Second, the panics that did occur took place either in the absence of a lender-of-last-resort mechanism or as a result of a major failure of the central bank to act as lender of last resort. Third, these panics did not generally precipitate economic downturns, although they often accompanied them.

In reviewing this evidence, I conclude that a system in which depositors are subject to greater risk of loss than they are today is probably more vulnerable to disruptive episodes—episodes in which a bank failure triggers runs on other banks perceived to be marginal. The risk of contagious runs on the banking system as a whole is small, provided such episodes are handled properly by the authorities. This involves managing failures in such a way that the liquidity of depositor accounts is preserved even if depositors are subject to losses and that solvent but illiquid banks have access to necessary reserves, preferably through open market operations but if necessary through the discount window.

Nonetheless, I doubt that private deposit insurance would become an important and permanent feature of our financial system even if O'Driscoll's proposed program were implemented. That is not to say there would be no private insurance of deposits; rather, there would be no extensive coverage.

Even without contagious runs, the banking system would be subject to macroeconomic disturbances—monetary shocks, velocity shocks, price-level shocks—that could affect a broad group of banks simultaneously. Although a bank system that is more diversified, both geographically and in terms of activities, would be less exposed to regional and industry shocks, such macroeconomic shocks are a nondiversifiable risk from the perspective of a private insurer, and they represent potentially enormous exposure.

Macroeconomic volatility over the past decade has been an important causal factor in explaining the rising rate of bank and thrift failures. Many of today's problems in financial markets are the result of the cycle of inflation and disinflation that began in the 1970s and of the accompanying volatility of interest rates and real returns. A private deposit insurer is simply not capable of insuring against such risks.

Other problems are posed by the transition to privately supplied deposit insurance. As long as a federal deposit insurance agency is the principal insurer, regulators presumably will not be willing to allow private insurance firms to determine when insolvent banks and thrifts should be closed or reorganized. Experience over the past decade, however, clearly shows that the extent of deposit insurance losses upon failure depends chiefly on how quickly insolvent firms are closed. Just as the loss exposure of a fire insurance underwriter depends upon the abilities of a community's fire fighters, the risk of loss to private deposit insurers would depend upon the ability and willingness of regulators to quickly close insolvent firms.

The deepest of our problems with the deposit insurance system result from the unwillingness of regulators to promptly close insolvent firms. Particularly when a large firm is in trouble, or when problems are widespread in an industry or region, the regulators have proven reluctant to incur the short-run disruptions and criticism that would result. Private insurance is not feasible unless the insurer has the power to close insolvent firms or to withdraw coverage, and I believe it is unlikely that the government would grant such powers to private insurers.

Another important transition problem relates to capacity constraints within the insurance industry. Presently, insured deposits amount to well over $2 trillion. Even if deposit insurance coverage is rolled back so that potential exposure is no more than, say, 2 percent of total deposits, this amounts to a staggering sum. One of the largest insurance packages ever assembled was designed to insure against losses from a nuclear accident. It took federal sponsorship and approximately 30 years of effort to bring the insurance pool up to $750 million.[1]

An attractive alternative to private insurance that may be more feasible to implement is a subordinated debt capital requirement. Subordinated notes play a role similar to that sought from private insurers: If losses exceed a bank's equity capital, note holders suffer a loss, just as a private deposit insurer would. The note holders, in effect, are "insuring" deposits up to the amount of their financial investment. Holders of such debt cannot withdraw their funds in times of trouble, yet they have incentives to provide important market discipline. Since they do not share in the higher returns that may result from risk taking, they are more inclined than stockholders toward conservative operations. To the extent the debt is rated and priced to reflect risk, it can provide a market signal of asset quality. A subordinated debt requirement would also not be particularly burdensome for healthy banks, since the marginal cost would be the difference between rates on uninsured notes and insured deposits on an after-tax basis.

In sum, I agree with O'Driscoll's emphasis on the value of diversification of activities and geographic markets for reducing risk in the U.S. banking system, but I am skeptical about the viability of

---

[1]See FDIC (1983) for further discussion of this point.

private deposit insurance, at least on a large scale. The federal deposit insurance system will be with us for some time. The important thing is to eliminate burdensome regulations that make banks more vulnerable to failure, as well as to correct the gross distortions resulting from current forbearance and failure resolution policies. The more bank and thrift regulators rely on market disciplines and prompt closure of firms that are insolvent on a market-value basis, the less regulation will be needed to protect the deposit insurer against losses.

References

Benston, George, and Kaufman, George. "Risks and Failures in Banking: Overview, History and Evaluation." In *Deregulating Financial Services: Public Policy in Flux,* pp. 49–78. Edited by George Kaufman and Roger Kormendi. Cambridge, Mass.: Ballinger Press, 1986.

Bordo, Michael. "Financial Crises, Banking Crises, Stock Market Crashes and the Money Supply." In *Financial Crises and the World Banking System,* pp. 190–248. Edited by Forrest Capie and Geoffrey Wood. London: Macmillan, 1985.

Cagan, Phillip. *Determinants and Effects of Changes in the Stock of Money 1875–1960.* Washington: National Bureau of Economic Research, 1965.

Federal Deposit Insurance Corporation (FDIC). *Deposit Insurance in a Changing Environment.* Washington: FDIC, 1983.

O'Driscoll, Gerald. "Deposit Insurance in Theory and Practice." Chap. 7 in this book.

Rolnick, Arthur, and Weber, Warren. "New Evidence on the Free Banking Era." *American Economic Review* (December 1983): 1080–91.

Schwartz, Anna J. "Real and Pseudo Financial Crises." In *Financial Crises and the World Banking System,* pp. 11–31. Edited by Forrest Capie and Geoffrey Wood. London: Macmillan, 1985.

8

FINANCIAL STABILITY AND FDIC INSURANCE

Roger W. Garrison, Eugenie D. Short, and Gerald P. O'Driscoll, Jr.

The Federal Deposit Insurance Corporation (FDIC) was created over five decades ago to increase the stability of the banking system. Questions of how and whether the FDIC enhances stability or welfare are now being raised in the economic literature. Buser et al. (1981) argue that deposit insurance has been deliberately underpriced so that the FDIC's package deal, which includes both insurance and regulation, will be attractive to banks. These authors identify a deadweight loss associated with this particular incentive structure. Campbell and Glenn (1984) discuss the determinants of the optimal policies regarding deposit-insurance pricing and bank closings. They show that appropriate policy depends in an important way on the nature of the mechanism for determining insolvency. Chan and Mak (1984) show that, given some exogenously determined constraint on the bank-failure rate, a risk-sensitive premium for deposit insurance may be ill-advised. These authors focus their analysis on the trade-off between depositors' welfare and the soundness of the insurance system.

In this chapter we identify the long-term effects of the FDIC's pricing policies and conclude that, coupled with partial deregulation, these policies are now a cause of—rather than a cure for—financial instability. While it is recognized in the literature that FDIC pricing policies subsidize risk-taking behavior,[1] we contribute to that literature by showing how different aspects of risk-taking behavior relate to specific banking regulations.

Roger W. Garrison is an assistant professor of economics at Auburn University; Eugenie D. Short is an assistant vice president and senior economist at the Federal Reserve Bank of Dallas; and Gerald P. O'Driscoll, Jr., is an assistant vice president and a senior economist at the Federal Reserve Bank of Dallas.

[1]Kareken and Wallace (1978, p. 413), for instance, employ state-preference theory to show, among other things, that "under an FDIC-type insurance scheme, the banking industry holds as risky a portfolio as regulators allow."

187

The next section presents a simple model with which to conveniently discuss the response of banks to the incentives they face. After that we will identify the market forces traditionally held in check by regulatory constraints. The section that follows will deal with these same market forces in a partially deregulated environment and show their relevance to the currently high and increasing bank-failure rate. The fourth section argues that the interaction between remaining regulations and market forces may result in long-term, or structural, instability. The final section summarizes our views.

A Simple Model

The profitability of the banking system as a whole reflects the rates of return to the asset portfolios that banks hold. These rates of return vary across banks and depend upon the quality of each bank's management as well as the particular environment in which the bank operates. For some banks, asset yields are so low as to result in bankruptcy. The likelihood of catastrophically low returns depends, in part, upon the individual bank's risk preferences—its willingness to risk its capital to increase the expected return to its assets.[2]

It is convenient to represent the profitability of the banking system—and hence the profit prospects for an individual bank—with a distribution of returns to the asset portfolios held by the different banks. A normal distribution, as used in Figure 1 and all subsequent figures, can represent the rates of return to asset portfolios across the banking system for a given accounting period. The actual rate of profit for that period will depend upon several other factors as well. For each bank the capital base, the cost of funds, and other operating costs all come into play. But to focus attention on the asset portfolios held by individual banks, we treat none of these other factors as stochastic variables in the model.

In the absence of any specific knowledge of the different banks' relative abilities, the location of any given bank along the rate-of-return spectrum will be attributed to random factors. The mean rate of return is consistent with the rates of profit in other industries. The variance of the distribution reflects the composition of the banks' portfolios. The location of a given bank on the distribution represents the return to its own portfolio—which itself reflects a distribution of

---

[2]See Short et al. (1985) for empirical evidence on the extent to which the level of risk exposure depends on the individual bank's portfolio choice. The likelihood of catastrophically low returns also depends upon the actions of policymakers and other systematic factors. The institutional considerations underlying these industrywide problems will be addressed below.

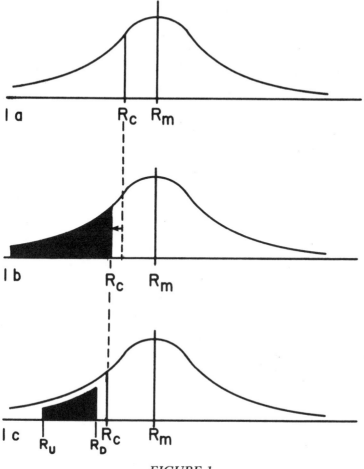

FIGURE 1

returns across the assets within that portfolio. Thus, Figure 1 and the subsequent figures have two different but complementary interpretations. Ex ante, the distributions depict the prospects of a representative bank; ex post, the distributions depict the portfolio rates of returns to the banking system as a whole.

Initially, we consider an unregulated banking system whose banks purchase deposit insurance from privately operated insurance companies. With due allowances for risk and other nonpecuniary considerations, the mean rate of return, indicated by Rm in Figure 1a, allows for a normal rate of profit. Each bank operates from a capital base that allows it to experience periods of below-average returns on its assets without jeopardy to the bank or its depositors. However, if a bank's portfolio yields a rate of return below some critical rate, Rc, the capital base is so seriously eroded that the bank faces bankruptcy. The difference, then, between Rc and Rm is a reflection of the bank's capital base. In the absence of deposit insurance, losses associated with rates of return below Rc would be suffered by the bank's depositors, up to the amount of their deposits. Stockholders are protected by limited liability law from losses in excess of their investment.

In response to the preferences of depositors, many—probably most—banks would choose to purchase deposit insurance. The cost of this insurance, if supplied competitively, reflects the portion of the rate-of-return distribution below Rc. In effect, the area of the distribution between negative infinity and Rc is "sold" to the insurer. The mean of the distribution remains unchanged; the purchasing of deposit insurance serves only to convert a portion of that distribution into its expected value. The capital base and deposit insurance, which are substitutes at the margin from the bank's point of view, are used in some combination to protect the depositors from losses. The capital base protects the depositors from minor losses that are likely to occur; deposit insurance protects them from catastrophic losses that are unlikely to occur. Rc marks the boundary between the two methods of protection.

The gains from pooling risks will be realized, in part, by a leftward shift of Rc as shown in Figure 1b. Risk-averse depositors will now be willing to accept a lower yield in exchange for added security. This lower yield to depositors means lower funding costs to banks, which allow the banks to survive lower asset yields.

As with all other areas in which insurance is provided, the problem of moral hazard does arise with deposit insurance. As one means of dealing with moral hazard, competitive insurance companies can be expected to stop short of providing full coverage. This practice will give the depositor an incentive to survey the policies of various banks before choosing one particular bank and then to monitor the behavior of that bank with respect to its portfolio management. Such surveys and monitoring services may be provided by some (public or private) bank-rating agency. Figure 1c, in which insured losses are confined to the shaded area, suggests several ways in which the insurance companies might intentionally leave the banks' depositors exposed to some risk. First, the insurer pays nothing unless the return on the bank's portfolio falls a prescribed distance below Rc, say, to Rd. This uninsured loss may be spread among depositors on a pro-rata basis. Second, over the range of portfolio returns for which the insurer has liability, from Rd down to Ru, the coverage is less than 100 percent. The depositor bears some percentage of the loss—say, 10 to 20 percent.[3] And third, if the bank's actual portfolio return is below Ru, the upper limit of the coverage, the insurer covers only the loss associated with Ru. This aspect of risk exposure provides an incentive for depositors to avoid banks that engage in shoot-the-moon investment strategies and hence discourages banks from adopting such strategies.

Figure 1c illustrates a possible outcome of the interaction between banks, bank depositors, and deposit insurers. And such an outcome would be a stable one—stable, at least, with respect to the parameters under consideration.[4] That is, even in the absence of regulation, none of the agents involved can take advantage of the circumstances depicted by altering that part of his own behavior that gave rise to those circumstances. This result suggests that there are no internal inconsistencies or inherent perversities in the competitive forces that govern deposit institutions in their relationship to depositors and deposit insurers. The competitive solution also provides a point of departure for the discussion of deposit insurance that is not provided competitively. Policies adopted by the FDIC, for instance, create incentives that are inconsistent with the results depicted in Figure 1. The particular ways in which the banks and the banks' depositors react to these incentives depend upon the regulatory environment they face. In the next two sections, we identify these reactions and their consequences in first a regulated, and then a partially deregulated, environment.

Subsidized Insurance in a Regulated Environment

The environment in which banks actually operate is substantially different from the one assumed in the discussion above. The actual environment is in some ways more favorable and in other ways less favorable to banks than a competitive environment is. Because of the pricing policies of the FDIC, the banks are able to buy deposit insurance for a fee that is not actuarially sound. The fee actually paid, then, does not reflect the true risk assumed by the insurer.

Recognizing that this would be a problem, Congress also established a number of regulatory constraints to offset the incentives generated by the public provision of deposit insurance. Those constraints included (1) interest-rate ceilings, (2) entry restrictions, (3)

[3]Strictly speaking, the vertical gap between the shaded area and the normal curve is measured in frequency units. But for our purposes, the unwillingness to insure 10 to 20 percent of the bank failures should be interpreted instead as the unwillingness to insure 10 to 20 percent of the loss associated with each failure.
[4]See White (1984) for a thorough treatment of the stability properties of competitive banking from both a theoretical and a historical perspective.

asset restrictions, and (4) capital-adequacy requirements. The model developed in the previous section can be used to discuss the incentives—and hence the market forces—created by subsidized deposit insurance in the context of these regulatory constraints.

By law, the FDIC charges a fixed-rate premium on domestic bank deposits. At present the FDIC collects from each insured bank a yearly premium of one-twelfth of 1 percent of all deposits. By pricing the insurance independent of the banks' portfolio decisions and providing coverage beyond the statutory limit, the FDIC virtually guarantees that banks' risk-taking behavior is effectively subsidized.[5] This subsidy is reinforced by the FDIC settlement practices for failed banks, which effectively provide de facto 100 percent insurance coverage to depositors of large banks.[6]

The qualitative impact of the FDIC subsidy can best be modeled by considering the polar case in which full coverage is provided at no cost. In terms of Figure 1a, the depositors are insured against any losses associated with portfolio rates of return below Rc. In effect, the expected value of that portion of the distribution, which is negative in magnitude, is removed from the depositors' consideration at no cost to the banks. Had the banks paid an actuarially sound premium for the insurance, the mean rate of return to their portfolios— net of the insurance premium—would have remained unchanged. (This was the case depicted in Figure 1b.) With a subsidized insurance premium (a zero premium in the polar case being modeled), however, the effective mean is increased from Rm to Rs as shown in Figure 2. That is, even if there are no changes in the banks' portfolios,

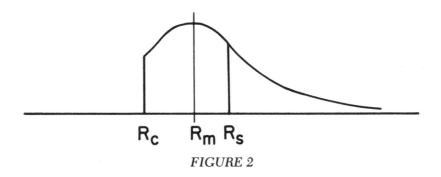

$$R_c \qquad R_m \; R_s$$

FIGURE 2

---

[5]See, for example, Kane (1985, p. 14).

[6]For a more comprehensive discussion of the provision of deposit insurance coverage and settlement practices for failed banks, see Short (1985), who concentrates on differences in settlement practices for large and small banks.

the relevant distribution of portfolio returns has been skewed to the right and the mean rate of return has been increased correspondingly.[7]

The new mean rate of return, Rs, reflects the skewing of the distribution and translates into supernormal profits to the banking industry. This is the direct effect of the deposit-insurance subsidy. To the extent that regulation prevents the individual banks from reacting to the subsidy, the banking system is safer (less risky) than it otherwise would be. In effect, the regulation is an attempt to minimize the losses that would otherwise diminish the banking industry's capital base. But the underpricing of the deposit insurance drives a wedge between the interests of the regulators and the interests of the individual banks. Only if the banks can be persuaded—or coerced—into acting against their own individual interests, will the regulators' efforts to control risks and hence losses be effective through time. What remains to be shown are the specific relationships between the various regulations and the subsidy created by the underpricing of deposit insurance.

The various regulations that banks currently face, or that they have faced in the past, all have histories of their own. The actual imposition of some of these regulations may have been unrelated, or only tangentially related, to the incentives created by subsidized deposit insurance. But the purposes of the present analysis will be served if each particular regulation is treated as if its objective were to prevent the individual banks from exploiting, or leveraging, the benefits of subsidized deposit insurance to the detriment of the banking system as a whole. The individual regulations can be identified in terms of the parameters of Figure 2. The following will discuss the effects of deregulation in terms of these same parameters.

Interest-Rate Ceilings. The supernormal profits made possible by subsidized insurance create an incentive for banks to bid for more funds from depositors in order to take fuller advantage of the subsidy. Until April 1986, Regulation Q placed interest-rate ceilings on a range of bank deposits.[8] This restriction prevented the subsidy from

---

[7]This result does not depend upon any special assumptions about market structure, liability rules, or risk preferences. It follows directly from the fact that the rate of return in this analysis is reckoned net of the insurance premium: An actuarially sound premium leaves the mean rate of return unaffected; a subsidized premium, especially one of zero, shifts the mean rate to the right of the mode.

[8]A provision of the Monetary Control Act of 1980 set in motion the process of phasing out interest rate restrictions on bank deposits. After April 1986, the only restriction remaining is on demand deposit accounts. In addition, businesses are not allowed to hold interest-bearing checking accounts. Additional discussion of this point is contained below.

being passed on to the depositors as a result of the competitive process. To the extent that they were effectively enforced, interest-rate ceilings held down the cost of bank funds and hence held down the portfolio rate of return needed to avoid bankruptcy. In terms of Figure 2, interest-rate ceilings prevented competitive forces from nudging Rc rightward.

Entry Restrictions. Those same supernormal profits would attract new entrants into the banking industry. If the profit levels are to be maintained, entry must be artificially restricted. In terms of Figure 2, entry restrictions prevent new entrants from driving Rs, along with the entire distribution of portfolio returns, leftward.[9] Note that the market forces impinging on Rc from the left and on Rs from the right are actually intertwined. More specifically, to the extent that banks can circumvent interest-rate ceilings and thereby attract more funds to invest, they bid down Rs. To the extent that new entrants increase the competition for loanable funds, they bid up Rc. For heuristic purposes, however, it is convenient to deal with interest-rate ceilings in terms of Rc and entry restrictions in terms of Rs. These effects would be completely absent only in a fully regulated environment in which interest-rate ceilings are all encompassing and perfectly enforced. Such an environment may never have existed.[10]

Asset Restrictions. The fact that the price of the deposit insurance is unrelated to the riskiness of the banks' portfolios creates a moral hazard problem. It is no longer in the interest of individual banks to limit their risk-taking behavior to portfolios whose returns are described by the distribution in Figure 2. Banks have an incentive to assume increased risks. Asset restrictions imposed by the regulatory authority prevent banks from altering this distribution in their effort to take fuller advantage of the underpriced insurance.[11] In effect, restrictions on assets restrain the market forces that determine the variance of the portfolio distribution.

Capital-Adequacy Requirements. The insurance subsidy, along with interest-rate ceilings and entry restrictions, creates an incentive for the individual banks to decrease their capital-to-asset ratios. That is, if interest-rate ceilings stand in the way of attracting more funds,

[9]The potential for banks, even collectively, to have this effect on the rates of return was assumed away by Kareken and Wallace (1978, p. 413): "[T]he banking industry is a monopoly supplier of deposit services, but is otherwise 'small'. . . ." The question of the empirical significance of this effect is addressed by neither Kareken and Wallace nor by the present authors.

[10]The classic article on the impact on entry restrictions is Peltzman (1963). Klein (1974) calls into question whether Regulation Q was ever effective.

[11]See Kane (1985, p. 19).

194

then the banks will attempt to overextend their existing capital base. Preventing such an overextension is the objective of capital-adequacy requirements.

The conflict between the interests of the individual banks and the interests of the regulatory authority can be stated in terms of the market value of bank charters. The value of the charter, which reflects the present value of all future supernormal profits, is part of the bank's capital so far as the individual bank is concerned, but it is not part of the capital that counts toward capital adequacy so far as the regulator is concerned. The purpose of capital-adequacy requirements is to force the banker to take the regulator's point of view when making decisions that affect the bank's capital-to-asset ratio.

By discussing the various regulations in terms of the parameters of Figure 2, we have identified the incentives created by the deposit-insurance subsidy and the corresponding market forces kept in check by the regulations. In the next section, we examine what happens when some of these restrictions are removed in the process of deregulation. As we will demonstrate, adjusting the parameters under deregulation has implications about the risk assumed (and created) by the FDIC and about the long-term stability of the banking system.

Subsidized Insurance under Partial Deregulation

The intended effect of any regulation is to hold in check some particular set of market forces, but the incentives underlying these market forces are not eliminated. If market participants are not allowed to respond directly to the incentives they face, then they will have an incentive to circumvent the regulations that stand in the way. At this stage in the regulatory process, deregulation may become inevitable. The wholesale removal of all the relevant regulations, however, means an abrupt restructuring of incentives. Market forces held in check for a period of years are suddenly unleashed. While the market concerned may have been a stable one in the absence of regulation, the response of market participants to deregulation may create short-term instability. Further, if some—but not all—of the interrelated regulations are removed, the market process that adjusts the deregulated aspects of the market to the circumstances created by the remaining regulations may give rise to both short- and long-term instability. This manner of characterizing the banking industry is consistent with a recent assessment by Kareken (1983, p. 203): "To deregulate further and never do anything about the FDIC would be to invite a crash."

Chart 1, which traces the bank-failure rate from 1946 to 1986, depicts the instability in a dramatic way. The divergence of this time series from its flat trend line calls for an explanation. The proximate cause can be found in developments in banking over the last two decades and in the government's reactions to these developments.

Beginning in the 1960s, rising inflation rates caused Regulation Q to become increasingly binding. The widening gap between the legally imposed interest-rate ceilings and market-clearing interest rates created strong incentives to find ways of skirting such regulations. The result was various forms of financial innovations. The clearest and most conspicuous example of efforts to circumvent interest-rate restrictions was the development of markets for certificates of deposit (CDs), including the unregulated Eurocurrency market.

By the 1980s, regulators and legislators began to adapt to these ongoing financial innovations. The Monetary Control Act of 1980 authorized the gradual elimination of interest-rate ceilings on domestic deposits. This process, which occurred over a period of six years, was accelerated by the Garn–St Germain Depository Institutions Act of 1982. By April 1986, interest rate restrictions were removed on all remaining deposit accounts except demand deposits. More comprehensive restrictions, however, remain on asset selection and entry.

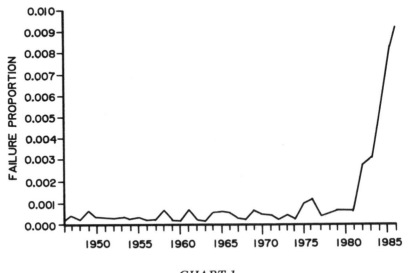

CHART 1

BANK FAILURES AS A PROPORTION OF NUMBER
OF BANKS

The equilibrium position that will be attained in this partially deregulated environment will not be the one depicted in Figure 1c, however, where the interests of bankers, bank depositors, and deposit insurers are all brought into balance. The result, instead, will balance the interests of bankers and bank depositors—given the insurance subsidy and the leverage made possible by that subsidy.[12]

It is difficult to separate and categorize all the different market forces that come into play when moving from a regulated to a partially deregulated environment. Some regulations put checks on several different market forces; and some forces are checked by more than one regulation. All these interacting forces are able to work themselves out partly in spite of regulation and partly because of deregulation. Further, the legislation enabling partial deregulation has occurred over time, and the market's reaction to the different aspects of deregulation requires different amounts of time. These considerations make it difficult to determine from historical perspective— from the observation of the ongoing process—what the end result is likely to be. To make this problem a more tractable one, the relevant market forces can be categorized in accordance with the analysis in the preceding section. They will be dealt with, then, in an analytical rather than a chronological sequence. However, the relationships between the market processes discussed and the circumstances that currently characterize the banking industry should be apparent

Figure 3a reproduces the distribution of portfolio returns depicted in Figure 2 with the lower tail included. The shading of the area to the left of Rc indicates the range of portfolio returns over which the FDIC is responsible for accommodating depositors. Because of the FDIC's assumption of this responsibility at a cost that does not depend on the banks' portfolio decisions, banks can continue to restrict their own attention to the unshaded area of the distribution.[13] The effects of deregulation can be discussed in terms of changes in the size of the shaded area of the distribution. And the discussion of these effects can take advantage of the relationships identified earlier between the various regulations and the parameters of the model.

---

[12]This assumes that the deposit insurers cannot effectively constrain behavior through bank supervision. For a more thorough discussion of the point, see Kane (1985, p. 19).
[13]Inattention to the shaded area does not imply that the banks are indifferent to whether the returns to their portfolios are in the shaded or the unshaded area of the distribution. It simply implies that they are indifferent as to how the shaded area is distributed. That is, given subsidized insurance and limited liability, they are indifferent about potential losses in excess of the banks' capital. From the banks' perspective, any point within the shaded area is equivalent to Rc.

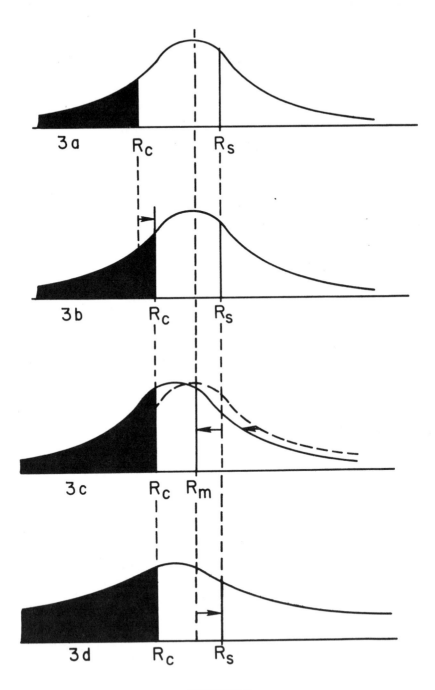

FIGURE 3

Figure 3b shows the effect of eliminating the ceilings on interest rates that banks pay their depositors. As Regulation Q was phased out, banks bid up interest rates in their attempts to attract more funds. Because of the higher cost of funds, the lowest survivable rate of return on assets is increased. Rc shifts rightward and the shaded area, the FDIC's exposure to risk, grows accordingly.[14]

Figure 3c shows the effect of relaxing entry restrictions. The supernormal rates of return are made possible by artificially restricting the number of bank charters granted and by forbidding nonbank institutions from competing directly with chartered banks. The actual extent of the relaxation of entry restrictions varies from state to state because the individual states as well as the federal government have the authority to issue bank charters. But the supernormal rate of return can be competed away partly by the expansion of the banking industry itself and partly by competition from such nonbank institutions as the money-market brokerage firms. Competing methods of amassing funds can allow nonbank institutions to bid for assets that may otherwise have been purchased by banks. The decreasing effectiveness of entry restrictions gets translated, at least in part, into decreasing rates of return to asset portfolios. In terms of Figure 3c, Rs, along with the entire portfolio distribution, is shifted leftward. A greater fraction of the distribution is pushed into the shaded region, reflecting an increase in the FDIC's risk exposure.

Figure 3d shows the effect of relaxing asset restrictions. Restrictions on asset selection, loan size, and credit standards have imposed binding constraints on banks' risk-taking behavior. As these aspects of banking become more deregulated, the banks are better able to respond to incentives to hold a riskier portfolio. Caught in the squeeze between rising costs and falling rates of return on traditional bank portfolios, banks are able to increase their rates of return by taking on more risk—without paying proportionately higher rates for deposit insurance.

In terms of Figure 3d, the increase in risk-taking behavior is represented by an increase in the variance of the distribution. Clearly, the banks' chances for a high portfolio return are increased. Rs, the mean of the unshaded portion of the distribution, is advanced to the right. But just as clearly, the chances for ruinously low return are increased as well. The shaded area grows still larger.

As we stated earlier, these effects, which have been separated for heuristic purposes in Figures 3b through 3d and in the discussion of

[14]See Keeton (1985) for a complementary treatment of the increased risk-taking behavior attributable to the removal of interest-rate ceilings.

the figures, are actually intertwined. That is, the nearly simultaneous relaxation of interest-rate ceilings, entry restrictions, and asset restrictions would have both direct and indirect effects on banks' funding costs and the composition and riskiness of their asset portfolios.[15] Lowered entry barriers, for example, may attract more adventuresome entrants who bid up the cost of bank funds in their efforts to take fuller advantage of eased asset restrictions. Also, the use of the normal curve, for which risk is measured by the variance, may seriously understate the risk that the FDIC is assuming. Subsidized deposit insurance coupled with deregulation could give rise to shoot-the-moon investment strategies. Depending on world events and foreign affairs, the rate of return to a shoot-the-moon portfolio is likely to be either extremely high, in which case the bank profits handsomely, or extremely low, in which case the FDIC absorbs the loss. Thus, under plausible assumptions the distribution in Figure 3d may be a bimodal distribution with the hit-the-moon mode lying far to the right and the miss-the-moon mode lying far to the left.

Given the incentives created by the FDIC, the analysis of investment strategy rightly focuses on the behavior of the banks rather than on the behavior of both the banks and their depositors. With deposits insured for a price that does not reflect risk, the depositor has little incentive to compare the investment strategies of different banks or to monitor the behavior of the bank in which his funds are deposited.[16] This task has fallen largely to the regulatory authorities. As indicated previously, monitoring the banks' capital and enforcing capital-adequacy requirements is one of the ways that the authorities may try to prevent the banks from further leveraging the insurance subsidy. Capital-adequacy requirements have not been discussed in the context of Figure 3 because this is one regulatory tool that has remained outside the gambit of deregulation. In fact, the regulation of this aspect of the behavior of banks has been stiffened in recent years as a means of partially offsetting the deregulation of the other

---

[15]As a matter of fact, only minimal changes in asset restrictions have been implemented at this time.

[16]Kareken (1981, p. 4) notes that "Casual observation indicates that [investors] are very much aware of what money market fund balance sheets are, much more aware than of what bank balance sheets are. Nor is it accidental that funds and banks differ so in their balance sheets." In a competitive environment, banks would tend to adopt the amount of financial conservatism consistent with the risk preferences of depositors; in a heavily regulated environment, banks come to be known as financially conservative institutions not because of their own or their depositors' risk preferences but because of the restrictions imposed by the regulatory authorities on the banks' asset selection.

aspects of the banks' behavior.[17] In the following section we discuss this and other ways in which regulatory authorities have coped—and may have to cope—with the long-term effects of partial deregulation.

Coping with the Long-Term Effects of Partial Deregulation

The incentives created by partial deregulation pit the immediate interests of banks against the immediate interests of the regulatory authorities. As is typical in this sort of environment, short-term expediency tends to take precedence over long-term stability. This trade-off between short- and long-term considerations can be seen in the efforts of the regulatory authorities to detect and ward off bank failures, to deal with the failures once they have occurred, and to correct the incentive structure that has given rise to the increasingly unstable banking environment. Coping with partial deregulation can be discussed under the headings of Capital Adequacy, Purchase and Assumption Agreements, Variable-Rate Insurance Premiums, and Privatization of Deposit Insurance.

Capital Adequacy

The standard indicator of a bank's capital adequacy is its capital-to-asset ratio. But this statistic, which ignores the riskiness of the bank's asset portfolio, is a suitable measure of capital adequacy over time only if risk-taking behavior on the part of the banks does not vary. Thinking in terms of the parameters of Figure 3, we can judge the bank's capital adequacy more clearly by considering the variance of the portfolio distribution and the location of Rc. The greater the variance, the greater the potential losses; the further Rc lies to the right, the more likely that losses will be incurred.

Comparing Figure 3a with Figure 3d suggests that even if the capital-to-asset ratios were the same for the two cases, the latter would represent less capital adequacy than the former. Banks with riskier portfolios need relatively larger capital bases. But under partial deregulation, banks have an incentive to decrease rather than increase their capital-to-asset ratios.

---

[17]A referee has pointed out that if the capital-adequacy requirements are sufficiently stringent, the elimination of interest ceilings, barriers to entry, and portfolio restrictions will not have the effects depicted in Figures 3b through 3d. This possibility is consistent with our understanding that the regulatory authorities are attempting to offset the increases in risk exposure by stiffening capital-adequacy requirements. But if banks were to respond to the increased stiffening by making still riskier loans, these attempts may be less than successful. In any case, the discussion in the next section suggests that actual changes in capital-adequacy requirements are far from offsetting.

The regulatory authorities have been aware of declining capital-to-asset ratios across the banking system. In their attempt to reverse—or at least to arrest—the trend, they are subjecting this aspect of banking to stricter enforcement than before deregulation. Beginning in late 1981, formal guidelines on capital adequacy were announced to replace the less formal, more discretionary procedures that were then being used. Significantly, as Wall (1983, p. 47) points out, one of the objectives of the new capital guidelines was "to address the long-term decline in capital ratios, particularly those of the multinational group."[18] In 1986, banking regulators proposed implementing a system of risk-based capital requirements. In 1987, this proposal was revised to incorporate comments received on the earlier proposal and through extensive discussion with the Bank of England in an attempt to establish minimum capital standards on an international basis.

The proposed system of capital guidelines attempts to link capital requirements to the actual risk of bank portfolios. Under this proposal, all banks (regardless of size) with portfolios deemed to be of comparable risk are required to hold the same proportion of capital. Risk is measured by the distribution of assets among five risk categories for which the weights are, respectively, 0, 10, 25, 50, and 100 percent. The weights increase according to the perceived risk of individual assets. For example, 0 capital would be required against cash equivalents, whereas 100 percent of the standard capital requirement would be held against commercial bank loans and other assets of standard risk. In addition, the revised proposal would implement capital adequacy standards for off-balance-sheet items held by larger banks.[19]

While this approach to capital requirements attempts to link capital guidelines to risk, it still suffers from fundamental deficiencies. Most notably, the weights assigned to each of the five risk categories do not price risk at all accurately. More specifically, risk within each category can vary as much as risk between categories. But the price of risk in terms of capital requirements remains the same within a single category. Hence, banks still have an incentive to increase expected return at the expense of incurring more risk. For example, banks can reallocate their loan portfolios to riskier credits without incurring a capital penalty.

The proposal, by moving toward risk-adjusted capital requirements, attempts to introduce greater market discipline. But by con-

[18]The article from which this quotation was taken is concerned with the impact of these guidelines on the development of interstate banking.

[19]For a more complete statement of these guidelines, see Federal Reserve System, Regulation Y; Docket No. R-0567.

tinuing to rely on categorical regulation, it fails to allow the market to reprice risk continuously. This failure is particularly noteworthy because the bond and equity holders expected to supply the required capital will continue to represent only a small proportion of total bank liabilities, and bank depositors, still protected by de facto 100 percent insurance coverage, will not provide effective constraints against risk taking. As such, the source of market discipline that is potentially most effective will continue to be held in check.

Purchase and Assumption Agreements

In some cases the problem of capital inadequacy turns into the problem of bank failure. When the bank can no longer keep its doors open, the FDIC is legally bound to make good on all the bank's unmet obligations to depositors for an amount up to $100,000 per account. But in most instances, the FDIC has provided full coverage to all depositors by arranging for the sale of the failed bank. Under its purchase and assumption policy, all liabilities of the failed bank, including uninsured deposits, are transferred to an assuming bank.

Dealing with failures in this way is to the short-term benefit not only of the technically uninsured depositors but also of the assuming bank. Even though the failed bank may have a negative present value net of "goodwill," the assuming bank is also the recipient of the "goodwill," an intangible asset that—especially in the case of a failed bank whose actual goodwill is minimal—reflects in large part the discounted value of the bank charter. What the FDIC sees as negative capital value is seen by the assuming bank as positive capital value. But this difference in perspective persists only so long as entry restrictions are maintained. Thus, the FDIC's ability to meet its obligations to a failed bank's depositors by soliciting the cooperation of other banks will be diminished over time as deregulation eats away at the entry restrictions.

Further, relying on purchase and assumption agreements as a short-term solution to the problem of bank failures is likely to aggravate the long-term problem for the banking system as a whole. Figure 3d suggests that subsidized deposit insurance, coupled with deregulation, increases the FDIC's exposure to risk. If the return on asset portfolios is increasingly likely to fall below Rc as deregulation proceeds, and if these portfolios are absorbed as a matter of FDIC policy by the surviving banks, then the surviving banks are more likely to experience returns that fall below Rc. The image that comes to mind is one of a dozen lifeboats on the high seas. All are loaded to capacity, and some have leaks. When one leaky boat sinks, the occupants are transferred into the boats that are still afloat. This short-term solution to the problem of one sinking boat may be irresistible—in spite of its compounding of the long-term problem. In an analogous way the purchase and assumption policy may be maintaining short-term stability at the price of long-term instability.

Variable-Rate Insurance Premiums

The FDIC has recognized the need to deal with the problem at its root, to change the incentives the banks face so as to decrease the banks' willingness to engage in risk-taking behavior. Accordingly, the FDIC (1983) recommended a system of variable-rate premiums based on three risk categories: normal, high, and very high. The vast majority of banks would be classified as normal. Banks with high exposure to either interest-rate or credit risk would be classified as high-risk banks. And banks with high exposure to both interest-rate and credit risk, or banks with dangerously low capital ratios would be classified as very high risk banks. After receiving considerable attention from both academics and policymakers, interest in the proposal waned. This largely reflected lack of legislative support for the introduction of variable-rate insurance premiums.[20]

The most noteworthy implication of the FDIC's proposal on deposit insurance reform is that it indicates the FDIC understands the nature of the problem. Solving the problem requires that the deposit insurance be priced in accordance with the risk assumed by the insurer. But adopting variable-rate premiums is just one small step toward that solution. It is analogous to the adoption of a three-tier minimum wage as a solution to the problem of unemployment caused by minimum-wage legislation. The FDIC has no way of knowing that banks should be divided into 3 risk categories rather than 13 or 30. It has no way of gauging the actuarial value of the insured risk of each of the categories. Thus, it has no way of calculating the appropriate insurance premium or of adjusting that premium as market conditions change. At best, variable-rate premiums represent an extremely crude approximation of a market solution to the problem.

Privatization of Deposit Insurance

The proposal of variable-rate premiums points the way toward one possible long-term solution to the problem: the privatization of deposit

---

[20]For a more thorough discussion of proposals to implement variable-rate deposit insurance premiums, see the papers on deposit insurance in the *Proceedings of a Conference on Bank Structure and Competition* sponsored by the Federal Reserve Bank of Chicago in May 1983.

insurance.[21] The incentive structure inherent in the provision of deposit insurance by private agencies would fundamentally reconfigure the relevant market forces. Banks would choose among competing insurers; insurers would compete with one another in terms of coverage offered and premiums charged. A market process can be expected to outperform a bureaucratic process whether the object of the process is determining the price of shoes or determining deposit insurance premiums.[22] The market test of profit and loss would allow for the establishment of actuarially sound premiums for the coverage provided. And that same market test would allow for less-than-full coverage that, while acceptable to both the banks and their depositors, would hold the problem of moral hazard in check. The long-term consequences of privatization ideally instituted are those depicted in Figure 1c.

In a deregulated and decentralized environment, banks could more fully diversify in terms of both geographic and product markets.[23] And they could compete with one another not only in terms of yields to depositors but also in terms of prudence. Competition of this sort would mean that banks with relatively low risk portfolios could actually gain in strength as a result of the perceived riskiness of more aggressive banks. Insurers could effectively pool their risks by insuring low-risk as well as high-risk banks. And unlike the FDIC, private insurers could further limit their risks by limiting deposit insurance to some small portion of their total underwritings.[24]

If complete deregulation were possible, including the decentralization of the banking system and the phasing out of the FDIC, market forces could bring into balance the interests of the banks, the bank's depositors, and the deposit insurers. But to opt for this long-term solution is to worsen the short-term problem. Institutional changes

[21]For a discussion of the possibility of private deposit insurance and of making the transition from FDIC to private insurers, see Kane (1983 and 1985) and Short and O'Driscoll (1983).

[22]Short and O'Driscoll (1983) suggest that the standard arguments for preferring a market solution to a bureaucratic solution apply to the problem of providing deposit insurance. Kane (1983, p. 271) argues that "bureaucrats are inherently slower in responding to changes in interest-rate volatility and other emerging forms of risk than private insurers would be."

[23]Wells and Scruggs (1984) show that historically geographic restrictions have been a source of instability of the banking system.

[24]A major concern regarding the viability of deposit insurance is the question of independence of risks of failure among banks, or what are known as contagion effects. For a comprehensive reassessment of this issue, see Benston et al. (1986, pp. 27–70). Further, it is necessary to distinguish between bank runs and bank failures. For a discussion of this point, see Gilbert and Wood (1986).

needed before the market can provide deposit insurance are fundamental and far-reaching. The period during which the banking system becomes adjusted to such a radically different set of incentives would undoubtedly be turbulent. Again, the trade-off between short- and long-term stability is illustrated.

Summary

There is no reason to believe that the business of banking is inherently unstable or that bank deposits are inherently uninsurable. Nor is there reason to doubt that regulatory authorities may be able to create a set of regulations and to make intermittent adjustments so as to avoid a banking crisis over some extended sequence of short runs.

But the current banking environment, in which some regulatory constraints are being eased or phased out while others are being maintained or even stiffened, is neither fish nor fowl. It does not require by law that the banks operate in the public interest; nor does it create the incentives that would entice them to do so. And barring a fortuitous counterbalancing of regulations, this hybrid environment of subsidized deposit insurance and partial deregulation gives rise to cumulative effects in the banking system that in the long term can result in financial instability.

References

Benston, George J., et al. *Perspectives on Safe and Sound Banking: Past, Present, and Future.* Cambridge, Mass.: MIT Press, 1986.

Buser, Stephen A., Chen, Andrew H., and Kane, Edward J. "Federal Deposit Insurance, Regulatory Policy, and Optimal Bank Capital." *The Journal of Finance* (March 1981): 51–60.

Campbell, Tim S., and Glenn, David. "Deposit Insurance in a Deregulated Environment." *The Journal of Finance* (July 1984): 775–87.

Chan, Yuk-Shee, and Mak, King-Tim. "Depositors' Welfare, Deposit Insurance, and Deregulation." Paper presented at the American Finance Association meetings, December 1984.

FDIC. *Deposit Insurance in a Changing Environment: A Study of the Current System of Deposit Insurance.* Washington, D.C.: FDIC, April 1983.

Gilbert, Alton, and Wood, Geoffrey E. "Coping with Bank Failures: Some Lessons from the United States and the United Kingdom." Federal Reserve Bank of St. Louis *Review* (December 1986): 5–14.

Kane, Edward J. "A Six-Point Program for Deposit-Insurance Reform." *Housing Finance Review* (July 1983): 269–78.

Kane, Edward J. *The Gathering Crisis in Federal Deposit Insurance.* Cambridge, Mass.: MIT Press, 1985.

Kareken, John A. "Deregulating Commercial Banks: The Watchword Should Be Caution." Federal Reserve Bank of Minneapolis *Quarterly Review* (Spring/Summer 1981): 1–5.

Kareken, John A. "The First Step in Bank Deregulation: What About the FDIC?" *American Economic Review* (May 1983): 198–203.

Kareken, John A., and Wallace, Neil. "Deposit Insurance and Bank Regulation: A Partial Equilibrium Exposition." *Journal of Business* (July 1978): 413–52.

Keeton, William R. "Deposit Insurance and Deregulation." Unpublished manuscript, Federal Reserve Bank of Kansas City, September 1985.

Klein, Benjamin. "Competitive Interest Payments on Bank Deposits and the Long-run Demand for Money." *American Economic Review* (December 1974): 931–49.

Peltzman, Sam. "Entry in Commercial Banking." *Journal of Law and Economics* (October 1963): 11–50.

Short, Eugenie D. "FDIC Settlement Practices and the Size of Failed Banks." Federal Reserve Bank of Dallas *Economic Review* (March 1985): 12–20.

Short, Eugenie D., and O'Driscoll, Gerald P., Jr. "Deregulation and Deposit Insurance." Federal Reserve Bank of Dallas *Economic Review* (September 1983): 11–22.

Short, Eugenie D., O'Driscoll, Gerald P., Jr., and Berger, Franklin D. "Recent Bank Failures: Determinants and Consequences." *Proceedings of a Conference on Bank Structure and Competition*, Federal Reserve Bank of Chicago, May 1985, pp. 150–65.

Wall, Larry D. "Will Capital Adequacy Requirements Slow the Development of Interstate Banking?" Federal Reserve Bank of Atlanta *Economic Review* (May 1983): 46–54.

Wells, Don R., and Scruggs, L. S. "Financial Deregulation, Deposit Insurance, Branch Banking and Free Banking: The Historical Implications." Paper presented at the Atlantic Economic Society meetings, October 1984.

White, Lawrence H. *Free Banking in Britain: Theory, History and Debate.* Cambridge: Cambridge University Press, 1984.

9

THE ROLE OF THE FEDERAL RESERVE IN RESERVE REQUIREMENT REGULATION

Mark Toma

Traditionally, economists have highlighted the macroeconomic consequences of reserve requirement regulation. A public-spirited central bank may impose reserve requirements to increase its control over the money supply. For a given money multiplier, the monetary authority controls the money supply through its production of reserves. Although the money multiplier may change over time, its variability decreases as the reserve requirement approaches one.

The traditional approach ignores the possibility that banks may be able to evade reserve requirement regulations by providing customers with nonreservable deposits. To enforce reserve requirement regulations, resources must be employed by some government agency. The enforcement authority may be a local agency or the central bank itself. For example, before 1980 a U.S. bank's choice of state agency or Federal Reserve System membership determined which authority would set and enforce reserve requirements. Edward Kane (1982) suggested that the ability of banks to choose their regulator constrained the Fed and state agencies to reduce reserve requirements to the "market" level. Kane's conclusion seems inconsistent with the traditional prediction that a central bank sets a high reserve requirement for monetary control reasons.

This paper attempts to explain the reserve requirement decisions of real world central banks by developing competitive and monopoly models of reserve requirement regulation. In the competitive model, local regulatory agencies compete with the central bank in setting and enforcing reserve requirements. After defining Kane's market reserve requirement, I specify the circumstances under which competition reduces the reserve requirement to this level.

I then modify the regulatory model along the lines suggested by the Depository Institutions Deregulation and Monetary Control Act

The author is a member of the department of economics at Miami University in Ohio.

of 1980. This act deregulated deposit interest rates in the United States and transformed the process of setting reserve requirements from a competitive one to a monopolistic one. For the first time, the Fed could set and enforce reserve requirements for *all* financial institutions that offered transaction accounts.

To contrast how a central bank sets reserve requirements under competitive and monopolistic conditions, I assume that the revenue consequences of money production motivate central bankers. Such an assumption may not be very useful in explaining the day-to-day actions of central bank decision makers, but it seems appropriate when viewing the Monetary Control Act as a change in the nation's monetary constitution. I argue that the act eliminated a constraint on the Fed's actions, and thereby enhanced its ability in the long run to raise revenue through money creation. Overall, the analysis suggests that changes in the incentives facing central bank decision makers, and not macroeconomic issues, determine long-run reserve requirement policy.

A History of Reserve Requirement Enforcement

The 1935 Banking Act gave the Federal Reserve System statutory authority to specify the amount of reserves banks were required to hold behind their deposits. This power, however, was not absolute because the Fed could impose reserve requirements only on deposits of its member banks. State agencies set requirements for other banks.

Although Fed member banks faced a set of reserve requirements that did not depend on their locational decision, before 1980 the requirements of nonmember institutions varied from state to state. Most state regulatory agencies imposed statutory requirements that were lower than Fed-mandated requirements (Gilbert and Lovati 1978). State agencies also were more lenient in what they defined as reserves. They generally allowed their members to count deposits at approved banks as reserves and often allowed government securities and cash items in process of collection to be counted as well. A few state agencies imposed no requirements. The relative leniency of state-imposed reserve requirements was a primary reason for the membership decline at the Fed after World War II. Responding to this decline, in 1959 the Fed allowed its members to count as reserves vault cash in addition to deposits at the Fed.[1]

Before 1980, a bank's decision to transfer membership from the Fed to a state agency affected the demand for Fed-produced reserves.

---

[1]See Goodfriend and Hargraves (1982) for a description of how the required reserve definition has changed over time.

Given generally lower state requirements, the membership change directly reduced aggregate (Fed member bank and other bank) reserve holdings. But even if aggregate reserve holdings did not change, the demand for Fed reserves would fall because state banks could satisfy requirements by holding assets (such as government securities) that were not produced by the Fed.

Banks' ability to evade reserve requirement regulations imposed another limitation on the regulatory powers of the Fed. Statutory authority to set reserve requirements has no practical implications if the Fed does not devote resources to enforcing reserve requirement regulations. The Fed has two margins along which it can change the intensity of enforcement. First, it monitors member bank liabilities that already are officially defined as reservable. If reserve holdings are found to be insufficient at prespecified intervals, then legal sanctions are imposed on the negligent bank.

Second, the Fed monitors the creation by member banks of new liabilities that initially lie outside the reserve classification. Through such activity, the Fed intends eventually to bring these innovations within its regulatory umbrella. Failure to act along either of the two enforcement margins would induce banks to hold no reserves behind accounts that legally are classified as deposits and/or to develop new liabilities that do not fall under reserve law as presently defined.

Recent advances in financial sector communications and information technology have made it more profitable for banks to produce nonreservable deposit-like accounts (Kane 1981a, Greenbaum 1983, Hester 1981). For example, commercial paper issued by a bank's parent holding company in the late 1960s was not treated as a deposit under the law. The holding company could issue the paper as a nonreservable liability and then distribute the funds to the subsidiary bank.

Also, with development of electronic wire transfer technology, large banks in 1968 began acquiring funds through repurchase agreements. Banks sold securities to corporate customers at the close of a business day and simultaneously agreed to repurchase the securities at the beginning of the next day. This transaction was attractive to banks because funds acquired through these agreements had no reserve requirements.

The markets for bank commercial paper and repurchase agreements expanded rapidly in the late 1960s and early 1970s. In response, the Fed worked to modify reserve law so that these bank liabilities would be treated as reservable deposits. On September 18, 1970, after only a year of regulatory deliberations, the Fed amended Regulation D on member bank reserve requirements to cover commercial paper sales by bank holding companies and their subsidiaries when the proceeds were used to supply funds to bank affiliates. In contrast, the banking sector was able to deflect the Fed's attempt to impose requirements on repurchase agreements.

Several factors affected the uneven pace of defining new bank liabilities as reservable. Banks, themselves, could influence the classification process by lobbying the Fed to ignore the innovations. The intensity of bank lobbying tended to reflect how closely the innovation substituted for simple deposit accounts. Innovations that were identical to deposits, except in name, would be relatively valuable to bank customers and would foster much bank lobbying.

Differential enforcement costs also affected the pace of regulation. The higher the costs of detecting a particular type of bank liability for reserve requirement purposes, the longer the lag between innovation and regulation. Finally, the Fed had to contend with the possibility that some state banking agency enforcement levels were more stringent than others. If an innovation originated in a state with relatively lenient enforcement, then the Fed would risk losing members in that state if it quickly imposed reserve requirements.

Just as the reserve requirements set by the Fed tended to be higher than state requirements, Fed enforcement efforts appeared to be more thorough than many state efforts (Gilbert and Lovati 1978). In general, state banking agencies devoted few resources to discovering and punishing those banks that failed to back reservable deposits. They also tended to be relatively tolerant of financial innovations designed to circumvent state regulations.

The 1980 Monetary Control Act strengthened the Fed's position in the regulatory hierarchy by expanding its power to impose reserve requirements (within certain statutory limits) not only on member banks of the Federal Reserve but also on nonmember depository institutions. These requirements covered transaction accounts, nonpersonal time deposits, and Eurodollar borrowings. While lowering the reserve requirements faced by Fed member banks, the act raised the requirements for other banks by enough to increase the overall reserve burden (Cacy and Winningham 1982).

Members of the Fed can satisfy the new requirements by holding vault cash and/or deposits at Federal Reserve Banks. Other financial institutions have additional pass-through options. Nonmember state banks, for example, can hold reserves in the form of deposits at designated institutions having accounts directly with the Fed. These designated institutions must hold vault cash or Fed deposits on a dollar-for-dollar basis behind their deposits from nonmember banks. Because of the pass-through option, every dollar of reserves held by nonmembers of the Fed increases the Fed's reserves by that full dollar.[2]

Under the Monetary Control Act, the Fed became a monopolist both in setting and enforcing reserve requirements. The act, for the first time, required all depository institutions periodically to report their deposit liabilities and reserves to the Fed. State agencies no longer were directly responsible for monitoring whether their members observed reserve requirement regulations.

The Market for Reserve Requirement Regulation

Any serious theory of reserve requirement regulation must generate predictions that are consistent with the history outlined in the previous section. At the very least, a theory should (1) define the so-called market reserve requirement and specify the circumstances when the actual requirement will be at or above this benchmark level, (2) explain why reserve requirements and enforcement activities in the United States varied across states before 1980 and why they tended to be higher with Fed membership, and (3) predict how the Monetary Control Act will affect the overall reserve-to-deposit ratio.

Identifying the objective function of the regulators and the constraints they face is a first step in developing a testable theory. Consider the objective function of the primary regulator of reserve requirements—the central bank. The long-run tendencies of the central bank as a money producer may be highlighted by assuming it manipulates its production rate along with the reserve requirement to maximize revenue for the government.

The annual revenue flow (seigniorage) equals the real amount of non-interest-bearing liabilities (the monetary base) produced by the central bank. To focus the analysis on reserve requirement regulation, I ignore the public's currency holdings and assume the private sector demands the central bank's monetary base only because it must be held by banks to satisfy reserve requirements on bank deposits. Also, deposits pay no interest and the base rate of production equals the inflation rate. These simplifying assumptions imply that seigniorage (S) equals

$$S = \Delta H = \pi H = \pi k D(i) \qquad (1)$$

where H is the real base, π is the inflation rate, k is the reserve

[2]Before 1980, a state bank might use correspondent balances as reserves. A dollar in state bank deposits increased correspondent balances by that dollar times the state requirement. Fed reserves increased by only the correspondent balance change times the Fed requirement.

213

requirement on real deposits, D, and i is the nominal interest rate on bonds. Equation (1) indicates that the public's real deposit holdings are a function of the nominal bond rate.

According to this standard formulation, the reserve requirement does not influence deposit demand.[3] Therefore, a seigniorage-maximizing central bank always benefits from increasing the requirement. If there are no political constraints, it sets the reserve requirement at one. Otherwise, the central bank raises the requirement as high as politically feasible and then selects the inflation rate that maximizes seigniorage. Viewing the reserve requirement as preset, Milton Friedman's (1953) well-known solution to this problem requires that the inflation rate be raised to the point where the inflation rate elasticity of base money demand equals a minus one.

The traditional approach makes a number of extreme assumptions about the nature of the regulatory market. Implicitly, it assumes that all banks choose central bank membership, or at least that both member and nonmember banks must back all of their deposits with central bank base. Furthermore, the traditional approach assumes the central bank devotes no resources to enforcing reserve requirement regulations. It is as if an automaton-like regulatory agency *costlessly* identifies and labels all bank money as deposits, subject to the prespecified reserve requirement. More generally, the seigniorage function should take into account that not all banks are required to hold reserves produced by the central bank, and those banks that are so required will comply with statutory requirements only if the central bank monitors their behavior.

To illustrate, consider two classes of banks. The law requires that central bank base support all the liabilities of class 1 banks. Class 2 banks fall outside the regulatory scope of the central bank, and therefore they do not hold central bank base. If z is the percent of total financial sector liabilities that the central bank legally can require be backed by its base (that is, z is the ratio of class 1 deposit liabilities to total deposit liabilities), then, with foolproof enforcement, the central bank can impose reserve requirements on zD of total deposits. With less than perfect enforcement, only a fraction, b, of zD will be detected for reserve requirement purposes.

Defining b as the enforcement (detection) ratio, the traditional seigniorage function can be reformulated as

$$S = \pi[bk + (1 - b)\hat{k}]zD(i) - C(a). \qquad (2)$$

The cost to the central bank of enforcing its reserve requirement is

---

[3]A more general formulation allows banks to pay interest on deposits. As Dwyer and Saving (1986) showed, reserve requirements then influence deposit demand.

C, and a represents units of the enforcement input used by the central bank to increase b. The symbol $\hat{k}$ represents the amount of (central bank) reserves class 1 banks voluntarily would hold behind a dollar of deposits even if the central bank did not enforce reserve requirements.

I interpret $\hat{k}$ as Kane's market reserve requirement. Without enforcement $(b = 0)$, $\hat{k}$ is the effective reserve requirement for class 1 banks. With foolproof enforcement $(b = 1)$, the effective requirement becomes the central bank's statutory requirement, k. With partial enforcement, the effective reserve requirement is a weighted average, $bk + (1 - b)\hat{k}$, of the statutory and market requirements. The central bank can change the effective reserve ratio either directly through an increase in the statutory reserve requirement, or indirectly by increasing a and thereby the enforcement ratio, b.

Given the reformulated seigniorage equation, a complete theory of reserve requirement regulation requires specifying the constraints facing the central agency. Kane (1981b, p. 132) indicates three sets of constraints that should be considered in modeling the operation of a regulatory market: "distributive politics that define a clientele to be serviced and place statutory limits on an agency's authority, opportunities for regulatee avoidance activity, and action undertaken by competing regulators."

With respect to reserve requirement regulations, local (state) regulatory agencies may compete with the central (bank) agency. A second group of participants in the regulatory market are the financial institutions that serve as the central bank's regulatees. Finally, Kane's reference to "distributive politics" suggests that a federal government and a network of local governments play at least some role in overseeing the operation of the central and local regulatory agencies.

I assume these groups interact within a federal region that is divided into n identical local jurisdictions. The local government in each region competes with other local governments in attracting financial institutions to its jurisdiction. Each of the n local governments establishes a regulatory agency that offers charters to financial institutions that choose to locate in the region. By choosing the local charter, banks automatically become members of the local banking agency and are bound by its regulations.[4] Alternatively, any bank may select central bank membership and regulation by choosing a central charter.

Only one local regulatory body regulates banks in a region at any one time. However, I model entry into the local regulatory market

---

[4] In the United States, bank selection of a state charter does not preclude Federal Reserve membership.

as contestable. A potential local regulator can replace the existing regulator in a jurisdiction at zero cost.

Having specified the structure of the regulatory market, the constraints faced by the central regulatory agency depend on the objective functions of the other actors in the regulatory market. Consider the objective function of competing local regulatory agencies. Unlike the central banking agency, local agencies do not have the right to produce monetary base. Without this revenue source, local agencies rely on budget appropriations from their local government each period.[5] Although not crucial to the analysis, for concreteness assume that agency employees want to maximize "excess" budgetary funds so as to engage in expense-preference behavior.

The actions of each local regulatory agency will be influenced by the preferences of its sponsor and its financial institution members. Initially, I make a simple assumption about the objective function of the sponsoring government. Each local government wants to maximize its local tax base in the form of total bank assets. Assuming homogeneous banks, the local government allocates budgets to its local agency so as to maximize the number of banks that choose to locate in the jurisdiction.

Finally, I assume that each financial institution confronts a dual-choice problem. Not only must it select a jurisdiction but, it also must decide whether to be a member of the local agency in that jurisdiction or the central agency. A representative bank will choose the regulatory agency that offers the most profits. When a bank receives the same profits with either agency, I assume the bank flips a coin to solve its membership problem.

To specify bank profits, assume that financial institutions have only non-interest-bearing transaction accounts as liabilities. Their assets consist of loans and reserves, and they always prefer to hold no excess reserves. Leaving aside intermediation costs, bank profits equal the revenue from loaning excess reserves on the market less any expenditures incurred in avoiding reserve requirement regulations.[6]

When a regulatory agency raises the effective reserve requirement, outstanding loans and therefore bank profits fall. Banks can react to this regulatory burden by varying the amount of resources used to hide or shelter their deposits from the regulator. The enforcement ratio, b, now depends on the intensity of bank sheltering, as well as

---

[5]Some state agencies also receive a fee from the banks they inspect.

[6]This bank profit definition ignores bank entry into the market over time. It also assumes that banks compete for deposits on neither a pecuniary nor a nonpecuniary basis. Finally, the definition assumes that banks use no resources in acquiring a charter.

the agency's choice of input, *a. Ceteris paribus,* an increase in sheltering activity causes the agency's enforcement ratio to fall.

A Pure Model of Competitive Regulation

The primary feature of a competitive market for reserve requirement regulation is the assumption of a system of local regulatory agencies that compete with the central bank in setting and enforcing reserve requirements. As indicated above, I assume that there is only one local regulatory agency for each jurisdiction. The local sponsoring government can, however, replace the existing regulatory agency with a new agency at zero cost. This section develops a "pure" model in the sense that competition among the n local governments to attract banks to their jurisdiction is perfect.

The competitive model also assumes that only central agency member banks hold central bank reserves. In contrast, each local agency mandates that reserves of its member institutions be in the form of non-interest-bearing liabilities provided by the private sector instead of the central bank. Local banks, therefore, are the class 2 banks of the previous section. Their deposits are not a source of central agency reserves.[7]

The central agency's problem of how to select the inflation rate, the reserve requirement, and its investment in enforcement inputs can be subdivided into smaller steps. Central to this problem is the determination of how competitive regulation at the local level constrains central bank actions. I first consider the budget the local government in a typical jurisdiction gives to its local regulatory agency. This budget allocation dictates the (maximum) level of local agency enforcement activity and allows banks to compute their profits when they choose local agency membership. The central bank then takes this profit condition into consideration in its decision problem. Specifically, the central bank maximizes net seigniorage subject to the constraint that profits promised its members are at least as great as profits those banks receive from local agency membership.

The assumption of perfect competition among local governments eliminates any discretion they might have in the budgetary process. Each local government will be driven by competition to grant its local agency a budget of zero. If, for example, a local government gives a budget that allows the regulatory agency to purchase some enforcement inputs, then bank profits in that jurisdiction will be lower than they potentially might be. This provides a neighboring

[7]Deposits at state agency banks generally had some effect on Federal Reserve base before 1980 (see *supra,* footnote 2).

local government with the opportunity to offer banks in its jurisdiction higher profits by granting its agency a lower enforcement budget. This budget-cutting process continues until budget appropriations in each jurisdiction equal zero. Ruling out subsidies to banks, local governments at this point have fully exploited their ability to attract banks to their jurisdiction.

The choice problem of the local regulatory agency follows trivially from this budgetary equilibrium. Without an enforcement budget, any attempt by the local agency to set a reserve requirement above the market level will be ignored by banks that are members of the local agency. Banks back their deposits with only the market level of reserves, and bank profits, designated as p^*, are the same as they would be in the absence of any formal regulatory structure.

Regulatory powers of the central bank are constrained by the condition that profits of its members be at least as great as p^*. Like the local regulatory agencies, therefore, the central bank is unable to enforce a reserve requirement higher than the market level. If the central bank tried to impose a statutory requirement higher than $\hat{k}$, no bank would take a central charter.[8]

Since bank profits are identical with local or central agency membership, each bank flips a coin to solve its membership problem. On average, half the banks join the central agency and the remainder some local agency. The percentage of total financial sector liabilities that the central bank legally can require be backed by its base, z, equals ½ in equilibrium.

Substituting $z = \frac{1}{2}$, $a = 0$ (which implies $b = 0$), and $k = \hat{k}$ into the central agency's seigniorage function (equation 2) results in

$$S = \pi\hat{k}(\frac{1}{2})D(i). \tag{3}$$

The central agency in this competitive regulatory setting has a decision problem that looks much like the traditional maximization problem depicted by equation (1). The main difference is that only a fraction (½) of banks are members of the central agency. As in the traditional case, seigniorage maximization implies that the central agency raises the inflation rate to the point where the inflation rate elasticity of money demand equals minus one.

One advantage of this competitive regulatory model, as compared with the traditional analysis, is that the reserve requirement is determined within the model. But the assumption of perfect competition

---

[8]I assume that local (central) agency banks hold local (central) agency reserves in the absence of enforcement. Also, the market reserve ratio is the same for all banks, regardless of their affiliation.

among the n local governments leads to the extreme conclusion that local regulatory agencies always set the reserve requirement at or below the market level. Competition at the local level forces the central agency to reduce its requirement accordingly.

Somewhat surprisingly, empirical work on the behavior of local agencies provides some support for the strong market implication. Alton Gilbert (1978, p. 19), for example, tested the effectiveness of state reserve requirements and concluded that "an overall assessment of results in this analysis supports the view that in general state reserve requirements are not effective."

Gilbert, however, found exceptions to this overall assessment. In states that do not allow banks to count cash items in process of collection as reserves, the reserve requirement influences nonmember bank behavior. More important, Fed membership across states is sensitive to the resources state agencies use to monitor and enforce requirements. These findings suggest not only that the *effective* reserve requirement exceeds the market level but also that requirements may differ across states.

The pure competitive model generates several other counterfactual conclusions. It implies that enforcement budgets can be no higher than zero and that central bank membership will be precisely one-half of the total number of banks. The following section reformulates the competitive interaction among local government sponsors in a way that allows (1) enforcement budgets greater than zero and, therefore, effective reserve requirements above the market level, (2) differences in statutory requirements between central and local agencies, (3) variations in effective requirements across localities, and (4) variations in central bank membership over time.

Competitive Regulation with Local Government Budget-Setting Power

Instead of assuming local government competition automatically drives enforcement budgets to zero, suppose local governments retain some budget-setting power. Each local government may use this power to induce local agency enforcement of a reserve requirement that is higher than the market requirement. This outcome presumes that over some range local governments prefer higher reserve requirements.

An interest group perspective suggests why a local government might have this preference. The local government may be responding to pressures from groups that benefit from higher local agency reserve requirements. For example, what if balances at specified correspondent banks and central government securities count as reserves? Reserve requirements then are a source of demand for these private and public obligations. Correspondent banks and the central government would have a common interest in lobbying (rewarding) the local government for using its budgetary authority in ways that lead to reserve requirement increases.[9]

The local government may favor higher reserve requirements for public interest considerations as well. Federal deposit insurance may induce banks to take too many risks in maximizing the value of their assets. In particular, banks may choose to reduce their reserve holdings below even market levels. This provides public-spirited local governments with the opportunity to use their budgetary powers to raise reserve requirements.

Whether interest group driven or public-spirited, a local government with budgetary power will grant a certain budget to its local agency with the expectation that the funds will be used to enforce an effective reserve requirement that is higher than the market level. However, because the local government directly observes only the statutory requirement, it cannot be sure that all the funds will be allocated strictly to production of a higher effective reserve requirement. The best the local government can do in these circumstances is to establish a target statutory requirement and rely on a contestable regulatory market to control local agency enforcement efforts.

What if a local agency used too few enforcement units and engaged in expense-preference behavior? With the appearance of any excess funds, outsiders would be prepared to take over management of the local regulatory agency. An efficient takeover market would ensure that enforcement activity would be raised to a level that cleared the market; that is, enforcement would increase to the point that exhausted excess funds.[10]

Bank profits will be lower when local agencies enforce requirements greater than market reserve requirements. Because local agency membership is less attractive, constraints on central bank actions are not as tight. The central agency will be able to raise its reserve requirement above the market level and devote resources to enforcement.

Consider the central bank decision problem when local agencies throughout the federal region receive identical enforcement budgets

[9]In addition, this section demonstrates that the central government's seigniorage extraction powers are enhanced with higher local agency reserve requirements.

[10]Without contestability, local governments must directly monitor agency shirking. Because such monitoring is not costless, some expense-preference behavior would be observed.

and set identical statutory reserve requirements (higher than $\hat{k}$). Although local bank profits will be the same in each jurisdiction, the central bank does not have to set its own control variables at precisely the levels established by the local regulatory agencies. It need only choose a reserve requirement and enforcement input combination such that the profits a bank receives from central bank membership equal the (now lower) profits a bank receives from local agency membership. The central agency may trade off a high (low) statutory reserve requirement for a low (high) level of enforcement activity.

With differential levels of local enforcement, profits of local agency members will differ across localities. The central bank now has an additional decision-making margin. Since there is no common local bank profit level, the central bank may choose to provide its members with either relatively low or high profits.[11] By choosing low levels of enforcement activity and low statutory reserve requirements, the central agency can induce banks in most states (that is, those with high effective reserve requirements) to choose central agency membership. Incrementally higher central bank activity levels and reserve requirements cause membership losses in marginal states. Instead of central bank membership being an all-or-nothing proposition, membership steadily declines as the effective reserve requirement rises.[12]

The extended competitive model avoids the factual anomalies associated with the pure model. Generally, the extended model predicts that both local and central regulatory agencies will enforce reserve requirements. To the extent that enforcement budgets differ among states, effective reserve requirements also differ. Given a continuum of local agency effective reserve requirements, the central agency can vary its effective reserve requirement within this range.

Monopoly Reserve Requirement Regulation

This section replaces competitive regulation with a setting suggested by the Depository Institutions Deregulation and Monetary Control Act of 1980. In particular, I assume here that the central agency has statutory authority to require all banks to hold reserves in the form of central bank–produced base. The central agency not only sets the reserve requirement for all banks but also is the only

---

[11]The central bank sets uniform statutory reserve requirements and enforcement activity levels across all states.

[12]In terms of seigniorage equation (2), z is now a function of activity level a and statutory requirement k.

enforcement agency. Local agencies no longer monitor local bank compliance with reserve requirements.

The seigniorage function of a central bank that has a monopoly in setting and enforcing reserve requirements becomes

$$S = \pi[bk + (1 - b)\hat{k}]D(i) - C(a). \tag{4}$$

The fraction, z, of total financial sector liabilities that the central bank legally can require be backed by its base automatically rises to one. Note also that the central bank no longer is constrained by a financial institution profit condition. Because the central bank regulates all policy variables (including reserve requirements for nonmembers), bank profits—and, therefore, central bank seigniorage—are not affected by the membership decision. In this pure monopoly setting, the central bank does not worry that the profits of its members may be lower than those of nonmembers.[13]

The absence of a bank profit constraint, however, does not imply that the central bank wants to raise reserve requirements and enforcement activities as high as possible. Increases in statutory reserve requirements and enforcement activities have negative as well as positive effects on central bank seigniorage. An increase in the reserve requirement, for example, increases seigniorage for a given enforcement ratio, b. But this positive effect will be at least partially offset by the increased bank-sheltering activity induced by the reserve requirement change. Similarly, although an increase in the amount of resources invested in enforcement activities raises seigniorage by increasing the enforcement ratio, it also raises enforcement costs. The monopoly central bank will be motivated to raise each of these control variables to the point where marginal benefits just equal marginal costs.

Comparison of Competitive and Monopoly Reserve Requirement Regulations

If local governments are modeled as having no budget-setting power, then the contrast between competitive and monopoly reserve requirement regulations is most striking. Even if the monopoly regulator does not enforce requirements higher than market reserve requirements, a comparison of equation (3) (where seigniorage becomes $\pi\hat{k}(\frac{1}{2})D$) with equation (4) (where seigniorage becomes

[13]Throughout the paper, I assume that banking agencies regulate only reserve requirements. This assumption is not descriptive of the U.S. regulatory market. After passage of the Monetary Control Act, for example, the relative attractiveness of Fed and state agency membership still depends on differences in other regulatory policies.

222

$\pi \hat{k} D)$ indicates that monopoly seigniorage will be twice as high as competitive seigniorage. More generally, this comparison understates the seigniorage difference because granting the central bank monopoly status transforms it from a "price taker," where it has no discretion over reserve requirement policy variables, into a "price setter." The effective reserve requirement will be raised from its market level to its monopoly level.

The ability of local governments to set their own budgets relaxes the price-taker constraints on the central bank. The central bank's decision problem in this modified competitive setting does not differ qualitatively from its problem in the pure monopoly setting. In both settings the central bank must search for policy instrument values that maximize seigniorage.

Under certain circumstances, the central bank's policy decisions will be identical in the competitive and monopoly settings. Consider the special case wherein all local governments happen to grant their local agencies uniformly "large" budgets. Bank profits from local agency membership will be correspondingly low. Profits may be so low that a central bank, acting as an unconstrained monopoly regulator, would choose to reduce them no lower. Because this type of competition places no effective constraint on central bank behavior, the central bank chooses the same reserve requirement and enforcement levels regardless of the regulatory structure.

Local governments generally do not grant such large enforcement budgets. Therefore, the bank profit constraint the central bank faces in the competitive setting usually will be binding. Making the central bank a monopoly regulator eliminates this constraint and induces it to raise its reserve requirement and enforcement activities above the (modified) competitive solution.

As with any market, monopoly in the market for reserve requirement regulations provides the producer with readily identifiable benefits. With respect both to statutory requirements and enforcement levels, the monopoly setting allows the central bank to raise the reserve requirement tax on banks. The monopolist's ability to exploit its position will be constrained by the opportunities banks have to evade reserve requirement regulations. Still, seigniorage at any inflation rate will be higher in the monopoly setting as compared with either the pure or modified competitive setting.

Conclusion

Economists have long known that reserve requirements create a demand for central bank base money. However, they have not formally acknowledged that resources must be invested in enforcement activities for these requirements to be effective. Earlier approaches tended to view the central bank as an automaton-like agency that costlessly identified bank liabilities as reservable. According to this view, the reserve requirement itself was either set by an unconstrained central bank or by unspecified political forces.

This paper has outlined a model of a seigniorage-maximizing central bank that controls its base rate of production, but whose ability to set and enforce reserve requirements may be constrained by competition from local regulatory agencies. The interaction between local governments and their local regulatory agencies helps define the political forces that constrain central bank actions. Several predictions emerge from this perspective.

First, the reserve requirement generally will not be set at the market level. The market solution emerges only in the special case where competition is so tight that local governments have no budget-setting powers. More generally, the local government provides its local regulatory agency with the budgetary inducement to expend some resources in enforcing a reserve requirement that is above the market benchmark.

Second, the reserve requirement and enforcement decisions of local agencies constrain the central bank's choice of policy variables in the competitive setting. Central bank regulations cannot leave a member bank with lower profits than that bank receives with membership in a local agency. If local agency regulations become less stringent, perhaps because of a tax revolt at the regional level, then the central bank must respond by a combination of reserve requirement and enforcement activity cuts. Overall, the regulatory model suggests that political "market" constraints, and not exogenous macroeconomic considerations, drive the central bank's reserve requirement decisions.

In the post–World War II period, reserve requirements of state agencies and the Federal Reserve System generally declined. State banking regulations, however, became progressively less stringent compared with Fed reserve requirement regulations. As a result, the Fed experienced a steady membership decline during the 1960s and 1970s. Continuation of this trend threatened to force the Federal Reserve out of the reserve requirement regulatory market. Partially in reaction to this threat, Congress passed the Depository Institutions Deregulation and Monetary Control Act of 1980.

The act changed the rules of the game by relaxing constraints on decision makers at the Fed. By giving the Fed the authority to impose reserve requirements on deposit liabilities of all financial institutions, the act eliminated local agencies as regulatory competitors, allowing the Fed to increase the stringency of its reserve requirement regulations and thereby extract more wealth through money production.

The model outlined in this paper does not predict that the Fed will immediately act as a profit-maximizing monopolist with passage of the Monetary Control Act. In particular, the Fed is a bureaucratic agency that does not have residual claimant rights to seigniorage. Furthermore, instead of allowing the Fed to set initial reserve requirement levels, the act directly defined new requirements.[14]

The Act does grant the Fed explicit powers to change reserve requirements in the future. The prediction of more stringent reserve requirement regulations, therefore, illustrates the long-run tendencies of a monetary authority that no longer is constrained by competition from other agencies in this regulatory market. In this sense the Monetary Control Act can be interpreted as a change in the nation's monetary constitution that enhances the wealth-extraction powers of the central government.

References

Cacy, J. A., and Winningham, Scott. "Reserve Requirements under the Depository Institutions Deregulation and Monetary Control Act of 1980." In *Issues in Monetary Policy*, vol. 2, pp. 68–81. Kansas City, Mo.: Federal Reserve Bank of Kansas City, 1982.

Dwyer, Gerald P., and Saving, Thomas R. "Government Revenue from Money Creation with Government and Private Money." *Journal of Monetary Economics* (March 1986): 239–50.

Friedman, Milton. "Discussion of the Inflationary Gap," In *Essays in Positive Economics*, pp. 251–62. Chicago: University of Chicago Press, 1953.

Gilbert, Alton R. "Effectiveness of State Reserve Requirements." Federal Reserve Bank of St. Louis *Review* (September 1978): 16–28.

Gilbert, Alton R., and Lovati, Jean M. "Bank Reserve Requirements and Their Enforcement: A Comparison across States." Federal Reserve Bank of St. Louis *Review* (March 1978): 22–33.

Goodfriend, Marvin, and Hargraves, Monica. "A Historical Assessment of the Rationales and Functions of Reserve Requirements." Federal Reserve Bank of Richmond *1982 Annual Report*, pp. 5–23.

Greenbaum, Stuart. "Legal Reserve Requirements: A Case Study in Bank Regulation." *Journal of Bank Research* (Spring 1983): 59–69.

Hester, Donald D. "Innovations and Monetary Control." In *Brookings Papers on Economic Activity*, pp. 141–89. Edited by William Brainard and George Perry. Washington, D.C.: Brookings Institution, 1981.

---

[14]Although the act lowered requirements for members of the Fed and raised them for nonmembers, on balance the reserve requirement burden increased (Cacy and Winningham 1982).

Kane, Edward. "Accelerating Inflation, Technological Innovation, and the Decreasing Effectiveness of Banking Regulation." *Journal of Finance* 36 (1981a): 355–67.

Kane, Edward. "Regulatory Policy for a Changing Financial Services Industry." In *Technological Innovation, Regulation, and the Monetary Economy,* pp. 125–43. Edited by Colin Lawrence and Robert P. Shay. Cambridge, Mass.: Ballinger, 1981b.

Kane, Edward. "Changes in the Provision of Correspondent-Banking Services and the Role of Federal Reserve Banks under the DIDMC Act." In *Monetary Regimes and Protectionism,* pp. 93–126. Edited by Karl Brunner and Allan H. Meltzer. Amsterdam: North-Holland, 1982.

FEDERAL RESERVE INTEREST RATE SMOOTHING

Marvin Goodfriend

Mark Toma's interesting paper on the theory of reserve requirement regulations explains such requirements as resulting from a government revenue-raising motive. I do not intend to address the details of Toma's argument or to comment directly on the plausibility of the view that reserve requirements are simply a tax. Nor will I discuss the specifics of his public choice theory explaining the structure of reserve requirements. Instead, this article focuses on a related topic, that of Federal Reserve interest rate smoothing. As shall become clear, the discussion here supports Toma's hunch on how to explain reserve requirements.

A discussion of interest rate smoothing is appropriate for a number of reasons. In recent years the theoretical feasibility of interest rate smoothing has been demonstrated in coherent rational expectations models. (See, for example, McCallum 1986 and Goodfriend 1987a.) This development has paved the way for sensibly interpreting the comments of Fed watchers who persistently characterize Federal Reserve policy as choosing the level of short-term interest rates. It also makes sense of the extensive institutional evidence that the Fed can and has smoothed interest rates throughout its history. (See Goodfriend 1987b.) In addition, empirical work by Miron (1986), Mankiw and Miron (1986), and Barro (1987) provides evidence of both seasonal and cyclical Fed interest rate smoothing. Giving interest rate smoothing a central place in thinking about monetary policy thereby reconciles analytical, financial market, institutional, and empirical evidence. The attractiveness of the interest rate smoothing view of monetary policy comes in part from this reconciliation.

The author is an economist and vice president at the Federal Reserve Bank of Richmond. The views expressed here do not necessarily reflect those of the Federal Reserve Bank of Richmond. This paper was written while the author was a visiting associate professor at the University of Rochester

As discussed below, the fact that the Fed has employed interest rate smoothing throughout its history implies that the standard rationale for reserve requirements—that they are necessary for monetary control—has been highly misleading. The interest rate smoothing characterization of monetary policy thereby provides indirect support that reserve requirements have functioned exclusively as a tax. This supports Toma's view that the structure of reserve requirements must be explained as a government revenue-maximizing motive.

In addition, pursuing the analytical and empirical implications of interest rate smoothing seems to be a promising way of developing a better understanding of monetary policy as it is actually conducted. In other words, it provides a realistic way of pursuing the positive theory of monetary policy. Historically, economists have emphasized the normative aspects of monetary policy, suggesting models of what the Fed ought to do, but they have found their advice largely ignored. Perhaps by using the interest rate smoothing view, economists can better understand the objectives and constraints facing the Fed so that policy advice can be made more relevant, tailored better to the realities of central banking, and have a better chance of being implemented.

How Interest Rate Smoothing Works

An oral tradition in monetary economics holds that the central bank cannot control nominal interest rates directly. For example, it asserts that the central bank cannot peg the nominal interest rate because doing so would make the price level unstable or indeterminant. This view dates back at least to Wicksell (1898, 1905). It was echoed by Friedman (1968) and received a more formal restatement in Sargent and Wallace (1975). This view, however, has been successfully challenged in recent years. First, McCallum (1981) showed that a monetary authority could run an adjustable nominal interest rate peg and generate a stable, determinate price level. The stability and determinacy of the price level under an absolute nominal interest rate peg was demonstrated by Dotsey and King (1983) and Canzoneri, Henderson, and Rogoff (1983). McCallum (1986) related these new developments to the real bills doctrine. Goodfriend (1987a) discussed the definitions, mechanics, and implications of interest rate smoothing in a positive theory of central bank behavior. It must be emphasized that these papers explain the feasibility of price level determinacy with *nominal* interest rate smoothing by the monetary authority. Whether the monetary authority can smooth real interest rates is a separate and more controversial matter. This discussion assumes that the monetary authority cannot influence real interest rates.

To understand the mechanics of nominal interest rate smoothing, consider Goodfriend's (1987a) model, which has three basic equations. First, it has a money demand function. Second, it has a Fisher equation relating the nominal interest rate to an ex ante real interest rate component plus an expected inflation component. It is helpful to conceive of the Fisher relation as an arbitrage condition equalizing expected real yields on nominal bonds with the real interest rate that clears the economywide goods market. Third, the model has a money supply rule that explains how the central bank generates the nominal money stock. The details of the money supply rule are unimportant for this discussion. What is important is that at each point in time, the money supply rule allows the public to form a determinate expectation of the future nominal money stock.

Interest rate smoothing works as follows. The money supply rule pins down the expected future nominal money stock each period. This, together with expected future real demand for money, implies an expected future price level. Suppose the central bank is pegging the nominal interest rate. The market sets the real expected yield on nominal debt equal to the goods market clearing real rate by bidding the current price level to the point where the pegged nominal rate less expected inflation just equals the required real interest rate.

A key feature of this equilibrium is that the current price level is determined by working backward from expectations about the future price level, through the expected inflation necessary to convert the nominal interest rate peg into the required real yield. Current nominal money growth, therefore, does not cause inflation under interest rate targeting. The current price level is determined by the level of the nominal interest rate peg, together with the goods market clearing real interest rate and future expected nominal money supply and demand.

Suppose the money supply rule were to pin down the future price level at a fixed target so that the price level were stationary. In this case, nominal interest rate smoothing would make the real interest rate shock move the current price level around. That is, the expected inflation or deflation required to convert the real yield on nominal debt into the required ex ante real rate would be achieved by bumping around the current price level.

In practice, central banks are uncomfortable allowing the current price level to be erratic. Long-term nominally denominated contracts in credit and labor markets may allow surprise price level movements to have potentially destabilizing effects. Goodfriend (1987a) has shown that a central bank wishing to minimize price level forecast error and smooth nominal interest rates can create the necessary inflation or deflation by moving the expected future price level around instead. Such a policy, however, makes both the price level nonstationary and the money stock exhibit "base drift." (See Goodfriend 1987b for a discussion of base drift.) It converts temporary real interest rate movements into permanent jumps in the money stock and price level. As the forecast horizon recedes, price level and money stock forecast error variance go to infinity. In this sense, interest rate smoothing creates macroeconomic instability. It appears that interest rate smoothing is a policy widely followed by world central banks because they believe that the financial stability it buys is worth the cost in increased price level instability. It remains unclear to me, however, whether this often-heard rationale for interest rate smoothing accords with its actual explanation. We need much future work on this question.

Finally, in this section, I want to apply the theory of interest rate smoothing to explain why reserve requirements are unnecessary for monetary control. The standard view is that reserve requirements are useful in enabling the central bank to better control the money stock. (See Friedman 1960, p. 50.) In this view, reserve requirements operate by stabilizing the money multiplier, thereby allowing the central bank to control bank deposit money with its total reserve instrument. But under interest rate smoothing as practiced by the Federal Reserve, the money multiplier does not play a causal role in nominal money stock or price level determination. Under interest rate smoothing, the current price level is determined by the chosen level of the nominal interest rate, the goods market clearing real interest rate, and the expected future price level. Current-period money demand, depending, of course, on the current price level, is accommodated by the central bank at the chosen current nominal interest rate. Reserve requirements simply help determine the quantity of monetary base that the central bank must supply currently to provide that accommodation. But reserve requirements do not help determine the money stock.

Institutional Means of Interest Rate Smoothing

The Federal Reserve has achieved its interest rate targets over the years in varied and somewhat complicated ways (Goodfriend 1987b). In the 1920s the Fed used relatively little nonprice rationing at the discount window. It forced the banking system to obtain a portion of monetary base demanded by borrowing at the window. But because there was little nonprice rationing, the discount rate, roughly speaking, provided a ceiling for other interest rates. The discount rate was raised and lowered to adjust the level of short-term interest rates, with appropriate adjustments to nonborrowed reserves so that banks were continually induced to borrow some monetary base at the window.

During most of the 1930s, the discount rate was above market rates, so borrowing at the window was negligible. From 1933 to the end of the decade, the Fed held its portfolio of government securities essentially constant. The Fed, therefore, could not be construed as smoothing interest rates during this period. Interest rates, however, were extremely low, less than 1 percent, and were more or less smoothed any way because they were near their lower bound of zero. So there would have been no need for the Fed actively to smooth interest rates. Later, in the 1940s, the Fed smoothed interest rates as part of its government security price pegging policy during and after World War II.

A procedure similar to that used in the 1920s was also used in the 1950s and 1960s after the Treasury–Federal Reserve Accord. The difference was that the target for borrowed reserves was varied more often to affect slight changes in the level of rates without always changing the discount rate. In the 1970s the Federal Reserve used an adjustable federal funds rate peg by establishing bands of 50 basis points, on average, within which it would keep the funds rate by appropriate open market operations whenever the limits of the band were hit.

The Fed's move to reserve targeting in October 1979 did not mean abandoning interest rate smoothing. Because reserve requirements were lagged (until February 1984), reserve demand was predetermined within a given reserve statement week. Hence, by choosing a nonborrowed reserve target in a given week, once again the Fed used a procedure whereby it essentially chose a quantity of reserves the banks would have to borrow at the discount window. Given Fed nonprice rationing, the demand for discount window borrowing is a function of the spread between the federal funds rate and the discount rate. By choosing the volume of forced borrowing together with the discount rate, the Fed in effect selected a level of the federal funds rate on a week-by-week basis. This procedure amounted to a kind of noisy interest rate smoothing because of the unpredictable variability in the demand schedule for discount window borrowing. Moreover, it was one in which reserve requirements played an inessential role; an identical path for the nominal interest rate could have been produced by choosing a level for the funds rate directly. Even since reserve requirements were made contemporaneous in February 1984, ostensibly to improve monetary control, the Fed has continued to target borrowed reserves or the federal funds rate, so the structure of reserve requirements has remained irrelevant to monetary control.

Empirical Evidence on Interest Rate Smoothing

I referred in the introduction to recent empirical evidence of interest rate smoothing. Miron (1986) has shown that the Fed removed a pronounced seasonal fluctuation in the nominal interest rate that ranged about 6 percentage points from 1890 to 1914. Of course, earlier authors such as Friedman and Schwartz (1963) recognized this. Mankiw and Miron (1986) cannot reject the view that the short-term interest rate is a random walk after the founding of the Fed, but not before. They suggest their finding represents interest rate smoothing behavior on the part of the Fed.

Barro (1987) used Goodfriend's (1987a) model of interest rate smoothing with a public finance view of the Fed's nominal interest rate target. Goodfriend assumed a constant nominal interest rate target to illustrate the mechanics and feasibility of interest rate smoothing. His simplifying assumptions made the nominal interest rate a serially uncorrelated white noise process. As mentioned above, Mankiw and Miron found it to be approximately a random walk. Barro appended a random walk nominal interest rate target generating equation to Goodfriend's model. In an earlier paper, Barro (1979) showed that optimal tax policy involves the government making the tax rate a random walk. Pointing out that the nominal interest rate is the tax rate on the monetary base, Barro justified his nominal rate random walk equation as optimal tax policy. His justification for the random walk interest rate target follows from and is empirically substantiated somewhat by Mankiw (1986).

Kimbrough's (1986) argument, however, weakens the optimal tax policy rationale. He showed that if money is explicitly modeled as an intermediate good that helps to affect the conversion of scarce resources into consumption goods, then it is not optimal to use an inflation tax to help generate revenue. Instead, optimal taxation calls for adopting the optimum quantity of money rule in which the government generates a rate of deflation that makes the nominal interest rate zero.

Nonetheless, with some additional modifications, Barro derives and tests joint restrictions on the inflation and monetary base generating processes implied by Goodfriend's model coupled with the random walk nominal interest rate target generating process. Barro's results are for the period 1890 to 1985. He rejects the model for the period before the establishment of the Fed, finds mixed results for the interwar period, but cannot reject the model for the post–World War II period. In short, his results are encouraging though preliminary.

Conclusion

This paper has argued that nominal interest rate smoothing has been an important feature of monetary policy as practiced by the Federal Reserve. It has drawn on recent theoretical, institutional, and empirical work to make the point. By documenting the interest rate smoothing view and by pointing out that reserve requirements serve no monetary policy purpose under it, the discussion has provided indirect support for the view that reserve requirements must be explained as a tax.

References

Barro, Robert. "On the Determination of the Public Debt." *Journal of Political Economy* (October 1979): 940–71.

Barro, Robert. "Interest Rate Smoothing." Unpublished manuscript. University of Rochester, February 1987.

Canzoneri, Matthew; Henderson, Dale; and Rogoff, Kenneth. "The Information Content of the Interest Rate and Optimal Monetary Policy." *Quarterly Journal of Economics* (November 1983): 545–66.

Dotsey, Michael, and King, Robert. "Monetary Instruments and Policy Rules in a Rational Expectations Environment." *Journal of Monetary Economics* (September 1983): 357–82.

Friedman, Milton. *A Program for Monetary Stability*. New York: Fordham University Press, 1960.

Friedman, Milton. "The Role of Monetary Policy." *American Economic Review* (March 1968): 1–17.

Friedman, Milton, and Schwartz, Anna. *A Monetary History of the United States*. Princeton, N.J.: Princeton University Press, 1963.

Goodfriend, Marvin. "Interest Rate Smoothing and Price Level Trend-Stationarity." *Journal of Monetary Economics* (May 1987a).

Goodfriend, Marvin. *Monetary Policy in Practice*. Federal Reserve Bank of Richmond, 1987b.

Kimbrough, Kent. "The Optimum Quantity of Money Rule in the Theory of Public Finance." *Journal of Monetary Economics* (November 1986): 277–84.

Mankiw, Gregory. "The Optimal Collection of Seigniorage: Theory and Evidence." Unpublished manuscript. Harvard University, November 1986.

Mankiw, Gregory, and Miron, Jeffrey. "The Changing Behavior of the Term Structure of Interest Rates." *Quarterly Journal of Economics* (May 1986): 211–28.

McCallum, Bennett. "Price Level Determinacy with an Interest Rate Policy Rule and Rational Expectations." *Journal of Monetary Economics* (November 1981): 319–29.

McCallum, Bennett. "Some Issues Concerning Interest Rate Pegging, Price Level Determinacy, and the Real Bills Doctrine." *Journal of Monetary Economics* (January 1986): 135–60.

Miron, Jeffrey. "Financial Prices, the Seasonality of the Nominal Interest Rate, and the Founding of the Fed." *American Economic Review* (March 1986): 125–40.

Sargent, Thomas, and Wallace, Neil. "Rational Expectations, the Optimal Monetary Instrument, and the Optimal Money Supply Rule." *Journal of Political Economy* (April 1975): 241–54.

Wicksell, Knut. *Interest and Prices.* 1898. Translated by R. F. Kahn. London: Macmillan, 1936.

Wicksell, Knut. *Lectures on Political Economy, Vol. 2.* 1905. Translated by Lionel Robbins. London: Routledge and Kegan Paul, 1935.

10

THE FSLIC IS "BROKE" IN MORE WAYS THAN ONE

Gillian Garcia

As a result of both the savings and loan industry crisis that began earlier in the decade and inappropriate regulatory policies, the FSLIC is now "broke." Its bankruptcy makes it principal among the thrift industry regulators because the plight of the FSLIC prevents it, as well as the other S&L regulators, from taking the actions needed to ensure the future prosperity of the industry. Regulators have been forced to make "second best" regulatory responses that are frequently so ineffective they render the system of regulatory policies itself "broke." In turn, this set of destitute policies, together with punitive actions from Congress and the administration requiring healthy thrifts to bear the burden of industry clean-up, could conceivably bankrupt the entire savings and loan industry.

The most important regulatory error, which will be the focus of this paper, is the decision to allow large numbers of insolvent and low-capital S&Ls to continue functioning, often for long periods of time and almost as a matter of course. The continued operation of these bankrupt institutions exposes the insurance corporation to moral hazard and the S&L industry to adverse selection as the owners and managers of insolvent insured thrifts are given the opportunity to enjoy any benefits from the gambles they undertake with depositors' funds while passing the losses to their insurer, healthy thrifts, or the taxpayer. These losses have proved heavy and are rapidly increasing the degree of the FSLIC's insolvency.

The continued operation of thrifts that have failed the market test of survival of the fittest, threatens the viability of the industry itself through adverse selection. Healthy thrifts must compete with weaker institutions enjoying regulatory preferences and subsidies. If this

The author directs a group of economists at the U.S. General Accounting Office and is an adjunct professor of finance at Georgetown University. She thanks Lawrence Cluff, Elizabeth Mays, Norman Miller, and Kevin Yeats of GAO's thrift team for assistance with the data. The views expressed are the author's and do not necessarily represent those of the General Accounting Office.

235

situation is allowed to continue indefinitely, the subsidized weak could bring down the marginally solvent and, ultimately, even the strong institutions, causing many more industry participants to fail.

Moreover, all thrifts are now paying higher insurance premiums in order to provide the FSLIC with the resources it needs to begin resolving the industry's problems. In this respect, the additional premiums put healthy thrifts at a disadvantage in competing with nonthrift depository institutions such as commercial banks, savings banks, and credit unions. The strongest thrifts are beginning to flee the industry by obtaining bank charters and shifting to the Federal Deposit Insurance Corporation, a stronger insurer. The viability of the S&L industry itself may be threatened as the strong flee while the weak and at least some of the marginal deteriorate.

Many argue that the new portfolio powers granted earlier in the decade have given thrifts opportunities to undertake exceptional risks. The call for reregulation has been made, therefore, and the Federal Home Loan Bank Board has responded by reimposing some portfolio restrictions. Indeed, it is inappropriate to allow insolvent firms to gamble at the FSLIC's expense, but while deregulation may have given insolvent S&Ls additional ways in which to gamble, it has also provided benefits to sound institutions, their borrowers, and depositors. Unless we are careful, sound as well as weak thrifts and the consumer could be forced to relinquish those gains. The exigencies of restraining the activities of failed S&Ls should be kept separate from the discussion of what powers are appropriate for sound depository institutions.

In short, the S&L industry has become polarized. Most of the strong institutions are prospering, but many insolvent thrifts are deteriorating rapidly, and some of the marginally solvent savings and loans are approaching failure. This situation has occurred at a time when the interest rate environment has been favorable for S&Ls (an advantage that may be departing as interest rates rose sharply during the second quarter of 1987). It is possible that a replay of the interest rate crisis that devastated the industry at the beginning of the decade will occur, making it all the more crucial that the existing problems be dealt with quickly.

On Being Broke

Traditionally, the FSLIC has imposed on federally insured S&Ls an annual insurance premium of one-twelfth of 1 percent of total deposits. For 50 years this premium was adequate to cover FSLIC expenses and the cost of resolving the problems of weak institutions.

However, the price of dealing with but some of the industry's recent problems has been so high that two years ago the FSLIC imposed an additional annual "special assessment" of one-eighth of one percent of total deposits, causing thrifts to pay 20.8 basis points to the FSLIC for each $100 of deposits. The special assessment raises S&L costs above those of the commercial banks, which currently pay to the FDIC only 8.5 basis points per $100 of deposits. Thus, because of their insurer's plight, S&Ls are at a competitive disadvantage when compared to banks and other depository institutions.

Despite the extra assessment, the FSLIC's primary and total reserves have declined since 1983 and have fallen far short of meeting its obligations, as Table 1 shows. Indeed, the General Accounting Office declared the Corporation insolvent early in 1987 and estimated it faced a negative net worth of $6 billion in May 1987.[1]

TABLE I

FSLIC INSURANCE FUND RESERVES
(in billions of dollars)
1980–85

December	Primary Reserves[a]	Secondary Reserves[b]	Total Reserves
1980	5.67	0.79	6.46
1981	5.70	0.60	6.30
1982	5.69	0.61	6.30
1983	5.76	0.66	6.42
1984	4.89	0.72	5.61
1985	3.78	0.77	4.55

[a]Primary reserves, in principle, are immediately usable by the FSLIC because they derive from the regular and special assessment premiums paid by thrifts to the FSLIC and from any interest earned on insurance fund investments.
[b]In the early 1960s, falling FSLIC reserves led to legislation requiring thrifts to prepay insurance premiums into a secondary reserve account. Although the requirement was eliminated in the 1970s, some prepaid premiums and accumulated interest remain. The secondary reserve was not readily available for FSLIC use as it remained an asset on S&L books. Thus, when GAO forced the FSLIC to write off the secondary reserve during the 1986 financial audit, it resulted in a dollar-for-dollar reduction in industry net worth, further increasing the difficulties of some problem thrifts.
SOURCES: *Examination of Financial Statements of the Federal Home Loan Bank Board and Related Agencies*, GAO/AFMD-82-58, March 1982; GAO/AFMD-83-65, April 1983; GAO/AFMD-84-47, May 1984; GAO/AFMD-85-60, July 1985; *Financial Audit Federal Savings and Loan Insurance Corporation's 1985 and 1984 Financial Statements*, GAO/AFMD-86-65, July 1986.

[1]See U.S. General Accounting Office (1987).

At the same time, estimates of the cost of resolving the problems facing the FSLIC have been rising. Table 2 shows that both the number of S&Ls that are insolvent using generally accepted accounting principles (GAAP) and the value of assets in failing thrifts rose each year from 1980 through 1985. The Federal Home Loan Bank Board (FHLBB) reports that the average cost of disposing of failed thrifts in 1984 was almost 15 cents per dollar of assets.[2] Extrapolating this average cost yields an estimated total cost of $16.9 billion for closing all thrifts that were insolvent in 1984.

To make matters worse, the FHLBB has said that the average cost of merging or liquidating failed thrifts has been rising lately, although it has not released recent point estimates of its costs. GAO has data showing that costs associated with liquidations have risen sharply since 1984, but it has no data on recent merger costs. Data in Table 3 indicate that the numbers of liquidations have been increasing relative to the numbers of mergers, even though mergers are usually less costly, so it would appear that average resolution costs have indeed been rising.

The number of insolvent thrifts and the value of their assets remained relatively constant during 1985 and 1986, but as the per dollar disposal cost has risen, total potential demands on the insurance fund have also soared. If average disposal costs have risen to, say, 25 cents per dollar of assets, total potential demands on the insurance fund in 1987 could exceed $28 billion. Early in 1987, the Bank Board estimated the cost of closing just the thrifts that were insolvent under the more lenient regulatory accounting principles (RAP) at $23.6 billion.

Resolution Options

The Bank Board uses three types of final resolution for failed S&Ls, all of which cause the insolvent institution to cease to exist. Liquidation is the first type of action listed in Table 3. The term is frequently understood to mean a payout to depositors. Today, however, payouts are rare because they are often costly, and the FSLIC does not have the necessary funds at hand. Recently, liquidations have involved passing insured deposits to another institution. The deposit liabilities are matched by both sound and unsound assets from the failed S&L or from some other firm, cash, or FSLIC promissory notes. Typically, the FSLIC takes over the worst assets.

Mergers have historically been the most cost-effective and, hence, the preferred way of disposing of failed thrifts. Two types of regu-

[2]See U.S. General Accounting Office (1986).

TABLE 2

ESTIMATES OF FSLIC LOSSES ON INSOLVENT INSTITUTIONS' ASSET PORTFOLIOS, 1980–86[a]
(in billions of dollars)

December	Number of Insolvent Institutions	Total Value of Assets	Potential Dollar Losses to the FSLIC[b]			
			5 Percent	15 Percent	25 Percent	35 Percent
1980	16	0.12	0.01	0.02	0.03	0.04
1981	53	11.82	0.59	1.77	2.96	4.14
1982	222	63.51	3.28	9.53	15.88	22.23
1983	281	77.76	3.89	11.66	19.44	27.21
1984	434	101.58	5.08	15.24	25.39	35.55
1985	449	112.93	5.65	16.94	28.23	39.52
1986[c]	445	112.76	5.64	16.91	28.19	39.47

[a]Insolvent institutions have zero or negative GAAP net worth. We have calculated the GAAP net worth of institutions by subtracting from their reported regulatory net worth those items not consistent with GAAP. Industry participants have questioned some FHLBB regulations related to the valuation of assets and reserves that may be more rigorous than would be required under GAAP. To the extent this is true, our estimates of GAAP net worth may be understated and, thus, the number of institutions insolvent under GAAP, overstated. Data to further refine our GAAP estimates are not collected by the Bank Board nor are they available elsewhere to our knowledge. Such adjustments to GAAP net worth as may be appropriate, therefore, cannot currently be done. While further research may be necessary, the Bank Board has said that such adjustments would not substantially alter the picture of the industry provided by currently available information.

[b]Dollar losses to the FSLIC assuming 5, 15, 25, and 35 percent losses on the assets of institutions that are liquidated or merged. In 1984, the average cost to the FSLIC of dealing with failed institutions was 14.7 percent of assets.

[c]Data are for September 1986.

SOURCE: FHLBB Semiannual and Quarterly Financial Statements, 1980–86.

TABLE 3
DISPOSITION OF INSOLVENT INSTITUTIONS[a] 1980–86

FSLIC Action	1980	1981	1982	1983	1984	1985	1986
Liquidations[b]	0	1	1	6	9	10[c]	21[d]
Supervisory Mergers[e]	21	56	166	31	13	11	4
FSLIC Mergers[f]	11	23	46	33	17	22	22
Total Resolutions	32	80	213	70	39	43	47
Allocations to MCP[g]	0	0	0	0	0	25	29 (17)[h]
Total Number of Insolvent Institutions[i]	16	53	222	281	434	449	445[j]

[a]An insolvent institution is defined to have GAAP net worth less than or equal to zero.
[b]Liquidations include depositor payoffs and transfers of deposits backed by cash, FSLIC assets or notes, or a combination of these to other, often newly created, institutions.
[c]In two 1985 liquidations, assets in receiverships were transferred to newly created S&Ls that became MCPs.
[d]Twelve institutions placed in liquidating receiverships in 1986 were actually transformed into newly created MCPs. Thus here and for two cases in 1985, the liquidating receivership was used, not to close institutions, but to create MCP institutions.
[e]In a supervisory merger, the Bank Board compels the institution to merge, typically without financial assistance, because the S&L failed to meet regulatory capital and other requirements.
[f]In a FSLIC merger, the insurance fund provides financial assistance as an inducement to the acquiring institution.
[g]Allocated initially to the management consignment program (MCP) in any given year.
[h]The MCP definition was changed early in 1987. Seventeen institutions originally classified as MCPs in 1986 were declared to be non-MCPs as of December 31, 1986, because they had not gone through conservatorship or receivership. These 17 institutions are *not* included in the 29 shown above as having been added to the program in 1986.
[i]At the end of the year, except 1986.
[j]By September 1986.
SOURCES: FHLBB and FSLIC.

latory merger are available to the Bank Board.[3] A supervisory merger is arranged by the Bank Board without financial assistance. The FHLBB has the power to force a thrift to merge if the institution becomes insolvent or if it is operating in an unsafe and unsound manner. In the second kind of regulatory merger, the FSLIC does provide assistance—in the form of assets, notes, or cash.

In the past two years, mergers have become more difficult to arrange. Bank holding companies and thrifts can now traverse state boundaries much more readily than before, and consequently the franchise value of a failed thrift in another state has been reduced. Connell (1987) has pointed out a second reason. The FSLIC can no longer afford to take over the problem assets of a failing thrift. But an "unclean bank," containing problem loans that will require considerable management effort to collect, is not an attractive acquisition target. These disadvantages are reflected in the reduced number of mergers,[4] particularly unassisted mergers. As shown in Table 3, unassisted mergers decreased from 166 in 1982 to 4 in 1986, and the number of assisted mergers declined from 46 in 1982 to 22 in 1986.

To take up the slack as the number of institutions needing attention was rising, the Bank Board introduced the management consignment program (MCP) in 1985. Under this program the managers of failing S&Ls are removed and replaced by tried and trusted officers, often from other, more successful thrifts. In 1985 and 1986, over one-third of Bank Board actions against failing institutions were allocations of S&Ls to the MCP. Such allocations cannot be regarded as problem resolutions, however, as participants in the program typically continue to be unprofitable and, hence, remain insolvent. Indeed, it is unclear that the program is stemming the FSLIC's economic losses in the way its creators had hoped.

The juxtaposition of rising demands and declining resources has inhibited FHLBB actions to correct the problems of insolvent and weak S&Ls. As Table 3 shows, 32 S&Ls were merged by supervisory action or with FSLIC assistance in 1980. At the end of that year only 16 GAAP insolvent thrifts remained in operation awaiting disposition. In 1981 and 1982, however, the numbers of problems and actions both rose dramatically, to 222 and 243, respectively, as the S&L crisis escalated with rising interest rates.

[3]Regulatory mergers should be distinguished from voluntary mergers organized without the regulators' involvement.

[4]The editors have pointed out two further reasons. Federal Reserve restrictions make bank holding company acquisitions of thrifts unattractive, and the FSLIC's insolvency makes the value of its indemnifications to acquirers of failed thrifts of questionable value.

Since 1982, the number of resolutions effected has decreased—to just 49 in 1985—as the number of insolvent institutions has risen—to peak at 449 at the end of 1985. Forbearance, a popular political platform in early 1987, was then being forced on a reluctant Bank Board because it lacked the money to deal with the problems facing it. In the mid-1980s, the FSLIC's impending bankruptcy prevented necessary actions from being taken and induced the Bank Board to adopt other, sometimes inappropriate, stop-gap policies.[5] At the same time, allowing insolvent thrifts to continue operating has given them opportunities to "go for broke." As the gamblers tend to lose, and to "lose big," more often than to gain, the demands on the FSLIC have escalated rapidly. Thus, the regulators have allowed an untenable situation—a vicious cycle of deterioration—to develop.

Delay

At the end of September 1986, 445 GAAP insolvent thrifts awaited disposition. Some had been allowed to operate without capital for extended periods of time. GAO (1987) has shown that of the 222 thrifts that were insolvent at the end of 1982, 145 continued to operate four years later, and 80 of them were still insolvent and incurring heavy losses despite the favorable interest rate environment they had experienced in the interim.

At the height of the S&L interest rate crisis in 1982, forbearance had appeared to be a viable policy. It would give thrifts time to use the new powers granted under the Depository Institutions Deregulation and Monetary Control Act of 1980 and the Garn-St Germain Depository Institutions Act of 1982 to adjust their portfolios and recover. It would also allow interest rates to fall as the business cycle progressed. The anticipated decline in rates was expected to reduce S&L costs more rapidly than their revenues, returning many to profitability and solvency. Furthermore, the market value of S&L assets would be increased by falling interest rates, reducing the FSLIC's costs of disposing of those institutions that did not recover.

So early in the 1980s, delaying the declaration of failure appeared to be an acceptable policy to Congress and the Bank Board. But this policy entailed risks. By definition, insolvency means that the value of an institution's liabilities (L) exceeds that of its assets (A). In this

---

[5]For example, the Bank Board proposed to severely restrict S&Ls', particularly state-chartered S&Ls', powers to make direct investments. It later revised its proposal to allow strongly capitalized thrifts more latitude. The Bank Board has severely curtailed growth. Its demands for faster loan-loss write-offs and higher appraisal standards have encountered strong opposition from the industry.

situation, it is difficult for a firm, especially one that is not growing, to earn profits and accumulate capital. Achieving these goals requires that the rate of return earned on assets (r) exceed that paid on liabilities (c) by a margin great enough to counterbalance the deficiency in assets.

Where an institution is solvent (A > L), any rate of return on assets greater than the rate paid on liabilities is sufficient to ensure profitability. But for an insolvent institution, r > c is a necessary but not sufficient condition for profitability. Absent capital gains or losses the sufficient condition is,

$$\frac{r}{c} > \frac{L}{A}.$$

That is, the greater the degree of insolvency, the higher the return on assets (r) needs to be in relation to the return on liabilities (c) to ensure positive profits.

In an efficient market, earning higher rates of return demands taking additional risks. Managers of solvent firms have their jobs and financial interests at stake, so they are likely to be risk-averse. But managers of insolvent firms have little at stake under the present system of deposit insurance. They expect the Bank Board to relieve them of their positions sooner or later anyway unless they recover. They may be willing to gamble in the hopes of recovery, therefore, because the losses they incur will be borne by others.

The Propensity to Take Risks

The FHLBB has asserted that some activities are more risky for S&Ls than others. In particular, the Bank Board's staff claims that investments in acquisition, development, construction, and commercial loans and direct investments in real estate and service corporations are particularly risky. Data to verify these claims are not publicly available. Moreover, modern finance theory reminds us that it is inappropriate to consider the variability of returns to a single asset in isolation. Rather, the effect of the activity on the risk of the portfolio as a whole is the relevant consideration for institutions deciding whether or not to undertake a new activity.

The fact that these activities became permissible for most S&Ls only recently suggests, however, that inexperience may lead S&Ls to make a larger than average number of mistakes. In this case the activities can be risky both in isolation and in the context of the portfolio as a whole.

The interest rate and credit risks inherent in traditional S&L mortgage lending are now well-known, and procedures are available for controlling them. But credit risks in the newer activities may be less well understood. Moreover, there may be an adverse selection problem facing S&Ls entering new markets—the good borrowers may well stay with their traditional lenders while the bad credit risks attempt to convince the new lenders to trust them.

Evidence on Risk Taking

Tables 4 and 5 present data on various forms of potential risk exposure for S&Ls. These tables examine the portfolio composition of thrifts nationwide and in the five states (California, Florida, Louisiana, Oklahoma, and Texas) that have experienced the most problems with their thrifts and/or their real estate markets during the mid-1980s. In the tables, S&Ls are divided into three groups: (1) GAAP insolvent, (2) low capital (that is, positive net worth below 3 percent of assets), and (3) well-capitalized thrifts (with net worth above 3 percent of assets).

Table 4 shows that there is a substantial variation among states in the percentage of assets devoted to direct investments and to acquisition and development loans.[6] Moreover, it tends to be the insolvent firms that engage most prominently in these "risky" activities. For example, insolvent thrifts nationwide and in 4 of the 5 states (but not in Oklahoma) held more commercial loans than the national average for S&Ls. Insolvent S&Ls as a group and in 4 of the 5 states (Louisiana being the exception) held more acquisition and development loans than the solvent institutions for the nation as a whole or in the individual states. Insolvent thrifts nationwide and in California, Oklahoma, and Texas, held a greater proportion of their assets as direct investments than the average S&L.

At the same time, insolvent thrifts also held fewer mortgage assets of all kinds: fewer total mortgages, fewer home mortgages, and fewer mortgage-backed securities. (See Table 5.) Judging exposure on interest rate risk is difficult because the Bank Board does not release the data that would allow estimates of the difference in the duration of assets and of liabilities. Given this limitation, exposure must be inferred from the division of the mortgage portfolio between fixed rate and adjustable rate instruments.

In general, insolvent thrifts nationally and in the states examined held both fewer fixed and fewer adjustable rate mortgages (FRMs and ARMs, respectively) than their solvent counterparts. Exceptions occurred in Florida and Oklahoma, however, where failed thrifts

---

[6]Data on construction loans are not included because they have not been released by the Bank Board.

TABLE 4
ASSET COMPOSITION FOR ALL FSLIC-INSURED INSTITUTIONS AS OF SEPTEMBER 30, 1986

Designation	Net Worth Category	Net Mortgage Loans and Contracts	Commercial Loans	Consumer Loans	A&D Loans[a]	Liquid Assets[b]	Direct Investments[c]	Deferred Losses	Goodwill
Total Industry	Less than or = to 0%	62.08	2.33	5.48	5.07	4.78	4.33	2.57	1.48
	Between 0 and 3%	71.76	1.58	4.36	3.65	4.72	3.19	0.60	2.29
	Greater than 3%	70.84	1.74	4.10	2.13	5.63	2.48	0.15	2.24
	Total Industry	70.21	1.76	4.30	2.80	5.32	2.84	0.50	2.18
California	Less than or = to 0%	58.54	1.85	2.32	1.82	3.09	12.14	0.55	0.68
	Between 0 and 3%	78.25	0.32	1.48	0.80	4.07	3.99	0.04	1.88
	Greater than 3%	73.54	1.05	3.40	1.09	4.61	3.88	0.07	1.71
	Total State	73.89	0.92	2.90	1.06	4.42	4.29	0.08	1.70
Florida	Less than or = to 0%	52.88	3.72	4.71	4.31	8.08	1.63	1.26	0.55
	Between 0 and 3%	71.56	2.22	5.73	4.28	4.64	1.67	0.25	2.29
	Greater than 3%	66.27	3.11	5.67	2.19	7.16	2.24	0.22	2.93
	Total State	66.36	2.95	5.60	2.89	6.63	2.05	0.32	2.56
Louisiana	Less than or = to 0%	59.08	3.18	6.79	3.93	5.50	1.05	1.66	0.79
	Between 0 and 3%	69.01	1.77	6.35	2.59	4.24	1.33	1.18	2.57
	Greater than 3%	66.71	0.58	7.00	9.35	3.90	8.37	0.29	2.65
	Total State	65.12	1.59	6.80	6.22	4.43	4.64	0.89	2.11
Oklahoma	Less than or = to 0%	69.99	1.33	7.18	2.84	3.47	1.44	3.48	0.09
	Between 0 and 3%	71.20	2.84	6.50	2.04	3.04	0.81	0.05	0.12
	Greater than 3%	72.35	2.13	6.29	2.49	5.10	1.07	0.04	0.25
	Total State	71.48	2.02	6.50	2.51	4.28	1.13	1.02	0.18
Texas	Less than or = to 0%	57.15	2.72	4.90	20.04	3.48	8.86	1.00	1.37
	Between 0 and 3%	67.27	3.07	3.70	15.02	3.82	7.86	0.15	2.58
	Greater than 3%	66.80	1.69	4.13	15.29	3.65	6.70	0.08	3.64
	Total State	65.35	2.48	4.10	15.98	3.70	7.58	0.27	2.78

[a]Acquisition and development loans.
[b]Cash, deposits, and investment securities excluding valuation allowances.
[c]Residential and nonresidential property and service corporations excluding valuation allowances.
SOURCE: FHLBB Quarterly Financial Statements, September 1986.

TABLE 5
COMPOSITION OF MORTGAGE ASSETS FOR ALL FSLIC-INSURED INSTITUTIONS, ON SEPTEMBER 30, 1986

Designation	Net Worth Category[a]	Net Mortgage Loans and Contracts[b]	Home Mortgages	Mortgage-backed Securities	Fixed-rate Mortgages	Adjustable Rate Mortgages
Total Industry	Less than or = to 0%	62.08	31.93	7.52	26.31	26.39
	Between 0 and 3%	71.76	34.88	17.46	36.83	26.62
	Greater than 3%	70.84	41.45	12.20	32.83	30.77
	Total Industry	70.21	38.89	13.21	33.17	29.31
California	Less than or = to 0%	58.54	26.30	4.85	19.16	31.34
	Between 0 and 3%	78.25	29.34	33.00	48.96	22.17
	Greater than 3%	73.54	40.45	9.60	20.68	43.88
	Total State	73.89	37.30	14.62	26.93	38.44
Florida	Less than or = to 0%	52.88	28.27	7.27	19.11	26.18
	Between 0 and 3%	71.56	45.15	7.23	32.90	29.95
	Greater than 3%	66.27	40.87	12.26	34.27	24.33
	Total State	66.36	40.78	10.59	32.58	25.86
Louisiana	Less than or = to 0%	59.08	33.52	6.47	24.66	21.80
	Between 0 and 3%	69.01	43.39	4.78	29.78	30.31
	Greater than 3%	66.71	43.18	3.98	30.76	21.10
	Total State	65.12	40.52	4.87	28.82	23.50
Oklahoma	Less than or = to 0%	69.99	38.62	5.98	24.43	32.50
	Between 0 and 3%	71.20	40.56	5.74	23.93	34.96
	Greater than 3%	72.35	43.10	8.00	32.68	27.61
	Total State	71.48	41.39	7.05	28.85	30.25
Texas	Less than or = to 0%	57.15	18.62	2.72	16.17	26.70
	Between 0 and 3%	67.27	23.77	7.22	18.56	37.07
	Greater than 3%	66.80	24.19	15.83	29.10	29.28
	Total State	65.35	23.05	9.80	22.22	32.28

[a]Rows do not sum to one because they encompass overlapping categories.
[b]Mortgages on 1 to 4 family residences.
SOURCE: FHLBB quarterly Financial Statements, 1986.

held more ARMs than the state average. The ratio of FRMs to ARMs is below unity (except in Louisiana) for insolvent thrifts, while it is often above one for solvent S&Ls. From these limited data, insolvent thrifts do not appear to be more exposed than the rest of the industry to interest rate risk, but they do potentially face more credit risk.

The Vicious Cycle

The insolvent savings and loans are typically incurrring heavy losses (see Table 6) causing the degree of their insolvency, and hence the FSLIC's need to redress the growing deficiency in assets, to continue increasing. As few insolvent thrifts recover, demands on the FSLIC's funds escalate. Insolvent thrifts were, for example, experiencing losses at an annual rate of 5 percent of assets in the third quarter of 1986 (Table 6). At this rate, delaying disposal of these thrifts by one year would add $5.6 billion to the FSLIC's resolution costs.

In the fall 1986, there were 3,234 S&Ls: 67.7 percent were well-capitalized with GAAP net worth of 3 percent or better, 18.5 percent were solvent but weak with capital below 3 percent, and 13.7 percent were insolvent.

The data presented in Table 6 show that two-thirds of the insolvent thrifts were incurring negative total and operating profits.[7] These losses occurred despite the fact that the economy was favorable during this period in most parts of the country. Interest rates were lower than at any other time in the decade, the economy was in its fourth year of an expansion, the demand for mortgages was strong, and funds were available to meet the demand.

In this environment, most well-capitalized thrifts, except those in markets depressed by the decline in energy and agricultural product prices, were profitable. For example, 66.9 of the solvent but weak thrifts and 88.4 percent of the well-capitalized savings and loans were profitable in the third quarter of 1986 despite the increasing loan loss write-offs that the Bank Board was imposing at that time.

Inappropriate Responses

This paper has shown that the S&L industry is polarized. The weaker section of the industry is exposed to credit risk, and because

---

[7]During the second half of 1986, the Bank Board required many S&Ls to take additional loan loss write-offs. Some analysts have explained the losses experienced by S&Ls at this time by referring to these write-offs. However, the present analysis shows that many S&Ls, particularly the insolvent ones, were incurring operating losses in addition to suffering from charges against nonoperating income.

247

TABLE 6
INCOME AND PROFITABILITY OF FSLIC-INSURED INSTITUTIONS IN SEPTEMBER 1986

Designation	Net Worth Category	Number of Institutions	Percent in Category	Total Assets (billions)	Average Return on Assets[a]	Total Industry Profits (billions)	Number Profitable	Percent Profitable	Net Operating Profit (billions)
Total Industry	Less than or = to 0%	445	13.70	112.70	-5.00	-1.40	148	33.26	-.74
	Between 0 and 3%	598	18.50	282.50	-0.09	-0.07	400	66.89	-.07
	Greater than 3%	2191	67.70	747.90	0.82	1.54	1936	88.36	1.92
	Total Industry	3234	100.00	1143.00	0.02	0.06	2484	76.81	1.10
California	Less than or = to 0%	30	13.70	13.90	-7.60	-0.26	4	13.33	-.19
	Between 0 and 3%	30	13.70	66.80	0.32	0.05	20	66.67	.00
	Greater than 3%	158	72.40	218.20	1.08	0.59	138	87.34	.73
	Total State	218	100.00	299.10	0.51	0.38	162	74.31	.55
Florida	Less than or = to 0%	19	12.90	7.40	-4.12	-0.07	4	21.05	-.04
	Between 0 and 3%	26	17.60	20.35	0.00	0.00	17	65.38	.01
	Greater than 3%	102	69.30	55.80	0.38	0.05	73	71.57	.06
	Total State	147	100.00	83.60	0.12	-0.02	94	63.95	.03
Louisiana	Less than or = to 0%	26	25.40	4.30	-3.50	-0.04	7	26.92	-.02
	Between 0 and 3%	23	22.50	3.70	-0.79	-0.01	12	52.17	.00
	Greater than 3%	53	51.90	7.50	1.12	0.02	43	81.13	.02
	Total State	102	100.00	15.60	-0.65	-0.03	62	60.78	.00
Oklahoma	Less than or = to 0%	14	26.40	2.80	-2.90	-0.02	0	0.00	-.01
	Between 0 and 3%	11	20.70	1.60	-1.10	0.00	1	9.09	.00
	Greater than 3%	28	52.80	5.40	-0.30	0.00	14	50.00	.00
	Total State	53	100.00	9.90	-1.19	-0.03	15	28.30	-.01
Texas	Less than or = to 0%	66	23.60	16.70	-15.50	-0.65	6	9.09	-.35
	Between 0 and 3%	74	26.50	43.10	-1.90	-0.21	21	28.38	-.20
	Greater than 3%	139	49.80	37.70	0.03	0.00	86	61.87	.00
	Total State	279	100.00	97.60	-3.50	-0.86	113	40.50	-.57

[a]Returns are annualized
SOURCE: FHLBB Quarterly Financial Statement, September 1986.

its gambles have been largely unsuccessful, it is deteriorating rapidly. The demise of the weaker S&Ls is imposing increasing demands on the FSLIC insurance fund, and at the same time it is prejudicing the successful operations of healthy thrifts. The FSLIC is insolvent and cannot provide the funds necessary to dispose of the problem S&Ls, so it is searching for other ways to contain the deteriorating situation it faces.

One response to the current problem is to reregulate the industry, asking Congress to remove some of the provisions of the 1980 and 1982 deregulation acts. The evidence in this paper suggests that insolvent thrifts should not be allowed *carte blanche* to engage in end-of-game plays. But it presents no evidence either for or against deregulation or reregulation for the industry as a whole. Restraining the weak does not imply that the strong necessarily should be similarly shackled. The question of what powers should be granted to healthy thrifts—or sound banks—is a separate one that is worthy of separate and careful consideration.

References

Barth, James R., and Regalia, Martin A. "The Evolving Role of Regulation in the Savings and Loan Industry." Chapter 6 of this book.

Connell, Lawrence. "Managing Insolvent Institutions." Paper presented at the Federal Reserve Bank of Chicago Conference on Bank Structure and Competition, May 1987.

Kane, Edward J. *The Gathering Crisis in Deposit Insurance.* Cambridge: MIT Press, 1985.

U.S. General Accounting Office. *Thrift Industry Problems: Potential Demands on the FSLIC Insurance Fund.* GAO/GDD-86-48BR. Washington, D.C., February 1986.

U.S. General Accounting Office. *Thrift Industry: Forbearance for Troubled Institutions 1982–1986.* GAO/GDD-87-78BR. Washington, D.C., May 1987.

11

NONBANK BANKS ARE NOT THE PROBLEM: OUTMODED REGULATIONS ARE
Catherine England

Nonbank banks have been the focus of much recent attention and debate. To some, limited-service banks are a shelter through which the parent organizations can conduct business critical to their continued profitability and even survival. To others, they are mongrel institutions born of efforts to evade legitimate strictures imposed by congressional intent as well as a threat to the interests of the traditional banks and their customers.

Exactly what are these organizations that have elicited such a fierce debate? Are they in fact free of regulation and oversight? Or are they a valid means of serving the interests of consumers?

The debate over nonbank banks has been marked by considerable misunderstanding—not surprising when one considers the name. To their individual customers, nonbank banks are banks like any other. Most offer checking and savings accounts as well as loans for cars, boats, houses, and educational expenses. Because most nonbank banks are federally insured, they are regulated by the Federal Deposit Insurance Corporation and subject to capital and reserve minimums and examinations much like those imposed on full-service banks. It is not the nonbank banks themselves that are unregulated; it is their parent organizations that enjoy more freedom than the owners of traditional banks, a fact that will be explained shortly.

As Congress sets out to deal with the "problem" of nonbank banks, it is particularly important for policymakers as well as the general public to set aside the myths and misconceptions and view the nonbank bank issue as objectively as possible. Because as complicated as the nonbank bank issue may seem, it is not the real problem facing Congress, the federal regulators, and the banking industry. Nonbank banks are a symptom of a much more serious malaise. The fundamental question is what long-term economic role banks and other financial institutions should play in an increasingly competitive envi-

---

The author is a Senior Policy Analyst at the Cato Institute.

ronment. Attempting to address the nonbank bank issue in isolation will only put off the day when the profound changes occurring in the domestic and international financial markets have to be reflected in the regulatory structure.

What Are Nonbank Banks?

To understand the genesis of nonbank banks, it is necessary to examine the Bank Holding Company Act of 1956, a key piece of legislation supplementing the banking regulation of the 1930s. The act, as amended, has two broad purposes: (1) to separate banking from commerce and from most other financial services, and (2) to prevent banking organizations from expanding across state lines through the device of wholly owned subsidiary banks.

The Bank Holding Company Act defines a bank as an organization that "accepts demand deposits and makes commercial loans." It then subjects corporations that own banks meeting that definition—bank holding companies—to regulation by the Federal Reserve Board, which is directed to determine what business activities a bank holding company may pursue, either through the parent organization or through its nonbank subsidiaries. Such activities must be "closely related to banking and a proper incident thereto." In addition, the Douglas amendment to the Bank Holding Company Act prohibits banking operations from establishing de facto interstate banking through the purchase of wholly owned subsidiary banks in other states unless such acquisitions are approved by the relevant state legislatures.

Both limited-service banks and the use of the term "nonbank banks" to describe them arose because of the word "and" in the Bank Holding Company Act's definition of a bank. If a financial institution either accepts demand deposits or makes commercial loans but does not do both, it is not a bank for the purposes of the Bank Holding Company Act.[1]

Because limited-service institutions fail to satisfy the legal definition of a bank, neither their parent corporations nor other subsidiaries are subject to the strictures imposed by the act. They may engage in any activities they wish, including activities that are closed to traditional banks and to bank holding companies—manufacturing, retailing, corporate securities underwriting, and insurance brokerage, to name a few. Not only can *anyone* acquire a nonbank bank,

---

[1] The Supreme Court has upheld this interpretation and has prevented the Federal Reserve Board from redefining either "commercial loans" or "demand deposits" in a way that would close the loophole.

but one can do so *anywhere*, thereby breaching the law's geographic restrictions as well.

Most nonbank banks accept deposits but make no commercial loans; they lend only to individuals.[2] Hence, their owners prefer the terms "limited-service banks" or "consumer banks." Companies in a wide range of industries have obtained limited-service banks—retailers, such as Sears, Roebuck and J. C. Penney; other financial institutions, such as Fidelity Federal Savings and Loan Association in California, Shearson/American Express, and Prudential Insurance; and conglomerates, such as Gulf & Western and Control Data Corporation—and they have done so for a variety of reasons. Gulf & Western, one of the first companies to acquire a limited-service bank, uses its nonbank bank to support its credit card and consumer lending activities. Merrill Lynch obtained its nonbank bank so that it could process its cash management account customers' check and credit card transactions in-house. Other firms have acquired nonbank banks in order to offer customers access to their funds through nationwide automatic teller machine networks.

The Case against Nonbank Banks

Those who oppose nonbank banks usually cite one of two reasons for doing so. They object to the absence of geographic restrictions on who may own nonbank banks, or they object to the powers that can be exercised by the parent companies of nonbank banks.[3]

Support for Geographic Restrictions

This country has the most decentralized banking system in the world. Maintaining that distinction has long required both state and federal legislation that restrains branch banking and attempts to shut

---

[2]The law is not absolutely clear about whether the personal loans made by nonbank banks must be confined to consumer loans—funds designated for car purchases, home improvements, and college tuition, for example—or whether they may be used by their recipients for business purposes. This ambiguity leads most limited-service banks to lend only for consumption purposes.

[3]Another reason sometimes cited for opposing nonbank banks involves congressional efforts to fashion a solution to the thrift crisis. It is argued that if nonbank banks exist as mechanisms through which other depository institutions can enter new geographic markets, fewer institutions will be willing to acquire the hundreds of insolvent S&Ls in the nation. The cost to the Federal Savings and Loan Insurance Corporation, the thrift industry, and the Treasury Department (that is, taxpayers) of resolving the industry's problems will increase, it is argued. That is no doubt true. But should public policy toward a wide range of financial firms and their customers be predicated on minimizing the costs that the federal authorities incur in their attempts to redress past regulatory and monetary policy mistakes?

down interstate banking innovations as they appear. And despite the regional banking compacts that are now eroding barriers to interstate banking, there remains much opposition to the "unregulated" geographic expansion of nonbank banks as many large regional and money-center banks own nonbank banks precisely because doing so allows them to attract and accept savings deposits and generate consumer loans outside their home markets. To the extent that nonbank banks are allowed to exist and expand, therefore, they hasten the demise of our highly decentralized banking system.

Many of those who oppose nonbank banks maintain that the deposits they gather are not likely to remain in the same community. Such opponents paint a scenario in which funds are gathered from the nation's small towns and used to support lending activities in its major cities, particularly those on the East Coast. The large money-center and regional banks that expand by purchasing nonbank banks are expected to offer higher interest rates on deposits, a wider range of services, and sometimes even lower interest rates on loans—enticements that will threaten the ability of locally based institutions to compete and survive. Once the local banks are gone, it is argued, service to consumers in less-populated areas will suffer as the owners of nonbank banks will turn their attention back to consumers in the big cities.

Those objections are not unfamiliar to anyone who has studied the struggle against interstate banking in this country. They echo 200-year-old populist concerns about the concentration of power and the evils perpetrated by money-center bankers. Not surprisingly, objections to the absence of geographic constraints for nonbank banks are often raised by the owners and managers of depositories in areas where new bank entry has been limited, and hence local market power protected, by restrictive branching laws.

Support for Powers Restrictions

Those who object to nonbank banks on the basis of the powers that can be exercised by their parent companies and other subsidiaries fall into two camps. The first supports the traditional separations between commerce and banking and between banking and other financial services. The second group contends that cordoning off banking into a narrowly defined set of activities is unnecessary and potentially destabilizing. Members of the second camp cite instead competitive inequities—owners of nonbank banks may provide their customers with a variety of services in a range of locations that traditional banks and bank holding companies cannot match.

Members of the first camp often assert that to protect the safety and soundness of the nation's banking system, the activities of banks and their parent corporations must be subject to federal scrutiny. Paul Volcker, chairman of the Federal Reserve Board until the summer of 1987, was one of the leading proponents of that position. It is his stated opinion that continuing to allow nonbank banks to operate would be indicative of a failure "to respect the uniqueness of banking." In that vein, he stated:

> The ensuing questions of conflict of interest, undue concentration of resources, unfair competition, and the transmission of unregulated risks to the financial system would hardly be consistent with long-standing public policy and the operation of the federal safety net.[4]

Such concerns frequently arise from the belief that it was excessive competition among banks and their participation in the securities markets in the 1920s and the early 1930s that made them particularly vulnerable during the Great Depression.[5]

An often-heard concern is that a nonbank bank might be forced to lend to its parent or to another subsidiary at preferential interest rates and without proper credit quality controls. Should such loans sour, they could endanger the bank. Even in the case of subsidiary banks that do not make commercial loans, it is feared that the public will nonetheless become concerned about the stability of a depository associated through a holding company with an ailing firm. Such concerns might lead to a bank run, it is argued, and because runs are widely believed to be contagious, it is feared that the resulting unease could spread throughout the system.[6]

Another oft-heard objection to the lack of regulation of nonbank banks' parent companies is that tie-in sales will result. Those who oppose retailing, insurance, and securities firms' ability to purchase banks frequently speculate that customers of those highly diversified firms will be coerced into buying goods and services they do not want at above-normal prices. That is, they envision a consumer loan being approved only if the customer agrees to buy his health insurance or his new carpeting from the insurance or retailing subsidiary of the bank's holding company.

---

[4]As quoted in "Nonbanks and Nonproblems," p. 9.

[5]For a recent discussion questioning many of the commonly accepted reasons for bank failures during the Great Depression, see Ely (1987).

[6]Recent examinations of historical evidence suggest that the "contagion effect"—bank runs spreading from insolvent to healthy institutions—was very rare before 1930. See, for example, Kaufman (1987).

There are also those who argue that it is unfair to allow banks, whose funds are guaranteed through federal deposit insurance, to become major participants in the securities and insurance markets. They contend that nonbank banks' government guarantees, implicit as well as explicit, give them an advantage over traditional securities and insurance firms in raising operating capital. In a similar vein, opponents of nonbank banks contend that allowing retailing, insurance, and securities firms to own federally insured banks gives them access to funds (raised as deposits) for which they will pay lower interest rates (because the deposits are perceived to embody less risk) than are paid for unguaranteed funds raised through the capital markets. Thus, such firms that own banks are believed to have an unfair advantage in attracting customers because they can afford to charge lower rates on extensions of credit.

Finally, even observers who generally advocate less regulation express anxiety over the prospect that if a nonfinancial parent begins to slide toward bankruptcy, regulators' fears that its failure will undermine the stability of the banking subsidiary will lead them to bail out the parent, its creditors, and other subsidiaries. Given that the federal deposit insurers—particularly the Federal Savings and Loan Insurance Corporation—are having difficulty handling depository failures alone, it is argued, the contingent liabilities that might result from expanded ownership of banks would create serious problems.

Of course, many argue that potential problems can be eliminated through laws and regulations limiting or prohibiting tie-in sales, intracorporate and affiliate lending, and federally sponsored financial aid to the parent firm and other subsidiaries of a holding company that includes a bank. Those who take this position, among them the owners of many large and mid-sized banks, maintain that the problem with nonbank banks lies not in the fact that securities firms, insurance companies, retailers, and manufacturers can own banks and engage in a wide range of other activities but in the fact that traditional bank holding companies are prohibited from responding to the competitive challenges that result.

The world in which banks compete has changed dramatically over the past 10 to 15 years. Telecommunications technology has advanced to the point where the international capital markets are rapidly becoming one. The highly volatile period of the 1970s and the early 1980s caused institutions of many stripes to develop and market innovative financial products designed to allow even middle-income individuals to achieve a greater return on their savings and investments. The competitive pressure on banks is heightened when nonbank financial firms can offer close substitutes for banking services (such as checkable accounts) and banks are prevented from responding with innovations of their own.

The Changing Financial Services Markets

Why have nonbank banks become such a widely debated policy topic over the past few years? The loophole has existed for 30 years, but the first nonbank bank was not established until 1980. Since then more than 200 nonbank banks have been formed, and more than 200 applications are pending. Are nonbank banks simply the latest fad in the financial services industry, or are substantial changes in the industry making them increasingly attractive?

One of the driving forces behind the nonbank bank movement is reflected in figures recently cited by Litan (1986, p. 6) in describing the competitive assault on banks and the important structural changes that are taking place in the financial services markets. Banks are losing many of their commercial loan customers, for example. Having supplied 85 percent of U.S. corporations' short- and intermediate-term credit in the 1950s, banks now provide only 60 percent of such credit, and the downward trend seems to be continuing. Nor can banks hope to make up those losses in the consumer markets, for they are no longer the primary source of individuals' credit. In 1985, consumers turned to finance companies, credit unions, retailers, and savings banks for 56 percent of their loans, up from 52 percent as recently as 1980.

What has caused these changes? For one thing, companies formed as specialized lenders are branching out. Ford and General Motors operate finance subsidiaries that are no longer interested in merely extending automobile loans. Both firms' subsidiaries are now heavily involved in mortgage banking, for example. General Electric Credit Corporation has become a leading business lender and, with its recent acquisition of Kidder Peabody, is positioning itself to become a major investment banker. Furthermore, the booming securities markets have encouraged an increasing number of firms to raise funds through the capital markets rather than borrow from banks.

Fundamental structural changes are driving such developments. At their root are two sets of events: the economic upheaval and the telecommunications revolution of the last decade.

The Consequences of the Economic Upheaval

The double-digit inflation and high interest rates of the late 1970s and the early 1980s had a significant impact on the financial services markets. They created additional demand for nonbanking financial services from bank customers, thereby generating an opportunity for new suppliers of financial services to enter markets in which they had not previously been competitive.

Specifically, with inflation soaring and interest rates rising and volatile, many individuals, whether in the course of managing their own financial affairs or their employers', began to reevaluate the service they were receiving from their banks. Often through no fault of their own, the banks were found wanting. They could not offer market rates of return on the funds traditionally deposited with them by low- and middle-income savers, nor could they offer new sources of working capital to their commercial customers. Consequently, as individuals and businesses sought to protect their interests in a period of economic uncertainty, they became accustomed to looking outside the banking community and dealing with other sources of financial services. Their financial sophistication increased accordingly.

Naturally, nonbank suppliers of financial services were happy to meet the needs of disenchanted bank customers. The results included innovations such as money market mutual funds for consumers seeking savings alternatives and commercial paper and non-investment-grade ("junk") bonds for companies seeking a less expensive source of debt capital. Furthermore, it was not only domestic financial firms that stepped into the gap created by U.S. bankers' inability to meet their customers' needs; foreign firms also eagerly contributed their services, through branches established in the United States and through the Eurodollar and Eurobond markets.

Although inflation has subsided substantially and, as a result of regulatory changes, banks are now able to offer higher rates of return on savings, the nonbank firms that have entered banking markets are not prepared to meekly step aside. Nor are former customers of banks complacently returning to the fold. Consequently, the markets to service the financial needs of businesses and individuals have become increasingly competitive. To retain their customers and attract new ones, financial services firms must offer attractive packages. Insured deposits, investment capabilities, access to affordable credit, and any number of other features may become part of the selection offered in the emerging financial services markets. Thus, in seeking to remain competitive, many nonbank financial companies have seized upon the nonbank bank as a means of providing a full range of services to their customers and of lowering their operating costs.

A more recent source of upheaval is the uneven economic performance during the current recovery. Industries in which participants had based investment decisions on the assumption that inflation would continue are now experiencing serious difficulties. Two of those, agriculture and energy, are causing particular concern in the banking industry because of their regional concentration. Many banks are inhibited by branching restrictions from adequately diversifying their loan portfolios and are consequently exposed to potentially devastating losses in the event of regional economic downturns.

Thus, the push among banks to expand across state lines and establish a presence in other markets through the device of nonbank banks has four motivations. First, banks are attempting to increase the diversification in their portfolios of consumer loans and thus reduce their risk of failure. Second, they are seeking to expand their base of relatively small deposits made by individuals and small businesses, which is the least expensive and most stable source of funding for banking operations. Third, banks are striving to match their competitors in the financial services industry—if not in the range of services offered, at least in the range of locations in which services are available. Finally, many banks are using nonbank banks to establish a presence in attractive locales in anticipation of expanding further after interstate barriers fall.

The Consequences of Telecommunications Advances

Telecommunications advances are playing a significant role in eliminating political boundaries (both state and national) as barriers to the flow of financial capital. More than any other industry, the network of money markets is becoming truly international in scope.

Community banks cannot hide from that fact at home. State restrictions are becoming increasingly ineffective. Not only are the barriers being assailed in state legislatures, but more and more consumers are able to use nationwide computer networks—whether at home or at automatic teller machines—to shop for and obtain banking services in the next town or the next state.

Consequently, newly chartered depositories are rethinking the traditional ways of doing business. For example, in January 1986, New England Federal Savings Bank set up shop in an upstairs Boston office. Its officials expected to operate almost entirely through the mails and by telephone. The absence of a physical branch network allows the institution to offer customers more attractive interest rates on deposits and to secure better returns for stockholders. Similarly, Greenwood Trust Company, the consumer bank owned by Sears, solicits deposits nationwide, promising savers higher returns that reflect the lower costs it incurs because of the absence of a physical branch network. There is no banking market into which such institutions cannot reach.

But it's not only individual customers that are finding more alternatives. The size of the businesses able to raise funds through the domestic and foreign capital markets is steadily decreasing as telecommunications advances allow information to be gathered and transmitted more cheaply and reduce the minimum size of transactions that can be handled easily in organized markets. The much talked about "junk" bonds are in fact primarily a mechanism through which mid-sized firms—not just the nation's largest corporations—are able to access the capital markets directly instead of being forced to raise debt capital only through bank loans. Non-investment-grade bonds allow such firms to borrow directly from lenders and reduce their capital costs in the process.

Furthermore, new communications technology is allowing an increasing number of U.S. firms to take their financial capital needs offshore; their officials can float debt issues in the Euromarkets without leaving their offices. U.S. banks with overseas branches can earn fees by aiding their corporate customers in that process, but such income must be little consolation to them, considering that until a few years ago they were providing the bulk of the credit themselves.[7]

In short, financial markets are evolving at a pace and in directions that could not possibly have been anticipated by legislators in 1933, in 1956, or as recently as a decade ago. Financial services firms that hope to survive and prosper in this rapidly changing environment must exhibit more flexibility than was required at any other time in history. Nonbank banks represent an attempt by many financial firms to attain such flexibility. But laws and regulations written for a different era in the name of safety and soundness constrain those financial firms in a way that may in fact threaten their long-term survival. It is little wonder, then, that financial institutions of all descriptions are straining at their regulatory chains, seeking any escape. Their situation argues not for tighter chains but for a reexamination of the need to constrain them at all.

The Case against Regulation

Opponents of geographic expansion and the liberalization of banks' powers rarely mention a desire to protect the local market power of existing depositories. Consequently, the following discussion focuses

---

[7]Of course, many of the nation's largest banks do have securities affiliates overseas, and the latter are able to underwrite the securities issues of U.S. firms that enter European markets. How is it in America's best interest, however, to force U.S. manufacturers and their banks offshore to conduct what is after all a legitimate business exercise?

on service to consumers and the safety and soundness of the banking industry.

Service to Consumers and Small-Business Owners

Among the charges of unfair competition brought by opponents of nonbank banks are that the parent companies can pay higher interest rates on deposits and charge lower interest rates on loans and credit card accounts financed through their limited-service banks. They are also said to have an unfair advantage because they can offer customers a broader range of services and wider access to funds. To whom are those practices unfair? No doubt providers of financial services that do not or cannot meet such challenges with their own innovations will be harmed, but how is that unfair to bank customers? Does the answer lie in restricting the behavior of firms that are attracting customers by offering better prices and services or in providing traditional depositories with more freedom to compete?

The latter alternative does not address concerns about an undue concentration of financial power, some will charge. As William Haraf of the American Enterprise Institute points out in an unsigned article on nonbank banks, however, those concerns have little basis in fact. If integrated financial services firms do gain market share at the expense of more specialized institutions, it must be because they are offering a better mix of services or offering the same services more efficiently or at a lower price.[8]

In fact, in most cases competition would be enhanced by removing the current restrictions. As a rule, the financial services sector is highly unconcentrated and very competitive. The major exception to that rule is not in New York or California, where the nation's largest banks and brokers operate and can range freely throughout the state, but rather in small rural communities, where there is often only one bank. Consider how much better served residents of such towns would be if a branch of a larger bank or a Sears catalogue store could offer them banking and insurance services. Consider how much broader the ownership of corporate stock would be if banks could offer their local customers advice on and access to the stock markets. And if new firms could enter small-town markets more easily, an institution that abused customers' trust and loyalty would soon face new competition.

Sen. William Proxmire (1987) has praised the small-business community for creating new jobs and for contributing much of the current vibrancy to the economy, and he is certainly right in doing so. But

---

[8]"Nonbanks and Nonproblems," p. 10.

his apparent assumption that we must have small banks to foster a healthy community of small businesses is misguided, for several reasons.

First, serving the small-business community is becoming the bread-and-butter activity of more and more banks, regardless of size. It is nice to land a large customer, but, by definition, there are few of those, and they can be fickle. To be assured of remaining in business, most banks must concentrate on the more stable customer base provided by small-business owners. In addition, more and more large and mid-sized firms are raising debt capital through the bond markets, which further increases the importance of small-business customers to bankers. Finally, one of the surest ways for a bank to obtain larger corporate customers is to foster the growth of small local businesses, and thereby gain their loyalty.

That brings us to a second reason greater regulatory freedom would aid rather than hinder small-business development. When a successful small business grows, its financial needs change. Its owners and directors may want to issue stock. They may want to raise debt capital from more than one source. They may want to open a manufacturing or distribution facility in another state or country and may therefore require a banking presence in their new location. To whom do they turn for advice? It is likely that they turn first to their local banker, who must refer them to someone else—someone who is less familiar with the history of their company. Accordingly, are we aiding or inhibiting the growth of the small-business community by maintaining the existing powers distinctions and geographic restrictions?

An issue generating increasing public concern is the role of U.S. businesses in world markets. Much has been said and written lately about the need to make U.S. goods more competitive overseas and the steps that might be taken to accomplish that goal.

It should be recognized that a major impediment to U.S. businesses' ability to enter overseas markets is the fragmented nature of our banking system. To whom should the owner of a local business— say, in Keokuk, Iowa—turn for financial advice should he learn of or seek to learn of opportunities to export his product? The manager of his locally owned and operated bank is unlikely to be of any help in explaining how he could hedge against fluctuations in the exchange rate, for example, or how he could establish the banking relationships he needs to compete in a foreign market. Owners of foreign-based companies seeking to expand into U.S. markets, on the other hand, often find that the same bankers who wrote their home mortgages and helped them raise the capital to start their businesses can provide them with the detailed advice and the services they need to launch their American operations.

The Question of Safety and Soundness

Everyone gains from a stable banking system, but efforts to protect each U.S. bank through laws that define acceptable activities and geographic markets narrowly may be undermining rather than enhancing the system's stability. Consider some of the current problems:

- The savings and loan industry is experiencing difficulties not because of its broader powers but because of regulations requiring S&Ls to fund long-term, locally concentrated, specialized asset portfolios with short-term liabilities. Serious and costly mistakes have certainly been made by S&L officials in pursuing new activities, but desperate gambles may seem necessary when one is attempting to recapitalize an insolvent institution.

- Banks in the farm and energy states are failing in record numbers, for the same reason that thousands of banks failed in the 1920s. The problem is not deregulation but restrictions that force those banks to bet their future on the continued economic health of narrowly defined regions. The banks cannot ride out short-term difficulties in certain sectors while continuing to provide support for the healthier elements of their communities. Their portfolios are so concentrated that losses in one sector quickly deplete their capital.

- Large banks are taking on more credit risks, and no one can predict the impact of the increase in their off-balance-sheet activities. Why these forays into unfamiliar territory? Banks are prevented by law from serving their traditional business and individual clients, who have found better-quality, more cost-effective services elsewhere. With large and mid-sized companies raising their debt capital through the services of other kinds of financial firms, the more heavily constrained banking industry must find new activities.

There is no evidence that combining depository institutions with commercial or other kinds of financial firms under the same holding company causes systemic problems.[9] Indeed, the increased diversification that results can help stabilize a holding company's earnings and profits over the business cycle. That mechanism could therefore represent an important way for locally operated banks that do not

---

[9]The restrictions preventing banks and commercial firms from being subsidiaries of the same parent company are in fact only 30 years old. See Huertas (1987).

become a part of a branching network to survive. Nondepository parent companies could be an excellent source of capital for depositories whose loan portfolios are concentrated in a single region.[10]

The very nature of its business requires the banking community to assume broader economic risks. After all, any loan, whether to a business or to an individual, carries the risk that a change in the borrower's exogenous economic circumstances—the emergence of new competitors, a reduction in the demand for a product, the loss of a job—will undermine his ability to repay his debt. There is no way to insulate the banking community from the risks faced by nonfinancial firms, but legal changes that allowed greater geographic and asset diversification would help them manage it more efficiently.

Conclusion

This study is not meant to provide a framework for the financial services industry of the 21st century. Nor is it meant to suggest that the dilemmas that policymakers must resolve are simple or straightforward; many of them involve very complicated economic and public policy principles. Rather, the purpose of this study is to suggest that the dilemmas faced by the financial services industry, federal and state regulators, and Congress will not be eliminated by closing loopholes without at the same time addressing the changes in the domestic and international financial markets that caused the loopholes to be exploited.

What is threatening the stability of the financial services system is not limited-service banks but rather the inflexibility of a regulatory structure that was designed 50 years ago. The economic (like the physical) world is in a state of constant flux, and financial institutions (like species of plants and animals) must adapt or die. But banks are kept by law from responding to the changes in their environment. Will the banking industry be strangled by the dead hand of Depression-era legislators?

References

Ely, Bert. "The Big Bust: The 1930–33 Banking Collapse—Its Causes, Its Lessons." Chapter 3 of this book.

Huertas, Thomas F. "Can Banking and Commerce Mix?" Chapter 13 of this book.

[10]In fact, if Congress is truly interested in minimizing the cost of closing or merging the many insolvent S&Ls, it ought to change its current policy. Instead of allowing only depository institutions to purchase them, it might consider allowing *any* firm able to recapitalize an ailing thrift to acquire one.

Kaufman, George G. "The Truth about Bank Runs." Chapter 2 of this book.

Litan, Robert E. "Taking the Dangers out of Banking Deregulation." *Brookings Review* (Fall 1986): 3–12.

"Nonbank Banks and Nonproblems." *Regulation* (September/October 1986): 8–11.

Proxmire, William. "The 'Nonbank Bank' Threat is Real." *Washington Post,* letter to the editor (March 10, 1987): A14.

PART III

THE FUTURE OF FINANCIAL SERVICES

12

REUNITING INVESTMENT AND COMMERCIAL BANKING

Robert E. Litan

Papers on the Glass-Steagall Act are difficult to write these days. Most economists who have examined the effects of the act have concluded that it has unwisely protected investment banks from competition and has been unnecessary to prevent banks from undertaking excessive risk. The legal profession, meanwhile, has created virtually a cottage industry in the discovery and exploitation of loopholes in the act that render its intended restrictions less and less relevant to the marketplace.

The key question, therefore, is not whether investment and commercial banking should be fully reunited, but how quickly and under what circumstances this marriage in activities will be permitted to occur. If history is any guide, Glass-Steagall will not be removed all at once but rather will continue to be eroded piecemeal, through liberalized interpretations by federal regulators and affirmative expansions of powers of state-chartered banks by state legislatures. Although the ultimate outcome of this process will be desirable—at some point, commercial and investment banking will be reunited—the process itself is less than ideal. During the transition, the economy will not only lose the benefits of unrestrained competition between commercial and investment banks, but the American financial industry as a whole will lose business to foreign competitors in markets abroad where commercial and investment banking are already combined.

I believe there is a way to accelerate removal of the Glass-Steagall restrictions. It lies in constructing a framework for allowing all types of financial organizations to diversify their activities without jeop-

The author is a Senior Fellow, The Brookings Institution; Of Counsel, Powell, Goldstein, Frazer & Murphy, Washington, D.C.; and Visiting Lecturer in Law, Yale Law School. Parts of this paper draw on Litan (1987), to be published by the Brookings Institution in the summer of 1987. The views expressed here are those of the author and not necessarily those of any officer, trustee, partner, or employee of the aforesaid institutions.

269

ardizing the deposit insurance system, and thus without running afoul of the key objections to financial product diversification that many opponents have raised. In this framework, firms that wish to own an insured depository may engage in any other kind of activity provided they confine the activities of the insured institution to accepting deposits and investing them only in liquid, safe securities. This approach is outlined briefly at the conclusion of this paper.

The Steady Erosion of the Glass-Steagall Restrictions

The principal objective of the sponsors of the Glass-Steagall Act, of course, was to sever ties between commercial and investment banks that, at the time, were believed to have contributed to the rash of bank failures experienced during the Depression. Several provisions of the act were instrumental. Sections 16 and 20 prohibited national and state-chartered banks belonging to the Federal Reserve System from underwriting corporate debt and equity securities. Similarly, section 21 made it unlawful for any entity underwriting the prohibited securities to accept deposits. And section 32 prohibited officer, director, or employee interlocks between member banks and securities underwriters.

What is not widely known—outside the legal establishment that specializes in the subject—is that by unwitting omission or design, the Glass-Steagall Act left open numerous ways in which banks could nevertheless participate in various facets of the securities business. Perhaps the longest recognized exception to the act's restrictions is the fact that the act does not bar banks from underwriting debt instruments of the federal government and general obligation bonds issued by states and municipalities.[1] Similarly, the prohibition on bank underwriting of corporate securities does not extend to securities issued abroad.[2] As a result, banks have become major underwriters in both permissible arenas.[3]

In recent years, bank interest in exploiting other cracks in the Glass-Steagall edifice has grown, particularly as securities houses

---

[1]The Housing and Urban Development Act of 1968 also enabled commercial banks to underwrite municipal revenue bonds used for housing, dormitory, and university purposes.

[2]The Federal Reserve Board, however, does limit American bank holding companies to $2 million in uncovered commitments of corporate equities in foreign securities markets. But the Board does not restrict corporate bond underwriting in foreign markets by bank holding companies.

[3]Banks currently underwrite about half of the total volume of general obligation municipal bonds. See Kaufman (1985).

have found ingenious ways to engage in banking.[4] In 1982 and 1983, the Comptroller of the Currency and the Federal Reserve Board approved bank entry into discount securities brokerage, or the execution of securities trades without the provision of investment advice.[5] Today, over 2,000 banking organizations offer discount brokerage services.

The spirit of Glass-Steagall was frontally assaulted in 1986 by several events. Among the most controversial was the Federal Reserve Board's approval of the purchase of a limited-partnership interest in one of America's leading private investment banks, Goldman Sachs, by one of the largest banks in the world, Sumitomo Bank of Japan.[6] Although foreign banks had already acquired minority ownership interests in two other leading American investment banking houses (First Boston; and Drexel, Burnham & Lambert), Sumitomo's application sparked considerable interest, given both the size of the commercial bank itself and the fact that the bank was headquartered in Japan.

The Federal Reserve Board also signed off during 1986 on a plan effectively allowing bank entry into the mutual fund business, an activity otherwise long off-limits to banks under Glass-Steagall.[7] To circumvent the act's underwriting restrictions, the commercial bank applicant (Bank of America) proposed that its discount brokerage subsidiary (Charles Schwab) would sell its customer list to an investment bank (Lazard Frères), which would market the mutual fund

---

[4]The two most prominent routes through which nonbanking firms have entered banking are by opening limited service (or "nonbank") banks and by owning and operating a single savings and loan. Under the first device, an organization may escape regulation as a bank holding company by operating an insured depository that only extends consumer (but not commercial) loans. The second device allows organizations that own a single thrift to escape the activity limitations imposed by the Savings and Loan Holding Company Act amendments.

[5]Both these decisions were upheld by the courts against challenge by the Securities Industry Association. See *Securities Industry Association* v. *Comptroller of the Currency*, FED. BANKING L. REP. (CCH) Par. 99,732 (September 23, 1983); and *Securities Industry Association* v. *Board of Governors of the Federal Reserve System*, 716 F.2d 92 (2d Cir. 1983), *aff'd*, 104 S.Ct. 1905 (1984).

[6]The purchase was effected through Sumitomo's American bank holding company headquartered in the United States. Although the Bank Holding Company Act permits bank holding companies to own no more than 5 percent of the voting securities of enterprises engaged in impermissible nonbank activities, the Federal Reserve Board approved Sumitomo's application, which proposed the acquisition of only a passive ownership interest in Goldman Sachs.

[7]Indeed, the Supreme Court's leading decision on the scope of the Glass-Steagall Act, *Investment Company Institute* v. *Camp*, 401 U.S. 617 (1971), reaffirmed the act's prohibition against bank offerings of mutual fund shares.

shares and inform potential customers that they could be bought through the discount brokerage affiliate of the commercial bank.

Perhaps the most significant blow to defenders of the Glass-Steagall restrictions in 1986, however, came in the last days of the year when a federal appellate court upheld a Federal Reserve ruling that banks were not prohibited under the act from privately placing commercial paper on behalf of corporate issuers.[8] This is a highly significant decision because major money center banks in recent years have lost many of their prime-quality corporate borrowers to the commercial paper market, which thus far has been dominated by investment banks. In 1975, for example, the nine largest money center banks extended 25 percent of all short- and intermediate-term commercial credit in the United States. By 1985, the money center share had fallen to just 15 percent. To compensate for the erosion in their competitive position in this market, banks have been forced to lend to borrowers with higher credit risks. The new court ruling allowing bank entry into commercial paper placement should enable at least some banks to reverse this trend.

Finally, the Federal Reserve Board issued a ruling in April 1987 that could punch the largest hole yet in the wall that Glass-Steagall was supposed to have erected between commercial and investment banking. The Board approved applications by Citicorp, J. P. Morgan, and Bankers Trust for permission to underwrite commercial paper, mortgage-backed securities, municipal revenue bonds, and securities backed by consumer installment debt (automobile loans and credit card receivables) through separate subsidiaries "not principally engaged" in these underwriting activities.[9] The "not principally engaged" exception was written into the Glass-Steagall Act, and the Federal Reserve Board is now in the process of more fully clarifying its meaning. The courts will have an opportunity to rule

[8]See *Securities Industry Association, v. Board of Governors of the Federal Reserve System*, slip. op. (D.C. Cir., December 23, 1986). Technically, this decision did not permit banks to underwrite commercial paper, that is, to purchase the securities and then resell them. Rather, the decision approved the narrow activity of banks placing commercial paper with ultimate purchasers for a fee without actually taking title to the securities.

[9]Significantly, the superintendent of banking for the State of New York issued a ruling in the closing days of 1986 permitting state-chartered banks in that state to underwrite otherwise impermissible corporate securities (as well as mortgage-backed securities, obligations backed by consumer receivables, and commercial paper) through separate subsidiaries of the banks, provided the underwriting of the otherwise impermissible securities constitutes no more than 25 percent of the affiliate's total underwriting activities.

on the Fed's actions because the Securities Industry Association has already challenged the new regulation in federal court.

If Glass-Steagall contains as many exceptions as it now appears, why has it taken banks so long to exploit them? A major reason, as already noted, is that not until recently have banks faced significant competition from nonbanking firms, particularly those engaged in securities brokerage and underwriting. With the advent of asset management accounts pioneered by Merrill Lynch, many securities firms now offer a full range of depository services in direct competition with banks. Not surprisingly, banks have attempted to counter the new competition by maneuvering through every loophole that Glass-Steagall permits and that the courts uphold.

Nevertheless, until the act is actually repealed, banks will continue to face some important barriers in competing with investment banks. For example, even though the Federal Reserve has allowed bank holding companies to underwrite various securities through separate subsidiaries, the "not principally engaged" limitation of the act will still impose costs on banking organizations that investment banks do not bear. More importantly, standard corporate debt and equity issues remain off-limits to bank underwriting affiliates, at least until the Federal Reserve broadens the "not principally engaged" exception to cover them as well. In short, while Glass-Steagall may continue to be construed by federal authorities in a progressively liberal fashion, the transition will be time-consuming and costly, both for banks seeking to engage in the broad spectrum of investment-banking activities and for society generally, which must continue to wait for the full benefits of unrestricted competition to materialize.

Benefits of Commercial Bank Entry into Investment Banking

Unrestricted bank entry into all facets of investment banking would prove to be socially beneficial primarily because it would strengthen competition in an industry that at present is imperfectly competitive in terms of a number of measures.

First, profits in investment banking outdistance those of all other financial services providers, including commercial banks. Between 1975 and 1984, securities underwriters as a group earned an after-tax return on equity (ROE) of 16.2 percent. Profits were even higher at the 10 largest investment banks, which recorded an after-tax ROE of 21.5 percent. By comparison, commercial banks during the 1975–84 period had an after-tax ROE of just 12.3 percent.[10]

[10]To be sure, investment bank earnings were more variable over this period than those

Second, as high as the profits among securities underwriters are, they conceal the high salaries and profit-sharing draws that investment banks pay their personnel, a fact consistent with the tendency of firms in imperfectly competitive markets to incur excessive costs. In the United States in 1985, for example, 5 of the top 25 highest paid executives at publicly held corporations were officers of investment banks (*Business Week* 1986, p. 49). That same year, personnel costs for the 10 leading investment banking firms averaged over $100,000 per employee, compared with approximately $50,000 for the two leading wholesale commercial banks (Bankers Trust and Morgan Guaranty), and $33,800 for all 12 money center banks.[11] Bank entry into the full range of securities activities would compress these differentials in personnel costs because it would reduce profits earned by investment banks as well as permit personnel now employed by commercial banking organizations to be involved in a broader range of investment banking activities.[12]

High profits and salaries, of course, do not mean that an industry is necessarily imperfectly competitive. If entry is relatively free— that is, if the market is "contestable"—excess profits will be driven down as new competitors arrive on the scene.[13] Precisely because of the Glass-Steagall restrictions, however, entry by commercial banks into investment banking is not costless, and in areas such as corporate securities underwriting, it is not even possible. Yet, in the absence of these restrictions, commercial banking organizations would be highly likely entrants into a broad range of investment banking activities. The skills used to evaluate credit risk in extending bank loans, for example, are readily transferable to underwriting securities. Simi-

---

of commercial banks. Still, the average ROE of the 10 largest investment banks stood at more than one standard deviation (7.7 percent) above the average bank ROE between 1975 and 1984. The data for all these profit calculations come from the annual editions of the *Securities Industry Association Yearbook* and the *Statistical Abstract of the United States.*

[11]Securities industry data are drawn from Securities Industry Association research reports. Banking industry data are drawn from Salomon Brothers (1986, p. 74).

[12]It is true, of course, that commercial banks now find it difficult to attract high-quality personnel from investment banks without paying the kind of six—and even seven— figure salaries these individuals now earn at investment banks. However, commercial banks are competing in a market in which investment banks still are protected from competition by the Glass-Steagall Act. If that protection were removed, the added competition should reduce profits from investment banking activities. This, in turn, would reduce the marginal revenue product generated by personnel employed by investment banks, which would cause salaries and profit shares to fall.

[13]The new literature on "contestability" demonstrates that even in a concentrated industry, market participants will behave competitively, provided entry is unrestricted. See Baumol et al. (1982).

larly, banks have networks of relationships with other financial institutions, as well as their own customers, that they can easily use to market securities. Finally, banks already trade government securities and, as discussed below, underwrite certain government obligations domestically, as well as a wide range of corporate securities abroad.

The anticompetitive effects of Glass-Steagall are clearly demonstrated by the fact that concentration levels are considerably lower in underwriting markets in which banks are permitted to participate than in the markets from which banks are excluded. As shown in Table 1, the top five investment banks in 1985 were lead managers for 70 percent of U.S. corporate securities sold in that year (up from 54 percent as recently as 1982) and for 96 percent of all commercial paper placed through dealers. As already noted, banks are effectively prohibited by Glass-Steagall from underwriting in either of these markets. In contrast, five firm concentration ratios in the Eurobond market, in which banks are permitted to participate, have been substantially lower, on the order of 33 to 41 percent. Similarly, the figures in Table 1 illustrate that in the United States, concentration levels have been far lower for underwritings of general obligation municipal bonds, which banks are allowed to underwrite, than for new issues of municipal revenue bonds, which remain off-limits to banks.

Collectively, the foregoing evidence suggests that added competition in investment banking would produce lower fees in each of the securities markets and in other investment banking activities that would be opened to new entry.

Revenue Bonds

Numerous studies have examined the potential benefits of bank underwriting of municipal revenue bonds by comparing underwriting spreads and fees in that market with those for underwritings of state and municipal general obligation bonds. For example, William Silber (1979) reported that all 12 of the studies that had addressed the issue up to that time had found underwriting costs in the municipal revenue bond market exceeded costs in the market for general obligation securities by 7 to 13 basis points. In 1979 that translated into $150 to $300 million in added costs to issuers of those securities. More recent studies making the same comparison come to similar conclusions (Pugel and White 1985, pp. 128–35).

Corporate Securities

It is unclear whether the competitive benefits of permitting bank entry into the underwriting of corporate securities would be of the

---

TABLE 1

MEASURES OF SECURITIES UNDERWRITING CONCENTRATION IN THE U.S. AND EUROPEAN SECURITIES MARKETS

	1980	1981	1982	1983	1984	1985
Markets In Which Banks May Not Underwrite Securities						
U.S. Corporate Securities[a]						
Top 5	59	64	54	56	71	70
Top 10	83	84	71	79	91	91
Municipal and State Revenue Bonds[b]						
Top 4	23	27	27	27	N/A	N/A
Top 10	43	50	50	49	N/A	N/A
Dealer-Placed Commercial Paper[d]						
Top 5	N/A	N/A	99	99	98	96
Markets In Which Banks May Underwrite Securities						
Eurobonds[c]						
Top 5	33	37	41	N/A	N/A	N/A
Top 10	47	52	57	N/A	N/A	N/A
Municipal and State General Obligations[b]						
Top 4	15	14	14	18	N/A	N/A
Top 10	31	29	29	32	N/A	N/A

N/A = Not available.
Note: Concentration data based on dollar volume of lead managers for securities offerings.
[a]Federal Reserve Bank of New York, *Recent Trends in Commercial Bank Profitability*, p. 364.
[b]Public Securities Association, *Statistical Yearbook of Municipal Finance: The New Issue Market* (1980–83 editions).
[c]Levich (1985, p. 273).
[d]Data supplied by the Federal Reserve Board.

same order of magnitude as the benefits estimated for bank underwritings of revenue bonds.

On the one hand, the fact that concentration is even higher in the market for corporate securities issues than it is for municipal and state revenue bonds would suggest that the potential benefits of bank entry into the corporate securities field would be even greater than those that have been estimated for the state and municipal bond market. On the other hand, competition among corporate securities underwriters appears to have intensified in recent years, despite the increase in market concentration, which suggests that less room is available for improvement. The new factor is Rule 415, introduced in 1982 by the Securities and Exchange Commission (SEC), which permits a company to register all securities of a particular type that the firm reasonably expects to issue over a two-year period. By allowing issuers to pull securities "off the shelf," Rule 415 dramatically reduces the time required to complete an underwriting. Although this provision has given larger investment bankers, which have the capabilities to perform "due diligence" reviews and to purchase entire issues on short notice, an advantage over their smaller competitors, Rule 415 has also made each security more of a "commodity" and thus has intensified competition among underwriters for business. Knowing the volumes of securities on the shelf, investment banks now actively solicit issuers for business, while issuers themselves appear more willing to shop around—tendencies that lead to more competitive bidding (Pugel and White 1985). Studies by the SEC confirm that, on balance, Rule 415 has had a procompetitive effect, lowering spreads on equity issues by roughly 1 percent and spreads on bonds by approximately 30 to 40 basis points (Pugel and' White 1985, p. 122).

Nevertheless, opportunities for lowering corporate securities underwriting spreads should remain. The competition is more vigorous among underwriters in the Euromarkets, in which banks are permitted to engage in investment banking, than it is in our own corporate securities markets, providing evidence that permitting bank entry here would strengthen competition.

Merger Advisory Services

Relaxing the Glass-Steagall restrictions against bank underwriting of corporate securities should also benefit corporate customers of advisory services now offered primarily by investment banks. As it is, securities underwriting makes up only a small portion of total revenues generated by investment banks. A far more sizable proportion of investment bank earnings arises out of advisory fees, particularly those collected in connection with mergers and acquisitions.[14]

[14]For example, of the $10 billion in revenues earned by the 10 largest investment banks in 1984, $6 billion originated from activities other than trading and underwriting; indeed, underwriting accounted for only $734 million, or little more than 7 percent of total revenues. Of all national full-line securities firms, only $1.5 billion of $13.1 billion in 1984 revenue was generated by underwriting activities. See Staff of the Federal Reserve Bank of New York 1986, p. 354.

It is true that the Glass-Steagall Act does not currently bar commercial banks from offering advisory services in competition with investment banks. However, firms allowed to offer both underwriting and advisory services simultaneously have a strong competitive advantage because many mergers and acquisitions require financing through additional securities offerings to the public, whether through debt or equity. The rapid rise of Drexel, Burnham & Lambert to the upper echelons of the investment banking elite, for example, was made possible by the marriage of that firm's merger and acquisition (M&A) advisory talent with its extraordinary ability to place sub-investment-grade securities (or "junk bonds") with investors. Because of the Glass-Steagall Act, however, banks face a severe disadvantage in competing for M&A business because they cannot underwrite securities and may be unwilling or unable to extend loans in the volumes required to complete the necessary financing.[15] Without this disadvantage, certain banks with extensive networks of customer relationships that they could use to market or place securities should be able to provide strong and effective competition for investment banks, and thus bring down advisory fees.

Effects on the U.S. Financial Services Industry

Finally, the early relaxation of the Glass-Steagall restrictions would have another not widely recognized benefit. As discussed further below, recent liberalizations in Great Britain have enabled large foreign banks to affiliate with securities firms headquartered in London and thus to underwrite securities in the London market. As competition for underwritings in London intensifies—and, in particular, as it lowers underwriting spreads—American borrowers should increasingly turn to offering their securities through underwriters operating in Great Britain rather than in New York. This would accelerate a trend that has already materialized toward Euromarket financings by American corporations.[16] Although some of this business will go to London-based securities affiliates of American banking organizations, a good portion can be expected to go to foreign

---

[15]It is not surprising, therefore, that between 1981 and 1984, banks participated as advisers in only 5 of the largest 100 merger transactions during a period of intensive merger activity (Staff of the Federal Reserve Bank of New York, p. 321).

[16]The limited evidence available indicates that in the recent past, underwriting spreads have been higher in the Eurobond market than in the United States, primarily because it has been essential for Eurobond underwriters to gain the participation of Continental banks (see Levich 1985, p. 277). However, with the entry of major American and Japanese banks into the Eurobond market through British securities subsidiaries, additional competition should bring down underwriting costs in the European securities markets.

financial organizations, particularly Japanese-owned financial institutions, which are now dominant in the world market and deeply involved in banking and securities activities in London.

Securities business that is lost to foreign competitors, of course, reduces income flows earned by American banking securities firms. Moreover, foreign-owned underwriters will inevitably want to leverage their ability to market the securities of American corporate issuers into capturing other banking and financial business of their corporate customers as well, thereby posing the threat of greater losses in market share for American-based financial institutions. Therefore, the sooner American banking organizations are allowed to compete in an unrestricted fashion in corporate securities underwriting activites in the United States, the more quickly this expected outflow of financial services jobs and income will be halted. Indeed, employment by foreign banks and securities houses operating in London jumped by over 11,000, or 26 percent, in 1986 alone, the largest single-year increase in the last two decades (Blanden 1986, p. 69). Citicorp already has 4,500 employees in Great Britain, Chase Manhattan has more than 2,000, and Security Pacific has more than 1,000 (*American Banker* 1986, p. 19). It is safe to say that many of these employees would be working in the United States rather than abroad if Glass-Steagall were repealed.

Risks of Combining Commercial and Investment Banking

Glass-Steagall was enacted—and has since been defended—primarily to protect banks against excessive risk. Banks, it has been said, would be able to exploit conflicts of interest if they were permitted to underwrite corporate securities, thereby threatening bank soundness and exposing securities customers to potential harm. In addition, securities underwriting itself has been alleged to be inherently too risky for banks to undertake. Finally, it has been argued that depositors' confidence in even a healthy bank could be undermined by bad news from affiliates of the same holding company. Each of these arguments will be discussed in turn below.

Conflicts of Interest

Recent research has cast a much different light on the conflict-of-interest argument than appeared at the time Glass-Steagall was adopted (Walter 1985). Much of the discussion about conflicts before the act was passed was conducted in hypothetical terms, centering on charges that affiliations between commercial banks "might" lead to the following practices: bank lending to securities purchasers to support buying of securities sold by the underwriting affiliate; bank lending to support issuers of securities underwritten by the affiliate; placement by banks of securities offered by the underwriting affiliate in bank trust accounts; and promotion by money center banks affiliated with underwriters of poor quality securities to correspondent banks.

Although congressional committees investigated these subjects before the Glass-Steagall Act was passed, the hearings centered on only a few banks and produced no evidence of large-scale, industry-wide abuse. In fact, Congress had rejected earlier variations of Glass-Steagall in previous sessions but was finally energized to take action in 1933 by the emergency atmosphere surrounding the bank holiday and by the disclosure that several leading bankers had evaded income taxes by failing to report substantial sums as income.

To be sure, many securities firms engaged in abusive practices during the 1930s, but these problems were hardly attributable to the securities-underwriting activities of banks. Congress addressed these evils in the Securities Act of 1933 and the Securities Exchange Act of 1934 by imposing strict disclosure and registration requirements on all securities firms. Recently, the Federal Deposit Insurance Corporation (FDIC) has added supplemental protection aimed specifically at the securities-underwriting affiliates of state-chartered banks, as discussed below.

Finally, and perhaps most important, banks are already actively engaged in the underwriting of corporate securities in Europe, where securities trading generally is subject to a less intensive regime of regulation than in the United States. Yet there is no evidence that banks have exploited conflicts of interest in that market (Levich 1985).

The Inherent Risks of Underwriting

The second argument supporting Glass-Steagall—that securities underwriting is inherently too risky for banks to undertake—is also flawed. In fact, the underwriting of corporate securities probably involves less risk than extending and holding loans. In a typical securities offering, the underwriter bears the risk of loss for only a few days, whereas a commercial bank bears the risk of a loan default until the loan is due. In addition, by definition, the underwriter deals in assets that are liquid and readily traded; despite the progressive securitization of commercial bank balance sheets, most bank loans remain illiquid because of their borrower-specific characteristics. Moreover, it is ironic that recent research has demonstrated that if anything, the risks of corporate securities underwriting are lower than for other types of securities that banks are already permitted to underwrite under exceptions written into Glass-Steagall (Giddy 1985; Saunders 1985).

In any event, as Ely (1987) discusses in a companion paper in this volume, it simply cannot be shown that bank affiliations with securities underwriting operations in the 1920s and 1930s were responsible for the rash of bank failures during the Depression. Less than 600 of the nation's 27,000 banks in 1930 were engaged in securities underwriting, yet 9,000 banks closed their doors between 1930 and 1933 (Peach 1940). Significantly, neither of the money center banks singled out for underwriting abuses in the congressional hearings held prior to the enactment of Glass-Steagall—Chase Manhattan and National City Bank (predecessor of Citibank)—failed.

Affiliation Risk

Although each of the most frequently mentioned risks of permitting banks to underwrite corporate securities is overstated, one risk cannot be dismissed. As discussed earlier, securities underwriting provides only a small portion of the revenues generated by investment banks. Among other activities related to underwriting, investment banks also engage extensively in trading, which can carry with it significant risk.[17] Although banks, too, currently engage in trading activities (related to their holdings of government securities and foreign exchange), the banking industry as a whole has historically displayed far less variability in its earnings than the investment banking industry.[18] Moreover, the earnings patterns of the two industries have been mildly related in recent years; that is, they have fluctuated somewhat together rather than in offsetting fashion.[19] In combination, these patterns suggest that through their affiliations with full-scale investment banking enterprises, some commercial banks may in fact expose themselves to greater risk, particularly as they enter new activities with which they have little experience.

---

[17]Between 1980 and 1984, for example, profits from securities trading accounted for roughly one-third of the revenues of the 10 largest investment banks (Staff of the Federal Reserve Bank of New York, p. 360).

[18]Based on the same data discussed in the text above, the standard deviation of after-tax ROE for the commercial banking industry between 1975 and 1984 was 1.3 percentage points (around a mean of 12.3 percent). By comparison, the standard deviation of the after-tax ROE for the 10 largest investment banks over this period was 7.7 percentage points (around a mean of 21.5 percent).

[19]Between 1975 and 1984, the correlation coefficient of after-tax ROE for commercial banking and all securities underwriters was .41; for the large investment banks, the correlation was .28.

The likelihood that certain depository organizations would diversify in a risk-enhancing fashion is not easily dismissed because of the moral hazard effects created by the current system of deposit insurance. Since the inception of the insurance programs, premiums have been assessed as a constant percentage of deposits.[20] As numerous commentators and the FDIC itself have observed, this feature of the insurance system encourages risk taking because it allows federally insured depositories to gather funds at costs that do not fully reflect the risks of the investments those institutions make (Benston 1983; FDIC 1983). Because there is ample evidence that managers of bank holding companies tend to view their organizations as integrated entities (Rhoades 1985; Eisenbeis 1983), the incentives that depository institutions have to take risks at the expense of the insurance agencies can also induce them to assume risks in diversifying into investment banking (as well as other nonbanking activities).

These risks should not be so great, however, that they warrant continuation or even strengthening of the Glass-Steagall restrictions. Moreover, they can be contained with appropriate safeguards to insulate banks from their troubled affiliates, as discussed further below.

Removing Glass-Steagall: The Policy Alternatives

The elimination of the remaining barriers separating commercial and investment banking is inevitable. The only important question is the manner in which this will occur, either in piecemeal fashion or in a clean break.

Piecemeal Erosion

For the past four years, Congress has been deadlocked over the issue of expanded bank powers, including the repeal of the Glass-Steagall Act. The stalemate reflects not only the reluctance of many legislators to settle what has thus far been widely portrayed as a "turf war" between banks, securities houses, insurance companies, and real estate firms, but also an uneasiness about permitting federally insured depositories, albeit through their holding companies, to venture into other businesses.

Even if this deadlock persists in the short run, the Glass-Steagall restrictions will continue to be assaulted from at least three directions.

First, the Federal Reserve itself has begun to gradually widen the exceptions to the act. The recent decision by the Federal Reserve

---

[20]The statutory insurance premium for both banks and thrifts is one-twelfth of 1 percent. In 1985, however, the Federal Home Loan Bank Board imposed an additional assessment of one-eighth of 1 percent on thrift deposits.

Board to allow Citicorp, J. P. Morgan, and Bankers Trust to underwrite otherwise prohibited noncorporate securities through subsidiaries "not principally engaged" in these activities laid the foundation for broadening that exception to cover corporate securities as well.

Second, it is inevitable that the states will liberalize the authorities of their state-chartered banks, just as they led the way toward deposit interest rate deregulation in the 1970s and thus far toward nationwide interstate banking in the 1980s. Indeed, a number of states have already permitted their state-chartered banks to underwrite corporate securities.[21] As the states finish eliminating the remaining geographic restrictions on banks and their holding companies, the liberalization of product-line authority for state-chartered banks will continue.

Indeed, the FDIC has already anticipated the movement toward broader state banking powers. In 1984, the agency issued a rule requiring state-chartered banks not belonging to the Federal Reserve System—or those directly supervised by the FDIC—to conduct any corporate securities underwriting their states may allow solely through "bona fide" subsidiaries.[22] According to the FDIC, a "bona fide" subsidiary is one that is capitalized at levels commensurate with the industry standard and that operates with employees, officers, directors, and a trade name different from that of the bank parent.[23] Significantly, the FDIC's 1984 rule also prohibited a bank affiliated with a firm engaged in underwriting from purchasing securities offered by that affiliate during the period in which the underwriting is carried out.

Finally, if liberalizations of Glass-Steagall by federal regulators and by the states are not sufficient by themselves to induce Congress to repeal the act at some point, financial deregulation abroad should do the trick. Other countries (notably West Germany and Switzerland) have long permitted their commercial banks to engage in the

[21]As noted earlier, the boldest step yet has come from New York. But several other states have also permitted banks at least some corporate securities underwriting; these include Alabama, Alaska, California, North Carolina, and Ohio.

[22]Although the FDIC insures both national and state-chartered banks, it supervises only those state-chartered banks that are not members of the Federal Reserve System. Significantly, the Glass-Steagall Act prohibits only national banks and state-chartered member banks from engaging (directly or indirectly) in securities underwriting. State-chartered banks not belonging to the Federal Reserve System are not so restricted.

[23]In addition, the offices of the subsidiary must be physically separate from the bank, although the two may be entered through a common lobby. In 1985, the FDIC proposed a similar rule that would require all insured banks to conduct any insurance underwriting or real estate development activities that their states may allow through bona fide subsidiaries. But as of this writing, the FDIC has not yet implemented this proposal.

full range of investment banking activities. Earlier this year, Great Britain opened up its securities business to foreign banks and removed its regulation of securities brokerage fees. The London financial markets are booming as a result. Canada is planning to allow its commercial and investment banks to combine later this year. Where commercial banks are able to engage in investment banking abroad, competition among underwriters is more intense—and growing more so—than in the United States. This has not escaped the attention of American corporations, which are turning increasingly to the Euro-markets for financing. This trend is certain to continue, and as it does, American financial institutions will lose business to foreign competitors, especially the Japanese banks that now dominate the list of the top 10 banking organizations in the world. In my view, Congress at some point will react to the expected erosion in the competitive positions of American-based financial institutions by either substantially modifying or repealing the Glass-Steagall Act.

Repealing Glass-Steagall: A Clean Break

The eventual demise of Glass-Steagall is good news for those who are waiting for the benefits of increased competition in investment banking. The bad news is that the piecemeal erosion of the act will take time. In the interim, corporate customers of investment banking services will not only lose the opportunity to obtain immediate benefits of the added competition, but financial business will continue to shift away from American shores.

I have outlined elsewhere a financial restructuring plan that I believe could end the political stalemate over expanded powers more quickly and, in the process, make a clean break with Glass-Steagall (Litan 1987; Litan 1986). Briefly, that plan calls for the creation of a new voluntary option for organizations that own or wish to own an insured depository and also wish to engage in an unrestricted set of nondepository activities (outside those permitted to bank and multithrift holding companies). In exchange for broader powers, those highly diversified institutions that want to operate an insured depository would have to confine the activities of their insured institution solely to accepting deposits (of any maturity) and investing the proceeds in safe, liquid securities.[24] This "narrow bank" could not make

---

[24]Under one version of the proposal, the permissible asset list would include all Treasury securities and federally insured bonds, which collectively amount to about $1.5 trillion, or twice the total amount of loans held by the top 35 bank holding companies combined. Under an alternative version, the permissible asset list could be expanded to include certain highly rated securitized instruments such as mortgage-backed securities and instruments backed by consumer installment loans (automobile loans and credit card receivables).

loans. All lending by these highly diversified organizations (as well as all other nondepository activities) would be conducted through separate affiliates, which would rely for funding on uninsured liabilities and equity (just as such nonbank lenders as General Electric Credit Corporation and Commercial Credit do today). No restrictions would be placed on the cross selling of services by these diversified supermarkets.

Several other features of the proposal are worth noting:

• Narrow banks would be eligible for deposit insurance, but at reduced premiums to reflect their lower risk. In addition, narrow banks could be required to report their financial status on a market value basis (rather than historical cost) and adhere to capital requirements on that basis.

• To avoid undue pressure on the securities markets, banking organizations would be allowed to diversify freely as long as they adhered to a 10-year schedule in transferring their loans out of their existing bank to a separate lending affiliate.

• The proposal would apply equally to both banks and thrift organizations, but the smallest banks and thrifts allowed by relevant state or federal law to diversify broadly would be exempted from the separation requirements.

This proposal, which has also been discussed and endorsed in general terms by several others (Wallich 1984; Angermueller 1985; Golembe and Mingo 1985; Karaken 1986), would address each of the concerns that opponents of broader bank powers—including broader securities powers—have raised. First, it would prevent a financial holding company from using the resources of its bank(s) to bail out "risky" nonbank affiliates. In the structure just outlined, deposit-taking subsidiaries would be limited to investing solely in high-quality, marketable instruments; they could not legally channel funds to support affiliated corporations or their customers. Second, the fact that deposits could not be used to finance loans should remove most of the concerns about potential conflicts of interest. Third, the proposed structure should ease qualms that these financial organizations would hold excessive concentrations of economic power. These fears stem in large part from the fact that deposit insurance allows banks to gather large pools of funds and thereby to exercise significant control over the allocation of credit. If the banks in financial holding companies could not fund loans with insured deposits, there would be much less reason to be concerned about the size of the holding company.

Finally, and perhaps most important, the proposed separation requirements have the political advantage of helping to move all of the interested financial industries beyond the stalemate that has surrounded the issue of expanded bank powers for the past several years. One does not have to buy my proposal to gain the repeal of Glass-Steagall, however. That day is coming. It is only a matter of time.

References

Angermueller, Hans. "The Emerging Shape of the Banking Business." Unpublished remarks at the Deutsche Bank Seminar, Frankfurt, West Germany, June 27, 1985.

Baumol, William J., Panzar, John C., and Willig, Robert D. *Contestable Markets and the Theory of Industrial Structure.* New York: Harcourt Brace Jovanovich, 1982.

Benston, George J. "Deposit Insurance and Bank Failures." Federal Reserve Bank of Atlanta *Economic Review* (March 1983): 4–17

"Big Bang Leads to Changes in U.S. Banks in London." *American Banker* (December 16, 1986): 18–19.

Blanden, Michael. "Bigger Role for Foreign Banks in the City." *The Banker* (November 1986): 69–73.

Eisenbeis, Robert A. "How Bank Holding Companies Should be Regulated." Federal Reserve Bank of Atlanta *Economic Review* (January 1983).

Ely, Bert. "The Big Bust: The 1930–33 Banking Collapse—Its Causes, Its Lessons." Chapter 3 of this book.

"Executive Pay: How the Boss Did in '85." *Business Week* (May 5, 1986): 48–52, 56–80.

Federal Deposit Insurance Corporation. *Deposit Insurance in a Changing Environment.* Washington: FDIC, 1983.

Giddy, Ian. "Is Equity Underwriting Risky for Commercial Banks?" In *Deregulating Wall Street,* pp. 145–69. Edited by Ingo Walter. New York: John Wiley & Sons, 1985.

Golembe, Carter H., and Mingo, John. "Can Supervision and Regulation Ensure Financial Stability?" In *The Search for Financial Stability: The Past Fifty Years.* San Francisco: Federal Reserve Bank of San Francisco, 1985.

Kareken, John. "Federal Bank Regulatory Policy: A Description and Some Observations." *Journal of Business* (January 1986): 3–48.

Kaufman, George C. "The Securities Activities of Commercial Banks." In *Handbook for Banking Strategy.* Edited by Richard Aspinwall and Robert Eisenbeis. Washington, D.C.: American Bankers Association, 1985.

Levich, Richard M. "A View from the International Capital Markets." In *Deregulating Wall Street,* pp. 255–92. Edited by Ingo Walter. New York: John Wiley & Sons, 1985.

Litan, Robert E. *What Should Banks Do?* Washington, D.C.: Brookings Institution, 1987.

Litan, Robert E. "Taking the Dangers Out of Bank Deregulation." *Brookings Review* (Fall 1986): 3–12

Peach, W. Nelson. *The Security Affiliates of National Banks.* Baltimore: Johns Hopkins Press, 1941.

Pugel, Thomas A., and White, Lawrence J. "An Analysis of the Competitive Effects of Allowing Commercial Bank Affiliates to Underwrite Corporate Securities." In *Deregulating Wall Street,* pp. 93–139. Edited by Ingo Walter. New York: John Wiley & Sons, 1985.

Rhoades, Stephen A. "Interstate Banking and Product Line Expansion: Implications from Available Evidence." *Loyola Law Review* (1985): 1115–45.

Salomon Brothers. *A Review of Bank Performance.* 1986.

Saunders, Anthony. "Bank Safety and Soundness and the Risks of Corporate Securities Activities." In *Deregulating Wall Street,* pp. 207–30. Edited by Ingo Walter. New York: John Wiley & Sons, 1985.

Silber, William L. *Municipal Revenue Bond Costs and Bank Underwriting: A Survey of the Evidence.* New York: Salomon Brothers Center for the Study of Financial Institutions, 1979.

Staff of the Federal Reserve Bank of New York. *Recent Trends in Commercial Bank Profitability.* 1986.

Wallich, Henry C. "A Broad View of Deregulation." In *Financial Policy and Reform in Pacific Basin Countries,* pp. 3–12. Edited by Hang-Sheng Cheng. Lexington, Mass.: Lexington Books, 1986.

Walter, Ingo, ed. *Deregulating Wall Street.* New York: John Wiley & Sons, 1985.

13

CAN BANKING AND COMMERCE MIX?

Thomas F. Huertas

The mixture of banking and commerce is hardly a revolutionary concept. Banking and commerce have been mixed in the United States since the birth of the republic, and they remain mixed today. The key questions therefore are: Should banking and commerce be permitted to continue to mix? If so, how should they be permitted to mix, and what regulation, if any, is required when they do mix? These are the questions for which this paper attempts to frame answers.

The Relevance of History

In some discussions of whether banking and commerce should mix, it is asserted that there exists a long tradition of separation between banking and commerce and that this tradition should continue to guide future policy (Volcker 1986; Corrigan 1987). But whatever this tradition says about the activities in which banks can engage directly, it says little about who can own a bank, or the activities in which the affiliate of a bank may engage.[1] Throughout American history, owners of banks have engaged in all types of business activities, including those that would not be permitted for banks themselves. Existing restrictions on what the owner of a bank may do are of relatively recent vintage. Indeed, as a Federal Reserve Board staff study has pointed out, it was not until 1956, when the Bank Holding Company Act prohibited nonbanking corporations from owning two or more commercial banks, that "the basic principle of separation of banking and commerce was established" (Savage 1978, p. 46). And since 1956, this principle has been applied only to some owners of some banks.

The author is a vice president at Citicorp/Citibank. He would like to thank Robert A. Eisenbeis for his comments as well as acknowledge useful discussions of the issues in this paper with George J. Benston, Franklin Edwards, Paul Horvitz, Edward Kane, and George G. Kaufman. Statements made in this paper are the responsibility of the author and do not necessarily reflect the position of Citicorp or Citibank.

[1]For a fuller discussion of the issues in this section, see Huertas (1986a).

In particular, the law has always permitted individuals to own controlling interests in both a bank and a commercial firm, and throughout American history individuals have simultaneously owned and in many cases managed both a bank and a commercial firm.[2] In the 19th century, for example, Moses Taylor was the chief executive and principal shareholder of National City Bank (the forerunner of Citibank) as well as the chief executive and principal shareholder of a trading company, a gas utility, and an iron and steel company.

Such individual control over banks and commercial firms continues today. For example, Joe L. Allbritton is chief executive and owns a controlling interest in Riggs National Corporation, the parent holding company for Riggs National Bank, the largest commercial bank in the District of Columbia. He also owns a controlling interest in five television stations. Another example is Sam Walton, the chairman, chief executive, and leading shareholder of Wal-Mart Department Stores. He also is the chairman, chief executive, and leading shareholder of Northwest Arkansas Bancshares, a bank holding company headquartered in Bentonville, Arkansas.

Similarly, the law has always permitted nonbank corporations to own some type of bank. Until 1956, any nonbank corporation could own any number of commercial banks.[3] Until 1970, any nonbank corporation could own a single commercial bank. Until 1969, any nonthrift corporation could own any number of thrifts. And any nonbank corporation remains able to own a single thrift.

In 1970, moreover, Congress created a class of commercial banks that could be owned by anybody (Felsenfeld 1985). It did so by redefining the term "bank" for the purposes of the Bank Holding

---

[2]One exception to this statement consists of the restrictions contained in the Glass-Steagall Act passed in 1933. Section 20 of the act prohibits individuals owning more than 50 percent of a member bank from owning more than 50 percent of an entity that is principally engaged in the underwriting and distribution of securities. Section 32 of the act prohibits an individual from simultaneously serving as an officer, director, or employee of a member bank and an entity that is primarily engaged in the underwriting and distribution of securities. The definitions of "primarily," "principally," and "securities" for the purposes of these sections are a matter of some dispute, but whatever their precise meaning, they are evidently consistent with an individual having a controlling influence over an investment bank, a member bank, and the bank holding company owning that member bank. One example of such an individual is Ira J. Kaufman, who is the chairman and chief executive of Exchange National Bank of Chicago, the chairman and chief executive of its parent holding company, Exchange International Corporation, and the chairman and chief executive of Rodman and Renshaw Capital Group, Inc., an investment bank that underwrites and deals in corporate debt and equity securities ineligible for underwriting directly by member banks.

[3]The National Bank Act of 1864 prohibited a national bank from owning stock in other corporations, but it did not prohibit a nonbank corporation from owning a national bank.

Company Act to be an institution that makes commercial loa' *and* accepts deposits payable on demand. Commercial banks that fulfilled one condition but not the other could be owned by any other corporation.

In sum, the law has always allowed some form of corporate affiliation between banks and commercial enterprises.

In practice, corporate affiliation between banks and commercial firms has a long tradition in the United States, dating back to at least 1799 when the Bank of the Manhattan Company was formed as a subsidiary of a company chartered to supply New York City with fresh water. Since then, commercial banks have at various times been affiliated with or owned by insurance companies, shipping companies, department stores, and manufacturers. Thrift institutions have been affiliated with or owned by retailers, insurance companies, securities firms, real estate developers, and electric utilities. And so-called nonbank banks are currently owned by a wide variety of commercial enterprises, including securities firms, insurance companies, and retailers.

Thus, the affiliation of banking and commerce has deep roots in American history. Individuals owning banks have at the same time owned commercial enterprises. Corporations owning banks have at the same time engaged in commerce or owned commercial enterprises. Thus, if history offers any guide to the question of whether banks should be affiliated with such firms, it points in the direction of allowing such affiliations.

The Benefits of Allowing Banking and Commerce to Mix

Competition among suppliers benefits customers in terms of lower prices and greater convenience, and it benefits society by boosting productivity and, ultimately, output. Free entry is the best way to promote competition, and allowing banking organizations to enter commerce, and commercial firms to enter banking, is certainly pro-competitive.

The benefits of allowing such free entry are primarily twofold. First, it would eliminate any market power that the current system of financial regulation may confer on financial firms. Second, free entry would allow financial firms to develop more comprehensive financial services that may offer improvements in convenience and/ or reductions in price.[4]

[4]Free entry would also allow financial firms to respond to market forces and to diversify their income, and this would potentially enhance the safety of financial instruments, including deposits, that they issue.

A trend toward allowing freer competition in financial services is already under way, and it has produced positive benefits. The customer now pays lower prices for financial services, receives higher rates of return on his savings, and is offered a greater choice among financial services. Subsidies from one group of customers to another have been reduced; the prices that customers pay are more in line with the cost that financial firms incur in producing the service. Financial firms have also been forced to become more efficient, to bring costs into line with the lower prices that customers pay (Bailey 1986). In sum, freer entry has made financial firms more competitive.

Entry into financial services is still not completely free, however. Restrictions on who may own a bank and on the activities in which the affiliates of banks may engage mean there still are significant barriers to entry into investment banking, insurance, and local deposit banking markets. These barriers raise the prices that customers pay for financial services. Specifically, limits on entry into investment banking tend to raise the underwriting fees that issuers must pay to float new securities (Silber 1979; Pugel and White 1985). Limits on entry into insurance raise the premiums that customers pay (Joskow 1973; Consumer Federation of America 1987). Limits on entry into local deposit banking markets raise loan rates and service fees and lower deposit rates, all to the detriment of banks' customers, especially small businesses and consumers who have few financing alternatives (Heggestad 1979).

Removing regulatory barriers to entry is the best way to ensure that markets will be competitive, that costs and profits will not be excessive, and that prices will be kept to a minimum. If anyone can legally enter the industry, no firm can exercise market power for very long unless there are natural barriers to entry (Bailey and Baumol 1984). And in financial services there do not appear to be any significant natural barriers to entry.

A second benefit to consumers of financial services would come from firms' passing along economies of scope to customers. Economies of scope arise when a factor needed to produce one product can be used at little or no additional cost to produce another. This means that a firm that produces the two products jointly can do so more cheaply than two independent firms that produce the two products separately. Customers therefore get a lower price on one or both of the two products, and firms that produce the products jointly tend to gain market share at the expense of firms that produce the products separately (Panzar and Willig 1981).

Financial services are particularly likely to be characterized by economies of scope, for information is a key factor in the production of financial services. Consulting information does not destroy it; the information remains intact and can be used to support other products. For example, many of the same data needed to grant a mortgage can be used to sell homeowner's insurance. The firm that offers both services need collect the information only once and can pass the resultant cost savings along to the consumer. In addition, the seller of the mortgage knows that the customer is a likely candidate for insurance, so that marketing expense can be much reduced. This saving can also be passed along to the consumer.[5]

In sum, allowing banking and commerce to mix would enhance economic efficiency. Benefits of economies of scope would be passed along to customers for financial services in the form of lower fees or higher rates of return on financial assets, such as deposits or securities, that customers purchase from or through financial firms. Because no financial firm would be protected from competition, no financial firm or group of firms would be able to earn excessive profits or incur unnecessary costs. Customers would be able to purchase the widest possible variety of financial services at the lowest possible price. Customers would decide for themselves, rather than have regulators decide for them, whether they were better served by specialized or by diversified financial firms.

Should Banking and Commerce Mix?

Restrictions on the affiliation between banking and commerce should be imposed only if such affiliations clearly threaten to impose costs on society that outweigh the benefits outlined above of allowing banking and commerce to mix. Opponents of allowing such mixing claim there is a clear threat. They allege that allowing banking and commerce to mix would make society undemocratic, the financial system unfair, the payments system unstable, and deposits unsafe. How clear and present are these dangers?

A Democratic Society

It is often claimed that allowing banking and commerce to mix would lead to an undue concentration of resources. The concern here is not about market power but about the size of firms themselves. The contention is that free entry would produce firms of great size, and that this would produce great evil, for it would confer on a firm or group of firms an undue influence over the political process.

---

[5]A case in point is Metropolitan Life's recent decision to originate mortgages, homeowner's insurance, and mortgage insurance through its real estate brokerage subsidiary, Century 21.

This argument has great populist appeal and is practically as old as the republic itself. It can be traced back at least to Andrew Jackson's "war" in the 1830s against the Second Bank of the United States, and elements of the argument were already present in the debates concerning the chartering of the nation's first banks during the late 18th and early 19th centuries (Hammond 1957, pp. 144–71; Schwartz 1947).

It is instructive to note that in the bank war of the 1830s, great numbers won out over great size, and that generally remains the rule in politics today. Fears that free entry into financial services would result in excessive political power seem overdrawn. Free entry may produce financial supermarkets, but no one financial supermarket will necessarily have political power. There will be many financial supermarkets, and each may have some political influence. To the extent that they will have such influence, however, it is likely to result from their acting as a group, much as members of trade associations now do.

In fact, allowing free entry into financial services is likely to reduce the concentration of political power that currently rests in specialized firms and their trade associations. Any law that restricts entry confers wealth on the people owning the entities that are protected from competition, and this tends to create a constituency in favor of the law (Stigler 1971). The current system of financial regulation is no exception. Regulation protects specialized financial firms from competition and increases their profit-making potential. Consequently, specialized firms have the incentive to reinvest some of the excess profits generated by regulation to lobby for a continuation of the very system of regulation that generates those excess profits. In this sense, excessive political power is far more likely to result from restricting entry, rather than from allowing entry, into financial services.

A Fair Financial System

How fair should the financial system be, and to whom should it be fair—to competitors or to customers? Much of the debate about financial regulation has been phrased in terms of fairness to competitors, creating a "level playing field" so that what is right for one firm is right for another. But many regulatory regimes might meet such a standard. The relevant question is, Which of these regimes is fairest to customers and to society as a whole?

By the standard of fairness to customers, it is hard to do better than allowing free entry into financial services. Allowing anyone to own a bank and allowing a bank's nonbank affiliates to engage in any type of activity affords customers the widest choice among financial services plus the prospect of paying lower prices for the financial services they do decide to buy. Some observers, however, contend that allowing free entry would inevitably lead to grave abuses involving conflicts of interest or to an undue concentration of market power in the hands of a few large financial firms, and that these adverse effects would outweigh the positive benefits of greater choice and lower cost resulting from free entry.

Conflicts of interest are universal, and so, therefore, is the possibility of abuse. In particular, all of the potential conflicts of interest that allowing free entry into financial services would allegedly create already exist within financial firms today. Is more competition within financial services likely to increase or reduce the possibility that abuses will arise?

In general, more competition reduces the possibility for abuse. It gives the customer more options and therefore makes him less vulnerable to the actions of any one vendor. The firm that provides many services must be careful in providing each, lest poor performance in one area lead the customer to take all of his business elsewhere (Peltzman 1979).

In particular, allowing free entry into financial services practically eliminates the possibility of abusive tie-ins. Tying is economically harmful only if a company has market power in at least one of the two products that are tied together.[6] Since free entry is the best way to minimize the market power that any firm may have, allowing free entry into financial services would help prevent abusive tie-ins and promote the beneficial bundling of banking and nonbanking services.

Free entry would also help prevent financial firms from amassing monopoly power, that is, from obtaining an undue concentration of economic resources.[7] Free entry into financial services does not mean that one firm will be permitted to become a financial supermarket, but that any firm will have the opportunity to do so. Consequently, free entry into financial services is likely to produce many financial supermarkets, none of which has monopoly power.[8]

[6]Tie-ins that are economically harmful are generally also illegal. See, for example, *Jefferson Parish Hospital District No. 2 et al. v. Hyde* 104 S.Ct. 1551 (1984).

[7]Indeed, barriers to entry are a precondition for market power. High concentration ratios are meaningful indicators of market power only if there exist barriers to entry into the relevant market. Conversely, if there are high barriers to entry to the relevant market, even extremely low concentration ratios are consistent with the possession of market power by firms in the market (Landes and Posner 1981).

[8]Free entry into financial services is unlikely to eliminate specialized, single-service financial firms. Indeed, as long as entry is free, specialized firms will retain the potential to skim the cream off any market that financial supermarkets show any sign of successfully monopolizing. Thus, financial firms may grow to a greater size as a result of freer entry into financial services, but no financial firm is likely to have any more market power than it does now. In fact, each financial firm is likely to have a good deal less.

Free entry, however, would force all financial firms to become more efficient. In other words, some specialist firms might have to reduce their prices (and costs) or improve the quality of their services, much as the vegetable store must offer fresher produce to compete with the supermarket. This is a more strenuous and perhaps less profitable world than many specialist firms enjoy today, and that prospect undoubtedly motivates many of them to oppose allowing free entry into financial services.

A Stable Payments System

Opponents of mixing banking and commerce cite risk to the payments system as a primary reason to restrict affiliations between banks and commercial enterprises (Volcker 1986; Corrigan 1987). But the stability of the payments system has nothing to do with who owns a bank or whether a bank does or does not have nonbank affiliates. Consequently, controls on who may own a bank or on the activities in which a bank's nonbank affiliates may engage are not required to assure stability in the payments system. If reforms in the payments system are needed, they concern changes in the way payments are settled.[9]

The payments system consists principally of two large electronic payments networks, FedWire and CHIPS (Clearing House Interbank Payments System). FedWire is the principal component of the domestic payments system; CHIPS is the principal component of the international dollar payments system. In terms of value, these two systems together process over 85 percent of all payments made in the United States each day.

Essentially the payments system is nothing more than a switching mechanism that routes funds from one bank to another. Risk in the payments system arises because banks extend credit to one another during the payment process. Controlling risk in the payment system therefore amounts to ensuring that banks adequately control the credit they grant to each other during the process.

Risk to the stability of the payments system is systemic risk. Such risk exists because the failure of one participant to settle its obligation to the payments system could lead other participants to be unable to settle and so lead to an interruption in the payments process.

There is no systemic risk on FedWire. FedWire cannot collapse because the Federal Reserve guarantees all payments made over

[9]For a fuller discussion of the issues in this section, see Huertas (1986b).

FedWire. Thus, if a bank fails, no other bank is affected. The system remains intact and stable, like the telephone network does when a single phone is disconnected.

The only party at risk on FedWire is the Federal Reserve or, more exactly, the Treasury, in that any losses sustained by the Federal Reserve as a result of its guarantee of payments made over FedWire would merely serve to reduce the Fed's net contribution to the Treasury. Thus, risk on FedWire should be compared to the risk that government expenditures and receipts may not come in at their budgeted levels and that the agency responsible for the shortfall may come under increased congressional scrutiny and/or executive branch supervision. But why should the Fed take this risk? Should the Fed guarantee payments over FedWire or even operate a payments system at all?

Some degree of systemic risk exists on CHIPS. CHIPS could collapse if one of its participating banks were to fail, but this systemic risk has nothing at all to do with the degree to which participants on CHIPS are or are not affiliated with nonbank enterprises.

On CHIPS the receiving bank is exposed to the sending bank for the net amount of payments due from the sending bank. Thus, the receiving bank is exposed to any risk that may be posed to the sending bank by its nonbank affiliates. The receiving bank controls for this risk, as well as all other risks that may be posed by the sending bank, by setting a limit on the net amount of payments that it agrees to receive from the sending bank (the bilateral credit limit). In addition, the system sets a limit on the total amount that any one bank can owe to all other banks on the system (net debit sender cap) that is equal to a fraction of the sum of the bilateral credit limits that the other banks in the system set for that bank. In this way receiving banks provide an independent assessment of the risk posed by sending banks, including any risk that may arise as a result of the sending bank's having nonbank affiliates.

The systemic risk on CHIPS arises solely from the provisional nature of the net settlement procedure used. Payments over CHIPS are not final when made, but contingent upon settlement at the end of the day. If one bank cannot settle, then others may not be able to settle either, and the payments involving one or more banks on the system may have to be deferred via a system delete or system unwind. Such procedures have never had to be invoked, and the system of bilateral credit limits and net debit sender caps makes it unlikely that they ever will. Nonetheless, there is a remote possibility that CHIPS could collapse, and to remove this possibility the members of CHIPS are currently considering the adoption of "settlement finality." Under settlement finality all payments made over CHIPS would be final as far as the sending and receiving banks are concerned. In the event that a bank with a net debit to the system fails, other participants on CHIPS would have to make good the failed bank's payment to the system so that settlement could occur.[10] In that case, the failure of one bank would not impair the ability to settle payments made on CHIPS. CHIPS would remain intact and stable.

In sum, risk to the stability of the payments system is not a reason to restrict who may own a bank or to limit the activities in which a bank's nonbank affiliates may engage. FedWire is inherently stable, and changes in the way CHIPS is settled will make CHIPS stable. Restricting who m y own a bank or restricting the activities in which a bank's affiliate may engage will not affect the stability of FedWire or CHIPS. Consequently, allowing the mixture of banking and commerce is perfectly consistent with maintaining the stability of the payments system.

Safe Deposits

One of the primary objectives of financial regulation is to enhance the safety of consumer deposits. But federal deposit insurance does this completely. Deposit insurance protects consumer deposits from all risk, including any risk that may arise as a result of a bank's affiliation with nonbank enterprises.[11] Consequently, allowing or prohibiting the mixture of banking and commerce has no effect on the safety of consumer deposits as far as consumers are concerned. Any risk to a bank that may arise from a bank's affiliation with nonbank enterprises is a risk borne by the deposit insurance fund and the bank's uninsured depositors and creditors.

That leads to the question of deposit insurance reform. Much of the debate about how to reform financial regulation centers around the question: In what activities should an institution that issues federally insured deposits be permitted to engage, either directly or through affiliates? Much of the debate about how to reform the deposit insurance system centers around the question: Is the financial guar-

---

[10]Adoption of such a rule requires the resolution of a number of issues, and these are currently under discussion among the members of the clearinghouse. The issues include fixing the rule by which the amount owed to the system by the failed bank would be apportioned among the other participants as well as establishing some provision to ensure the liquidity of the settlement (so that the banks obligated to cover the position of the failed bank could make available the necessary funds promptly enough for settlement to occur).

[11]It should be noted that an individual can insure a truly staggering amount of deposits. By depositing $100,000 in each of the nation's 14,000 banks a consumer or corporation could obtain up to $1.4 billion in FDIC-insured deposits.

antee provided by deposit insurance worth more or less than the premium paid to the deposit insurance agency? Are these two questions related, and if so, what light does this shed on the question of mixing banking and commerce?[12]

Deposit insurance is a financial guarantee given to insured deposits. The price of this guarantee is the premium paid to the deposit insurance agency; in the case of FDIC insurance, it is one-twelfth of 1 percent of the bank's domestic deposits.[13] The value of the guarantee is equivalent to the value of a put option on the stock of the bank. This value depends on whether regulators allow such a put option to go "in the money"—that is, on whether they allow banks to operate with negative net worth. If regulators do not—if banks are promptly reorganized or recapitalized if and when they become insolvent—the value of the guarantee given by deposit insurance is zero, and consequently less than the positive premium paid for it. If the value of deposit insurance is less than the premium paid for it, deposit insurance cannot be said to subsidize banks or to induce banks to take excessive risk, either directly or indirectly, through their affiliation with nonbank enterprises.

Promptly reorganizing or recapitalizing banks if and when they become insolvent, is precisely what bank regulators are supposed to do. If there is a problem in the deposit insurance system, it has arisen for two reasons. One is that regulators have permitted banks to operate with negative net worth. The other reason is that regulators on occasion have resolved bank failures so as to protect uninsured depositors and creditors of the bank and, in some instances, so as to protect creditors of the parent holding company as well. Such ex post extensions of insurance to liabilities that are de jure uninsured have led some observers to contend that investors regard these uninsured liabilities to be de facto or ex ante insured. As a consequence, these same observers assert, the value of the guarantee given by deposit insurance exceeds the premium paid for it, so that deposit insurance is alleged to subsidize banks and to induce banks to take excessive risk.

Regardless of whether such assertions are true or false (and there is evidence to suggest that they are false [Huertas and Strauber 1986c]), the source of the alleged problem is not deposit insurance per se, but bank failure determination and resolution policies. Con-

---

[12]For a fuller discussion of the issues in this section, see Huertas and Strauber (1986a).
[13]Note that only the first $100,000 of a depositor's domestic deposits are insured. Since the premium is due on all domestic deposits, the premium rate relative to insured deposits is higher for banks that fund with uninsured domestic deposits.

sequently, the key to reforming deposit insurance is to reform the way in which bank failures are determined and resolved. Banks should be promptly reorganized or recapitalized when they become insolvent, and bank failures should be resolved in a manner that does not protect the creditors of the bank's parent holding company or of its nonbank affiliates.

Such reforms in policies for resolving bank failures would solve the problems facing the deposit insurance system. Separating banking and commerce does not. Thus, deposit insurance cannot be cited as a reason to prevent the affiliation of banking and commerce.[14]

In sum, the public would benefit from allowing free entry into financial services. Customers would benefit in terms of greater convenience and lower cost. The stability of the payments system would be unaffected. Consumer deposits would remain safe. The potential for abuses caused by conflicts of interest would be reduced, as would the potential for firms or groups of firms to amass excessive political power.

These results hold regardless of the type of nonbank firm that would affiliate itself with a bank or own a bank. Consequently, there is no reason to restrict who may own a bank or to limit the activities in which a bank's nonbank affiliates may engage. Banking and commerce should be allowed to mix.

What Should Banks Do?

If banking and commerce should be permitted to mix, is there any rationale for limiting what a bank can do? What should constitute "banking," or what should banks be permitted to do directly?

---

[14]The objection that deposit insurance gives firms affiliated with banks an unfair advantage over other firms is also no reason to prevent affiliation between banking and commerce. As long as any firm can own a bank, deposit insurance would be an advantage open to all, and therefore no competitive advantage at all. Moreover, if banks are promptly reorganized or recapitalized when they become insolvent, deposit insurance is not an advantage to anyone, in the sense that there would be no subsidy from deposit insurance. Thus, deposit insurance could not be used by anybody to subsidize entry into anything.

Similarly, there is the notion that allowing the affiliation of banking and commerce would somehow aggravate the "too big to fail" problem. But this is not the case. The issue of whether a firm is too big to fail does not depend on whether that firm is a bank. At various times automobile companies (Chrysler), defense contractors (Lockheed), and securities firms (Bache) have been considered too big to fail. Moreover, it is possible to solve the problem as it may apply to banks, first by resolving all bank failures in a manner that does not protect the creditors of a bank's parent or nonbank affiliates, and second, by promptly reorganizing or recapitalizing banks when they become insolvent. Such steps are possible even for very large banking organizations. For details on how this can be done, see Huertas and Strauber (1986a).

If there is a rationale for limiting the activities of banks, it must be based on distinctions between banks and other firms. Perhaps the most important such distinction is that a different closure rule applies to banks. Unlike other firms, banks do not declare bankruptcy; indeed, the bankruptcy code does not apply to banks. Instead, the chartering agencies are responsible for monitoring the solvency of banks and for ensuring that banks that become insolvent are promptly reorganized or recapitalized.[15] And as noted above, if the chartering agency is able to reorganize or recapitalize a bank at the point where its net worth is equal to zero, the deposits of the bank will be safe.

This suggests that what a bank should be permitted to do should depend on how easy it is to monitor the solvency of the bank. That in turn depends on whether others, in addition to the chartering agency, monitor the bank. Currently, the chartering agencies share responsibility for monitoring the solvency of the bank with uninsured depositors and general creditors. If these investors expect they will be exposed to loss in the event the bank fails, then they will monitor the solvency of the bank. In particular, no uninsured creditor will lend funds to a bank he considers to be insolvent, and banks that are close to insolvency will find it increasingly difficult to fund their activities with uninsured liabilities. Consequently, uninsured creditors could give an early warning to regulators as to when a bank is becoming insolvent.[16] Thus, if a bank largely funds itself through uninsured liabilities, there is little need to define what the bank can or cannot do. That can be left for the market to determine. In effect, the bank will have to confine itself to activities that yield returns sufficiently high and sufficiently stable to ensure the degree of safety desired by depositors.

A similar result would hold if the bank issued subordinated debt. Holders of such debt would monitor the condition of the bank, for

[15]Other distinctions between banks and nonbank firms, such as deposit insurance and access to the discount window, are really part and parcel of the different closure rule applied to banks. Deposit insurance is in effect a performance bond given to small, and presumably unsophisticated, depositors that chartering agencies will reorganize or recapitalize banks whose net worth has been exhausted. The small depositor therefore need not be concerned that the chartering agency will fail to close a bank that has become insolvent. Access to the discount window is supposed to prevent a bank that is solvent but temporarily illiquid from failing. Nonbank firms, however, can fail solely because they are illiquid (that is, cannot refund maturing liabilities).

[16]Uninsured depositors will provide such an early warning by reducing the volume of funds they are willing to place with the bank and/or by raising the rate of return they demand on their deposits. They will exert such discipline if they expect to be exposed to the possibility of loss (of principal and/or liquidity) in the event the bank should fail. And regulators can reinforce such expectations by resolving the bank failures that do occur in a manner that exposes uninsured depositors and general creditors to loss.

they would bear the first portion of any loss the bank incurred after its equity was exhausted. To protect themselves, investors in subordinated debt would build in covenants allowing them a greater say in the bank's affairs when the net worth of the bank declined to zero or close to zero. Thus, subordinated debt would make it easier for the chartering agency to determine when the bank was close to insolvency, and it would also provide a cushion of additional protection to deposits, thereby making deposits safer.

Moreover, if such subordinated debt were required to be convertible into equity when the net worth of the bank reached zero (or some small positive amount), it could provide for an automatic recapitalization of the bank in the event the bank "failed" (that is, in the event its equity capital were exhausted).[17] In effect, mandatory convertible subordinated debt would provide a parachute that would ensure a soft landing for the payments system and deposit insurance funds. The covenants on the debt that trigger the mandatory conversion into equity would be the ripcord.

With such a safeguard in place, there would be no need to restrict the activities in which a bank could engage. Once again, that could be left for the market to determine. Banks that engaged in overly risky activities would find themselves unable to issue subordinated debt at reasonable rates. And if banks were required to fund a certain percentage of their assets with subordinated debt, they could not expand unless they could issue additional subordinated debt.

If a bank does not issue subordinated debt, and if it funds itself exclusively through insured deposits, then the chartering agency will be the only entity responsible for monitoring the solvency of the bank. To this end, the chartering agency has various tools at its disposal, including periodic reporting requirements and on-site examinations. Are restrictions on the activities in which a bank may engage also required?

Strictly speaking, such restrictions are not necessary if the chartering agency can monitor the solvency of banks under its supervision so that banks can be promptly reorganized or recapitalized when

---

[17]See, for example, Benston et al. (1986, pp. 192–95). Such subordinated debt could be issued either to outside investors or to the bank's parent holding company. In the latter case, the market discipline exerted on the bank would be indirect, through discipline exerted by debt holders of the holding company. Since dividends and interest from the bank to the holding company would service the holding company debt, and assuming there would continue to be minimum equity requirements and dividend restrictions on the subsidiary bank, the mandatory conversion of subordinated debt into equity in the bank could jeopardize the ability of the bank to pay dividends to the holding company and of the holding company to service its debt. This would induce investors in the holding company's debt to monitor the condition of subsidiary banks.

they become insolvent. If current reporting and examination techniques are insufficient, they could be improved through on-line reporting, statistical analysis, more frequent examinations, and a greater emphasis during examinations on detecting fraud (which remains the primary cause of bank failures). Another method would involve allowing the chartering agency to take over the administration of the bank through a conservatorship if the bank's capital fell below a minimal positive level (say 1 percent of assets), or if the bank had to borrow some multiple of its capital from the discount window over an extended period of time.

Thus, tightly defining what a bank can do directly does not seem necessary, particularly for banks that issue subordinated debt or derive a large proportion of their funding from uninsured liabilities. In such banks, the uninsured creditors can be expected to keep a sharp eye on the solvency of the bank and to refuse to fund any bank they believe to be insolvent or close to being insolvent. In such cases, regulators can take their cue from the market as to when a bank becomes insolvent and needs to be reorganized or recapitalized.

In sum, what banks should do, or what should constitute "banking," does not appear to be susceptible to easy definition. Perhaps the best that can be said is that it does not much matter what banks are permitted to do as long as the activities themselves are lawful and banks are promptly reorganized or recapitalized when they become insolvent.

How Should Banking and Commerce Be Allowed to Mix?

If banking and commerce do mix, should the owner be required to conduct all activities within the bank itself, or should the owner be free to structure the corporation in any manner he chooses, provided the entity that issues deposits is regulated as a bank? The analysis of the previous section suggests that all activities could be conducted within the bank itself, and the private banks of the 19th century and today's universal banks are examples of this.

There is, however, no reason to require that all activities be conducted within the bank itself. As long as the condition of the bank can be monitored and banks that become insolvent are promptly recapitalized or reorganized, any corporation should be free to own a bank; a bank's nonbank affiliates or subsidiaries should be able to engage in any activity whatsoever; and the owner of the bank should be free to decide which activities to conduct within the bank and which activities to conduct in nonbank affiliates or subsidiaries.

If some activities are conducted outside the bank, what restrictions should be imposed on transactions between the bank and its nonbank affiliates? Strictly speaking, no such restrictions are necessary if the bank funds itself largely through uninsured deposits or if it issues subordinated debt. In such cases, the uninsured depositors or creditors would monitor all the risk to which the bank might be exposed, including any risk that might result from its affiliation with nonbank enterprises. It could be left to the market to determine what restrictions, if any, are appropriate, and, over time, banks and investors would develop various sets of covenants regarding transactions with affiliates that would protect depositors and/or subordinated debtors, much as covenants in debt issued by nonbanks protect bondholders.

Thus, if restrictions on interaffiliate transactions are needed, they are required only to the extent that the bank funds itself with insured deposits and only to facilitate regulators' ability to monitor the solvency of the bank. However, overly restrictive limitations on interaffiliate transactions, by limiting the ability of banking organizations to serve their customers effectively, could actually increase the likelihood that the bank will become insolvent. Thus, in designing restrictions on interaffiliate transactions, a balance must be struck between ease of monitoring and ease of conducting business.[18]

Where should that balance be struck? One approach is to err on the side of safety, to impose restrictions that would enable the bank regulator to confine its monitoring activity to the bank itself and to ensure that the deposits of a bank with affiliates are at least as safe as the deposits of a bank without affiliates. The following represents one set (and not necessarily the only set) of restrictions on interaffiliate transactions that would fulfill these criteria:

1. Impose limits on dividends from the bank to the parent, such as those imposed on national banks. Coupled with the requirement that all banks, regardless of parentage, maintain minimum capital, this would prevent a bank from upstreaming an excessive amount of resources to its parent. It would also give depositors and general creditors what amounts to a first lien on the assets of the bank.

---

[18]Volcker (1986) asserts that restrictions should completely insulate all banks from all risk that might be assumed by nonbank affiliates. Strictly speaking, this standard implies that the equity as well as the deposits of the bank should be protected, and that it is more important to protect deposits completely from the risks assumed by nonbank affiliates than to protect deposits against risks, such as credit risk, that are directly assumed by the bank itself. For a fuller discussion of this and the other issues in this section, see Huertas (1986c).

2. Impose a requirement that all extensions of credit by a bank to its parent or affiliates be fully and adequately collateralized.[19] This restriction removes the need for the bank regulator to monitor the condition of the affiliate to which the bank may extend credit, and it would actually make credits extended to affiliates considerably safer than credits extended to nonbank affiliates.

3. Impose a requirement that all other transactions between a bank and its parent or affiliates be conducted on an arm's-length basis, that is, on terms that are at least as favorable to the bank as those that would prevail in comparable transactions between the bank and unaffiliated third parties. This restriction would make it impossible for the parent or nonbank affiliates to siphon off an excessive amount of resources from the bank. But it would leave the parent and the nonbank affiliates free to transact with the bank on terms that do not harm the bank or that plainly favor the bank. Again, such a restriction removes the need for the bank regulator to monitor the condition of the nonbank affiliates.

4. Impose a requirement that a bank's parent and its nonbank affiliates explicitly state to investors that their liabilities are not deposits and are not covered by federal deposit insurance. This restriction would go beyond full disclosure to require that banking organizations give investors fair warning they are not buying a deposit when they buy a security issued by a bank's parent or its nonbank affiliates. This extra precaution would act to preserve the reputation of the bank should either its parent or nonbank affiliates get into trouble.

Together, these four restrictions confine the bank regulator's monitoring task to the bank itself, and they would more than adequately protect the deposits issued by a bank with affiliates, in the sense that they would make those deposits at least as safe as the deposits issued by a bank without any affiliates at all. In fact, under such restrictions the deposits of a bank with affiliates would likely be a good deal safer than the deposits of a bank without affiliates because the bank with affiliates could potentially draw on a "hidden reserve"—the resources of those affiliates.

Aside from these four restrictions, no further restrictions on a bank's relationship with its parent or nonbank affiliates are necessary. In particular, no further restrictions need be placed on cross marketing or on operating the bank and its nonbank affiliates in tandem with

---

[19]An exception to the collateralization requirement could be made in the case of intraday overdrafts by affiliates of their accounts on the bank. On CHIPS the risk to the sending bank of such overdrafts is monitored by the receiving bank, and on FedWire the overdraft limit of the bank itself vis-à-vis the Fed may be a more efficient monitoring mechanism than the collateralization of the overdrafts.

one another. No requirements need be imposed on the capital that the parent holding company must maintain. All that is required is that the above restrictions be enforced. And as noted above, even these restrictions are not necessary if the bank issues subordinated debt or if the bank funds itself largely through uninsured liabilities.

Conclusion

Regardless of what banks should be permitted to do, anyone should be permitted to own a bank, and banks should be permitted to affiliate themselves with any type of nonbank enterprise. Affiliations between banking and commerce have been common throughout American history, and they continue today. They are beneficial and fair to customers. They do not jeopardize the safety of consumer deposits or threaten the stability of the payments system. Consequently, banking and commerce should be permitted to mix.

References

Angermueller, Hans H. Statement before the Commerce, Consumer and Monetary Affairs Subcommittee of the Committee on Government Operations, U.S. House of Representatives, Washington, D.C., December 17, 1986.

Bailey, Elizabeth E. "Price and Productivity Change Following Deregulation: The U.S. Experience." *Economic Journal* 96 (1986): 1–17.

Bailey, Elizabeth E., and Baumol, William J. "Deregulation and the Theory of Contestable Markets." *Yale Journal on Regulation* 1 (1984): 111–37.

Benston, George J.; Eisenbeis, Robert A.; Horvitz, Paul M.; Kane, Edward J.; and Kaufman, George G. *Perspectives on Safe and Sound Banking: Past, Present and Future.* Cambridge, Mass: MIT Press, 1986.

Consumer Federation of America. "The Potential Costs and Benefits of Allowing Banks to Sell Insurance." Mimeographed. Washington, D.C., 1987.

Corrigan, E. Gerald. *Financial Market Structure: A Longer View.* New York: Federal Reserve Bank of New York, 1987.

Edwards, Franklin R., ed. *Issues in Financial Regulation.* New York: McGraw-Hill, 1979.

Felsenfeld, Carl. "Non-Bank Banks: An Issue in Need of a Policy." *The Business Lawyer* 41 (1985): 99–123.

Hammond, Bray. *Banks and Politics in America from the Revolution to the Civil War.* Princeton, N.J.: Princeton University Press, 1957.

Heggestad, Arnold A. "Market Structure, Competition and Performance in Financial Industries: A Survey of Banking Studies." In *Issues in Financial Regulation,* pp. 449–90. Edited by Franklin R. Edwards. New York: McGraw-Hill, 1979.

Huertas, Thomas F. "The Union of Banking and Commerce in American History." Appendix B to Statement of Hans Angermueller, U.S. House of Representatives, December 17, 1986a.

Huertas, Thomas F. "Risk in the Payments System." Appendix D to Statement of Hans Angermueller, U.S. House of Representatives, December 17, 1986b.

Huertas, Thomas F. "The Protection of Deposits from Risks Assumed by Non-Bank Affiliates." Appendix C to Statement of Hans Angermueller, U.S. House of Representatives, December 17, 1986c.

Huertas, Thomas F., and Strauber, Rachel. "An Analysis of Alternative Proposals for Deposit Insurance Reform." Appendix E to Statement of Hans Angermueller, U.S. House of Representatives, December 17, 1986a.

Huertas, Thomas F., and Strauber, Rachel. "The Competitive Environment Facing Banks." Appendix A to Statement of Hans Angermueller, U.S. House of Representatives, December 17, 1986b.

Huertas, Thomas F., and Strauber, Rachel. "Deposit Insurance: Overhaul or Tune-Up?" *Issues in Bank Regulation* 9 (1986c): 3–24.

Joskow, Paul L. "Cartels, Competition and Regulation in the Property-Liability Insurance Industry." *Bell Journal of Economics* 3 (1973): 375–427.

Landes, William M., and Posner, Richard A. "Market Power in Anti-Trust Cases." *Harvard Law Review* 94 (1981): 937–96.

Panzar, J. C., and Willig, R. D. "Economies of Scope." *American Economic Review* 71 (1981): 268–72.

Peltzman, Sam. "Commentary." In *Issues in Financial Regulation*, pp. 155–61. Edited by Franklin R. Edwards. New York: McGraw-Hill, 1979.

Pugel, Thomas A., and White, Lawrence J. "An Analysis of the Competitive Effects of Allowing Commercial Bank Affiliates to Underwrite Corporate Securities." In *Deregulating Wall Street: Commercial Bank Penetration of the Corporate Securities Market*, pp. 93–139. Edited by Ingo Walter. New York: John Wiley and Sons, 1985.

Savage, Donald T. "History of the Bank Holding Company Movement, 1900–1978." In *The Bank Holding Company Movement to 1978: A Compendium*. Washington, D.C.: Federal Reserve Board, 1978.

Schwartz, Anna J. "Beginning of Competitive Banking in Philadelphia." *Journal of Political Economy* 55 (1947): 417–31.

Silber, William L. *Municipal Revenue Bond Costs and Bank Underwriting: A Survey of the Evidence.* New York: New York University Graduate School of Business Administration, 1979.

Stigler, George J. "The Theory Of Economic Regulation." *Bell Journal of Economics and Management Science* 1 (1971): 3–21.

Volcker, Paul A. Statement before the Commerce, Consumer and Monetary Affairs Subcommittee of the Committee on Government Operations, U.S. House of Representatives. Washington, D.C., June 11, 1986.

COMMENT ON "CAN BANKING AND COMMERCE MIX?"

Robert A. Eisenbeis

The paper by Thomas Huertas (1987) on commingling banking and commerce is useful because it raises a number of interesting and important issues relevant to the present debate over expanded powers for banking organizations—issues that are on the minds of both policy makers and those in the financial services industry.

The paper has several key sections. The first is a history section that attempts to answer the question posed in the title of the paper "Can Banking and Commerce Mix?" Not surprisingly, the conclusion is yes. More important, however, is the fact that the conclusion follows logically from the historical review that indicates these activities always have been mixed.

Huertas's analysis debunks the notion found elsewhere that there has been a traditional separation between banking and commerce.[1] The evidence shows there have never been restrictions on individuals owning or having substantial interests in banks and nonbanking firms. Moreover, throughout the 19th century, there were numerous instances of corporate affiliations between banks and a wide range of commercial enterprises, including public utilities, water companies, railroads, chemical companies, and other nonfinancial and financial firms. The paper documents and illustrates quite well the various kinds of affiliations that existed.

The present separation between banking and commerce is very recent, dating back to the Bank Holding Company Act of 1956.[2] That act broke up the Transamerica Corporation and prohibited any firm owning two or more banks from owning companies other than those

---

The author is the Wachovia Professor of Banking at the University of North Carolina at Chapel Hill.

[1]See, for example, Corrigan (1987), Volcker (1986), and Fein (1986).

[2]The principal exception, as Huertas points out, is the prohibition of the combining of investment and commercial banking in the 1933 Glass-Steagall Act.

whose business was closely related to banking. The subsequent rise of one-bank holding companies, which were not subject to the activity prohibitions in the 1956 act and thus free to acquire commercial affiliates, caused great congressional concern during 1968–69 and culminated in passage of the 1970 amendments to the Bank Holding Company Act of 1956.[3] The 1970 amendments prohibited any company owning a bank that both accepted demand deposits and made commercial loans from engaging in any financial or commercial activity that was not "so closely related to banking . . . as to be a proper incident thereto." The interesting question following from Huertas's analysis is why there has never been similar concern about the commingling of banking and commerce through individual ownership that seems to have accompanied corporate ownership of banking and commercial firms.

A small quibble is possible with one portion of this history section. In discussing the 1970 amendments, Huertas suggests that, by revising the definition of a bank, Congress purposefully created a class of banks that could be owned by any individual or corporation outside of the activity restrictions of the act. Review of the legislative history of the 1966 and 1970 amendments to the 1956 Bank Holding Company Act suggests a different interpretation.[4] The original 1956 act defined a bank so as to include both savings banks and nondeposit trust companies. Experience with the act suggested that this definition was too broad. The 1966 amendments modified that definition so as to exclude savings banks and trust companies by defining a bank to be any company that accepted demand deposits. The Senate report on this change indicated that the intent of the act was to limit undue concentration and control of bank credit and to prevent abuses of bank subsidiaries by bank holding companies to the benefit of nonbank subsidiaries. It further stated that this purpose could be achieved without extending the act to savings banks.[5] Natter (1983) indicates that even with the revision, coverage was too broad, so further modifications were made in the 1970 amendments. Fischer (1986, p. 159) notes that the Senate report explained:

> The definition of "bank" adopted by Congress in 1966 was designed to include commercial banks and exclude those institutions not engaged in commercial banking, since the purpose of the act was to restrain undue concentration of commercial banking resources and to prevent possible abuses related to the control of commercial

[3]See Fischer (1986).
[4]This discussion is based on Natter (1983) and Fischer (1986).
[5]Senate Report No. 89-1179, 89th Congress, 2d sess., 1966.

310

credit. However, the Federal Reserve Board has noted that this definition may be too broad and may include institutions which are not in fact engaged in the business of commercial banking in that they do not make commercial loans. The committee, accordingly, adopted a provision which would exclude institutions that are not engaged in the business of making commercial loans.

Given this history, it is unlikely that Congress was attempting to open up bank ownership to nonbanking organizations. Rather, Congress apparently intended to exclude from coverage of the act institutions like the Boston Safe Deposit Corporation that were not primarily engaged in commercial banking.[6] In making such refinements, Congress unintentionally opened the possibility for commingling commerce and insured deposit taking.

In the second main section of his paper, Huertas shifts his attention to a general discussion of the benefits of permitting the commingling of banking and commerce. The conclusion that positive social benefits would result is rooted in a theoretical discussion of the benefits of increased competition and the preservation of free entry into markets. The only empirical evidence cited suggests that some of the markets that banking organizations would be most likely to enter if permitted (for example, insurance and investment banking) have been characterized by abnormally high profits and prices. Presumably, prices would fall and abnormal profits would disappear if bank entry were permitted. There is no evidence cited, however, on the actual experience in those nonbanking markets in which banking organizations have been permitted under existing provisions of the Bank Holding Company Act.[7]

Turning from the theoretical discussion to the present debate over whether banking and commerce should be permitted to mix, Huertas suggests that restrictions could be justified only if the social costs exceed the benefits. He examines four common arguments about why these social costs might be high. Net social costs might result because free entry might (1) lead to bigness and the abuse of political power, (2) lead to inequities in the functioning of markets, (3) pose a threat to the safety of the payments system, or (4) adversely affect the safety of bank deposits.

With respect to the issues of fairness, which include the first two sources of social costs mentioned, Huertas correctly points out that much of the present concern with fairness is from the perspective of

---

[6]Boston Safe was subsequently acquired by American Express and became an entry vehicle for American Express into the deposit taking business in the U.S.

[7]For reviews of this evidence see Fischer (1986) or Federal Reserve Board (1978).

competitors and not customers. He argues, and I agree, that the focus should be on fairness to customers more than competitors.[8] One of the best ways to ensure fairness is through increased competition and free entry. Interestingly, however, much of the existing financial legislation enacted to promote fairness to competitors does so by imposing differential costs and handicapping certain institutions relative to others. Such regulation promotes inequity and unfairness to achieve redistributions of resources and wealth and allocations of credit different from what an unfettered market would offer.[9]

With respect to the safety and soundness considerations that might arise from commingling banking and commerce, the third and fourth sources of social costs discussed, Huertas breaks down the issues into two broad categories: those pertaining to the implications for the payments system and those related to the protection of customer deposits. In the payments system area, he notes that the bulk of the dollar volume of payments is large and flows through CHIPS (the Clearing House Interbank Payments System) and FedWire.

FedWire is essentially a riskless system from the customers' perspective because once a transaction enters the system, the Federal Reserve guarantees that payment will be received, even if the initiator of the transaction defaults. There are some very interesting questions here that are worthy of further consideration. These concern the appropriateness of the Fed assuming the credit risk in such cases without charging for that risk. Should the federal government even operate a payments system at all?

In the case of CHIPS, Huertas argues that because of the provisional way that transactions are settled, funds received may be reversed if the sender defaults. This policy makes the system vulnerable to systemic risk. Huertas suggests that adoption of "settlement finality" would deal with that problem, but he does not discuss how likely

[8]We already have general statutes in the form of the Robinson-Patman Act that prevent predatory and unfair competitive practices.

[9]In contrast, antidiscrimination laws and regulations attempt to ensure that all customers have access to financial services based on their economic capabilities and are not denied access on the basis of race, creed, etc. One should be careful to distinguish between these types of consumer regulations and those designed to promote credit allocation. Regulation Q ceilings, for example, were neither fair to consumers nor fair to competitors. See Kane (1981). During the Cato Institute's February 1987 conference, it was pointed out repeatedly that most financial regulation has been anticompetitive and designed to reallocate market shares rather than to promote competition. Attempts to promote competition appear to be almost an afterthought in the bank merger and bank holding company acts, which require that proposed mergers and acquisitions pass muster under the antitrust laws of the country. But these requirements are an attempt to correct the anticompetitive consequences of restrictive branching laws and home office protection provisions in state law.

this is to come about or whether finality of settlement should be required for CHIPS to continue operation. Huertas asserts, but does not discuss, that activities engaged in by system participants do not affect the risks facing these two major payments systems. Here, his analysis is incomplete and needs further development to be convincing.

In the case of protecting customer deposits, Huertas argues that federal deposit insurance has accomplished this end because any risks arising from the commingling of banking and commerce would be borne by the federal deposit insurance agencies. He suggests, consistent with both Benston (1987) and Kaufman (1987), that the principal risks arising from expanding the activities permitted to banking organizations result from failure of the insurance agencies to close institutions when their economic net worth goes to zero, and this closure risk exists independent of the activities banks are permitted to pursue. I agree with this argument completely.[10] The key to protecting the insurance agencies from losses due to activity risks are accurate monitoring and prompt closure policies.[11] In fact, with accurate monitoring and prompt closure policies, there is no need to be concerned about the mix of banking and nonbanking activities engaged in by insured entities from a risk perspective.

In the third major section of his paper, having established that banking and commerce have never truly been separated and that the risk associated with these activities should not be of major concern, Huertas addresses the question of how banking and commerce should be mixed. This section is divided into two parts. The first focuses on the activities that should be permitted to banks, and the second deals with the restrictions that should be placed on the activities of the corporate owners of banks (bank holding companies).

If one accepts, as I do, that prompt closure policies can protect the deposit insurance fund, then the principal reason for limiting banking activities rests on the ease of monitoring the activity. The innovation in the first part of this section lies in Huertas' pointing out that effective monitoring depends not only on the capabilities of the regulators (the lack of which might be used as an excuse for limiting activities) but also on the incentives that other agents, such as debt holders and uninsured depositors, have to monitor the bank.[12] He suggests that these incentives would be enhanced by requiring all

[10]See Benston et al. (1986, pp. 103–06).

[11]Adoption of current value accounting is a key element in accurate monitoring by either the regulators or the market.

[12]Kaufman (1987) points out that in periods before federal deposit insurance, banks were required by market forces to maintain substantially higher levels of capital than at present.

banks to maintain a minimum proportion of their liabilities in subordinated debt that would be converted into equity when net worth reached zero. Huertas fails, however, to present a more complete discussion of this interesting recommendation.[13]

The next part of this section investigates restrictions on the activities of corporate owners of banks that choose to conduct activities outside of commercial bank subsidiaries. The goal of these restrictions presumably is to limit risk shifting between an insured bank and a nonbank parent or affiliate. Again, the main issues pertain to the ease of monitoring transactions and risk shifting. Regulation is justified if it facilitates monitoring and, I would add, settlement of claims in the event of default. Huertas does not address either how the regulations are justifiable or the more important issue of what closure policies should be used for banks in a holding company system.[14] Should, for example, the agencies close a bank holding company or require a recapitalization when its net worth falls to zero, even if its subsidiary banks are solvent? More generally, whose capital and what uninsured claims support the bank and protect the insurance fund? Only the bank's, or all the resources of the holding company? Can one really separate subsidiary banks from risk taking in the rest of the organization, and would properly designed closure policies stimulate market discipline and enhance monitoring? These are only a few of the questions that arise from this interesting paper.

References

Benston, George. Luncheon remarks, presented at the Cato Institute Conference on the Financial Services Revolution, Washington, D.C., February 26, 1987.

Benston, George J. "The Regulation of Financial Services." In *Financial Services: The Changing Institutions and Government Policy.* Edited by George J. Benston. Englewood Cliffs, N.J.: Prentice-Hall, 1983.

Benston, George J.; Eisenbeis, Robert A.; Horvitz, Paul M.; Kane, Edward J.; and Kaufman, George G. *Perspectives on Safe and Sound Banking: Past, Present and Future.* Cambridge, Mass.: MIT Press, 1986.

Cornyn, Anthony; Hanweck, Gerald; Rhoades, Steven; and Rose, John. "An Analysis of the Concept of Corporate Separateness in BHC Regulation from an Economic Perspective." Appendices to the statement by Paul A. Volcker, chairman, Board of Governors of the Federal Reserve System, before the Subcommittee on Commerce, Consumer and Monetary Affairs

---

[13]This role of uninsured creditors in monitoring and the possibility of requiring the issuance of subordinated debt has been suggested recently in Benston et al. (1986).

[14]The FDIC has already had to face some of these issues in its restructuring of Continental and First Oklahoma. Here the FDIC did make claims on the resources of the parent company and affiliates in resolving the problems.

of the Committee on Government Operations, U.S. House of Representatives, June 11, 1986.

Corrigan, E. Gerald. *Financial Market Structure: A Longer View*. New York: Federal Reserve Bank of New York, 1987.

Federal Reserve Board. *The Bank Holding Company Movement to 1978: A Compendium*. Washington, D.C.: Board of Governors of the Federal Reserve System, 1978.

Fein, Melanie L. "The Separation of Banking and Commerce in American Banking History." Appendices to the statement by Paul A. Volcker, chairman, Board of Governors of the Federal Reserve System, before the Subcommittee on Commerce, Consumer and Monetary Affairs of the Committee on Government Operations, U.S. House of Representatives, June 11, 1986.

Fischer, Gerald C. *The Modern Bank Holding Company: Development, Regulation, and Performance*. Philadelphia: Temple University, 1986.

Huertas, Thomas F. "Can Banking and Commerce Mix?" Chapter 13 of this book.

Kane, Edward J. "Accelerating Inflation, Technological Innovation, and the Decreasing Effectiveness of Bank Regulation." *Journal of Finance* (May 1981): 355–67.

Kaufman, George. "The Truth About Bank Runs." Chapter 2 of this book.

Natter, Raymond. "Formation and Powers of National Banking Associations—A Legal Primer." Prepared by the American Law Division, Congressional Research Service, Library of Congress, for the Committee on Banking, Finance and Urban Affairs, U.S. House of Representatives, 98th Congress, 1st sess., May 1983.

Volcker, Paul A. Statement before the Subcommittee on Commerce, Consumer and Monetary Affairs of the Committee on Government Operations, U.S. House of Representatives, June 11, 1986.

14

AGENCY COSTS AND UNREGULATED BANKS: COULD DEPOSITORS PROTECT THEMSELVES?
Catherine England

Advocates of federal regulation often argue that individual depositors lack the information necessary to choose a stable institution or to monitor its continued performance. Bankers are presumed to have neither the incentives nor the means to communicate accurate information about the market value and long-term stability of their asset portfolios, and depositors are believed to have no other sources of accurate data. Without government oversight, it is argued, consumers would fall victim to unscrupulous or inefficient bankers who would take depositors' funds and use them to make unsound or illegal investments. The so-called contagion effect, in which the failure of one or more unsound banks can undermine confidence in healthy institutions, is an outgrowth of this presumption that the banking industry is marked by insufficient and asymmetric information.

Federal regulation and supervision of banks is supported, therefore, both as a means of protecting "innocent" bank customers and as a means of protecting "innocent" banks from the negative effects often associated with the failure of other banks. These arguments are widely accepted as describing market failures that prevent the development of a stable unregulated banking system. But there is reason to question their validity.

Most markets can be described as suffering from incomplete and/or asymmetric information. Yet in many cases some individuals turn over to others control of specified assets—either financial or physical—for a period of time, just as bank depositors hand over their funds to bank managers. The literature about agency costs focuses on the arrangements principals (those who entrust the management of some resource to another) make with their agents (those who are entrusted). Contractual terms outline what is expected of the agents

The author is a senior policy analyst at the Cato Institute. She would like to thank Thomas Huertas, Charles Smithson, and Charles Maurice for helpful comments on earlier drafts.

317

and the penalties for nonperformance, and provisions are often made for monitoring the agents' performance. Further, agents have reason to make an effort to signal potential principals about the quality of their effort. The problems and solutions identified by the agency cost literature are directly applicable to the problems expected to arise in an unregulated banking environment.

In the next section of this paper, applying insights available from agency cost literature, we will try to predict how bank managers and customers would behave if there were no federal regulation or federal deposit insurance.[1] To provide support for the theory developed, we will then discuss the performance of banks in Scotland and the United States during their so-called free banking periods when banks were not subject to today's extensive regulatory network. A case can be made that unregulated banking would prove more stable than many observers believe, that information and monitoring systems would develop to guide depositors in the selection of a bank, and that consumers would find ways to protect their funds.

Agency Costs and Unregulated Banking

The agency costs literature argues that both agents and principals are aware of the potential conflicts of interest and abuses that can arise in an agency relationship. But neither group is expected to passively accept the limitations imposed by the potential problems and inefficiencies. The recognition of agency costs creates incentives for both groups to take steps to minimize and control the problem.

To protect their interests, principals have reason to develop and incorporate contractual terms designed to channel the behavior of agents in desirable directions and/or to limit their ability to engage in unacceptable activities. In addition, principals setting a value on agents' services will consider the costs associated with the principal/ agent relationship and reduce accordingly the compensation that would be paid to agents in a world of perfect information. Faced with the possibility of reduced compensation, agents will not only agree to contractual terms that reassure principals, but will also develop mechanisms that tend to make principals more confident.

It is not important whether agency cost control mechanisms are initiated by agents or principals. Many common contractual arrangements can be explained in terms of controlling agency costs. Markets do develop means for protecting the interests of principals.

---

[1]We will assume throughout this paper that there is no federal deposit insurance in an unregulated setting.

In their initial work on agency costs, Jensen and Meckling (1976) discussed the position of bondholders in relation to owner-managers as one example of an agency relationship. This is particularly applicable to the issue of unregulated banking as the depositors of a bank can be viewed as being in a position similar to that of bondholders. Deposits are liabilities of the bank and depositors are creditors of the firm.[2] Viewing a depositor as a type of creditor raises agency cost questions as depositors (the principals) give control of their funds to bank managers (the agents) in return for specified services (for example, a convenient means of paying bills) and/or a positive return on the money balances deposited (that is, interest).

Bank managers may not share all the concerns of depositors or hold them with the same intensity, however; the two groups may operate under different sets of incentives. Consequently, depositors must be concerned that bank managers may (in the view of depositors) misuse the funds entrusted to them. This raises certain questions: In an unregulated, uninsured setting, can depositors be reasonably assured that deposited funds will be available when they seek to withdraw them? What mechanisms might banking customers develop to protect their interests and encourage desirable behavior on the part of depository institution managers? What reassurances would bank managers and stockholders develop to attract and hold depositors? In other words, how might agency costs be controlled in an unregulated banking relationship?

Incentives

While it is theoretically possible that, without regulation, the fundamental form of banking organizations could change, following Fama and Jensen (1983) we assume here that the corporate form of banking would continue. Therefore we must consider the incentives and effective power of the bank's stockholders, managers, and depositors.

---

[2]Under current banking practices, influenced no doubt by the overarching bank regulatory structure, the many bank customers who hold demand deposits and passbook savings accounts are able to require repayment of their funds on demand rather than having a contractually specified date for the return of their money. It is often argued, therefore, that bank managers face greater day-to-day uncertainty about the continued availability of a large part of their operating funds than do managers of nonfinancial firms. But the proportion of bank deposits payable on demand, especially at larger banks, is declining. The bulk of bank funds is now made up of short-dated time deposits, analogous to the commercial paper that funds the operation of relatively unregulated finance companies. Furthermore, as discussed below, the possibility exists that unregulated banks and their customers would use contractual changes to further limit the extent to which deposits payable on demand make up the institution's liabilities.

The stockholders. As currently regulated, banks are among the more highly leveraged firms in the country, obtaining 94 to 95 percent of their operating funds from deposits, that is, as debt capital. Whether such low equity capital ratios could or would be maintained if there were no government supervision will be discussed below. Certainly stockholders have reason, other things being equal, to economize on equity capital.

As Jensen and Meckling (1976) have pointed out, however, when the bulk of a firm's operating capital is obtained as debt, the owners have an incentive to make investments that promise high payoffs, even if the probability of collecting final payment is relatively low. Bondholders and other creditors of the firm receive a fixed return on their investment and no share of any extraordinary profits, so the owner-manager of a highly leveraged firm can retain most of the gains from successful investments while sharing with the firm's creditors a large part of the costs of its failure. This tendency for more highly leveraged firms to take on more risk is especially true with corporations. Stockholders, by the nature of their limited investment, are better able to diversify their holdings across firms and sectors of the economy than are single entrepreneurs. Thus, while stockholders certainly do not want their bank to fail, they have an incentive to encourage risk-taking on the part of bank managers as they seek to maximize their total expected return. The more highly leveraged the bank, the more risk it can afford to pursue.

Depositors. We assume here that the bank's depositors are the most risk averse of the three groups considered (though of course, many individual depositors may be less risk averse than some bank stockholders). The depositors' primary interest, we postulate, is the eventual repayment of deposited funds (to themselves or to a designated recipient) and any interest that has been promised. Assuming depositors follow the norm for creditors in other markets, a bank's deposit customers would stand to gain relatively little from the institution's rapid growth or the pursuit of relatively risky profits with high potential payoffs. On the other hand, the depositors could suffer significant losses if the bank failed.

Bank managers. The fundamental goal of professional managers, we are assuming, is to maximize the expected value of their future income streams. In that pursuit, they will try to enhance the prestige associated with the positions they currently hold and to avoid failures that would generate charges of fraud or mismanagement. Because the long-term income and prestige of a bank's managers are more closely tied to the success or failure of a particular institution than is the financial security of the average stockholder, bank managers are likely to be more risk averse than corporate owners. (See, for example, Leonard and Zeckhauser 1985.) The precise degree of a bank manager's risk aversion will depend on the operation of the market for bank management talent and the degree to which individual managers are viewed as responsible for institutions' successes and failures.

The assumption that bank managers seek to maximize the expected value of a future stream of income implies that their risk-taking propensities can be affected by the policies of those who compensate them for their services. The exact position of bank managers on the continuum of risk-taking behavior that places stockholders at one end and depositors at the other, will depend, therefore, on the reward and punishment structures devised by stockholders and depositors. As the ultimate success or failure of the depository depends largely on the decisions made by bank managers, the question is, who will exercise the greater influence over their behavior: stockholders or depositors? The answer will depend on which group is in the better position to reward (or punish) behavior of which it approves (or disapproves). This suggests an inherent conflict between a bank's stockholders, who would encourage more risk, and its depositors, who would urge more caution.

Stockholders vs. Depositors. Stockholders, through the board of directors, will attempt to influence the behavior of bank managers principally through a structure of direct rewards—promotions, salary, bonuses, and other perquisites—established for the institution. Control also can be exercised indirectly through the stock market and the market for corporate control.

Thus, shareholders have at hand both internal and external mechanisms for controlling agency costs and managerial behavior. The methods of stockholders are potentially powerful and fairly well developed as a result of extended experience through time and across industries. But depositors responding to an unregulated banking system could, contrary to common perception, exercise even more influence.

The existing system of government regulation and insurance has stifled the development of market mechanisms through which depositors might control bankers' behavior. But bank depositors, particularly those controlling relatively large accounts, are in a position to exercise relatively direct control over the bank's managers. When a depositor removes his funds from a bank, he directly reduces the resources available to the depository, even though no immediate sale of assets may be required. Given existing deposit contracts, if enough depositors became dissatisfied and responded by closing their accounts, the ensuing run could force a bank into failure in a relatively short time (if there were no government intervention), something disgruntled stockholders would find it much more difficult to do. Because of the potentially serious (even institutionally fatal) consequences of depositor displeasure, a bank's managers and stockholders could be expected not only to agree to, but also to attempt to develop, contractual terms that protect and reassure depositors.

An increased emphasis on safety. We assume that while the customers of unregulated banks might demand a wider range of financial services or nationwide access to their funds, their primary concern would be safety. Before considering how such a concern might manifest itself, it is worth noting that existing federal guarantees mute competition in this area.

Except in the wake of a large local bank failure or a widely publicized problem, bankers rarely discuss with depositors or potential depositors the relative stability of their banks. To indicate it is safe, a bank merely reminds customers that it is a member of the Federal Deposit Insurance Corporation and/or that deposits are "federally insured to $100,000." Indeed, banks have been exempted from many disclosure requirements imposed on other institutions,[3] but the main reason there is little information about the relative stability of individual institutions is that because of federal deposit insurance the public demand for such information is sharply reduced.

Widespread apathy about the details of the banking business or about the investment decisions of any particular bank is rational given the existing deposit insurance system. For depositors placing accounts of less than $100,000, there is no practical reason to care about the future prospects of an institution, and even individuals depositing more than $100,000 often find their funds protected as federal officials handling troubled institutions have demonstrated a preference for purchase and assumption agreements (that is, mergers) that fully protect all depositors.

If there were no government guarantees and oversight, however, individual depositors would find it more worthwhile to gather information about the business practices of individual depositories. There would also be more reason for depositors to develop ways of moni-

---

[3]There have been recent moves to force more disclosure from banks—on the subject of loans to Third World countries, for example. There has also been a good deal of discussion about increasing the disclosure of relevant information both from banks and federal regulators as a means of enhancing the market's discipline of banks taking excessive risks.

toring and controlling the actions of particular banks. Huertas and Strauber (1986, p. 9) have argued that bank regulation and supervision limit the amount and type of discipline the market would otherwise impose because regulators are believed to fulfill the function that creditors or their trustees fulfill when loans are made to a non-depository firm.

Control Mechanisms

Even with improved public knowledge about depository institutions, not every consumer would need to study banks' balance sheets and loan portfolios before deciding where to place his funds. Many small stockholders rarely, if ever, read an annual report or follow the daily developments that affect companies in which they have invested. Neither do bondholders rely on their individual resources to discipline the firms to whom they lend money. Covenants designed to protect the interests of bondholders are developed by the managing underwriters, and the covenants are monitored and enforced by the trustees for the issue and by the bond rating services (Huertas and Strauber 1986, p. 9).

The first, and simplest, step individuals could take to protect their financial interests in the face of unregulated banking would be to better diversify their personal financial portfolios. That is, even without detailed information about the stability of any specific bank, depositors could reduce their risk by placing their savings account(s) in a bank (or banks) other than the one that held their checking account. In addition, however, it is logical to expect mechanisms to develop through which depositors as a group could monitor and control unregulated banks. Possible control mechanisms can be considered in three broad, though not entirely exclusive, categories: 1) sources that provide information about particular institutions, 2) parties other than the bank's stockholders or depositors who can monitor the behavior of bankers, and 3) contractual terms that expand or more fully define the legal obligations of bank stockholders and managers to depositors in the event the bank fails.

Sources of information. Independent sources of information about the relative stability of individual depositories could include independent bank rating services, money brokerage services, and/or financial auditors.[4] Bank rating and money brokerage services could

---

[4]Bank rating services already exist, both independently and as parts of larger brokerage firms, to advise investors regarding bank stocks, nondeposit bank debt issues, and bank CDs. Such services, and others like them, could be expanded and developed as more depositors sought information about the relative stability of various institutions.

provide comparative analyses about banks' relative returns, services, and risk to clients. Some might act as agents themselves, placing the funds of clients in institutions that exhibit the desired risk/return trade-offs. In addition, the broadcast and print media as well as public libraries would be likely to subscribe to summary versions of such analyses in order to provide their customers with basic financial information. In fact, bank rating services might provide some information through news releases to establish name recognition and attract potential clients.

To substantiate their advantage, relatively stable banks would readily provide data to these third-party monitors, and banks that had performed particularly well in independent rankings would use that information in their promotional materials to confirm their claims of superiority.[5] This willingness on the part of healthy banks to distribute information would place competitive pressures on those institutions that otherwise would be inclined to be less forthcoming.

Independent auditors could also play an important role in analyzing financial data about the health of depository institutions. Currently accepted accounting procedures allow auditors to base their reports on the book values of assets, which permit them to ignore or gloss over the true condition of many institutions. Indeed, the primary purpose of auditors' reports is currently not so much to evaluate the overall health of an institution as it is to ensure that the firm is complying with accepted procedures in preparing financial reports and income statements. If there were no government guarantees, however, depositors would have greater incentive to encourage independent auditors to issue more candid reports and to go beyond the job they do today. This could be accomplished through explicit or implicit contracts between auditors and depositors that held the auditors legally responsible for losses suffered by depositors because of inaccurate, incomplete, or misleading reports.[6] Or depositors could prove willing to deposit significant sums only in those depositories that had received a favorable audit from an accounting firm with a reputation for accurate reports.

Another source of readily available information would be the prices charged for the funds made available to banks, that is, the interest rates banks paid to attract deposits. Market prices reflect the per-

---

[5] A. M. Best's rating of insurance companies is often used as a marketing tool by those firms that perform well.

[6] Independent audits can be used to provide the necessary information to control the behavior of bankers. Swiss banking supervisors do not employ bank examiners of their own. They rely entirely on the reports produced by the banks' independent auditors.

ceived risk attached to various investments, and without government guarantees, the market for bank debt would undoubtedly become even more sensitive to relative depository risk. As the market's perception of the risk associated with deposits in an institution rose, the interest rate that depository would need to offer to attract and hold funds would also rise.[7]

Outside monitors. In addition to new sources of information, depositors might also employ third party monitors to influence the activities of bank managers. In some cases, the function of providing information and the use of third-party monitors would be closely related; in others, large depositors in particular might include covenants in deposit contracts that required agreed upon third-party monitoring of the bank in question.

Consider the role of money brokers mentioned earlier. Money brokers now place large deposits where they will earn the highest return. Since the FDIC guarantees accrued interest as well as principal, this brokering process represents a no-lose situation for risk-averse individuals who break up larger sums into $100,000 deposits.

Under the no-regulation, no-federal-insurance scenario, money brokers might still place deposits for their customers, but the purpose would be to reduce the risks of depositors through diversification and to take advantage of the brokers' relative expertise in evaluating and monitoring individual depository performance. Thus brokers would probably compete, in part, on their ability to accurately measure risk and anticipate changes in the prospects of depositories in which they placed clients' funds. Successful brokers would not only identify those institutions paying the highest rates, they would also need to consider the risks associated with different depositories.

In an unregulated market, depositors might also demand private deposit insurance, sold either to depository institutions or to individual depositors. For private deposit guarantors to manage their own risk exposure, they would need to develop a means for accurately assessing the risk embodied in individual banks. If private insurance were provided through the depository, as federal guarantees are now, insurance premiums would vary with the expected future health of the client institution, raising or lowering the costs of operating the bank depending on the managers' investment decisions. Further, the guarantor could develop contractual mechanisms for controlling the risk taken on by bank managers—capital or reserve minimums, for

---

[7]This is true to some extent today. Interest on certificates of deposit exceeding $100,000 vary with the perceived soundness of the institution offering the CD.

example, or requirements that certain actions be approved by the insurer before being undertaken.[8]

Selling deposit insurance policies directly to bank customers would not eliminate the need for guarantors to monitor the financial health of individual banks. It would, however, provide depositors with another index to the relative health of various institutions. The managers of banks assuming greater than average risk would offer higher interest rates to attract funds, but customers seeking to insure those deposits would also have to pay higher insurance premiums.[9]

The activities of banks not subject to government oversight could also be monitored through self-regulatory organizations formed by bank managers and stockholders who believe that the stability of their institution is at least partly dependent on the stability of other depositories. Industry-sponsored monitors could be local, regional, or nationwide collections of institutions that agreed to make funds available to troubled members under contractually specified conditions. The emergency funds could be deposited in advance in a common pool managed by representatives of the member institutions, or membership agreements might specify the conditions under which healthy institutions would be expected to make a loan to or buy assets from an illiquid fellow member. To minimize the risk associated with such agreements, participating bankers would want to be sure other member institutions maintained certain prudent standards of behavior, so a self-regulatory organization might establish minimum capital and reserve requirements, for example, and/or "prudent" lending standards. It could also develop ways to monitor member performance and to expel members who failed to meet minimum requirements. Self-regulatory mutual support organizations might develop a logo or trademark that member institutions could use to signal depositors about the standards of banking practice adhered to and the extent of external support available in the event of trouble.[10]

[8]For a more complete discussion of how private deposit insurance might work, see England and Palffy (1983), England (1985), or Ely (1985).

[9]Similarly, insurance premiums now provide individuals with some information about the relative structural soundness of competing car brands, for example, or of the relative hazard associated with different careers.

[10]The Best Western motel chain, for example, is actually made up of independently owned and operated firms. To use the name "Best Western," these hotels must meet specified standards for size of rooms, quality of service, cleanliness, etc. Thus, "Best Western" was designed to provide customers with information about the quality of certain independently operated models, and the continuing value of this "name brand capital" depends on how well the private supervisor enforces established standards of operation.

Contractual relationships. The contractual relationships between bank stockholders or managers and depositors in an unregulated banking environment could also change. If the objective of depositors is to limit risk-taking, they should attempt to reduce the gains associated with successful risk-taking and/or to increase the costs of failure as measured by bank managers and stockholders. Of course, this generally will not be accomplished through individually negotiated contracts between depositors and their banks. While some very large depositors might exercise such direct power, most changes would arise as bank managers and stockholders offered different combinations of contracts and organizational structures in an attempt to attract more depositors. A successful contractual innovation that better protected the interests of depositors would attract customers (and hence funds) from other banks. These banks, to protect their market positions, would either match the innovative contract or attempt to improve on it. In this way, the market would evolve in a manner that reflects the concerns of depositors.

For example, unregulated banks might find it advantageous to increase their paid-in capital above what is currently enforced by federal regulators. As Modigliani and Miller (1958) established, individuals and firms (including banks) lending to highly leveraged companies compensate for the additional risk by increasing the interest rate charged. In the absence of government regulation and deposit insurance this same principle would apply to banks. Thus, unregulated depositories would find their cost of funds reduced as their equity capital increased, other things being equal. Of course, the optimal mix of debt and equity capital would vary from bank to bank depending on the risk associated with different asset portfolios, the stability and long-term prospects of the markets and industries served by individual banks, and the risk-taking characteristics of the customers of the various institutions.

Another possibility would involve extending the shareholders' liability in a failure beyond their investment in the bank's stock. This would give depositors a claim against assets of the shareholders beyond the paid-in capital of the bank. Recent proposals have suggested that shareholders should be required to contribute an additional amount up to the par value of their investment to cover any losses. This "double liability" should increase shareholders' incentives to encourage bank managers to avoid failure.[11]

[11]The oldest and most widely known form of banking in Switzerland is the so-called private bank. These institutions cater to a wealthy international clientele and emphasize investment management, brokerage, underwriting, placement of securities, and related bank functions. The owners of these banks, viewed as among the most stable in the world, accept unlimited liability in the event of failure (Corti, p. 4.6.10).

As an alternative to requiring extended liability for stockholders, depositors in an unregulated environment might choose to patronize only banks that included a portion of subordinated debt in their capital accounts. As fellow creditors, the interests of subordinated debtholders are more closely aligned with depositors than with stockholders or bank managers but, by definition, such debt does not threaten the ability of depositors to recover their funds in the event of a failure. If the debt were structured so that a portion matured at regular intervals, the sale of subordinated debt would provide depositors with regularly updated information about the market's assessment of the health of the bank in question.[12]

Depositors might also be willing to accept innovations that would help protect against occasional illiquidity. For example, a bank caught short on cash, but generally recognized as solvent, might convince a customer seeking access to his funds to delay his request for a specified period while the banker generated additional liquidity. Alternatively, the banker might issue a "promise to pay" that would be accepted as a cash substitute by local merchants or other depositories. In return for the forbearance of the depositor or for acceptance of the promissory note, the banker would provide an interest bonus or forgo some fee. In fact, the contractual terms applied to demand and savings deposits might be changed in a way that would give bank managers the option to limit withdrawals for a specified period of time or to require prenotification before an account was closed.[13]

Such a clause is more than a means of protecting the bank's stockholders and managers. It would also protect bank customers, for it would remove the threat that either an unexpectedly large demand for cash or a panic-driven run would impose disproportionate losses on those who did not react quickly. Because the bank's managers and/or directors could delay payments, those depositors who believed the institution to be solvent would have no reason to join and reinforce a panic even if others attempted to close their accounts. And if the bank were truly insolvent, it could be closed and liquidated in a

---

[12]While it is generally accepted that the use of subordinated debt as part of a bank's capital structure would tend to reduce bank risk, Black et al. (1978) observed that in at least one respect the use of subordinated debt would tend to increase the marginal incentives for risk-taking. By allowing banks to substitute subordinated debt for equity capital, stockholders would further increase the leverage of the firm. As noted, stockholders of a highly leveraged firm generally are less risk averse than they would be if their contribution to the firm's working capital were proportionately greater.

[13]Before 1933, savings banks had a clause in their deposit contracts requiring depositors to provide a 60-day notice prior to withdrawing their funds. Generally, this notice was waived, but during panics or cash shortages, the savings banks would invoke the requirement.

more orderly manner than is possible in the face of a run. There would no longer be any significant advantage to being first in line and hence no reason concern among some bank customers should generate a panic that could become a self-fulfilling prophecy.

Finally, to protect their funds, depositors placing large sums or money brokers acting on behalf of clients might place contractual constraints on the behavior of bank managers. For example, in an unregulated, uninsured banking system, it might be that only those institutions with deposits backed by easily marketable assets would survive, that is, mutual funds-type organizations. (See Fama 1980.) Other constraints might limit the life of loans made by depositories, the ability of bankers to concentrate loan portfolios in a particular region or industry, or the size of loan bankers could make to any one lender.

Much of the foregoing discussion about the sources of information and contractual protections that might develop without government oversight is, of necessity, speculative. It is difficult to predict exactly what form changes designed to control agency costs between depositors and bankers would take. Clearly, however, no one directly involved benefits from a run on a solvent institution. In an unregulated, non-federally-insured banking environment, therefore, bank managers and stockholders would have good reason to accept, even initiate, changes in contractual arrangements that would generate a sense of confidence among depositors. Those institutions able to develop attractive, effective protection mechanisms for depositors and incorporate them into their operations would attract funds from other banks less attuned to the concerns of consumers.

Naturally, it is unlikely that an unregulated banking industry would develop the uniformity of contractual terms apparent in today's highly controlled environment. That is, some depository institutions could be expected to cater to the most risk-averse depositors. These banks might offer deposits backed only by highly liquid assets, for example. Other, less risk averse individuals would be attracted by institutions offering a wider range of services and higher rates of return. In short, if there were no federally enforced standards of uniformity, the banking industry would be expected to become more heterogeneous than it now is. Each institution would attract subsets of the broad spectrum of consumers whose needs and preferences best matched its mix of contractual terms and risk/return trade-offs.

Failures

In the absence of government regulation, bail outs, and deposit insurance, the potential for more frequent bank failures exists, so two

329

questions must be addressed: 1) What response, if any, would the failure of one institution elicit from stockholders and managers of other banks? and 2) What response, if any, would the failure of one institution elicit from depositors of other banks?

Other bankers' reaction to failure. How the managers and stock-holders of healthy institutions might respond to the actual or imminent failure of another bank will depend on many variables—the size of the failed bank, the extent of losses to depositors, its membership or nonmembership in a mutual support organization, and the publicly accepted reasons for the bank's failure, to name but a few.

Healthy depositories would attempt to distance their operations from those of the failed bank. Bank managers would make an effort to explain how their operations were different, how their management was superior, or how their portfolios were safer than those of the defunct depository. The point would be to convince depositors that the failure of one institution implied no more than that bad decisions were made at that bank. The remaining, healthy institutions could even gain by the demise of a competitor, and they would want to make sure their customers understood that.

If bankers believe that all depositors are more likely to panic when any one institution fails, then sound banks might take steps to facilitate the quiet, orderly liquidation of a troubled institution. Solvent banks could work together to evaluate and purchase the assets of the troubled bank, including its physical assets and its loan portfolio. Healthy institutions individually might take steps to minimize the costs of failure to the affected depositors. To attract as new customers the depositors of an institution forced to close, for example, remaining banks might offer loans backed by individuals' claims on the insolvent depository.

Mutual support or self-regulatory organizations would have even more reason to facilitate the liquidation of and protect the depositors of an insolvent member institution as the confidence instilled by their operation under an organizational umbrella would depend in part on how the organization handled such a crisis. Therefore, such organizations might develop methods of distributing assets to fellow members so that funds could be raised promptly and depositors paid.

Other depositors' response to failure. Panic-generated runs are presumed to occur because depositors are unable to differentiate healthy from unhealthy institutions. When some weakness causes the failure of one bank, it is believed that consumers will ascribe similar frailties to other institutions and that they will question the stability of all remaining banks. If enough depositors are sufficiently concerned to withdraw their funds from the banking *system* while awaiting additional information, a general collapse can ensue.[14] Therefore, the important question is whether depositors in an unregulated setting would have confidence in their ability to differentiate healthy banks from unsound ones. If depositors felt they could make such distinctions, they would be unlikely to remove funds from one bank solely because another had failed, and funds that were removed from questionable depositories would be quickly redeposited in other institutions.

Without federal regulation and insurance, the returns to depositors investing in information about the banking industry generally and about specific depository institutions would increase. This increased interest among depositors in the relative strength of banks would lead to an increase in the availability of both comparative and absolute information. In an unregulated setting, then, there would be a greater demand for and a greater supply of information about the strengths and weaknesses of various institutions than now exists.

Consequently, depositors as a group would be better informed about the business of banking as well as about the health of any particular depository than they are under the existing system. While increased information about banks would not eliminate the possibility of a run based on unfounded fears, additional knowledge should work to reduce the probability of such a scenario.

Reinforcing the argument that an unregulated banking system could be a stable one is the presumption that banks would become more differentiated, more heterogeneous in an unregulated environment. In an effort to identify the bank(s) that best met their individual needs, bank customers would compare (or hire someone to compare for them) the range of services, the returns offered, and the safety embodied in individual institutions. Through this shopping process, consumers would begin to differentiate among depositories rather than viewing them as similar in their essential characteristics. Given such differentiation, weaknesses uncovered at one depository need not lead depositors to assume that all or any other banks are likely to incorporate similar flaws. Thus, the more heterogeneous an unregulated banking system became and the more this heterogeneity was communicated to depositors, the more stable the industry could be expected to be.

---

[14]Runs on individual banks, even solvent banks, cannot threaten the system if the money is redeposited in other depositories. Indeed, such shifting of deposits will provide the banks receiving a net inflow of funds with the liquidity to extend loans to or buy assets from solvent, but illiquid competitors. It is a run on the *system*, when withdrawn funds are hoarded, that creates a cause for concern.

Of course, a serious weakness revealed through one failure could be reflected in other institutions, and confidence in similarly situated depositories could, then, be undermined, generating depositor runs on all such banks. But such runs should be self-contained as the market would reject only those institutions exhibiting attributes determined to be undesirable.[15] Further, those consumers removing funds from the suspect depositories should prove willing to redeposit them in another bank exhibiting different characteristics. The banking system would not be threatened, only certain banks.

The Historical Evidence

In an attempt to determine whether there is any validity to the foregoing predictions about depositors' ability to protect themselves, we will now examine the "free banking" periods in Scotland and the United States. The Scottish free banking era lasted roughly from 1716 until 1845. It was the less regulated of the two systems as there was neither a Scottish central bank nor government oversight of banking activities—including entry and exit. The U.S. "free banking" experiments occurred between 1836 and 1863. During this period, the federal government played no role in banking, so regulatory decisions were made at the state level. Many states instituted a system of relatively free entry. Anyone meeting the minimum capital and collateral requirements could obtain a bank charter and issue bank notes. It would be a mistake to view these banks as unregulated, however, as the various states imposed branching restrictions and reserve requirements, for example. Still, there were fewer restrictions than exist today and, of course, there was no federal deposit insurance.[16]

---

[15]It can be argued that just such a situation touched off runs on state-insured savings and loans in Ohio and Maryland during the spring of 1985. As it became apparent that the state insurance funds had failed to adequately police the behavior of managers at Home State in Ohio and Old Court in Maryland, depositors feared that similar ill-advised and/or illegal practices were taking place at other state-insured institutions. Once there was reason to doubt the efficacy of the formerly trusted supervision structure, depositors were no longer willing to leave their funds in the thrifts in question. Support for this thesis arises from the facts that, first, uninsured savings and loans in Ohio were not threatened by the runs and, second, at least during the Ohio crisis, other state systems remained largely unscathed.

[16]For a description of the Scottish free banking system and its performance, see White (1984). For a description of the various U.S. "free banking" systems, see, for example, Rockoff (1975).

Deposit banking played a much less important role during the 18th and 19th centuries than it does today.[17] Instead, each bank issued its own currency and the concern was whether a bank's notes would be accepted by others and/or whether they could be redeemed for specie (gold or silver coin). Further, the claim of noteholders against the assets of a failed bank superseded depositors' claims. As Hildreth (p. 155), writing in the early 19th century, explained, "[I]t is a voluntary thing for [depositors of a bank] to become such, and they may properly be left to select a depository for themselves, and stand any loss which that voluntary selection may involve." Noteholders received somewhat more sympathy because it was more difficult to control the selection of notes one held at any particular moment in time.

Recent historical evidence indicates that these earlier banking systems were not as chaotic and unstable as they are often portrayed.[18] Much of the explanation may lie in the markets' responses to the agency costs discussed above.

Sources of Information and Third-Party Monitors

The restrictions on branch banking in the United States led the 19th-century money brokers to locate in larger towns and commercial centers so they could buy and sell notes from across town or across the country. "Foreign" notes could be exchanged for either local currencies or for specie. Not all bank notes circulated in every location at par, of course, and the discount attached to a particular issue, its "specie price," was determined by the local money brokers. The market value of a particular bank's notes generally depended on the bank's location (particularly its distance from the broker setting the discount) and available information about the condition of the issuing bank (Rockoff 1974, p. 143).[19]

Information about the discount rates attached by the brokers to specific note issues was published in "bank note reporters." These

---

[17]This is evident in debates over whether demand deposits constituted part of the money supply (see Mints, pp. 127–28) as well as in the general lack of concern about the losses suffered by depositors as opposed to noteholders in the event of a bank failure.

[18]See, for example, White (1984) and Kaufman (1987).

[19]Jay Cooke began his career as a bank note expert for E. W. Clark and Company of Philadelphia, for example. As an expert on bank notes, Cooke could "recognize at sight notes from all over the country, could distinguish the spurious and the counterfeit, and knew the varying value of those that had value" (Hammond, p. 702). In describing his company's brokerage activities during 1839 and 1840, Cooke wrote, "Our office is continually crowded with customers, and we do a tremendous business. We buy and sell at from ⅛ to ¼ for commission and thus in doing $50,000 per day you will see it pays well" (Hammond, p. 703).

newspaper-like periodicals, usually published weekly, listed each bank by state and county along with the discount on its notes in the city for which the reporter was published. The reporter also described and identified all counterfeit notes and notes from banks that had failed. This was a cumulative list, reporting failures that had occurred and counterfeits that had been removed from circulation years before. Merchants and bankers not only could readily determine the market value of any unfamiliar notes presented in payment for goods or in exchange for other notes or specie, they also were protected from attempts by others to reintroduce notes earlier deemed valueless. (See Hammond, p. 703; Rockoff 1974, p. 143.)[20]

In addition to providing a service to travelers and local bankers by exchanging notes issued by out-of-town banks, the brokers also provided an important disciplinary function by returning notes for redemption—even when they circulated outside a bank's home market. When Minnesota suspended construction on its railroad in 1859, the value of its railroad bonds fell sharply. State officials proved reluctant to reduce the legal price of the depreciating state debt and force banks to contract their note issues or contribute more capital to support their operations; the money brokers provided the discipline.[21] Within six months, brokers in St. Paul began a systematic attack on those banks holding large sums of railroad bonds as backing for their notes. The brokers collected and returned the notes for redemption, thus forcing the banks to improve the quality of their collateral by threatening to drive them out of business (Rockoff 1975, p. 110). In 1858, Chicago brokers imposed discipline on Wisconsin wildcat banks when they refused to accept the notes of 27 specific Wisconsin banks that had "located at inaccessible points, having no capital, doing no banking business, providing no means whatever for the redemption of their issues" (Hammond, p. 618).[22]

---

[20]Many scholars have viewed the heterogeneity of the 18th- and 19th-century currencies as increasing the costs of doing business and potentially slowing overall economic growth. In fact, verifying the value of an unknown bank note in 19th-century America was probably similar to the process associated with verifying the validity of a customer's Mastercard or Visa today.

[21]When the Minnesota banking authority sought guidance from the state's attorney general in dealing with the depreciating state railroad bonds, the attorney general replied that while the banking authorities had no legal obligation to accept the railroad bonds for more than their market value, in his opinion, they had a *moral* obligation to do so. (See Rockoff 1975, p. 108.)

[22]The system did not always work, however, especially when the state interfered with the brokers' efforts to impose discipline. In Maryland in 1841, banks were explicitly released by the state from the legal obligation to redeem notes presented by brokers. The legislature took the view that "evil brokers" were seeking to carry off the com-

In Scotland, where wider branching and a nationwide note exchange system made money brokers less valuable, the banks themselves sometimes provided information about their financial health. In 1704 and again in 1728 when unexpected illiquidity forced the Bank of Scotland to temporarily suspend specie payments, the bank was able to satisfy its customers and maintain public confidence in its notes by publishing its accounts to demonstrate its solvency. In 1836, the Glasgow Union Bank began to regularly publicize its asset and liability status as a means of attracting customers. It thus became the first British bank to issue a detailed annual balance sheet, but others soon followed suit.

The note exchanges and clearinghouses. In 1751, the Bank of Scotland and the Royal Bank agreed to accept and regularly exchange one another's notes. The Aberdeen and the Perth United banks initiated a similar system of mutual acceptance and exchange in 1761 to encourage merchants doing business between the two cities to hold the notes of the two banks. Perth United soon entered into a similar arrangement with Dundee Banking Company. By 1771, a nationwide note exchange system had developed in Scotland (White, pp. 30–31).

This note exchange system benefited both the bankers and the public. The acceptance by banks of one another's notes at par reduced the public's costs of accepting and using bank notes, which enhanced the participating banks' name brand capital and hence their ability to expand their note issues. But the Scottish note exchange system also provided a form of industry-imposed discipline.

The most dramatic example of this discipline was the failure of Douglas, Heron and Company, better known as the Ayr Bank, established in 1769. Through its note issues, the Ayr Bank extended a great quantity of bad credit. The note exchange system, to which the Ayr Bank belonged, rapidly returned the bank's notes to it and, lacking the specie to settle its accounts with fellow members, the bank was forced to turn to the London money markets to raise funds. The Ayr Bank floated an increasingly large sum of "bills of accommodation" with London banks, but when the loans it had made in Scotland began to sour, the Ayr Bank found it could not roll over, let alone retire, its debt obligations in London. In 1772, the Ayr Bank was forced into liquidation when brokers and bankers in London

---

munity's specie to other parts of the country (Hammond, p. 691). And a Boston money broker was brought before a grand jury in Vermont for attempting to redeem in specie the notes of a Vermont bank. The Vermont attorney general maintained the broker was guilty of an indictable offense (Dewey, p. 74).

refused to buy its paper (White, pp. 30–32). Thus, while the Scottish free banking system could not prevent the establishment of a bank with poor management, it could cause its failure within a fairly short period of time.

Similarly, the clearinghouses that developed in the United States during the 19th century were in a position to monitor the performance of member banks.[23] Redlich (1968, vol. 2, pp. 46–47) observed that through the regular exchange of notes and settlement of balances, the stronger banks could compel weaker institutions to adhere to accepted standards of prudent banking behavior. Hepburn (1903, pp. 157–58), no great fan of free banking, nevertheless reported of the antebellum clearinghouse associations that:

> The clearing-house fixed a cash reserve and bound each member to maintain the same; took the public into its confidence by publishing weekly reports of condition showing the standing of each bank. This action, more than any legislation, more than anything else, aided in building up a sense of moral responsibility to the public on the part of banks throughout the country, in restraining the undue expansion of note issues and the many other reprehensible practices which characterized the banking of that period.

The "sense of moral responsibility" admired by Hepburn was more probably effective market discipline imposed by noteholders armed with information.

Probably the best known example of a clearinghouse acting as a self-regulatory organization was the Suffolk System begun in 1824.[24] According to Trivoli (1979, p. 17), "The most striking achievement of the Suffolk System for Boston was the ultimate elimination of the discount on country bank notes. . . . The Suffolk System worked as an effective protection of the public against unsound banks." The

---

[23]As the role of clearinghouses developed in the United States, one bank in the association would be assigned the administrative role of clearing other member banks' accounts. Each member bank kept part of its specie on deposit with this "central" bank, which in turn issued clearinghouse certificates of an equivalent amount to be used in the settlement of daily balances. (See Timberlake 1984, p. 3.)

[24]The Suffolk Bank of Boston entered the business of clearing country banks' notes as a profit-making venture, unlike the more typical cooperative associations established by member banks. The Suffolk Bank hoped to force the country banks to limit their note issues circulating within Boston and, thus, to create a larger market for its own notes. Further, the Suffolk Bank was interested primarily in collecting and clearing the notes of banks outside of Boston—in the surrounding countryside and in other New England states—as opposed to clearing the intracity notes, though it eventually did that too. Despite these differences with the more typical clearinghouses, the Suffolk System provides a good example of private regulation of the banking system. For a more complete description of the operation of the Suffolk System, see Trivoli (1979, pp. 13–15).

Suffolk Bank did not automatically accept any bank as a member of its system. Bankers that followed practices which could be expected to lead to an overexpansion of their notes were not included. The ability to monitor and control country banks' account "overdrafts" gave the Suffolk Bank considerable power over the loan policies of these banks. Through the power to insist on immediate payment in specie of notes sent back to the issuing bank and through the threat to remove a bank from its list of New England banks in "good standing," the Suffolk Bank effectively imposed its standards on the banks throughout New England. (See Trivoli, p. 19.)

Before it came to an end in 1858, the system compiled an impressive record. By 1850, the Suffolk Bank either directly or through other Boston banks cleared notes for about 500 New England banks, or basically all those considered sound (Hammond 1957, pp. 551–54). The banking standards imposed by the Suffolk System improved the performance and stability of the banks that were members. In the panic of 1837, for example, not one Connecticut bank failed or found it necessary to suspend specie payments. Similarly, in 1857, when the state of Maine declared a suspension of specie payments, all but three banks, almost all members of the Suffolk System, continued to redeem their notes in specie (Rothbard, p. 218). Even Bray Hammond (p. 556), a critic of free banking generally, admitted the Suffolk System worked:

> The operation of the Suffolk Bank showed *laisser faire* at its best. With no privileges or sanctions whatever from the government, private enterprise developed in the Suffolk an efficient regulation of bank credit that was quite as much in the public interest as government regulation could be.

Though not as geographically widespread as the Suffolk System, other successful clearinghouses were also established. In New York City, for example, sixty banks established the New York Clearing House in October 1853.

After the panic of 1857, 42 New York City banks agreed to maintain specific reserve requirements (Hammond, p. 713). This voluntary reserve requirement soon became effectively binding on all members of the New York Clearing House. In 1858, James Gibbons, summarizing the overall impact of the New York Clearing House, reported the clearinghouse had "put an end to speculative banking in New York. It has exerted a powerful influence to arrest speculative commerce" (Hammond, p. 706).

Timberlake (1984, p. 2) viewed the development of the 19th century U.S. clearinghouse associations as a mutual defense system against illiquidity. The panic of 1857 provides an example of the ability of the clearinghouse association to protect individual banks and their customers. Reserves in the New York banks began to decline in August 1857, and when a prominent bank failed a full blown panic seemed likely. At first the New York banks wanted to curtail loans, the usual means of responding to a specie drain. But the clearing-house banks agreed to "increase their loans so that the clearing-house balances of all of them would be increased proportionately and would cancel each other without reducing the slender stock of specie" (Timberlake, p. 3).

Meanwhile, the country banks had drawn down the balance of specie held with the New York banks and against which their notes were cleared. A policy committee of the New York Clearing House Association authorized the issuance of "clearing house loan certificates." These loan certificates were backed by the unredeemed notes of country banks which were held by the central bank of the association. The loan certificates were issued to the creditor city banks that had received country bank notes in the course of doing business. The loan certificates were used by members of the clearinghouse in lieu of specie in settling interbank balances.

The loan certificates differed from the usual clearinghouse certificates in that the latter were issued strictly in lieu of specie or other legal reserves while the loan certificates were extensions of credit by the clearinghouse policy committee to member banks during the emergency. The country banks that could not redeem their notes immediately agreed to pay 6 percent interest on the loans thus granted by their city bank correspondents. The city banks then used the country bank notes, still backed by securities deposited with the New York state authorities, as collateral for the new clearinghouse loan certificates. The city banks were, thus, able to furnish more of their own notes to pay depositors and extend loans. (See Timberlake, pp. 3–4.) The clearinghouse had found a way to conserve the specie held by its members and to avoid the expected panic.

Contractual Terms

Of course, the definition of free banking in the United States represented a change in the contractual terms under which notes were issued. Paid-in capital took the form of specified securities held by state banking authorities for safekeeping. In addition, stockholders of free banks in Massachusetts faced unlimited liability in the event of failure (Rockoff 1975, p. 125) as did bank shareholders in Scotland (White, pp. 32–41).[25]

---

[25]Furthermore, stockholders of all national banks and of many state banks were subject to double liability until 1937. In fact, double liability was not completely eliminated for U.S. banks until after 1950.

The Scottish banks used unlimited stockholder liability as a means of competing to provide "safety" to their customers and noteholders. Limited liability became an option in Scotland 20 years before any banks adopted it. Apparently, bank owners and directors feared a loss of confidence would result if they included "Limited" after their names. To further bolster confidence, 18th-century Scottish bankers often posted with the town clerk a personal bond guaranteeing payment of the bank's notes in the event of failure (White, p. 41).

In 1730 the Bank of Scotland, to increase the bank's flexibility in the event of an unexpected demand for specie by noteholders, began inserting an "option clause" into the obligation printed on its notes. The bank's pound note then promised to the bearer "one pound sterling on demand, or in the option of the Directors one pound and sixpence sterling at the end of six months after the day of demand" (White, p. 26). (This represented an annual interest rate of 5 percent.) Noteholders were apparently willing to accept the option as a means of protecting their interests in the event of illiquidity, and the bank did not exercise the option for more than 30 years after it was introduced.

Failures

Finally, there is evidence that failures did not prove as destabilizing during the Scottish and American free banking periods as many have supposed.

The failure of the Ayr Bank in Scotland in 1772 was the most spectacular during the Scottish free banking period, but it did not appear to imperil the banking system. Because of the nationwide note exchange system, few banks held many Ayr Bank notes at the time of its collapse. Although the public's demand for specie did increase in Edinburgh on the day of the Ayr Bank's demise, this "run" lasted for less than a full day. Eight smaller banks with close business ties to the Ayr Bank also failed, but for the most part the negative repercussions from the failure were short-lived. The Bank of Scotland and the Royal Bank in Edinburgh helped calm any public fears by offering to accept at face value the notes of the defunct bank. In addition to helping maintain public confidence, the two banks were able to attract new depositors and increase their note issues. The Bank of Scotland and the Royal Bank also advanced specie to the three Glasgow banks to meet unexpected cash demands immediately following the Ayr Bank failure. In the end, the unlimited liability of the Ayr Bank's shareholders meant that the demands of all creditors were met in full (White, pp. 32, 45).

Rolnick and Weber (1986) examined the U.S. free banking period using data collected from state auditor reports in New York, Wisconsin, Indiana, and Minnesota (chosen to reflect a range of experiences with free banking). They sought to determine whether bank failures that occurred in clusters were evidence of a general loss of confidence in sound banks. In other words, did such failures indicate the presence of "contagion" or "spillover" effects often associated with unregulated banking systems?

Rolnick and Weber found four "clusters" of failures between 1841 and 1861. Notably, each group of failures was limited to a single state, leading Rolnick and Weber to look for explanations in the states' policies toward banks and/or state-specific events. In fact, Rolnick and Weber were able to explain three of the four clusters of failures by identifying real shocks that rightfully undermined the public's confidence in the banks that failed. When construction on the Minnesota railroad was suspended in the spring of 1859, those banks whose notes were backed by Minnesota railroad bonds failed. In Wisconsin and Indiana, Minnesota railroad bonds were eligible securities for backing bank notes but, in fact, no banks in these states held these securities to any great extent in their portfolios. Apparently the public was aware of the securities actually held by these banks, for there was no increase in bank failures in these states (Rolnick and Weber 1986, pp. 884–86).

Wisconsin's problems occurred, by contrast, on the eve of the Civil War—between June 1860 and June 1861. Wisconsin accepted bonds from several southern states as bank note collateral. As the Civil War approached, the value of the bonds issued by states likely to secede fell rapidly in northern markets. Again, the public had good reason to reevaluate the stability of those banks that had deposited significant portions of southern bonds as backing for their notes. Among the banks and in the states where southern bonds were not accepted, there were no similar adverse affects (Rolnick and Weber 1986, pp. 886–87).

In short, the evidence presented by Rolnick and Weber (1986) indicates that during the free banking era consumers did differentiate among those banks exhibiting different portfolio characteristics. Bank customers could and did force the closure of several banks in a short period of time when the stability of those banks appeared threatened by changing conditions. But there is no evidence that runs then spread to institutions with markedly different and stable securities portfolios. That the market appeared to reject almost simultaneously several banks marked by undesirable traits should be viewed as a demonstration of market-imposed discipline and stability rather than as a sign of instability.

Conclusions

The agency costs literature suggests that in the absence of government guarantees and regulations, market forces would encourage the development of mechanisms designed to limit the costs to bank customers entrusting their funds to depository institutions. It has been argued that readily available sources of information would arise in response to consumers' demands for intelligence about the relative stability of competing banks. Furthermore, it would be in the interest of the stockholders and managers of banks to develop contractual terms and other mechanisms to reassure customers about the safety of their investments. Such "competition in safety," if communicated to consumers of bank services, would allow the banks that employed them to gain market share and to increase the stability of their institutions as depositors would be less likely to panic in the face of adverse news.

The periods of "free banking" in Scotland and the United States provide evidence to support these predictions. These banking systems, established in the late 18th and early 19th century in Scotland and in the mid-19th century in the U.S., were chosen as representing periods of relatively unregulated banking, though the Scottish system was much less regulated than the American system was. While deposit banking was of less importance during the 18th and 19th centuries than it is today, in some ways the important role bank notes played as bank liabilities creates an even more stringent test for the conclusions drawn from the agency costs literature. It can be argued, as it was during the free banking periods, that an individual has less control over the selection of bank notes he holds than over the bank(s) in which he deposits his funds.

It appears that bank customers in Scotland and the U.S. did have access to information about the relative stability of individual banks. Furthermore, in both countries the self-regulatory activities of note exchange systems and clearinghouse associations provided noteholders with information about member banks. Noteholders also benefited from contractual terms designed to reassure bank customers. These differences were most apparent in Scotland, perhaps because it was considerably less regulated than the U.S. free banking system.

Finally, these banking systems appeared to be more stable than is commonly believed. Evidence indicates that when a cluster of bank failures did occur, it did so for reasons connected to the practices of or the securities held by the institutions. The public appeared able to discriminate between those banks that exhibited undesirable characteristics and those that did not.

In short, during the U.S. and Scottish experiences with free banking, the problems often associated with unregulated banking seem to be, if not absent, at least not as extensive as common lore would indicate. Bank customers were reasonably well informed, and the market developed mechanisms for protecting their interests in the face of incomplete information.

References

Black, Fischer; Miller, Merton H.; and Posner, Richard. "An Approach to the Regulation of Bank Holding Companies." *Journal of Business* 51 (July 1978): 379–411.

Corti, Mario A. *Switzerland: Banking, Money and Bond Markets.* Reprinted from George-Giddy: International Finance Handbook, Section 4.6, Volume 1, pp. 1–50.

Dewey, Davis R. *State Banking Before the Civil War.* New York: Johnson Reprint Company, 1972.

Ely, Bert. "Yes—Private Sector Depositor Protection is a Viable Alternative to Federal Deposit Insurance!" *Proceedings of a Conference on Bank Structure and Competition.* Federal Reserve Bank of Chicago, 1985, pp. 338–53.

England, Catherine. "Private Deposit Insurance: Stabilizing the Banking Industry." *Policy Analysis* No. 54. Washington, D.C.: Cato Institute, June 21, 1985.

England, Catherine, and Palffy, John. "Replacing the FDIC: Private Insurance for Deposits." *Backgrounder* No. 229. Washington, D.C.: Heritage Foundation, December 2, 1982.

Fama, Eugene F. "Banking in the Theory of Finance." *Journal of Monetary Economics* 6 (January 1980): 39–57.

Fama, Eugene F., and Jensen, Michael C. "Agency Problems and Residual Claims." *Journal of Law and Economics* 26 (June 1983): 327–49.

Hammond, Bray. *Banks and Politics in America: From the Revolution to the Civil War.* Princeton: Princeton University Press, 1957.

Hepburn, A. Barton. *History of Coinage and Currency in the United States and the Perennial Contest for Sound Money.* New York: Macmillan Co., 1903.

Hildreth, Richard. *Banks, Banking, and Paper Currencies.* New York: Greenwood Press, 1968.

Huertas, Thomas F., and Strauber, Rachel L. S. "Deposit Insurance: Overhaul or Tune-Up?" *Issues in Bank Regulation* (Winter 1986): 3–24.

Jensen, Michael C., and Meckling, William H. "Theory of the Firm: Managerial Behavior, Agency Costs and Ownership Structure." *Journal of Financial Economics* (October 1976): 305–60.

Kaufman, George G. "The Truth about Bank Runs." Chapter 2 of this book.

Leonard, Herman B., and Zeckhauser, Richard J. "Financial Risk and the Burdens of Contracts." *American Economic Review* (May 1985): 375–80.

Mints, Lloyd W. *A History of Banking Theory in Great Britain and the United States.* Chicago: University of Chicago Press, 1945.

Modigliani, Franco, and Miller, Merton H. "The Cost of Capital, Corporation Finance, and the Theory of Investment." *American Economic Review* 48 (June 1958): 261–97.

Redlich, Fritz. *The Molding of American Banking: Parts I and II.* New York: Johnson Reprint Company, 1968.

Rockoff, Hugh. "The Free Banking Era: A Reexamination." *Journal of Money, Credit and Banking* (May 1974): 141–67.

Rockoff, Hugh. *The Free Banking Era.* New York: Arno Press, 1975.

Rolnick, Arthur J., and Weber, Warren E. "Inherent Instability in Banking: The Free Banking Experience." *Cato Journal* 5 (Winter 1986): 877–90.

Rothbard, Murray. *The Mystery of Banking.* New York: Richardson and Snyder, 1983.

Timberlake, Richard H. "The Central Banking Role of Clearing Associations." *Journal of Money, Credit and Banking* (February 1984): 1–15.

Trivoli, George. *The Suffolk Bank: A Study of a Free Enterprise Clearing System.* London: Adam Smith Institute, 1979.

White, Lawrence H. *Free Banking in Britain: Theory, Experience and Debate, 1800–1845.* Cambridge: Cambridge University Press, 1984.

EVOLUTION IN BANKING

A. James Meigs

Catherine England (1987) argues that in an unregulated banking system without deposit insurance, various services and institutions would evolve to do what many people now think must be done by government. These new services and institutions would protect innocent bank customers from unscrupulous or inefficient bankers who otherwise would use depositors' funds for unsound or illegal investments, and would protect innocent banks from the contagious effects of other banks' failures.

Then she reviews the experience of free banking systems in Scotland and the United States and finds that such services and institutions did in fact evolve in those periods, much as her theoretical arguments would have predicted.

I found all of this most agreeable and plausible. I would not change any of it.

Her paper raises some intriguing questions:

1. If the system she describes would be so efficient and stable, why has it not already evolved?
2. Why do we have instead the unsatisfactory system we have met here to complain about?
3. How should we expect the system to evolve in the future?

She did not try to answer those questions here. They were not in her assignment for this conference, although she undoubtedly has thought a lot about how we may get from where we are now to the system she describes. She said in her opening remarks that she was going to talk about what would happen the day after the revolution. But evolution of the new services and institutions would take more than one day. Therefore, I believe she has raised a problem in understanding the evolution of complex systems.

The author is an independent scholar and consultant who lives in Princeton, New Jersey.

My observations on this problem will apply not only to England's paper but to most of the papers presented at this conference. For help on this problem I turn to the work of Stephen Jay Gould (1987), who teaches biology, geology, and the history of science at Harvard. He recently illustrated the problem of understanding evolution with a homey example, the typewriter keyboard. He did this with the help of Paul A. David (1986), professor of American economic history at Stanford.

Probably everyone in this room types on the QWERTY keyboard, which is named for the first six letters on the top line. As Gould says, it is "drastically suboptimal." Some of the most frequently used letters are in hard-to-reach positions or are under the weakest fingers. There have been many competitors, including the Dvorak Simplified Keyboard (DSK). DSK is much faster.[1] But no competitors have ever dented the dominance of QWERTY.

Why? This is like our problem with banking. We have a "drastically suboptimal" banking system, even though a superior system might have evolved—or may yet evolve—as England argues. The QWERTY keyboard actually was designed to keep typists from typing too fast, to keep the keys from jamming on a primitive early machine invented around 1867. But why did QWERTY win out over all of its competitors after other machines came onto the market?

According to Gould and Day, a crucial speed typing contest was won on a QWERTY keyboard in 1888 by a typist who had the novel idea of memorizing the keyboard instead of using hunt-and-peck. He had invented touch typing. But the wide publicity his victory received led manufacturers and typing schools to standardize on QWERTY from then on. In short, an accident shaped the course of typing history.[2]

The story of QWERTY illustrates two commonplaces of history, says Gould:

1. *Contingency.* Mammals, or QWERTY, or our heavily regulated banking system are the chancy results of long strings of unpredictable antecedents, rather than the necessary outcomes of natural laws. Evolution is not a simple, linear process. Chance events can nudge

---

[1]There is software for shifting modern computer terminals to a DSK keyboard virtually at a keystroke. However, Apple reports little use of this high-speed alternative on its machines. One person from the audience at the Cato Monetary Conference told me that he had bought software to convert his IBM PC to DSK.

[2]As Gould says, competitions that would have tested QWERTY against other keyboards and other styles of typing were never held. In public perception and in the eyes of those who published typing manuals, QWERTY had proved its superiority.

a process into a new pathway with "cascading consequences that produce an outcome vastly different from any alternative."

Two examples of such pivotal events in the history of the banking system that were stressed by several speakers at the conference are the establishment of the Federal Reserve System in 1913 and the Great Depression of the 1930s. Without the first, we would not have had the second, but the two combined had powerful effects on the evolution of banking.

2. *Incumbency.* The second of these commonplaces of history, incumbency, reinforces the stability of a pathway once such chance events push a sequence into a new channel. As Gould says, "Suboptimal politicians often prevail nearly forever once they gain office and grab the reins of privilege." That sounds more like a statement from the Center for the Study of Public Choice than the view of a Harvard professor of biology, but that is what he said.

He went on to say, "If every typist in the world stopped using QWERTY tomorrow and began to learn Dvorak, we would all be winners, but who will bell the cat, or start the ball rolling?" It is not easy. In banking, for each banker or regulator who wants to change the system there are probably ten opposed.

Where does all of this leave us? At the moment, we are stuck with a QWERTY banking system. It is the end result of a long chain of accidents. England as well as others have told us a better keyboard is available. However, because of the power of incumbency, a change of course will be difficult. We should not be too optimistic. After all, says Gould, "Mammals waited 100 million years to become the dominant animals on land and only got a chance because dinosaurs succumbed during a mass extinction."

I hope we don't have to wait for a mass extinction before we can move to Catherine England's more stable system. Fortunately, we are not like those little mammals waiting for the dinosaurs to die out. We can nudge history. In sum, I think we can read England's argument two ways.

In the first, which I call the Gradualist Approach, she says we should not be afraid to take any opportunity for moving even a little way in the direction of her ideal system. For example, we could reduce deposit insurance coverage to introduce more market discipline or take other measures discussed here. The system would not fall apart.

In the second, which I call the Big Bang, she assures us that if we do have a cataclysm, such as the extinction of the FSLIC and the thrift industry, we would be ready to propose shifting the direction of evolution heavily toward a freer, more efficient system.

References

David, Paul A. "Understanding the Economics of QWERTY: The Necessity of History." In *Economic History and the Modern Economist*, pp. 30–49. Edited by W. N. Parker. New York: Basil Blackwell Inc., 1986.

England, Catherine. "Agency Costs and Unregulated Banks: Could Depositors Protect Themselves?" Chapter 14 in this book.

Gould, Stephen Jay. "The Panda's Thumb of Technology." *Natural History* (January 1987): 14–23.

INDEX